Henry James Byron

The works of Lord Byron

Volume V: The Doge of Venice

Henry James Byron

The works of Lord Byron
Volume V: The Doge of Venice

ISBN/EAN: 9783742840424

Manufactured in Europe, USA, Canada, Australia, Japa

Cover: Foto ©Andreas Hilbeck / pixelio.de

Manufactured and distributed by brebook publishing software (www.brebook.com)

Henry James Byron

The works of Lord Byron

COLLECTION
OF
BRITISH AUTHORS.
VOL. XII.

THE WORKS OF LORD BYRON.

IN FIVE VOLUMES.

VOL. V.

THE WORKS

OF

LORD BYRON

COMPLETE IN FIVE VOLUMES.

Second Edition.

VOL. V.

LEIPZIG

BERNHARD TAUCHNITZ

1866.

CONTENTS

OF VOLUME V.

	Page
MARINO FALIERO, DOGE OF VENICE; AN HISTORICAL TRAGEDY, in Five Acts	1
Preface	1
Appendix	121
THE TWO FOSCARI. AN HISTORICAL TRAGEDY	135
SARDANAPALUS, A TRAGEDY	208
Dedication	208
Preface	209
WERNER, OR, THE INHERITANCE. A TRAGEDY	312
Preface	312
Dedication	314
APPENDIX. A FRAGMENT (Vampire)	432
PARLIAMENTARY SPEECHES	435

MARINO FALIERO,
DOGE OF VENICE;

AN HISTORICAL TRAGEDY,
IN FIVE ACTS.

"Dux inquieti turbidus Adriæ." — HORACE.

PREFACE.

THE conspiracy of the Doge Marino Faliero is one of the most remarkable events in the annals of the most singular government, city, and people of modern history. It occurred in the year 1355. Every thing about Venice is, or was, extraordinary — her aspect is like a dream, and her history is like a romance. The story of this Doge is to be found in all her Chronicles, and particularly detailed in the "Lives of the Doges," by Marin Sanuto, which is given in the Appendix. It is simply and clearly related, and is perhaps more dramatic in itself than any scenes which can be founded upon the subject.

Marino Faliero appears to have been a man of talents and of courage. I find him commander in chief of the land forces at the siege of Zara, where he beat the King of Hungary and his army of eighty thousand men, killing eight thousand men, and keeping the besieged at the same time in check; an exploit to which I know none similar in history, except that of Cæsar at Alesia, and of Prince Eugene at Belgrade. He was afterwards commander of the fleet in the same war. He took Capo d'Istria. He was ambassador at Genoa and Rome, — at which last he received the news of his election to the dukedom; his absence being a proof that he sought it by no intrigue, since he was apprized of his predecessor's death and his own succession at the same moment. But he appears to have been of an ungovernable temper. A story is told by Sanuto, of his having, many years before, when podesta and captain at Treviso, boxed the ears of the bishop, who was somewhat tardy in bringing the Host. For this, honest Sanuto "saddles him with a judgment," as Thwackum did Square; but he does not tell us whether he was punished or rebuked by the Senate for this outrage at the time of its commission. He seems, indeed, to have been afterwards at peace with the church, for we find him ambassador at Rome, and invested with the fief of Val di Marino, in the march of Treviso, and with the title of Count, by Lorenzo Count-bishop of Ceneda. For these facts my authorities are Sanuto, Vettor Sandi, Andrea Navagero, and the account of the siege of Zara, first published by the indefatigable Abate Morelli, in his "Monumenti Veneziani di varia Letteratura," printed in 1796, all of which I have looked over in the original language. The moderns, Darù, Sismondi, and Laugier, nearly agree with the ancient chroniclers. Sismondi attributes the conspiracy to his *jealousy;* but I find this nowhere asserted by the national historians. Vettor Sandi, indeed, says, that "Altri scrissero che ..... dalla gelosa suspizion di esso Doge siasi fatto (Michel Steno) staccar con violenza," &c. &c.; but this appears to have been by no means the general opinion, nor is it alluded to by Sanuto or by Navagero; and Sandi himself adds, a moment after, that "per altre Veneziane memorie traspiri, che non il *solo* desiderio di vendetta lo dispose alla congiura ma anche la innata abituale ambizion sua, per cui anelava a farsi principe independente." The first motive appears to have been excited by the gross affront of the words written by Michel Steno on the ducal chair, and by the light and inadequate sentence of the Forty on the offender, who was one of their "tre Capi." The attentions of Steno himself appear to have been directed towards one of her damsels, and not to the "Dogaressa" herself, against whose fame not the slightest insinuation appears, while she is praised for her beauty, and remarked for her youth. Neither do I find it asserted (unless the hint of Sandi be an assertion), that the Doge was actuated by jealousy of his wife; but rather by respect for her, and for his own honour, warranted by his past services and present dignity.

I know not that the historical facts are alluded to in English, unless by Dr. Moore in his View of Italy. His account is false and flippant, full of stale jests about old men and young wives, and wondering at so great an effect from so slight a cause. How so acute and severe an observer of mankind as the author of Zeluco could wonder at this is inconceivable. He knew that a basin of water spilt on Mrs. Masham's gown deprived the Duke of Marlborough of his command, and led to the inglorious peace of Utrecht — that Louis XIV. was plunged into the most desolating wars, because his minister was nettled at his finding fault with a window, and wished to give him another occupation — that Helen lost Troy — that Lucretia expelled the Tarquins from Rome — and that Cava brought the Moors to Spain — that an insulted husband led the Gauls to Clusium, and thence to Rome — that a single verse of Frederick II. of Prussia on the Abbé de Bernis, and a jest on Madame de Pompadour, led to the battle of Rosbach — that the elopement of Dearbhorgil with Mac Murchad conducted the English to the slavery of Ireland — that a personal pique between Maria Antoinette and the Duke of Orleans precipitated the first expulsion of the Bourbons — and, not to multiply instances, that Commodus, Domitian, and Caligula fell victims not to their public tyranny, but to private vengeance — and that an order to make Cromwell disembark from the ship in which he would have sailed to America destroyed both king and commonwealth. After these instances, on the least reflection, it is indeed extraordinary in Dr. Moore to seem surprised that a man used to command, who had served and swayed in the most important offices, should fiercely resent, in a fierce age, an unpunished affront, the grossest that can be offered to a man, be he prince or peasant. The age of Faliero is little to the purpose, unless to favour it —

> "The young man's wrath is like straw on fire,
> But like red hot steel is the old man's ire."

> "Young men soon give and soon forget affronts,
> Old age is slow at both."

Laugier's reflections are more philosophical: — "Tale fù il fine ignominioso di un' uomo, che la sua nascita, la sua età, il suo carattere dovevano tener lontano dalle passioni produttrici di grandi delitti. I suoi *talenti* per lungo tempo esercitati ne' maggiori impieghi, la sua capacità sperimentata ne' governi e nelle ambasciate, gli avevano acquistato la stima e la fiducia de' cittadini, ed avevano uniti i suffragj per collocarlo alla testa della repubblica. Innalzato ad un grado che terminava gloriosamente la sua vita, il risentimento di un' ingiuria leggiera insinuò nel suo cuore tal veleno che bastò a corrompere le antiche sue qualità, e a condurlo al termine dei scellerati; serio esempio, che prova *non esservi età, in cui la prudenza umana sia sicura, e che nell' uomo restano sempre passioni capaci a disonorarlo, quando non invigili sopra se stesso.*"*

Where did Dr. Moore find that Marino Faliero begged his life? I have searched the chroniclers, and find nothing of the kind; it is true that he avowed all. He was conducted to the place of torture, but there is no mention made of any application for mercy on his part; and the very circumstance of their having taken him to the rack seems to argue any thing but his having shown a want of firmness, which would doubtless have been also mentioned by those minute historians, who by no means favour him: such, indeed, would be contrary to his character as a soldier, to the age in which he lived, and *at* which he died, as it is to the truth of history. I

* Laugier, Hist. de la Répub. de Venise, Italian translation, vol. iv. p. 30.

know no justification, at any distance of time, for calumniating an historical character: surely truth belongs to the dead, and to the unfortunate; and they who have died upon a scaffold have generally had faults enough of their own, without attributing to them that which the very incurring of the perils which conducted them to their violent death renders, of all others, the most improbable. The black veil which is painted over the place of Marino Faliero amongst the Doges, and the Giants' Staircase where he was crowned, and discrowned, and decapitated, struck forcibly upon my imagination; as did his fiery character and strange story. I went, in 1819, in search of his tomb more than once to the church San Giovanni e San Paolo; and, as I was standing before the monument of another family, a priest came up to me and said, "I can show you finer monuments than that." I told him that I was in search of that of the Faliero family, and particularly of the Doge Marino's. "Oh," said he, "I will show it you;" and conducting me to the outside, pointed out a sarcophagus in the wall with an illegible inscription. He said that it had been in a convent adjoining, but was removed after the French came, and placed in its present situation; that he had seen the tomb opened at its removal; there were still some bones remaining, but no positive vestige of the decapitation. The equestrian statue of which I have made mention in the third act as before that church is not, however, of a Faliero, but of some other now obsolete warrior, although of a later date. There were two other Doges of this family prior to Marino; Ordelafo, who fell in battle at Zara in 1117 (where his descendant afterwards conquered the Huns), and Vital Faliero, who reigned in 1082. The family, originally from Fano, was of the most illustrious in blood and wealth in the city of once the most wealthy and still the most ancient families in Europe. The length I have gone into on this subject will show the interest I have taken in it. Whether I have succeeded or not in the tragedy, I have at least transferred into our language an historical fact worthy of commemoration.

PREFACE.

It is now four years that I have meditated this work; and before I had sufficiently examined the records, I was rather disposed to have made it turn on a jealousy in Faliero. But, perceiving no foundation for this in historical truth, and aware that jealousy is an exhausted passion in the drama, I have given it a more historical form. I was, besides, well advised by the late Matthew Lewis on that point, in talking with him of my intention at Venice in 1817. "If you make him jealous," said he, "recollect that you have to contend with established writers, to say nothing of Shakspeare, and an exhausted subject;—stick to the old fiery Doge's natural character, which will bear you out, if properly drawn; and make your plot as regular as you can." Sir William Drummond gave me nearly the same counsel. How far I have followed these instructions, or whether they have availed me, is not for me to decide. I have had no view to the stage; in its present state it is, perhaps, not a very exalted object of ambition; besides, I have been too much behind the scenes to have thought it so at any time. And I cannot conceive any man of irritable feeling putting himself at the mercies of an audience. The sneering reader, and the loud critic, and the tart review, are scattered and distant calamities; but the trampling of an intelligent or of an ignorant audience on a production which, be it good or bad, has been a mental labour to the writer, is a palpable and immediate grievance, heightened by a man's doubt of their competency to judge, and his certainty of his own imprudence in electing them his judges. Were I capable of writing a play which could be deemed stage-worthy, success would give me no pleasure, and failure great pain. It is for this reason that, even during the time of being one of the committee of one of the theatres, I never made the attempt, and never will.* But surely there

---

* While I was in the sub-committee of Drury Lane Theatre, I can vouch for my colleagues, and I hope for myself, that we did our best to bring back the legitimate drama. I tried what I could to get "De Montfort" revived, but in vain, and equally in vain in favour of Sotheby's "Ivan," which was thought an acting play; and I endeavoured also to

is dramatic power somewhere, where Joanna Baillie, and Millman, and John Wilson exist. The "City of the Plague" and the "Fall of Jerusalem" are full of the best "*materiel*" for tragedy that has been seen since Horace Walpole, except passages of Ethwald and De Montfort. It is the fashion to underrate Horace Walpole; firstly, because he was a nobleman, and secondly, because he was a gentleman; but, to say nothing of the composition of his incomparable letters, and of the Castle of Otranto, he is the "Ultimus Romanorum," the author of the Mysterious Mother, a tragedy of the highest order, and not a puling love-play. He is the father of the first romance and of the last tragedy in our language, and surely worthy of a higher place than any living writer, be he who he may.

In speaking of the drama of Marino Faliero, I forgot to mention, that the desire of preserving, though still too re-

wake Mr. Coleridge to write a tragedy. Those who are not in the secret will hardly believe that the "School for Scandal" is the play which has brought *least money*, averaging the number of times it has been acted since its production; so Manager Dibdin assured me. Of what has occurred since Maturin's "Bertram" I am not aware; so that I may be traducing, through ignorance, some excellent new writers: if so, I beg their pardon. I have been absent from England nearly five years, and, till last year, I never read an English newspaper since my departure, and am now only aware of theatrical matters through the medium of the Parisian Gazette of Galignani, and only for the last twelve months. Let me then deprecate all offence to tragic or comic writers, to whom I wish well, and of whom I know nothing. The long complaints of the actual state of the drama arise, however, from no fault of the performers. I can conceive nothing better than Kemble, Cooke, and Kean in their very different manners, or than Elliston in *gentleman's* comedy, and in some parts of tragedy. Miss O'Neill I never saw, having made and kept a determination to see nothing which should divide or disturb my recollection of Siddons. Siddons and Kemble were the *ideal* of tragic action; I never saw any thing at all resembling them even in *persons*: for this reason, we shall never see again Coriolanus or Macbeth. When Kean is blamed for want of dignity, we should remember that it is a grace, and not an art, and not to be attained by study. In all, *not* SUPER-natural parts, he is perfect; even his very defects belong, or seem to belong, to the parts themselves, and appear truer to nature. But of Kemble we may say, with reference to his acting, what the Cardinal de Retz said of the Marquis of Montrose, "that he was the only man he ever saw who reminded him of the heroes of Plutarch."

mote, a nearer approach to unity than the irregularity, which is the reproach of the English theatrical compositions, permits, has induced me to represent the conspiracy as already formed, and the Doge acceding to it; whereas, in fact, it was of his own preparation and that of Israel Bertuccio. The other characters (except that of the Duchess), incidents, and almost the time, which was wonderfully short for such a design in real life, are strictly historical, except that all the consultations took place in the palace. Had I followed this, the unity would have been better preserved; but I wished to produce the Doge in the full assembly of the conspirators, instead of monotonously placing him always in dialogue with the same individuals. For the real facts, I refer to the Appendix.

DRAMATIS PERSONÆ.

MEN.

MARINO FALIERO, *Doge of Venice.*
BERTUCCIO FALIERO, *Nephew of the Doge.*
LIONI, *a Patrician and Senator.*
BENINTENDE, *Chief of the Council of Ten.*
MICHEL STENO, *One of the three Capi of the Forty.*
ISRAEL BERTUCCIO, *Chief of the Arsenal,*
PHILIP CALENDARO,
DAGOLINO,
BERTRAM,
} *Conspirators.*

Signor of the Night, { *"Signore di Notte," one of the Officers belonging to the Republic.*
First Citizen.
Second Citizen.
Third Citizen.
VINCENZO,
PIETRO,
BATTISTA,
} *Officers belonging to the Ducal Palace.*
Secretary of the Council of Ten.
Guards, Conspirators, Citizens, The Council of Ten, The Giunta, &c. &c.

WOMEN.

ANGIOLINA, *Wife to the Doge.*
MARIANNA, *her Friend.*

Female Attendants, &c.

Scene VENICE — in the year 1355.

MARINO FALIERO.

ACT I.

SCENE I.

An Antechamber in the Ducal Palace.

PIETRO *speaks, in entering, to* BATTISTA.

Pie. Is not the messenger return'd?
Bat.   Not yet;
I have sent frequently, as you commanded,
But still the Signory is deep in council,
And long debate on Steno's accusation.
    Pie. Too long — at least so thinks the Doge.
    Bat.   How bears he
These moments of suspense?
    Pie.   With struggling patience.
Placed at the ducal table, cover'd o'er
With all the apparel of the state; petitions,
Despatches, judgments, acts, reprieves, reports,
He sits as rapt in duty; but whene'er
He hears the jarring of a distant door,
Or aught that intimates a coming step,
Or murmur of a voice, his quick eye wanders,
And he will start up from his chair, then pause,
And seat himself again, and fix his gaze
Upon some edict; but I have observed
For the last hour he has not turn'd a leaf.
    Bat. 'Tis said he is much moved, — and doubtless 'twas
Foul scorn in Steno to offend so grossly.
    Pie. Ay, if a poor man: Steno's a patrician,
Young, galliard, gay, and haughty.
    Bat.   Then you think
He will not be judged hardly?
    Pie.   'Twere enough

He be judged justly; but 'tis not for us
To anticipate the sentence of the Forty.
  Bat. And here it comes.—What news, Vincenzo?

            Enter VINCENZO.
  Vin.   'Tis
Decided; but as yet his doom's unknown:
I saw the president in act to seal
The parchment which will bear the Forty's judgment
Unto the Doge, and hasten to inform him.   [*Exeunt.*

                SCENE II.
            The Ducal Chamber.

MARINO FALIERO, *Doge; and his Nephew,* BERTUCCIO FALIERO.
  Ber. F. It cannot be but they will do you justice.
  Doge. Ay, such as the Avogadori did,
Who sent up my appeal unto the Forty
To try him by his peers, his own tribunal.
  Ber. F. His peers will scarce protect him; such an act
Would bring contempt on all authority.
  Doge. Know you not Venice? Know you not the Forty?
But we shall see anon.
  Ber. F. (*addressing* VINCENZO, *then entering.*)
                How now—what tidings?
  Vin. I am charged to tell his highness that the court
Has pass'd its resolution, and that, soon
As the due forms of judgment are gone through,
The sentence will be sent up to the Doge;
In the mean time the Forty doth salute
The Prince of the Republic, and entreat
His acceptation of their duty.
  Doge.   Yes—
They are wond'rous dutiful, and ever humble.
Sentence is pass'd, you say?
  Vin.   It is, your highness:
The president was sealing it, when I
Was call'd in, that no moment might be lost

In forwarding the intimation due
Not only to the Chief of the Republic,
But the complainant, both in one united.
    Ber. F. Are you aware, from aught you have perceived,
Of their decision?
    Vin.   No, my lord; you know
The secret custom of the courts in Venice.
    Ber. F. True; but there still is something given to guess,
Which a shrewd gleaner and quick eye would catch at;
A whisper, or a murmur, or an air
More or less solemn spread o'er the tribunal.
The Forty are but men—most worthy men,
And wise, and just, and cautious—this I grant—
And secret as the grave to which they doom
The guilty; but with all this, in their aspects —
At least in some, the juniors of the number—
A searching eye, an eye like yours, Vincenzo,
Would read the sentence ere it was pronounced.
    Vin. My lord, I came away upon the moment,
And had no leisure to take note of that
Which pass'd among the judges, even in seeming;
My station near the accused too, Michel Steno,
Made me—
    Doge (abruptly). And how look'd *he?* deliver that.
    Vin. Calm, but not overcast, he stood resign'd
To the decree, whate'er it were;—but lo!
It comes, for the perusal of his highness.

                   Enter the SECRETARY *of the Forty.*

    Sec. The high tribunal of the Forty sends
Health and respect to the Doge Faliero,
Chief magistrate of Venice, and requests
His highness to peruse and to approve
The sentence pass'd on Michel Steno, born
Patrician, and arraign'd upon the charge
Contain'd, together with its penalty,
Within the rescript which I now present.

ACT I.   13

Doge. Retire, and wait without.
            [*Exeunt* SECRETARY *and* VINCENZO.
                    Take thou this paper:
The misty letters vanish from my eyes;
I cannot fix them.
    Ber. F.   Patience, my dear uncle:
Why do you tremble thus?—nay, doubt not, all
Will be as could be wish'd.
    Doge.   Say on.
    Ber. F. (reading).   "Decreed
In council, without one dissenting voice,
That Michel Steno, by his own confession,
Guilty on the last night of Carnival
Of having graven on the ducal throne
The following words—"
    Doge.   Would'st thou repeat them?
Would'st *thou* repeat them—*thou*, a Faliero,
Harp on the deep dishonour of our house,
Dishonour'd in its chief—that chief the prince
Of Venice, first of cities?—To the sentence.
    Ber. F. Forgive me, my good lord; I will obey—
(*Reads.*) "That Michel Steno be detain'd a month
In close arrest."
    Doge.   Proceed.
    Ber. F.   My lord, 'tis finish'd.
    Doge. How, say you?—finish'd! Do I dream?—'tis
        false—
Give me the paper—(*Snatches the paper and reads*)—"'Tis
        decreed in council
That Michel Steno"—Nephew, thine arm!
    Ber. F.   Nay,
Cheer up, be calm; this transport is uncall'd for—
Let me seek some assistance.
    Doge.   Stop, sir—Stir not—
'Tis past.
    Ber. F. I cannot but agree with you
The sentence is too slight for the offence—

It is not honourable in the Forty
To affix so slight a penalty to that
Which was a foul affront to you, and even
To them, as being your subjects; but 'tis not
Yet without remedy: you can appeal
To them once more, or to the Avogadori,
Who, seeing that true justice is withheld,
Will now take up the cause they once declined,
And do you right upon the bold delinquent.
Think you not thus, good uncle? why do you stand
So fix'd? You heed me not:—I pray you, hear me!
  Doge (*dashing down the ducal bonnet, and offering to trample*
    upon it, exclaims, as he is withheld by his nephew)
Oh! that the Saracen were in Saint Mark's!
Thus would I do him homage.
  Ber. F.   For the sake
Of Heaven and all its saints, my lord—
  Doge.   Away!
Oh, that the Genoese were in the port!
Oh, that the Huns whom I o'erthrew at Zara
Were ranged around the palace!
  Ber. F.   'Tis not well
In Venice' Duke to say so.
  Doge.   Venice' Duke!
Who now is Duke in Venice? let me see him,
That he may do me right.
  Ber. F.   If you forget
Your office, and its dignity and duty,
Remember that of man, and curb this passion.
The Duke of Venice—
  Doge (*interrupting him*). There is no such thing—
It is a word—nay, worse—a worthless by-word:
The most despised, wrong'd, outraged, helpless wretch,
Who begs his bread, if 'tis refused by one,
May win it from another kinder heart;
But he, who is denied his right by those
Whose place it is to do no wrong, is poorer

Than the rejected beggar—he's a slave—
And that am I, and thou, and all our house,
Even from this hour; the meanest artisan
Will point the finger, and the haughty noble
May spit upon us:—where is our redress?
    Ber. F. The law, my prince?—
    Doge (interrupting him). You see what it has done—
I ask'd no remedy but from the law—
I sought no vengeance but redress by law—
I call'd no judges but those named by law—
As sovereign, I appeal'd unto my subjects,
The very subjects who had made me sovereign,
And gave me thus a double right to be so.
The rights of place and choice, of birth and service,
Honours and years, these scars, these hoary hairs,
The travel, toil, the perils, the fatigues,
The blood and sweat of almost eighty years,
Were weigh'd i' the balance, 'gainst the foulest stain,
The grossest insult, most contemptuous crime
Of a rank, rash patrician—and found wanting!
And this is to be borne!
    Ber. F.   I say not that:—
In case your fresh appeal should be rejected,
We will find other means to make all even.
    Doge. Appeal again! art thou my brother's son?
A scion of the house of Faliero?
The nephew of a Doge? and of that blood
Which hath already given three dukes to Venice?
But thou say'st well—we must be humble now.
    Ber. F. My princely uncle! you are too much moved:—
I grant it was a gross offence, and grossly
Left without fitting punishment: but still
This fury doth exceed the provocation,
Or any provocation: if we are wrong'd,
We will ask justice; if it be denied,
We'll take it; but may do all this in calmness—
Deep Vengeance is the daughter of deep Silence.

I have yet scarce a third part of your years,
I love our house, I honour you, its chief,
The guardian of my youth, and its instructor—
But though I understand your grief, and enter
In part of your disdain, it doth appal me
To see your anger, like our Adrian waves,
O'ersweep all bounds, and foam itself to air.

   Doge. I tell thee—*must* I tell thee—what thy father
Would have required no words to comprehend?
Hast thou no feeling save the external sense
Of torture from the touch? hast thou no soul—
No pride—no passion—no deep sense of honour?

   Ber. F. 'Tis the first time that honour has been doubted,
And were the last, from any other sceptic.

   Doge. You know the full offence of this born villain,
This creeping, coward, rank, acquitted felon,
Who threw his sting into a poisonous libel,
And on the honour of—Oh God!—my wife,
The nearest, dearest part of all men's honour,
Left a base slur to pass from mouth to mouth
Of loose mechanics, with all coarse foul comments,
And villanous jests, and blasphemies obscene;
While sneering nobles, in more polish'd guise,
Whisper'd the tale, and smiled upon the lie
Which made me look like them—a courteous wittol,
Patient—ay, proud, it may be, of dishonour.

   Ber. F. But still it was a lie—you knew it false,
And so did all men.

   Doge.   Nephew, the high Roman
Said, "Cæsar's wife must not even be suspected,"
And put her from him.

   Ber. F.   True—but in those days—

   Doge. What is it that a Roman would not suffer,
That a Venetian prince must bear? Old Dandolo
Refused the diadem of all the Cæsars,
And wore the ducal cap I trample on,
Because 'tis now degraded.

ACT I.

Ber. F.   'T is even so.
   Doge. It is — it is; — I did not visit on
The innocent creature thus most vilely slander'd
Because she took an old man for her lord,
For that he had been long her father's friend
And patron of her house, as if there were
No love in woman's heart but lust of youth
And beardless faces; — I did not for this
Visit the villain's infamy on her,
But craved my country's justice on his head,
The justice due unto the humblest being
Who hath a wife whose faith is sweet to him,
Who hath a home whose hearth is dear to him,
Who hath a name whose honour's all to him,
When these are tainted by the accursing breath
Of calumny and scorn.
   Ber. F.   And what redress
Did you expect as his fit punishment?
   Doge. Death! Was I not the sovereign of the state —
Insulted on his very throne, and made
A mockery to the men who should obey me?
Was I not injured as a husband? scorn'd
As man? reviled, degraded, as a prince?
Was not offence like his a complication
Of insult and of treason? — and he lives!
Had he instead of on the Doge's throne
Stamp'd the same brand upon a peasant's stool,
His blood had gilt the threshold; for the carle
Had stabb'd him on the instant.
   Ber. F.   Do not doubt it,
He shall not live till sunset — leave to me
The means, and calm yourself.
   Doge.   Hold, nephew: this
Would have sufficed but yesterday; at present
I have no further wrath against this man.
   Ber. F. What mean you? is not the offence redoubled
By this most rank — I will not say — acquittal;

For it is worse, being full acknowledgment
Of the offence, and leaving it unpunish'd?
 Doge. It is *redoubled*, but not now by him:
The Forty hath decreed a month's arrest—
We must obey the Forty.
 Ber. F.   Obey *them!*
Who have forgot their duty to the sovereign?
 Doge. Why yes;—boy, you perceive it then at last:
Whether as fellow citizen who sues
For justice, or as sovereign who commands it,
They have defrauded me of both my rights
(For here the sovereign is a citizen);
But, notwithstanding, harm not thou a hair
Of Steno's head—he shall not wear it long.
 Ber. F. Not twelve hours longer, had you left to me
The mode and means: if you had calmly heard me,
I never meant this miscreant should escape,
But wish'd you to suppress such gusts of passion,
That we more surely might devise together
His taking off.
 Doge. No, nephew, he must live;
At least, just now—a life so vile as his
Were nothing at this hour; in th' olden time
Some sacrifices ask'd a single victim,
Great expiations had a hecatomb.
 Ber. F. Your wishes are my law: and yet I fain
Would prove to you how near unto my heart
The honour of our house must ever be.
 Doge. Fear not; you shall have time and place of proof:
But be not thou too rash, as I have been.
I am ashamed of my own anger now;
I pray you, pardon me.
 Ber. F.   Why that's my uncle!
The leader, and the statesman, and the chief
Of commonwealths, and sovereign of himself!
I wonder'd to perceive you so forget

All prudence in your fury at these years,
Although the cause —
    Doge.   Ay, think upon the cause —
Forget it not: — When you lie down to rest,
Let it be black among your dreams; and when
The morn returns, so let it stand between
The sun and you, as an ill-omen'd cloud
Upon a summer-day of festival:
So will it stand to me; — but speak not, stir not, —
Leave all to me; — we shall have much to do,
And you shall have a part. — But now retire,
'Tis fit I were alone.
    Ber. F. (*taking up and placing the ducal bonnet on the table*).
                Ere I depart,
I pray you to resume what you have spurn'd,
Till you can change it haply for a crown.
And now I take my leave, imploring you
In all things to rely upon my duty
As doth become your near and faithful kinsman,
And not less loyal citizen and subject.
                              [*Exit* BERTUCCIO FALIERO.
    Doge (*solus*). Adieu, my worthy nephew. — Hollow bauble!
                              [*Taking up the ducal cap.*
Beset with all the thorns that line a crown,
Without investing the insulted brow
With the all-swaying majesty of kings;
Thou idle, gilded, and degraded toy,
Let me resume thee as I would a vizor.   [*Puts it on.*
How my brain aches beneath thee! and my temples
Throb feverish under thy dishonest weight.
Could I not turn thee to a diadem?
Could I not shatter the Briarean sceptre
Which in this hundred-handed senate rules,
Making the people nothing, and the prince
A pageant? In my life I have achieved
Tasks not less difficult — achieved for them,
Who thus repay me! — Can I not requite them?

Oh for one year! Oh! but for even a day
Of my full youth, while yet my body served
My soul as serves the generous steed his lord,
I would have dash'd amongst them, asking few
In aid to overthrow these swoln patricians;
But now I must look round for other hands
To serve this hoary head;—but it shall plan
In such a sort as will not leave the task
Herculean, though as yet 'tis but a chaos
Of darkly brooding thoughts: my fancy is
In her first work, more nearly to the light
Holding the sleeping images of things
For the selection of the pausing judgment.—
The troops are few in—

Enter Vincenzo.

Vin. There is one without
Craves audience of your highness.
Doge. I'm unwell—
I can see no one, not even a patrician—
Let him refer his business to the council.
Vin. My lord, I will deliver your reply;
It cannot much import—he's a plebeian,
The master of a galley, I believe.
Doge. How! did you say the patron of a galley?
That is—I mean—a servant of the state:
Admit him, he may be on public service.
[*Exit* Vincenzo.
Doge (solus). This patron may be sounded; I will try him.
I know the people to be discontented:
They have cause, since Sapienza's adverse day,
When Genoa conquer'd: they have further cause,
Since they are nothing in the state, and in
The city worse than nothing—mere machines,
To serve the nobles' most patrician pleasure.
The troops have long arrears of pay, oft promised,
And murmur deeply—any hope of change

Will draw them forward: they shall pay themselves
With plunder:—but the priests—I doubt the priesthood
Will not be with us; they have hated me
Since that rash hour, when, madden'd with the drone,
I smote the tardy bishop at Treviso,*
Quickening his holy march; yet, ne'ertheless,
They may be won, at least their chief at Rome,
By some well-timed concessions; but, above
All things, I must be speedy: at my hour
Of twilight little light of life remains.
Could I free Venice, and avenge my wrongs,
I had lived too long, and willingly would sleep
Next moment with my sires; and, wanting this,
Better that sixty of my fourscore years
Had been already where—how soon, I care not—
The whole must be extinguish'd;—better that
They ne'er had been, than drag me on to be
The thing these arch-oppressors fain would make me.
Let me consider—of efficient troops
There are three thousand posted at—

Enter VINCENZO *and* ISRAEL BERTUCCIO.

 Vin.   May it please
Your highness, the same patron whom I spake of
Is here to crave your patience.
 Doge.   Leave the chamber,
Vincenzo.—   [*Exit* VINCENZO.
    Sir, you may advance—what would you?
 I. Ber. Redress.
 Doge.   Of whom?
 I. Ber.   Of God and of the Doge.
 Doge. Alas! my friend, you seek it of the twain
Of least respect and interest in Venice.
You must address the council.
 I. Ber.   'Twere in vain;
For he who injured me is one of them.

   * An historical fact. See Marin Sanuto's Lives of the Doges.

Doge. There's blood upon thy face—how came it there?
I. Ber. 'Tis mine, and not the first I've shed for Venice,
But the first shed by a Venetian hand:
A noble smote me.
  Doge.   Doth he live?
  I. Ber.   Not long—
But for the hope I had and have, that you,
My prince, yourself a soldier, will redress
Him, whom the laws of discipline and Venice
Permit not to protect himself;—if not—
I say no more.
  Doge.   But something you would do—
Is it not so?
  I. Ber. I am a man, my lord.
  Doge. Why so is he who smote you.
  I. Ber.   He is call'd so;
Nay, more, a noble one—at least, in Venice:
But since he hath forgotten that I am one,
And treats me like a brute, the brute may turn—
'Tis said the worm will.
  Doge.   Say—his name and lineage?
  I. Ber. Barbaro.
  Doge.   What was the cause? or the pretext?
  I. Ber. I am the chief of the arsenal, employ'd
At present in repairing certain galleys
But roughly used by the Genoese last year.
This morning comes the noble Barbaro
Full of reproof, because our artisans
Had left some frivolous order of his house,
To execute the state's decree; I dared
To justify the men—he raised his hand;—
Behold my blood! the first time it e'er flow'd
Dishonourably.
  Doge.   Have you long time served?
  I. Ber. So long as to remember Zara's siege,
And fight beneath the chief who beat the Huns there,
Sometime my general, now the Doge Faliero.—

ACT I.

Doge. How! are we comrades?—the state's ducal robes
Sit newly on me, and you were appointed
Chief of the arsenal ere I came from Rome;
So that I recognised you not. Who placed you?

I. Ber. The late Doge; keeping still my old command
As patron of a galley: my new office
Was given as the reward of certain scars
(So was your predecessor pleased to say):
I little thought his bounty would conduct me
To his successor as a helpless plaintiff;
At least, in such a cause.

Doge.   Are you much hurt?

I. Ber. Irreparably in my self-esteem.

Doge. Speak out; fear nothing: being stung at heart,
What would you do to be revenged on this man?

I. Ber. That which I dare not name, and yet will do.

Doge. Then wherefore came you here?

I. Ber.   I come for justice,
Because my general is Doge, and will not
See his old soldier trampled on. Had any,
Save Faliero, fill'd the ducal throne,
This blood had been wash'd out in other blood.

Doge. You come to me for justice—unto *me!*
The Doge of Venice, and I cannot give it;
I cannot even obtain it—'twas denied
To me most solemnly an hour ago!

I. Ber. How says your highness?

Doge.   Steno is condemn'd
To a month's confinement.

I. Ber.   What! the same who dared
To stain the ducal throne with those foul words,
That have cried shame to every ear in Venice?

Doge. Ay, doubtless they have echo'd o'er the arsenal,
Keeping due time with every hammer's clink
As a good jest to jolly artisans;
Or making chorus to the creaking oar,
In the vile tune of every galley-slave,

Who, as he sung the merry stave, exulted
He was not a shamed dotard like the Doge.
 I. Ber. Is 't possible? a month's imprisonment!
No more for Steno?
 Doge.   You have heard the offence,
And now you know his punishment; and then
You ask redress of *me!* Go to the Forty,
Who pass'd the sentence upon Michel Steno;
They'll do as much by Barbaro, no doubt.
 I. Ber. Ah! dared I speak my feelings!
 Doge.   Give them breath.
Mine have no further outrage to endure.
 I. Ber. Then, in a word, it rests but on your word
To punish and avenge—I will not say
My petty wrong, for what is a mere blow,
However vile, to such a thing as I am?—
But the base insult done your state and person.
 Doge. You overrate my power, which is a pageant.
This cap is not the monarch's crown; these robes
Might move compassion, like a beggar's rags;
Nay, more, a beggar's are his own, and these
But lent to the poor puppet, who must play
Its part with all its empire in this ermine.
 I. Ber. Wouldst thou be king?
 Doge.   Yes—of a happy people.
 I. Ber. Wouldst thou be sovereign lord of Venice?
 Doge.   Ay,
If that the people shared that sovereignty,
So that nor they nor I were further slaves
To this o'ergrown aristocratic Hydra,
The poisonous heads of whose envenom'd body
Have breathed a pestilence upon us all.
 I. Ber. Yet, thou wast born, and still hast lived, patrician.
 Doge. In evil hour was I so born; my birth
Hath made me Doge to be insulted: but
I lived and toil'd a soldier and a servant
Of Venice and her people, not the senate;

ACT I.

Their good and my own honour were my guerdon.
I have fought and bled; commanded, ay, and conquered;
Have made and marr'd peace oft in embassies,
As it might chance to be our country's 'vantage;
Have traversed land and sea in constant duty,
Through almost sixty years, and still for Venice,
My fathers' and my birthplace, whose dear spires,
Rising at distance o'er the blue Lagoon,
It was reward enough for me to view
Once more; but not for any knot of men,
Nor sect, nor faction, did I bleed or sweat!
But would you know why I have done all this?
Ask of the bleeding pelican why she
Hath ripp'd her bosom? Had the bird a voice,
She'd tell thee 'twas for *all* her little ones.
    I. Ber. And yet they made thee duke.
    Doge.   *They made* me so;
I sought it not, the flattering fetters met me
Returning from my Roman embassy,
And never having hitherto refused
Toil, charge, or duty for the state, I did not,
At these late years, decline what was the highest
Of all in seeming, but of all most base
In what we have to do and to endure:
Bear witness for me thou, my injured subject,
When I can neither right myself nor thee.
    I. Ber. You shall do both, if you possess the will;
And many thousands more not less oppress'd,
Who wait but for a signal—will you give it?
    Doge. You speak in riddles.
    I. Ber.   Which shall soon be read
At peril of my life; if you disdain not
To lend a patient ear.
    Doge.   Say on.
    I. Ber.   Not thou,
Nor I alone, are injured and abused,
Contemn'd and trampled on; but the whole people

Groan with the strong conception of their wrongs:
The foreign soldiers in the senate's pay
Are discontented for their long arrears;
The native mariners, and civic troops,
Feel with their friends; for who is he amongst them
Whose brethren, parents, children, wives, or sisters,
Have not partook oppression, or pollution,
From the patricians? And the hopeless war
Against the Genoese, which is still maintain'd
With the plebeian blood, and treasure wrung
From their hard earnings, has inflamed them further:
Even now—but, I forget that speaking thus,
Perhaps I pass the sentence of my death!
    Doge. And suffering what thou hast done—fear'st thou
        death?
Be silent then, and live on, to be beaten
By those for whom thou hast bled.
    I. Ber.   No, I will speak
At every hazard; and if Venice' Doge
Should turn delator, be the shame on him,
And sorrow too; for he will lose far more
Than I.
    Doge. From me fear nothing; out with it!
    I. Ber. Know then, that there are met and sworn in secret
A band of brethren, valiant hearts and true;
Men who have proved all fortunes, and have long
Grieved over that of Venice, and have right
To do so; having served her in all climes,
And having rescued her from foreign foes,
Would do the same from those within her walls.
They are not numerous, nor yet too few
For their great purpose; they have arms, and means,
And hearts, and hopes, and faith, and patient courage.
    Doge. For what then do they pause?
    I. Ber.   An hour to strike.
    Doge (*aside*). Saint Mark's shall strike that hour!*

* The bells of San Marco were never rung but by order of the Doge.

I. Ber.   I now have placed
My life, my honour, all my earthly hopes
Within thy power, but in the firm belief
That injuries like ours, sprung from one cause,
Will generate one vengeance: should it be so,
Be our chief now—our sovereign hereafter.
   Doge. How many are ye?
   I. Ber.   I'll not answer that
Till I am answer'd.
   Doge.   How, sir! do you menace?
   I. Ber. No; I affirm. I have betray'd myself;
But there's no torture in the mystic wells
Which undermine your palace, nor in those
Not less appalling cells, the "leaden roofs,"
To force a single name from me of others.
The Pozzi and the Piombi were in vain;
They might wring blood from me, but treachery never.
And I would pass the fearful "Bridge of Sighs,"
Joyous that mine must be the last that e'er
Would echo o'er the Stygian wave which flows
Between the murderers and the murder'd, washing
The prison and the palace walls: there are
Those who would live to think on't, and avenge me.
   Doge. If such your power and purpose, why come here
To sue for justice, being in the course
To do yourself due right?
   I. Ber.   Because the man,
Who claims protection from authority,
Showing his confidence and his submission
To that authority, can hardly be
Suspected of combining to destroy it.
Had I sate down too humbly with this blow,
A moody brow and mutter'd threats had made me
A mark'd man to the Forty's inquisition;
But loud complaint, however angrily

One of the pretexts for ringing this alarm was to have been an announcement of the appearance of a Genoese fleet off the Lagune.

It shapes its phrase, is little to be fear'd,
And less distrusted. But, besides all this,
I had another reason.
  Doge.   What was that?
  I. Ber. Some rumours that the Doge was greatly moved
By the reference of the Avogadori
Of Michel Steno's sentence to the Forty
Had reach'd me. I had served you, honour'd you,
And felt that you were dangerously insulted,
Being of an order of such spirits, as
Requite tenfold both good and evil: 'twas
My wish to prove and urge you to redress.
Now you know all; and that I speak the truth,
My peril be the proof.
  Doge.   You have deeply ventured;
But all must do so who would greatly win:
Thus far I'll answer you—your secret's safe.
  I. Ber. And is this all?
  Doge.   Unless with all intrusted,
What would you have me answer?
  I. Ber.   I would have you
Trust him who leaves his life in trust with you.
  Doge. But I must know your plan, your names, and
    numbers;
The last may then be doubled, and the former
Matured and strengthen'd.
  I. Ber.   We're enough already;
You are the sole ally we covet now.
  Doge. But bring me to the knowledge of your chiefs.
  I. Ber. That shall be done upon your formal pledge
To keep the faith that we will pledge to you.
  Doge. When? where?
  I. Ber.   This night I'll bring to your apartment
Two of the principals; a greater number
Were hazardous.
  Doge. Stay, I must think of this.

What if I were to trust myself amongst you,
And leave the palace?
    I. Ber.   You must come alone.
    Doge. With but my nephew.
    I. Ber.   Not were he your son.
    Doge. Wretch! darest thou name my son? He died in arms
At Sapienza for this faithless state.
Oh! that he were alive, and I in ashes!
Or that he were alive ere I be ashes!
I should not need the dubious aid of strangers.
    I. Ber. Not one of all those strangers whom thou doubtest,
But will regard thee with a filial feeling,
So that thou keep'st a father's faith with them.
    Doge. The die is cast. Where is the place of meeting?
    I. Ber. At midnight I will be alone and mask'd
Where'er your highness pleases to direct me,
To wait your coming, and conduct you where
You shall receive our homage, and pronounce
Upon our project.
    Doge.   At what hour arises
The moon?
    I. Ber. Late, but the atmosphere is thick and dusky,
'Tis a sirocco.
    Doge.   At the midnight hour, then,
Near to the church where sleep my sires; the same,
Twin-named from the apostles John and Paul;
A gondola*, with one oar only, will
Lurk in the narrow channel which glides by.
Be there.
    I. Ber. I will not fail.
    Doge.   And now retire —
    I. Ber. In the full hope your highness will not falter
In your great purpose. Prince, I take my leave.
                                      [*Exit* Israel Bertuccio.

---

* A gondola is not like a common boat, but is as easily rowed with one oar as with two (though, of course, not so swiftly), and often is so from motives of privacy; and, since the decay of Venice, of economy.

Doge (solus). At midnight, by the church Saints John and
    Paul,
Where sleep my noble fathers, I repair—
To what? to hold a council in the dark
With common ruffians leagued to ruin states!
And will not my great sires leap from the vault,
Where lie two doges who preceded me,
And pluck me down amongst them? Would they could!
For I should rest in honour with the honour'd.
Alas! I must not think of them, but those
Who have made me thus unworthy of a name
Noble and brave as aught of consular
On Roman marbles; but I will redeem it
Back to its antique lustre in our annals,
By sweet revenge on all that's base in Venice,
And freedom to the rest, or leave it black
To all the growing calumnies of time,
Which never spare the fame of him who fails,
But try the Cæsar, or the Catiline,
By the true touchstone of desert—success.

ACT II.

SCENE I.

An Apartment in the Ducal Palace.

ANGIOLINA (*wife of the* DOGE) *and* MARIANNA.

Ang. What was the Doge's answer!
  Mar.   That he was
That moment summon'd to a conference;
But 'tis by this time ended. I perceived
Not long ago the senators embarking;
And the last gondola may now be seen
Gliding into the throng of barks which stud
The glittering waters.
  Ang.   Would he were return'd!
He has been much disquieted of late;

And Time, which has not tamed his fiery spirit
Nor yet enfeebled even his mortal frame,
Which seems to be more nourish'd by a soul
So quick and restless that it would consume
Less hardy clay—Time has but little power
On his resentments or his griefs. Unlike
To other spirits of his order, who,
In the first burst of passion, pour away
Their wrath or sorrow, all things wear in him
An aspect of eternity: his thoughts,
His feelings, passions, good or evil, all
Have nothing of old age; and his bold brow
Bears but the scars of mind, the thoughts of years,
Not their decrepitude: and he of late
Has been more agitated than his wont.
Would he were come! for I alone have power
Upon his troubled spirit.

 Mar.   It is true,
His highness has of late been greatly moved
By the affront of Steno, and with cause:
But the offender doubtless even now
Is doom'd to expiate his rash insult with
Such chastisement as will enforce respect
To female virtue, and to noble blood.

 Ang. 'Twas a gross insult; but I heed it not
For the rash scorner's falsehood in itself,
But for the effect, the deadly deep impression
Which it has made upon Faliero's soul,
The proud, the fiery, the austere—austere
To all save me: I tremble when I think
To what it may conduct.

 Mar.   Assuredly
The Doge can not suspect you?

 Ang.   Suspect *me!*
Why Steno dared not: when he scrawl'd his lie,
Grovelling by stealth in the moon's glimmering light,
His own still conscience smote him for the act,

And every shadow on the walls frown'd shame
Upon his coward calumny.
  Mar.   'Twere fit
He should be punish'd grievously.
  Ang.   He is so.
  Mar. What! is the sentence pass'd? is he condemn'd?
  Ang. I know not that, but he has been detected.
  Mar. And deem you this enough for such foul scorn?
  Ang. I would not be a judge in my own cause,
Nor do I know what sense of punishment
May reach the soul of ribalds such as Steno;
But if his insults sink no deeper in
The minds of the inquisitors than they
Have ruffled mine, he will, for all acquittance,
Be left to his own shamelessness or shame.
  Mar. Some sacrifice is due to slander'd virtue.
  Ang. Why, what is virtue if it needs a victim?
Or if it must depend upon men's words?
The dying Roman said, "'twas but a name:"
It were indeed no more, if human breath
Could make or mar it.
  Mar.   Yet full many a dame,
Stainless and faithful, would feel all the wrong
Of such a slander; and less rigid ladies,
Such as abound in Venice, would be loud
And all-inexorable in their cry
For justice.
  Ang.   This but proves it is the name
And not the quality they prize: the first
Have found it a hard task to hold their honour,
If they require it to be blazon'd forth;
And those who have not kept it, seek its seeming
As they would look out for an ornament
Of which they feel the want, but not because
They think it so; they live in others' thoughts,
And would seem honest as they must seem fair.
  Mar. You have strange thoughts for a patrician dame.

Ang. And yet they were my father's; with his name,
The sole inheritance he left.
 Mar.   You want none;
Wife to a prince, the chief of the Republic.
 Ang. I should have sought none though a peasant's bride,
But feel not less the love and gratitude
Due to my father, who bestow'd my hand
Upon his early, tried, and trusted friend,
The Count Val di Marino, now our Doge.
 Mar. And with that hand did he bestow your heart?
 Ang. He did so, or it had not been bestow'd.
 Mar. Yet this strange disproportion in your years,
And, let me add, disparity of tempers,
Might make the world doubt whether such an union
Could make you wisely, permanently happy.
 Ang. The world will think with worldlings; but my heart
Has still been in my duties, which are many,
But never difficult.
 Mar.   And do you love him?
 Ang. I love all noble qualities which merit
Love, and I loved my father, who first taught me
To single out what we should love in others,
And to subdue all tendency to lend
The best and purest feelings of our nature
To baser passions. He bestow'd my hand
Upon Faliero: he had known him noble,
Brave, generous; rich in all the qualities
Of soldier, citizen, and friend; in all
Such have I found him as my father said.
His faults are those that dwell in the high bosoms
Of men who have commanded; too much pride,
And the deep passions fiercely foster'd by
The uses of patricians, and a life
Spent in the storms of state and war; and also
From the quick sense of honour, which becomes
A duty to a certain sign, a vice
When overstrain'd, and this I fear in him.

And then he has been rash from his youth upwards,
Yet temper'd by redeeming nobleness
In such sort, that the wariest of republics
Has lavish'd all its chief employs upon him,
From his first fight to his last embassy,
From which on his return the dukedom met him.

 Mar. But previous to this marriage, had your heart
Ne'er beat for any of the noble youth,
Such as in years had been more meet to match
Beauty like yours? or since have you ne'er seen
One, who, if your fair hand were still to give,
Might now pretend to Loredano's daughter?

 Ang. I answer'd your first question when I said
I married.

 Mar. And the second?

 Ang.   Needs no answer.

 Mar. I pray you pardon, if I have offended.

 Ang. I feel no wrath, but some surprise: I knew not
That wedded bosoms could permit themselves
To ponder upon what they *now* might choose,
Or aught save their past choice.

 Mar.   'Tis their past choice
That far too often makes them deem they would
Now choose more wisely, could they cancel it.

 Ang. It may be so. I knew not of such thoughts.

 Mar. Here comes the Doge—shall I retire?

 Ang.   It may
Be better you should quit me; he seems rapt
In thought.—How pensively he takes his way!

          [*Exit* MARIANNA.

    Enter the DOGE *and* PIETRO.

 Doge (*musing*). There is a certain Philip Calendaro
Now in the Arsenal, who holds command
Of eighty men, and has great influence
Besides on all the spirits of his comrades:
This man, I hear, is bold and popular,

ACT II.

Sudden and daring, and yet secret; 'twould
Be well that he were won: I needs must hope
That Israel Bertuccio has secured him,
But fain would be—
    Pie.   My lord, pray pardon me
For breaking in upon your meditation;
The Senator Bertuccio, your kinsman,
Charged me to follow and enquire your pleasure
To fix an hour when he may speak with you.
    Doge. At sunset.—Stay a moment—let me see—
Say in the second hour of night.   [*Exit* PIETRO.
    Ang.   My lord!
    Doge. My dearest child, forgive me—why delay
So long approaching me?—I saw you not.
    Ang. You were absorb'd in thought, and he who now
Has parted from you might have words of weight
To bear you from the senate.
    Doge.   From the senate?
    Ang. I would not interrupt him in his duty
And theirs.
    Doge.   The senate's duty! you mistake;
'Tis we who owe all service to the senate.
    Ang. I thought the Duke had held command in Venice.
    Doge. He shall.—But let that pass.—We will be jocund.
How fares it with you? have you been abroad?
The day is overcast, but the calm wave
Favours the gondolier's light skimming oar;
Or have you held a levee of your friends?
Or has your music made you solitary?
Say—is there aught that you would will within
The little sway now left the Duke? or aught
Of fitting splendour, or of honest pleasure,
Social or lonely, that would glad your heart,
To compensate for many a dull hour, wasted
On an old man oft moved with many cares?
Speak, and 'tis done.
    Ang.   You're ever kind to me.

I have nothing to desire, or to request,
Except to see you oftener and calmer.
 Doge. Calmer?
 Ang.   Ay, calmer, my good lord.—Ah, why
Do you still keep apart, and walk alone,
And let such strong emotions stamp your brow,
As not betraying their full import, yet
Disclose too much?
 Doge.   Disclose too much!—of what?
What is there to disclose?
 Ang.   A heart so ill
At ease.
 Doge. 'Tis nothing, child.—But in the state
You know what daily cares oppress all those
Who govern this precarious commonwealth;
Now suffering from the Genoese without,
And malcontents within—'tis this which makes me
More pensive and less tranquil than my wont.
 Ang. Yet this existed long before, and never
Till in these late days did I see you thus.
Forgive me; there is something at your heart
More than the mere discharge of public duties,
Which long use and a talent like to yours
Have render'd light, nay, a necessity,
To keep your mind from stagnating. 'Tis not
In hostile states, nor perils, thus to shake you;
You, who have stood all storms and never sunk,
And climb'd up to the pinnacle of power
And never fainted by the way, and stand
Upon it, and can look down steadily
Along the depth beneath, and ne'er feel dizzy.
Were Genoa's galleys riding in the port,
Were civil fury raging in Saint Mark's,
You are not to be wrought on, but would fall,
As you have risen, with an unalter'd brow—
Your feelings now are of a different kind;
Something has stung your pride, not patriotism.

ACT II.

Doge. Pride! Angiolina? Alas! none is left me.
Ang. Yes—the same sin that overthrew the angels,
And of all sins most easily besets
Mortals the nearest to the angelic nature:
The vile are only vain; the great are proud.
Doge. I *had* the pride of honour, of *your* honour,
Deep at my heart—But let us change the theme.
Ang. Ah no!—As I have ever shared your kindness
In all things else, let me not be shut out
From your distress: were it of public import,
You know I never sought, would never seek
To win a word from you; but feeling now
Your grief is private, it belongs to me
To lighten or divide it. Since the day
When foolish Steno's ribaldry detected
Unfix'd your quiet, you are greatly changed,
And I would soothe you back to what you were.
Doge. To what I was!—Have you heard Steno's sentence?
Ang. No.
Doge.   A month's arrest.
Ang.   Is it not enough?
Doge. Enough!—yes, for a drunken galley slave,
Who, stung by stripes, may murmur at his master;
But not for a deliberate, false, cool villain,
Who stains a lady's and a prince's honour
Even on the throne of his authority.
Ang. There seems to me enough in the conviction
Of a patrician guilty of a falsehood:
All other punishment were light unto
His loss of honour.
Doge.   Such men have no honour;
They have but their vile lives—and these are spared.
Ang. You would not have him die for this offence?
Doge. Not *now:*—being still alive, I'd have him live
Long as *he* can; he has ceased to merit death;
The guilty saved hath damn'd his hundred judges,
And he is pure, for now his crime is theirs.

Ang. Oh! had this false and flippant libeller
Shed his young blood for his absurd lampoon,
Ne'er from that moment could this breast have known
A joyous hour, or dreamless slumber more.

Doge. Does not the law of Heaven say blood for blood?
And he who *taints* kills more than he who sheds it.
Is it the *pain* of blows, or *shame* of blows,
That make such deadly to the sense of man?
Do not the laws of man say blood for honour?
And, less than honour, for a little gold?
Say not the laws of nations blood for treason?
Is 't nothing to have fill'd these veins with poison
For their once healthful current? is it nothing
To have stain'd your name and mine — the noblest names?
Is 't nothing to have brought into contempt
A prince before his people? to have fail'd
In the respect accorded by mankind
To youth in woman, and old age in man?
To virtue in your sex, and dignity
In ours? — But let them look to it who have saved him.

Ang. Heaven bids us to forgive our enemies.

Doge. Doth Heaven forgive her own? Is Satan saved
From wrath eternal?

Ang. Do not speak thus wildly —
Heaven will alike forgive you and your foes.

Doge. Amen! May Heaven forgive them!

Ang. And will you?

Doge. Yes, when they are in heaven!

Ang. And not till then?

Doge. What matters my forgiveness? an old man's,
Worn out, scorn'd, spurn'd, abused; what matters then
My pardon more than my resentment, both
Being weak and worthless? I have lived too long. —
But let us change the argument. — My child!
My injured wife, the child of Loredano,
The brave, the chivalrous, how little deem'd
Thy father, wedding thee unto his friend,

That he was linking thee to shame!—Alas!
Shame without sin, for thou art faultless. Hadst thou
But had a different husband, *any* husband
In Venice save the Doge, this blight, this brand,
This blasphemy had never fallen upon thee.
So young, so beautiful, so good, so pure,
To suffer this, and yet be unavenged!

  Ang. I am too well avenged, for you still love me,
And trust, and honour me; and all men know
That you are just, and I am true: what more
Could I require, or you command?
  Doge.   'Tis well,
And may be better; but whate'er betide,
Be thou at least kind to my memory.
  Ang. Why speak you thus?
  Doge.   It is no matter why;
But I would still, whatever others think,
Have your respect both now and in my grave.
  Ang. Why should you doubt it? has it ever fail'd?
  Doge. Come hither, child; I would a word with you.
Your father was my friend; unequal fortune
Made him my debtor for some courtesies
Which bind the good more firmly: when, oppress'd
With his last malady, he will'd our union,
It was not to repay me, long repaid
Before by his great loyalty in friendship;
His object was to place your orphan beauty
In honourable safety from the perils,
Which, in this scorpion nest of vice, assail
A lonely and undower'd maid. I did not
Think with him, but would not oppose the thought
Which soothed his death-bed.
  Ang.   I have not forgotten
The nobleness with which you bade me speak
If my young heart held any preference
Which would have made me happier; nor your offer
To make my dowry equal to the rank

Of aught in Venice, and forego all claim
My father's last injunction gave you.
 Doge.   Thus,
'Twas not a foolish dotard's vile caprice,
Nor the false edge of aged appetite,
Which made me covetous of girlish beauty,
And a young bride: for in my fieriest youth
I sway'd such passions; nor was this my age
Infected with that leprosy of lust
Which taints the hoariest years of vicious men,
Making them ransack to the very last
The dregs of pleasure for their vanish'd joys;
Or buy in selfish marriage some young victim,
Too helpless to refuse a state that's honest,
Too feeling not to know herself a wretch.
Our wedlock was not of this sort; you had
Freedom from me to choose, and urged in answer
Your father's choice.
 Ang.   I did so; I would do so
In face of earth and heaven; for I have never
Repented for my sake; sometimes for yours,
In pondering o'er your late disquietudes.
 Doge. I knew my heart would never treat you harshly;
I knew my days could not disturb you long;
And then the daughter of my earliest friend,
His worthy daughter, free to choose again,
Wealthier and wiser, in the ripest bloom
Of womanhood, more skilful to select
By passing these probationary years
Inheriting a prince's name and riches,
Secured, by the short penance of enduring
An old man for some summers, against all
That law's chicane or envious kinsmen might
Have urged against her right; my best friend's child
Would choose more fitly in respect of years,
And not less truly in a faithful heart.
 Ang. My lord, I look'd but to my father's wishes,

Hallow'd by his last words, and to my heart
For doing all its duties, and replying
With faith to him with whom I was affianced.
Ambitious hopes ne'er cross'd my dreams; and should
The hour you speak of come, it will be seen so.

 Doge. I do believe you; and I know you true:
For love, romantic love, which in my youth
I knew to be illusion, and ne'er saw
Lasting, but often fatal, it had been
No lure for me, in my most passionate days,
And could not be so now, did such exist.
But such respect, and mildly paid regard
As a true feeling for your welfare, and
A free compliance with all honest wishes;
A kindness to your virtues, watchfulness
Not shown, but shadowing o'er such little failings
As youth is apt in, so as not to check
Rashly, but win you from them ere you knew
You had been won, but thought the change your choice;
A pride not in your beauty, but your conduct,—
A trust in you—a patriarchal love,
And not a doting homage—friendship, faith—
Such estimation in your eyes as these
Might claim, I hoped for.

 Ang.   And have ever had.

 Doge. I think so. For the difference in our years
You knew it, choosing me, and chose: I trusted
Not to my qualities, nor would have faith
In such, nor outward ornaments of nature,
Were I still in my five and twentieth spring;
I trusted to the blood of Loredano
Pure in your veins; I trusted to the soul
God gave you—to the truths your father taught you—
To your belief in heaven—to your mild virtues—
To your own faith and honour, for my own.

 Ang. You have done well.—I thank you for that trust,

Which I have never for one moment ceased
To honour you the more for.

   Doge.   Where is honour,
Innate and precept-strengthen'd, 'tis the rock
Of faith connubial: where it is not — where
Light thoughts are lurking, or the vanities
Of worldly pleasure rankle in the heart,
Or sensual throbs convulse it, well I know
'Twere hopeless for humanity to dream
Of honesty in such infected blood,
Although 'twere wed to him it covets most:
An incarnation of the poet's god
In all his marble-chisell'd beauty, or
The demi-deity, Alcides, in
His majesty of superhuman manhood,
Would not suffice to bind where virtue is not;
It is consistency which forms and proves it:
Vice cannot fix, and virtue cannot change.
The once fall'n woman must for ever fall;
For vice must have variety, while virtue
Stands like the sun, and all which rolls around
Drinks life, and light, and glory from her aspect.

   Ang. And seeing, feeling thus this truth in others,
(I pray you pardon me;) but wherefore yield you
To the most fierce of fatal passions, and
Disquiet your great thoughts with restless hate
Of such a thing as Steno?

   Doge.   You mistake me.
It is not Steno who could move me thus;
Had it been so, he should — but let that pass.

   Ang. What is't you feel so deeply, then, even now?

   Doge. The violated majesty of Venice,
At once insulted in her lord and laws.

   Ang. Alas! why will you thus consider it?

   Doge. I have thought on't till — but let me lead you back
To what I urged; all these things being noted,

I wedded you; the world then did me justice
Upon the motive, and my conduct proved
They did me right, while yours was all to praise:
You had all freedom — all respect — all trust
From me and mine; and, born of those who made
Princes at home, and swept kings from their thrones
On foreign shores, in all things you appear'd
Worthy to be our first of native dames.

   Ang. To what does this conduct?

   Doge.   To thus much — that
A miscreant's angry breath may blast it all —
A villain, whom for his unbridled bearing,
Even in the midst of our great festival,
I caused to be conducted forth, and taught
How to demean himself in ducal chambers;
A wretch like this may leave upon the wall
The blighting venom of his sweltering heart,
And this shall spread itself in general poison;
And woman's innocence, man's honour, pass
Into a by-word; and the doubly felon
(Who first insulted virgin modesty
By a gross affront to your attendant damsels
Amidst the noblest of our dames in public)
Requite himself for his most just expulsion
By blackening publicly his sovereign's consort,
And be absolved by his upright compeers.

   Ang. But he has been condemn'd into captivity.

   Doge. For such as him a dungeon were acquittal;
And his brief term of mock-arrest will pass
Within a palace. But I've done with him;
The rest must be with you.

   Ang.   With me, my lord?

   Doge. Yes, Angiolina. Do not marvel; I
Have let this prey upon me till I feel
My life cannot be long; and fain would have you
Regard the injunctions you will find within

This scroll (*Giving her a paper*)—Fear not; they are for your
Read them hereafter at the fitting hour.   [advantage:
   Ang. My lord, in life, and after life, you shall
Be honour'd still by me: but may your days
Be many yet—and happier than the present!
This passion will give way, and you will be
Serene, and what you should be—what you were.
   Doge. I will be what I should be, or be nothing;
But never more—oh! never, never more,
O'er the few days or hours which yet await
The blighted old age of Faliero, shall
Sweet Quiet shed her sunset! Never more
Those summer shadows rising from the past
Of a not ill-spent nor inglorious life,
Mellowing the last hours as the night approaches,
Shall soothe me to my moment of long rest.
I had but little more to take, or hope,
Save the regards due to the blood and sweat,
And the soul's labour through which I had toil'd
To make my country honour'd. As her servant—
Her servant, though her chief—I would have gone
Down to my fathers with a name serene
And pure as theirs; but this has been denied me.—
Would I had died at Zara!
   Ang.   There you saved
The state; then live to save her still. A day,
Another day like that would be the best
Reproof to them, and sole revenge for you.
   Doge. But one such day occurs within an age;
My life is little less than one, and 'tis
Enough for Fortune to have granted *once*,
That which scarce one more favour'd citizen
May win in many states and years. But why
Thus speak I? Venice has forgot that day—
Then why should I remember it?—Farewell,
Sweet Angiolina! I must to my cabinet;
There's much for me to do—and the hour hastens.

Ang. Remember what you were.
Doge. It were in vain!
Joy's recollection is no longer joy,
While Sorrow's memory is a sorrow still.

Ang. At least, whate'er may urge, let me implore
That you will take some little pause of rest:
Your sleep for many nights has been so turbid,
That it had been relief to have awaked you,
Had I not hoped that Nature would o'erpower
At length the thoughts which shook your slumbers thus.
An hour of rest will give you to your toils
With fitter thoughts and freshen'd strength.

Doge. I cannot—
I must not, if I could; for never was
Such reason to be watchful: yet a few—
Yet a few days and dream-perturbed nights,
And I shall slumber well—but where?—no matter.
Adieu, my Angiolina.

Ang. Let me be
An instant—yet an instant your companion!
I cannot bear to leave you thus.

Doge. Come then,
My gentle child—forgive me; thou wert made
For better fortunes than to share in mine,
Now darkling in their close toward the deep vale
Where Death sits robed in his all-sweeping shadow.
When I am gone—it may be sooner than
Even these years warrant, for there is that stirring
Within—above—around, that in this city
Will make the cemeteries populous
As e'er they were by pestilence or war,—
When I *am* nothing, let that which I *was*
Be still sometimes a name on thy sweet lips,
A shadow in thy fancy, of a thing
Which would not have thee mourn it, but remember;—
Let us begone, my child—the time is pressing.

[*Exeunt.*

SCENE II.

A retired Spot near the Arsenal.

ISRAEL BERTUCCIO *and* PHILIP CALENDARO.

Cal. How sped you, Israel, in your late complaint?
I. Ber. Why, well.
Cal. Is't possible! will he be punish'd?
I. Ber. Yes.
Cal. With what? a mulct or an arrest?
I. Ber. With death!—
Cal. Now you rave, or must intend revenge,
Such as I counsell'd you, with your own hand.
I. Ber. Yes; and for one sole draught of hate, forego
The great redress we meditate for Venice,
And change a life of hope for one of exile;
Leaving one scorpion crush'd, and thousands stinging
My friends, my family, my countrymen!
No, Calendaro; these same drops of blood,
Shed shamefully, shall have the whole of his
For their requital—But not only his;
We will not strike for private wrongs alone:
Such are for selfish passions and rash men,
But are unworthy a tyrannicide.
Cal. You have more patience than I care to boast.
Had I been present when you bore this insult,
I must have slain him, or expired myself
In the vain effort to repress my wrath.
I. Ber. Thank Heaven, you were not—all had else been
marr'd:
As 'tis, our cause looks prosperous still.
Cal. You saw
The Doge—what answer gave he?
I. Ber. That there was
No punishment for such as Barbaro.
Cal. I told you so before, and that 'twas idle
To think of justice from such hands.
I. Ber. At least,

It lull'd suspicion, showing confidence.
Had I been silent, not a sbirro but
Had kept me in his eye, as meditating
A silent, solitary, deep revenge.

    Cal. But wherefore not address you to the Council?
The Doge is a mere puppet, who can scarce
Obtain right for himself. Why speak to him?

    I. Ber. You shall know that hereafter.
    Cal.   Why not now?
    I. Ber. Be patient but till midnight. Get your musters,
And bid our friends prepare their companies:—
Set all in readiness to strike the blow,
Perhaps in a few hours; we have long waited
For a fit time—that hour is on the dial,
It may be, of to-morrow's sun: delay
Beyond may breed us double danger. See
That all be punctual at our place of meeting,
And arm'd, excepting those of the Sixteen,
Who will remain among the troops to wait
The signal.

    Cal.   These brave words have breathed new life
Into my veins; I am sick of these protracted
And hesitating councils: day on day
Crawl'd on, and added but another link
To our long fetters, and some fresher wrong
Inflicted on our brethren or ourselves,
Helping to swell our tyrants' bloated strength.
Let us but deal upon them, and I care not
For the result, which must be death or freedom!
I'm weary to the heart of finding neither.

    I. Ber. We will be free in life or death! the grave
Is chainless. Have you all the musters ready?
And are the sixteen companies completed
To sixty?

    Cal.   All save two, in which there are
Twenty-five wanting to make up the number.

    I. Ber. No matter; we can do without. Whose are they?

Cal. Bertram's and old Soranzo's, both of whom
Appear less forward in the cause than we are.
　　I. Ber. Your fiery nature makes you deem all those
Who are not restless cold: but there exists
Oft in concentred spirits not less daring
Than in more loud avengers.　Do not doubt them.
　　Cal. I do not doubt the elder; but in Bertram
There is a hesitating softness, fatal
To enterprise like ours: I've seen that man
Weep like an infant o'er the misery
Of others, heedless of his own, though greater;
And in a recent quarrel I beheld him
Turn sick at sight of blood, although a villain's.
　　I. Ber. The truly brave are soft of heart and eyes,
And feel for what their duty bids them do.
I have known Bertram long; there doth not breathe
A soul more full of honour.
　　Cal.　　　　　　　It may be so:
I apprehend less treachery than weakness;
Yet as he has no mistress, and no wife
To work upon his milkiness of spirit,
He may go through the ordeal; it is well
He is an orphan, friendless save in us:
A woman or a child had made him less
Than either in resolve.
　　I. Ber.　　　　　Such ties are not
For those who are call'd to the high destinies
Which purify corrupted commonwealths;
We must forget all feelings save the *one*—
We must resign all passions save our purpose—
We must behold no object save our country—
And only look on death as beautiful,
So that the sacrifice ascend to heaven,
And draw down freedom on her evermore.
　　Cal. But if we fail—
　　I. Ber.　　　　　They never fail who die
In a great cause: the block may soak their gore;

Their heads may sodden in the sun; their limbs
Be strung to city gates and castle walls—
But still their spirit walks abroad. Though years
Elapse, and others share as dark a doom,
They but augment the deep and sweeping thoughts
Which overpower all others, and conduct
The world at last to freedom: What were we,
If Brutus had not lived? He died in giving
Rome liberty, but left a deathless lesson—
A name which is a virtue, and a soul
Which multiplies itself throughout all time
When wicked men wax mighty, and a state
Turns servile: he and his high friend were styled
"The last of Romans!" Let us be the first
Of true Venetians, sprung from Roman sires.

Cal. Our fathers did not fly from Attila
Into these isles, where palaces have sprung
On banks redeem'd from the rude ocean's ooze,
To own a thousand despots in his place.
Better bow down before the Hun, and call
A Tartar lord, than these swoln silkworms masters!
The first at least was man, and used his sword
As sceptre: these unmanly creeping things
Command our swords, and rule us with a word
As with a spell.

I. Ber. It shall be broken soon.
You say that all things are in readiness:
To-day I have not been the usual round,
And why thou knowest; but thy vigilance
Will better have supplied my care: these orders
In recent council to redouble now
Our efforts to repair the galleys, have
Lent a fair colour to the introduction
Of many of our cause into the arsenal,
As new artificers for their equipment,
Or fresh recruits obtain'd in haste to man
The hoped-for fleet.—Are all supplied with arms?

Cal. All who were deem'd trust-worthy: there are some
Whom it were well to keep in ignorance
Till it be time to strike, and then supply them;
When in the heat and hurry of the hour
They have no opportunity to pause,
But needs must on with those who will surround them.
   I. Ber. You have said well. Have you remark'd all such?
   Cal. I've noted most; and caused the other chiefs
To use like caution in their companies.
As far as I have seen, we are enough
To make the enterprise secure, if 'tis
Commenced to-morrow; but, till 'tis begun,
Each hour is pregnant with a thousand perils.
   I. Ber. Let the Sixteen meet at the wonted hour.
Except Soranzo, Nicoletto Blondo,
And Marco Giuda, who will keep their watch
Within the arsenal, and hold all ready
Expectant of the signal we will fix on.
   Cal. We will not fail.
   I. Ber.   Let all the rest be there;
I have a stranger to present to them.
   Cal. A stranger! doth he know the secret?
   I. Ber.   Yes.
   Cal. And have you dared to peril your friends' lives
On a rash confidence in one we know not?
   I. Ber. I have risk'd no man's life except my own —
Of that be certain: he is one who may
Make our assurance doubly sure, according
His aid; and if reluctant, he no less
Is in our power: he comes alone with me,
And cannot 'scape us; but he will not swerve.
   Cal. I cannot judge of this until I know him:
Is he one of our order?
   I. Ber.   Ay, in spirit,
Although a child of greatness; he is one
Who would become a throne, or overthrow one —
One who has done great deeds, and seen great changes;

No tyrant, though bred up to tyranny;
Valiant in war, and sage in council; noble
In nature, although haughty; quick, yet wary:
Yet for all this, so full of certain passions,
That if once stirr'd and baffled, as he has been
Upon the tenderest points, there is no Fury
In Grecian story like to that which wrings
His vitals with her burning hands, till he
Grows capable of all things for revenge;
And add too, that his mind is liberal,
He sees and feels the people are oppress'd,
And shares their sufferings. Take him all in all.
We have need of such, and such have need of us.

 Cal. And what part would you have him take with us?
 I. Ber. It may be, that of chief.
 Cal.   What! and resign
Your own command as leader?
 I. Ber.   Even so.
My object is to make your cause end well,
And not to push myself to power. Experience,
Some skill, and your own choice, had mark'd me out
To act in trust as your commander, till
Some worthier should appear: if I have found such
As you yourselves shall own more worthy, think you
That I would hesitate from selfishness,
And, covetous of brief authority,
Stake our deep interest on my single thoughts,
Rather than yield to one above me in
All leading qualities? No, Calendaro,
Know your friend better; but you all shall judge.—
Away! and let us meet at the fix'd hour.
Be vigilant, and all will yet go well.

 Cal. Worthy Bertuccio, I have known you ever
Trusty and brave, with head and heart to plan
What I have still been prompt to execute.
For my own part, I seek no other chief;
What the rest will decide I know not, but

I am with you, as I have ever been,
In all our undertakings. Now farewell,
Until the hour of midnight sees us meet.   [*Exeunt.*

ACT III.

SCENE I.

Scene, the Space between the Canal and the Church of San Giovanni e San Paolo. An equestrian Statue before it.—A Gondola lies in the Canal at some distance.

Enter the Doge *alone, disguised.*

Doge (*solus*). I am before the hour, the hour whose voice,
Pealing into the arch of night, might strike
These palaces with ominous tottering,
And rock their marbles to the corner-stone,
Waking the sleepers from some hideous dream
Of indistinct but awful augury
Of that which will befall them. Yes, proud city!
Thou must be cleansed of the black blood which makes thee
A lazar-house of tyranny: the task
Is forced upon me, I have sought it not;
And therefore was I punish'd, seeing this
Patrician pestilence spread on and on,
Until at length it smote me in my slumbers,
And I am tainted, and must wash away
The plague-spots in the healing wave. Tall fane!
Where sleep my fathers, whose dim statues shadow
The floor which doth divide us from the dead,
Where all the pregnant hearts of our bold blood,
Moulder'd into a mite of ashes, hold
In one shrunk heap what once made many heroes,
When what is now a handful shook the earth—
Fane of the tutelar saints who guard our house!
Vault where two Doges rest—my sires! who died
The one of toil, the other in the field,
With a long race of other lineal chiefs

And sages, whose great labours, wounds, and state
I have inherited,—let the graves gape,
Till all thine aisles be peopled with the dead,
And pour them from thy portals to gaze on me!
I call them up, and them and thee to witness
What it hath been which put me to this task—
Their pure high blood, their blazon-roll of glories,
Their mighty name dishonour'd all *in* me,
Not *by* me, but by the ungrateful nobles
We fought to make our equals, not our lords:—
And chiefly thou, Ordelafo the brave,
Who perish'd in the field, where I since conquer'd,
Battling at Zara, did the hecatombs
Of thine and Venice' foes, there offer'd up
By thy descendant, merit such acquittance?
Spirits! smile down upon me; for my cause
Is yours, in all life now can be of yours,—
Your fame, your name, all mingled up in mine,
And in the future fortunes of our race!
Let me but prosper, and I make this city
Free and immortal, and our house's name
Worthier of what you were, now and hereafter!

Enter ISRAEL BERTUCCIO.

I. Ber. Who goes there?
Doge.   A friend to Venice.
I. Ber.   'Tis he.
Welcome, my lord,—you are before the time.
Doge. I am ready to proceed to your assembly.
I. Ber. Have with you.—I am proud and pleased to see
Such confident alacrity. Your doubts
Since our last meeting, then, are all dispell'd?
Doge. Not so—but I have set my little left
Of life upon this cast: the die was thrown
When I first listen'd to your treason—Start not!
That is the word; I cannot shape my tongue
To syllable black deeds into smooth names,

Though I be wrought on to commit them. When
I heard you tempt your sovereign, and forbore
To have you dragg'd to prison, I became
Your guiltiest accomplice: now you may,
If it so please you, do as much by me.

 I. Ber. Strange words, my lord, and most unmerited;
I am no spy, and neither are we traitors.

 Doge. We — *Wel* — no matter — you have earn'd the right
To talk of *us*. — But to the point. — If this
Attempt succeeds, and Venice, render'd free
And flourishing, when we are in our graves,
Conducts her generations to our tombs,
And makes her children with their little hands
Strew flowers o'er her deliverers' ashes, then
The consequence will sanctify the deed,
And we shall be like the two Bruti in
The annals of hereafter; but if not,
If we should fail, employing bloody means
And secret plot, although to a good end,
Still we are traitors, honest Israel; — thou
No less than he who was thy sovereign
Six hours ago, and now thy brother rebel.

 I. Ber. 'Tis not the moment to consider thus,
Else I could answer. — Let us to the meeting,
Or we may be observed in lingering here.

 Doge. We *are* observed, and have been.
 I. Ber.   We observed!
Let me discover — and this steel —

 Doge.   Put up;
Here are no human witnesses: look there —
What see you?

 I. Ber.   Only a tall warrior's statue
Bestriding a proud steed, in the dim light
Of the dull moon.

 Doge.   That warrior was the sire
Of my sire's fathers, and that statue was

Decreed to him by the twice rescued city:—
Think you that he looks down on us or no?

 I. Ber. My lord, these are mere fantasies; there are
No eyes in marble.
 Doge.   But there are in Death.
I tell thee, man, there is a spirit in
Such things that acts and sees, unseen, though felt;
And, if there be a spell to stir the dead,
'Tis in such deeds as we are now upon.
Deem'st thou the souls of such a race as mine
Can rest, when he, their last descendant chief,
Stands plotting on the brink of their pure graves
With stung plebeians?
 I. Ber.   It had been as well
To have ponder'd this before,—ere you embark'd
In our great enterprise.—Do you repent?
 Doge. No—but I *feel*, and shall do to the last.
I cannot quench a glorious life at once,
Nor dwindle to the thing I now must be,
And take men's lives by stealth, without some pause:
Yet doubt me not; it is this very feeling,
And knowing *what* has wrung me to be thus,
Which is your best security. There's not
A roused mechanic in your busy plot
So wrong'd as I, so fall'n, so loudly call'd
To his redress: the very means I am forced
By these fell tyrants to adopt is such,
That I abhor them doubly for the deeds
Which I must do to pay them back for theirs.
 I. Ber. Let us away—hark—the hour strikes.
 Doge.   On—on—
It is our knell, or that of Venice—On.
 I. Ber. Say rather, 'tis her freedom's rising peal
Of triumph—This way—we are near the place.
              [*Exeunt.*

SCENE II.

The House where the Conspirators meet.

DAGOLINO, DORO, BERTRAM, FEDELE TREVISANO, CALENDARO, ANTONIO DELLE BENDE, &c. &c.

    Cal. (entering). Are all here?
    Dag.   All with you; except the three
On duty, and our leader Israel,
Who is expected momently.
    Cal.   Where's Bertram?
    Ber. Here!
    Cal.   Have you not been able to complete
The number wanting in your company?
    Ber. I had mark'd out some: but I have not dared
To trust them with the secret, till assured
That they were worthy faith.
    Cal.   There is no need
Of trusting to their faith: *who*, save ourselves
And our more chosen comrades, is aware
Fully of our intent? they think themselves
Engaged in secret to the Signory,*
To punish some more dissolute young nobles
Who have defied the law in their excesses;
But once drawn up, and their new swords well-flesh'd
In the rank hearts of the more odious senators,
They will not hesitate to follow up
Their blow upon the others, when they see
The example of their chiefs, and I for one
Will set them such, that they for very shame
And safety will not pause till all have perish'd.
    Ber. How say you? *all!*
    Cal.   Whom would'st thou spare?
    Ber.   *I spare?*
I have no power to spare. I only question'd,
Thinking that even amongst these wicked men

---

* An historical fact. See APPENDIX, Note (A).

There might be some, whose age and qualities
Might mark them out for pity.
  Cal.   Yes, such pity
As when the viper hath been cut to pieces,
The separate fragments quivering in the sun,
In the last energy of venomous life,
Deserve and have. Why, I should think as soon
Of pitying some particular fang which made
One in the jaw of the swoln serpent, as
Of saving one of these: they form but links
Of one long chain; one mass, one breath, one body;
They eat, and drink, and live, and breed together,
Revel, and lie, oppress, and kill in concert,—
So let them die as *one!*
  Dag.   Should *one* survive,
He would be dangerous as the whole; it is not
Their number, be it tens or thousands, but
The spirit of this aristocracy
Which must be rooted out; and if there were
A single shoot of the old tree in life,
'Twould fasten in the soil, and spring again
To gloomy verdure and to bitter fruit.
Bertram, we must be firm!
  Cal.   Look to it well,
Bertram; I have an eye upon thee.
  Ber.   Who
Distrusts me?
  Cal. Not I; for if I did so,
Thou wouldst not now be there to talk of trust:
It is thy softness, not thy want of faith,
Which makes thee to be doubted.
  Ber.   You should know
Who hear me, who and what I am; a man
Roused like yourselves to overthrow oppression;
A kind man, I am apt to think, as some
Of you have found me; and if brave or no,
You, Calendaro, can pronounce, who have seen me

Put to the proof; or, if you should have doubts,
I'll clear them on your person!
  Cal.   You are welcome,
When once our enterprise is o'er, which must not
Be interrupted by a private brawl.
  Ber. I am no brawler; but can bear myself
As far among the foe as any he
Who hears me; else why have I been selected
To be of your chief comrades? but no less
I own my natural weakness; I have not.
Yet learn'd to think of indiscriminate murder
Without some sense of shuddering; and the sight
Of blood which spouts through hoary scalps is not
To me a thing of triumph, nor the death
Of men surprised a glory. Well—too well
I know that we must do such things on those
Whose acts have raised up such avengers; but
If there were some of these who could be saved
From out this sweeping fate, for our own sakes
And for our honour, to take off some stain
Of massacre, which else pollutes it wholly,
I had been glad; and see no cause in this
For sneer, nor for suspicion!
  Dag.   Calm thee, Bertram;
For we suspect thee not, and take good heart.
It is the cause, and not our will, which asks
Such actions from our hands: we'll wash away
All stains in Freedom's fountain!

   Enter Israel Bertuccio, *and the* Doge, *disguised.*

  Dag.   Welcome, Israel.
  Consp. Most welcome.—Brave Bertuccio, thou art late—
Who is this stranger?
  Cal.   It is time to name him.
Our comrades are even now prepared to greet him
In brotherhood, as I have made it known
That thou wouldst add a brother to our cause,

Approved by thee, and thus approved by all,
Such is our trust in all thine actions. Now
Let him unfold himself.
  I. Ber.   Stranger, step forth!
          [*The* Doge *discovers himself.*
  Consp. To arms!—we are betray'd—it is the Doge!
Down with them both! our traitorous captain, and
The tyrant he hath sold us to.
  Cal. (*drawing his sword*). Hold! hold!
Who moves a step against them dies. Hold! hear
Bertuccio—What! are you appall'd to see
A lone, unguarded, weaponless old man
Amongst you?—Israel, speak! what means this mystery?
  I. Ber. Let them advance and strike at their own bosoms,
Ungrateful suicides! for on our lives
Depend their own, their fortunes, and their hopes.
  Doge. Strike!—If I dreaded death, a death more fearful
Than any your rash weapons can inflict,
I should not now be here:—Oh, noble Courage!
The eldest born of Fear, which makes you brave
Against this solitary hoary head!
See the bold chiefs, who would reform a state
And shake down senates, mad with wrath and dread
At sight of one patrician!—Butcher me,
You can; I care not.—Israel, are these men
The mighty hearts you spoke of? look upon them!
  Cal. Faith! he hath shamed us, and deservedly
Was this your trust in your true chief Bertuccio,
To turn your swords against him and his guest?
Sheathe them, and hear him.
  I. Ber.   I disdain to speak.
They might and must have known a heart like mine
Incapable of treachery; and the power
They gave me to adopt all fitting means
To further their design was ne'er abused.
They might be certain that whoe'er was brought

By me into this council had been led
To take his choice—as brother, or as victim.
 Doge. And which am I to be? your actions leave
Some cause to doubt the freedom of the choice.
 I. Ber. My lord, we would have perish'd here together,
Had these rash men proceeded; but, behold,
They are ashamed of that mad moment's impulse,
And droop their heads; believe me, they are such
As I described them—Speak to them.
 Cal.   Ay, speak;
We are all listening in wonder.
 I. Ber. (*addressing the Conspirators*). You are safe,
Nay, more, almost triumphant—listen then,
And know my words for truth.
 Doge.   You see me here,
As one of you hath said, an old, unarm'd,
Defenceless man; and yesterday you saw me
Presiding in the hall of ducal state,
Apparent sovereign of our hundred isles,
Robed in official purple, dealing out
The edicts of a power which is not mine,
Nor yours, but of our masters—the patricians.
Why I was there you know, or think you know;
Why I am *here*, he who hath been most wrong'd,
He who among you hath been most insulted,
Outraged and trodden on, until he doubt
If he be worm or no, may answer for me,
Asking of his own heart what brought him here?
You know my recent story, all men know it,
And judge of it far differently from those
Who sate in judgment to heap scorn on scorn.
But spare me the recital—it is here,
Here at my heart the outrage—but my words,
Already spent in unavailing plaints,
Would only show my feebleness the more,
And I come here to strengthen even the strong,
And urge them on to deeds, and not to war

With woman's weapons; but I need not urge you.
Our private wrongs have sprung from public vices
In this—I cannot call it commonwealth
Nor kingdom, which hath neither prince nor people,
But all the sins of the old Spartan state
Without its virtues—temperance and valour.
The Lords of Lacedæmon were true soldiers,
But ours are Sybarites, while we are Helots,
Of whom I am the lowest, most enslaved;
Although dress'd out to head a pageant, as
The Greeks of yore made drunk their slaves to form
A pastime for their children. You are met
To overthrow this monster of a state,
This mockery of a government, this spectre,
Which must be exorcised with blood,—and then
We will renew the times of truth and justice,
Condensing in a fair free commonwealth
Not rash equality but equal rights,
Proportion'd like the columns to the temple,
Giving and taking strength reciprocal,
And making firm the whole with grace and beauty,
So that no part could be removed without
Infringement of the general symmetry.
In operating this great change, I claim
To be one of you—if you trust in me;
If not, strike home,—my life is compromised,
And I would rather fall by freemen's hands
Than live another day to act the tyrant
As delegate of tyrants: such I am not,
And never have been—read it in our annals;
I can appeal to my past government
In many lands and cities; they can tell you
If I were an oppressor, or a man
Feeling and thinking for my fellow men.
Haply had I been what the senate sought,
A thing of robes and trinkets, dizen'd out
To sit in state as for a sovereign's picture;

A popular scourge, a ready sentence-signer,
A stickler for the Senate and "the Forty,"
A sceptic of all measures which had not
The sanction of "the Ten," a council-fawner,
A tool, a fool, a puppet,—they had ne'er
Foster'd the wretch who stung me. What I suffer
Has reach'd me through my pity for the people;
That many know, and they who know not yet
Will one day learn: meantime I do devote,
Whate'er the issue, my last days of life—
My present power such as it is, not that
Of Doge, but of a man who has been great
Before he was degraded to a Doge,
And still has individual means and mind;
I stake my fame (and I had fame)—my breath—
(The least of all, for its last hours are nigh)
My heart—my hope—my soul—upon this cast!
Such as I am, I offer me to you
And to your chiefs, accept me or reject me,
A Prince who fain would be a citizen
Or nothing, and who has left his throne to be so.

    Cal. Long live Faliero!—Venice shall be free!
    Consp. Long live Faliero!
    I. Ber.   Comrades! did I well?
Is not this man a host in such a cause?
    Doge. This is no time for eulogies, nor place
For exultation. Am I one of you?
    Cal. Ay, and the first amongst us, as thou hast been
Of Venice—be our general and chief.
    Doge. Chief!—general!—I was general at Zara,
And chief in Rhodes and Cyprus, prince in Venice:
I cannot stoop—that is, I am not fit
To lead a band of—patriots: when I lay
Aside the dignities which I have borne,
'Tis not to put on others, but to be
Mate to my fellows—but now to the point:

ACT III.

Israel has stated to me your whole plan—
'Tis bold, but feasible if I assist it,
And must be set in motion instantly.
    Cal. E'en when thou wilt. Is it not so, my friends?
I have disposed all for a sudden blow;
When shall it be then?
    Doge.   At sunrise.
    Ber.   So soon?
    Doge. So soon?—so late—each hour accumulates
Peril on peril, and the more so now
Since I have mingled with you;—know you not
The Council, and "the Ten?" the spies, the eyes
Of the patricians dubious of their slaves,
And now more dubious of the prince they have made one?
I tell you, you must strike, and suddenly,
Full to the Hydra's heart—its heads will follow.
    Cal. With all my soul and sword, I yield assent.
Our companies are ready, sixty each,
And all now under arms by Israel's order;
Each at their different place of rendezvous,
And vigilant, expectant of some blow;
Let each repair for action to his post!
And now, my lord, the signal?
    Doge.   When you hear
The great bell of Saint Mark's, which may not be
Struck without special order of the Doge
(The last poor privilege they leave their prince),
March on Saint Mark's!
    I. Ber.   And there?—
    Doge.   By different routes
Let your march be directed, every sixty
Entering a separate avenue, and still
Upon the way let your cry be of war
And of the Genoese fleet, by the first dawn
Discern'd before the port; form round the palace,
Within whose court will be drawn out in arms
My nephew and the clients of our house,

Many and martial; while the bell tolls on,
Shout ye, "Saint Mark!—the foe is on our waters!"
    Cal. I see it now—but on, my noble lord.
    Doge. All the patricians flocking to the Council,
(Which they dare not refuse, at the dread signal
Pealing from out their patron saint's proud tower,)
Will then be gather'd in unto the harvest,
And we will reap them with the sword for sickle.
If some few should be tardy or absent them,
'Twill be but to be taken faint and single,
When the majority are put to rest.
    Cal. Would that the hour were come! we will not scotch,
But kill.
    Ber. Once more, sir, with your pardon, I
Would now repeat the question which I ask'd
Before Bertuccio added to our cause
This great ally who renders it more sure,
And therefore safer, and as such admits
Some dawn of mercy to a portion of
Our victims—must all perish in this slaughter?
    Cal. All who encounter me and mine, be sure,
The mercy they have shown, I show.
    Consp.   All! all!
Is this a time to talk of pity? when
Have they e'er shown, or felt, or feign'd it?
    I. Ber.   Bertram,
This false compassion is a folly, and
Injustice to thy comrades and thy cause!
Dost thou not see, that if we single out
Some for escape, they live but to avenge
The fallen? and how distinguish now the innocent
From out the guilty? all their acts are *one*—
A single emanation from one body,
Together knit for our oppression! 'Tis
Much that we let their children live; I doubt
If all of these even should be set apart:
The hunter may reserve some single cub

ACT III.

From out the tiger's litter, but who e'er
Would seek to save the spotted sire or dam,
Unless to perish by their fangs? however,
I will abide by Doge Falicro's counsel:
Let him decide if any should be saved.

Doge. Ask me not—tempt me not with such a question—
Decide yourselves.

I. Ber. You know their private virtues
Far better than we can, to whom alone
Their public vices, and most foul oppression,
Have made them deadly; if there be amongst them
One who deserves to be repeal'd, pronounce.

Doge. Dolfino's father was my friend, and Lando
Fought by my side, and Marc Cornaro shared
My Genoese embassy: I saved the life
Of Veniero—shall I save it twice?
Would that I could save them and Venice also!
All these men, or their fathers, were my friends
Till they became my subjects; then fell from me
As faithless leaves drop from the o'erblown flower,
And left me a lone blighted thorny stalk,
Which, in its solitude, can shelter nothing;
So, as they let me wither, let them perish!

Cal. They cannot co-exist with Venice' freedom!

Doge. Ye, though you know and feel our mutual mass
Of many wrongs, even ye are ignorant
What fatal poison to the springs of life,
To human ties, and all that's good and dear,
Lurks in the present institutes of Venice:
All these men were my friends; I loved them, they
Requited honourably my regards;
We served and fought; we smiled and wept in concert;
We revell'd or we sorrow'd side by side;
We made alliances of blood and marriage;
We grew in years and honours fairly,—till
Their own desire, not my ambition, made
Them choose me for their prince, and then farewell!

Farewell all social memory! all thoughts
In common! and sweet bonds which link old friendships,
When the survivors of long years and actions,
Which now belong to history, soothe the days
Which yet remain by treasuring each other,
And never meet, but each beholds the mirror
Of half a century on his brother's brow,
And sees a hundred beings, now in earth,
Flit round them whispering of the days gone by,
And seeming not all dead, as long as two
Of the brave, joyous, reckless, glorious band,
Which once were one and many, still retain
A breath to sigh for them, a tongue to speak
Of deeds that else were silent, save on marble—
Oime! Oime!—and must I do this deed?

 I. Ber. My lord, you are much moved: it is not now
That such things must be dwelt upon.
 Doge.   Your patience
A moment—I recede not: mark with me
The gloomy vices of this government.
From the hour that made me Doge, the *Doge* THEY *made*
  me—
Farewell the past! I died to all that had been,
Or rather they to me: no friends, no kindness,
No privacy of life—all were cut off:
They came not near me, such approach gave umbrage;
They could not love me, such was not the law;
They thwarted me, 'twas the state's policy;
They baffled me, 'twas a patrician's duty;
They wrong'd me, for such was to right the state;
They could not right me, that would give suspicion;
So that I was a slave to my own subjects;
So that I was a foe to my own friends;
Begirt with spies for guards—with robes for power—
With pomp for freedom—gaolers for a council—
Inquisitors for friends—and hell for life!
I had one only fount of quiet left,

And *that* they poison'd! My pure household gods
Were shiver'd on my hearth, and o'er their shrine
Sate grinning Ribaldry and sneering Scorn.

I. Ber. You have been deeply wrong'd, and now shall be
Nobly avenged before another night.

Doge. I had borne all—it hurt me, but I bore it—
Till this last running over of the cup
Of bitterness—until this last loud insult,
Not only unredress'd, but sanction'd; then,
And thus, I cast all further feelings from me—
The feelings which they crush'd for me, long, long
Before, even in their oath of false allegiance!
Even in that very hour and vow, they abjured
Their friend and made a sovereign, as boys make
Playthings, to do their pleasure—and be broken!
I from that hour have seen but senators
In dark suspicious conflict with the Doge,
Brooding with him in mutual hate and fear;
They dreading he should snatch the tyranny
From out their grasp, and he abhorring tyrants.
To me, then, these men have no *private* life,
Nor claim to ties they have cut off from others;
As senators for arbitrary acts
Amenable, I look on them—as such
Let them be dealt upon.

Cal. And now to action!
Hence, brethren, to our posts, and may this be
The last night of mere words: I'd fain be doing!
Saint Mark's great bell at dawn shall find me wakeful!

I. Ber. Disperse then to your posts: be firm and vigilant;
Think on the wrongs we bear, the rights we claim.
This day and night shall be the last of peril!
Watch for the signal, and then march. I go
To join my band; let each be prompt to marshal
His separate charge: the Doge will now return
To the palace to prepare all for the blow.
We part to meet in freedom and in glory!

5*

Cal. Doge, when I greet you next, my homage to you
Shall be the head of Steno on this sword!
Doge. No; let him be reserved unto the last,
Nor turn aside to strike at such a prey,
Till nobler game is quarried: his offence
Was a mere ebullition of the vice,
The general corruption generated
By the foul aristocracy: he could not—
He dared not in more honourable days
Have risk'd it. I have merged all private wrath
Against him in the thought of our great purpose.
A slave insults me—I require his punishment
From his proud master's hands; if he refuse it,
The offence grows his, and let him answer it.
 Cal. Yet, as the immediate cause of the alliance
Which consecrates our undertaking more,
I owe him such deep gratitude, that fain
I would repay him as he merits; may I?
 Doge. You would but lop the hand, and I the head;
You would but smite the scholar, I the master;
You would but punish Steno, I the senate.
I cannot pause on individual hate,
In the absorbing, sweeping, whole revenge,
Which, like the sheeted fire from heaven, must blast
Without distinction, as it fell of yore,
Where the Dead Sea hath quench'd two cities' ashes.
 I. Ber. Away, then, to your posts! I but remain
A moment to accompany the Doge
To our late place of tryst, to see no spies
Have been upon the scout, and thence I hasten
To where my allotted band is under arms.
 Cal. Farewell, then,—until dawn!
 I. Ber.   Success go with you!
 Consp. We will not fail—Away! My lord, farewell!
   [*The Conspirators salute the* Doge *and* Israel Ber-
     tuccio, *and retire, headed by* Philip Calendaro.
     The Doge *and* Israel Bertuccio *remain.*

ACT III.

I. Ber. We have them in the toil—it cannot fail!
Now thou'rt indeed a sovereign, and wilt make
A name immortal greater than the greatest:
Free citizens have struck at kings ere now;
Cæsars have fallen, and even patrician hands
Have crush'd dictators, as the popular steel
Has reach'd patricians: but, until this hour,
What prince has plotted for his people's freedom?
Or risk'd a life to liberate his subjects?
For ever, and for ever, they conspire
Against the people, to abuse their hands
To chains, but laid aside to carry weapons
Against the fellow nations, so that yoke
On yoke, and slavery and death may whet,
Not glut, the never-gorged Leviathan!
Now, my lord, to our enterprise;—'tis great,
And greater the reward; why stand you rapt?
A moment back, and you were all impatience!

   Doge. And is it then decided! must they die?
   I. Ber. Who?
   Doge.   My own friends by blood and courtesy,
And many deeds and days—the senators?
   I. Ber. You pass'd their sentence, and it is a just one.
   Doge. Ay, so it seems, and so it is to *you;*
You are a patriot, plebeian Gracchus—
The rebel's oracle, the people's tribune—
I blame you not—you act in your vocation;
They smote you, and oppress'd you, and despised you;
So they have *me:* but *you* ne'er spake with them;
You never broke their bread, nor shared their salt;
You never had their wine-cup at your lips;
You grew not up with them, nor laugh'd, nor wept,
Nor held a revel in their company;
Ne'er smiled to see them smile, nor claim'd their smile
In social interchange for yours, nor trusted
Nor wore them in your heart of hearts, as I have:
These hairs of mine are grey, and so are theirs,

The elders of the council: I remember
When all our locks were like the raven's wing,
As we went forth to take our prey around
The isles wrung from the false Mahometan;
And can I see them dabbled o'er with blood?
Each stab to them will seem my suicide.

   I. Ber. Doge! Doge! this vacillation is unworthy
A child; if you are not in second childhood,
Call back your nerves to your own purpose, nor
Thus shame yourself and me. By heavens! I'd rather
Forego even now, or fail in our intent,
Than see the man I venerate subside
From high resolves into such shallow weakness!
You have seen blood in battle, shed it, both
Your own and that of others; can you shrink then
From a few drops from veins of hoary vampires,
Who but give back what they have drain'd from millions?

   Doge. Bear with me! Step by step, and blow on blow,
I will divide with you; think not I waver:
Ah! no; it is the *certainty* of all
Which I must do doth make me tremble thus.
But let these last and lingering thoughts have way,
To which you only and the Night are conscious,
And both regardless; when the hour arrives,
'Tis mine to sound the knell, and strike the blow,
Which shall unpeople many palaces,
And hew the highest genealogic trees
Down to the earth, strew'd with their bleeding fruit,
And crush their blossoms into barrenness:
This will I — must I — have I sworn to do,
Nor aught can turn me from my destiny;
But still I quiver to behold what I
Must be, and think what I have been! Bear with me.

   I. Ber. Re-man your breast; I feel no such remorse,
I understand it not: why should you change?
You acted, and you act, on your free will.

   Doge. Ay, there it is — *you* feel not, nor do I,

Else I should stab thee on the spot, to save
A thousand lives, and, killing, do no murder;
You *feel* not—*you* go to this butcher-work
As if these high-born men were steers for shambles!
When all is over, you'll be free and merry,
And calmly wash those hands incarnadine;
But I, outgoing thee and all thy fellows
In this surpassing massacre, shall be,
Shall see and feel—oh God! oh God! 'tis true,
And thou dost well to answer that it was
"My own free will and act," and yet you err,
For I *will* do this! Doubt not—fear not; I
Will be your most unmerciful accomplice!
And yet I act no more on my free will,
Nor my own feelings—both compel me back;
But there is *hell* within me and around,
And like the demon who believes and trembles
Must I abhor and do. Away! away!
Get thee unto thy fellows, I will hie me
To gather the retainers of our house.
Doubt not, Saint Mark's great bell shall wake all Venice,
Except her slaughter'd senate: ere the sun
Be broad upon the Adriatic there
Shall be a voice of weeping, which shall drown
The roar of waters in the cry of blood!
I am resolved—come on.

   I. Ber.   With all my soul!
Keep a firm rein upon these bursts of passion;
Remember what these men have dealt to thee,
And that this sacrifice will be succeeded
By ages of prosperity and freedom
To this unshackled city: a true tyrant
Would have depopulated empires, nor
Have felt the strange compunction which hath wrung you
To punish a few traitors to the people.
Trust me, such were a pity more misplaced
Than the late mercy of the state to Steno.

Doge. Man, thou hast struck upon the chord which jars
All nature from my heart. Hence to our task!
[*Exeunt.*

ACT IV.

SCENE I.

Palazzo of the Patrician LIONI. LIONI *laying aside the mask and cloak which the Venetian Nobles wore in public, attended by a Domestic.*

Lioni. I will to rest, right weary of this revel,
The gayest we have held for many moons,
And yet, I know not why, it cheer'd me not;
There came a heaviness across my heart,
Which, in the lightest movement of the dance,
Though eye to eye, and hand in hand united
Even with the lady of my love, oppress'd me,
And through my spirit chill'd my blood, until
A damp like death rose o'er my brow; I strove
To laugh the thought away, but 'twould not be;
Through all the music ringing in my ears
A knell was sounding as distinct and clear,
Though low and far, as e'er the Adrian wave
Rose o'er the city's murmur in the night,
Dashing against the outward Lido's bulwark:
So that I left the festival before
It reach'd its zenith, and will woo my pillow
For thoughts more tranquil, or forgetfulness.
Antonio, take my mask and cloak, and light
The lamp within my chamber.
    Ant.   Yes, my lord:
Command you no refreshment?
    Lioni.   Nought, save sleep,
Which will not be commanded. Let me hope it,
[*Exit* ANTONIO.
Though my breast feels too anxious; I will try
Whether the air will calm my spirits: 'tis

ACT IV.

A goodly night; the cloudy wind which blew
From the Levant hath crept into its cave,
And the broad moon has brighten'd. What a stillness!
            [*Goes to an open lattice.*
And what a contrast with the scene I left,
Where the tall torches' glare, and silver lamps'
More pallid gleam along the tapestried walls,
Spread over the reluctant gloom which haunts
Those vast and dimly-latticed galleries
A dazzling mass of artificial light,
Which show'd all things, but nothing as they were.
There Age essaying to recall the past,
After long striving for the hues of youth
At the sad labour of the toilet, and
Full many a glance at the too faithful mirror,
Prank'd forth in all the pride of ornament,
Forgot itself, and trusting to the falsehood
Of the indulgent beams, which show, yet hide,
Believed itself forgotten, and was fool'd.
There Youth, which needed not, nor thought of such
Vain adjuncts, lavish'd its true bloom, and health,
And bridal beauty, in the unwholesome press
Of flush'd and crowded wassailers, and wasted
Its hours of rest in dreaming this was pleasure,
And so shall waste them till the sunrise streams
On sallow cheeks and sunken eyes, which should not
Have worn this aspect yet for many a year.
The music, and the banquet, and the wine—
The garlands, the rose odours, and the flowers—
The sparkling eyes, and flashing ornaments—
The white arms and the raven hair—the braids
And bracelets; swanlike bosoms, and the necklace,
An India in itself, yet dazzling not
The eye like what it circled; the thin robes,
Floating like light clouds 'twixt our gaze and heaven;
The many-twinkling feet so small and sylphlike,
Suggesting the more secret symmetry

Of the fair forms which terminate so well —
All the delusion of the dizzy scene,
Its false and true enchantments — art and nature,
Which swam before my giddy eyes, that drank
The sight of beauty as the parch'd pilgrim's
On Arab sands the false mirage, which offers
A lucid lake to his eluded thirst,
Are gone. — Around me are the stars and waters —
Worlds mirror'd in the ocean, goodlier sight
Than torches glared back by a gaudy glass;
And the great element, which is to space
What ocean is to earth, spreads its blue depths,
Soften'd with the first breathings of the spring;
The high moon sails upon her beauteous way,
Serenely smoothing o'er the lofty walls
Of those tall piles and sea-girt palaces,
Whose porphyry pillars, and whose costly fronts,
Fraught with the orient spoil of many marbles,
Like altars ranged along the broad canal,
Seem each a trophy of some mighty deed
Rear'd up from out the waters, scarce less strangely
Than those more massy and mysterious giants
Of architecture, those Titanian fabrics,
Which point in Egypt's plains to times that have
No other record. All is gentle: nought
Stirs rudely; but, congenial with the night,
Whatever walks is gliding like a spirit.
The tinklings of some vigilant guitars
Of sleepless lovers to a wakeful mistress,
And cautious opening of the casement, showing
That he is not unheard; while her young hand,
Fair as the moonlight of which it seems part,
So delicately white, it trembles in
The act of opening the forbidden lattice,
To let in love through music, makes his heart
Thrill like his lyre-strings at the sight; the dash
Phosphoric of the oar, or rapid twinkle

Of the far lights of skimming gondolas,
And the responsive voices of the choir
Of boatmen answering back with verse for verse;
Some dusky shadow checkering the Rialto;
Some glimmering palace roof, or tapering spire,
Are all the sights and sounds which here pervade
The ocean-born and earth-commanding city—
How sweet and soothing is this hour of calm!
I thank thee, Night! for thou hast chased away
Those horrid bodements which, amidst the throng,
I could not dissipate: and with the blessing
Of thy benign and quiet influence,—
Now will I to my couch, although to rest
Is almost wronging such a night as this—
                    [*A knocking is heard from without.*
Hark! what is that? or who at such a moment?

              Enter ANTONIO.

  Ant. My lord, a man without, on urgent business,
Implores to be admitted.
  Lioni.   Is he a stranger?
  Ant. His face is muffled in his cloak, but both
His voice and gestures seem familiar to me;
I craved his name, but this he seem'd reluctant
To trust, save to yourself; most earnestly
He sues to be permitted to approach you.
  Lioni. 'Tis a strange hour, and a suspicious bearing!
And yet there is slight peril: 'tis not in
Their houses noble men are struck at; still,
Although I know not that I have a foe
In Venice, 'twill be wise to use some caution.
Admit him, and retire; but call up quickly
Some of thy fellows, who may wait without.—
Who can this man be?—
            [*Exit* ANTONIO, *and returns with* BERTRAM *muffled.*
  Ber.   My good lord Lioni,

I have no time to lose, nor thou — dismiss
This menial hence; I would be private with you.
    Lioni. It seems the voice of Bertram — Go, Antonio.
                                                [*Exit* ANTONIO.
Now, stranger, what would you at such an hour?
    Ber. (*discovering himself*). A boon, my noble patron; you
        have granted
Many to your poor client, Bertram; add
This one, and make him happy.
    Lioni.   Thou hast known me
From boyhood, ever ready to assist thee
In all fair objects of advancement, which
Beseem one of thy station; I would promise
Ere thy request was heard, but that the hour,
Thy bearing, and this strange and hurried mode
Of suing, gives me to suspect this visit
Hath some mysterious import — but say on —
What has occurred, some rash and sudden broil? —
A cup too much, a scuffle, and a stab? —
Mere things of every day; so that thou hast not
Spilt noble blood, I guarantee thy safety;
But then thou must withdraw, for angry friends
And relatives, in the first burst of vengeance,
Are things in Venice deadlier than the laws.
    Ber. My lord, I thank you; but —
    Lioni.   But what? You have not
Raised a rash hand against one of our order?
If so, withdraw and fly, and own it not;
I would not slay — but then I must not save thee!
He who has shed patrician blood —
    Ber.   I come
To save patrician blood, and not to shed it!
And thereunto I must be speedy, for
Each minute lost may lose a life; since Time
Has changed his slow scythe for the two-edged sword,
And is about to take, instead of sand,

ACT IV.   77

The dust from sepulchres to fill his hour-glass!—
Go not *thou* forth to-morrow!
    Lioni.   Wherefore not?—
What means this menace?
    Ber.   Do not seek its meaning,
But do as I implore thee;—stir not forth,
Whate'er be stirring; though the roar of crowds—
The cry of women, and the shrieks of babes—
The groans of men—the clash of arms—the sound
Of rolling drum, shrill trump, and hollow bell,
Peal in one wide alarum!—Go not forth
Until the tocsin's silent, nor even then
Till I return!
    Lioni.   Again, what does this mean?
    Ber. Again, I tell thee, ask not; but by all
Thou holdest dear on earth or heaven—by all
The souls of thy great fathers, and thy hope
To emulate them, and to leave behind
Descendants worthy both of them and thee—
By all thou hast of bless'd in hope or memory—
By all thou hast to fear here or hereafter—
By all the good deeds thou hast done to me,
Good I would now repay with greater good,
Remain within—trust to thy household gods,
And to my word for safety, if thou dost
As I now counsel—but if not, thou art lost!
    Lioni. I am indeed already lost in wonder;
Surely thou ravest! what have *I* to dread?
Who are my foes? or if there be such, *why*
Art *thou* leagued with them?—*thou!* or if so leagued,
Why comest thou to tell me at this hour,
And not before?
    Ber.   I cannot answer this.
Wilt thou go forth despite of this true warning?
    Lioni. I was not born to shrink from idle threats,
The cause of which I know not: at the hour

Of council, be it soon or late, I shall not
Be found among the absent.
 Ber.   Say not so!
Once more, art thou determined to go forth?
 Lioni. I am. Nor is there aught which shall impede me!
 Ber. Then Heaven have mercy on thy soul!—Farewell!
              [*Going.*
 Lioni. Stay—there is more in this than my own safety
Which makes me call thee back; we must not part thus:
Bertram, I have known thee long.
 Ber.   From childhood, signor,
You have been my protector: in the days
Of reckless infancy, when rank forgets,
Or, rather, is not yet taught to remember
Its cold prerogative, we play'd together;
Our sports, our smiles, our tears, were mingled oft;
My father was your father's client, I
His son's scarce less than foster-brother; years
Saw us together—happy, heart-full hours!
Oh God! the difference 'twixt those hours and this!
 Lioni. Bertram, 'tis thou who hast forgotten them.
 Ber. Nor now, nor ever; whatsoe'er betide,
I would have saved you: when to manhood's growth
We sprung, and you, devoted to the state,
As suits your station, the more humble Bertram
Was left unto the labours of the humble,
Still you forsook me not; and if my fortunes
Have not been towering, 'twas no fault of him
Who ofttimes rescued and supported me
When struggling with the tides of circumstance
Which bear away the weaker: noble blood
Ne'er mantled in a nobler heart than thine
Has proved to me, the poor plebeian Bertram.
Would that thy fellow senators were like thee!
 Lioni. Why, what hast thou to say against the senate?
 Ber. Nothing.
 Lioni.   I know that there are angry spirits

And turbulent mutterers of stifled treason,
Who lurk in narrow places, and walk out
Muffled to whisper curses to the night;
Disbanded soldiers, discontented ruffians,
And desperate libertines who brawl in taverns;
Thou herdest not with such: 'tis true, of late
I have lost sight of thee, but thou wert wont
To lead a temperate life, and break thy bread
With honest mates, and bear a cheerful aspect.
What hath come to thee? in thy hollow eye
And hueless cheek, and thine unquiet motions,
Sorrow and shame and conscience seem at war
To waste thee.

 Ber.   Rather shame and sorrow light
On the accursed tyranny which rides
The very air in Venice, and makes men
Madden as in the last hours of the plague
Which sweeps the soul deliriously from life!

 Lioni. Some villains have been tampering with thee,
   Bertram;
This is not thy old language, nor own thoughts;
Some wretch has made thee drunk with disaffection:
But thou must not be lost so; thou *wert* good
And kind, and art not fit for such base acts
As vice and villany would put thee to:
Confess—confide in me—thou know'st my nature—
What is it thou and thine are bound to do,
Which should prevent thy friend, the only son
Of him who was a friend unto thy father,
So that our good-will is a heritage
We should bequeath to our posterity
Such as ourselves received it, or augmented;
I say, what is it thou must do, that I
Should deem thee dangerous, and keep the house
Like a sick girl?

 Ber.   Nay, question me no further:
I must be gone.—

Lioni. And I be murder'd!—say,
Was it not thus thou said'st, my gentle Bertram?

Ber. Who talks of murder? what said I of murder?—
'Tis false! I did not utter such a word.

Lioni. Thou didst not; but from out thy wolfish eye,
So changed from what I knew it, there glares forth
The gladiator. If *my* life's thine object,
Take it—I am unarm'd,—and then away!
I would not hold my breath on such a tenure
As the capricious mercy of such things
As thou and those who have set thee to thy task-work.

Ber. Sooner than spill thy blood, I peril mine;
Sooner than harm a hair of thine, I place
In jeopardy a thousand heads, and some
As noble, nay, even nobler than thine own.

Lioni. Ay, is it even so? Excuse me, Bertram;
I am not worthy to be singled out
From such exalted hecatombs—who are they
That *are* in danger, and that *make* the danger?

Ber. Venice, and all that she inherits, are
Divided like a house against itself,
And so will perish ere to-morrow's twilight!

Lioni. More mysteries, and awful ones! But now,
Or thou, or I, or both, it may be, are
Upon the verge of ruin; speak once out,
And thou art safe and glorious; for 'tis more
Glorious to save than slay, and slay i' the dark too—
Fie, Bertram! that was not a craft for thee!
How would it look to see upon a spear
The head of him whose heart was open to thee,
Borne by thy hand before the shuddering people?
And such may be my doom; for here I swear,
Whate'er the peril or the penalty
Of thy denunciation, I go forth,
Unless thou dost detail the cause, and show
The consequence of all which led thee here!

Ber. Is there no way to save thee? minutes fly,

ACT IV.

And thou art lost!—*thou!* my sole benefactor,
The only being who was constant to me
Through every change. Yet, make me not a traitor!
Let me save thee—but spare my honour!

   Lioni. Where
Can lie the honour in a league of murder?
And who are traitors save unto the state?

   Ber. A league is still a compact, and more binding
In honest hearts when words must stand for law;
And in my mind, there is no traitor like
He whose domestic treason plants the poniard
Within the breast which trusted to his truth.

   Lioni. And *who* will strike the steel to mine?

   Ber. Not I;
I could have wound my soul up to all things
Save this. *Thou* must not die! and think how dear
Thy life is, when I risk so many lives,
Nay, more, the life of lives, the liberty
Of future generations, *not* to be
The assassin thou miscall'st me;—once, once more
I do adjure thee, pass not o'er thy threshold!

   Lioni. It is in vain—this moment I go forth.

   Ber. Then perish Venice rather than my friend!
I will disclose—ensnare—betray—destroy—
Oh, what a villain I become for thee!

   Lioni. Say, rather thy friend's saviour and the state's!—
Speak—pause not—all rewards, all pledges for
Thy safety and thy welfare; wealth such as
The state accords her worthiest servants; nay,
Nobility itself I guarantee thee,
So that thou art sincere and penitent.

   Ber. I have thought again: it must not be—I love thee—
Thou knowest it—that I stand here is the proof,
Not least though last; but having done my duty
By thee, I now must do it by my country!
Farewell—we meet no more in life!—farewell!

Lord Byron. V.

Lioni. What, ho!—Antonio—Pedro—to the door!
See that none pass—arrest this man!—

Enter ANTONIO *and other armed Domestics, who seize* BERTRAM.

 Lioni (continues).   Take care
He hath no harm; bring me my sword and cloak,
And man the gondola with four oars—quick—

                 [*Exit* ANTONIO.

We will unto Giovanni Gradenigo's,
And send for Marc Cornaro:—fear not, Bertram;
This needful violence is for thy safety,
No less than for the general weal.
 Ber.   Where wouldst thou
Bear me a prisoner?
 Lioni.   Firstly to "the Ten;"
Next to the Doge.
 Ber.   To the Doge?
 Lioni.   Assuredly:
Is he not chief of the state?
 Ber.   Perhaps at sunrise—
 Lioni. What mean you?—but we'll know anon.
 Ber.   Art sure?
 Lioni. Sure as all gentle means can make; and if
They fail, you know "the Ten" and their tribunal,
And that St. Mark's has dungeons, and the dungeons
A rack.
 Ber. Apply it then before the dawn
Now hastening into heaven.—One more such word,
And you shall perish piecemeal, by the death
You think to doom to me.

       Re-enter ANTONIO.

 Ant.   The bark is ready,
My lord, and all prepared.
 Lioni.   Look to the prisoner.
Bertram, I'll reason with thee as we go
To the Magnifico's, sage Gradenigo.   [*Exeunt.*

SCENE II.

The Ducal Palace.—The Doge's Apartment.

The DOGE *and his nephew* BERTUCCIO FALIERO.

Doge. Are all the people of our house in muster?
 Ber. F. They are array'd, and eager for the signal,
Within our palace precincts at San Polo.*
I come for your last orders.
 Doge. It had been
As well had there been time to have got together,
From my own fief, Val di Marino, more
Of our retainers—but it is too late.
 Ber. F. Methinks, my lord, 'tis better as it is:
A sudden swelling of our retinue
Had waked suspicion; and, though fierce and trusty,
The vassals of that district are too rude
And quick in quarrel to have long maintain'd
The secret discipline we need for such
A service, till our foes are dealt upon.
 Doge. True; but when once the signal has been given,
These are the men for such an enterprise;
These city slaves have all their private bias,
Their prejudice *against* or *for* this noble,
Which may induce them to o'erdo or spare
Where mercy may be madness; the fierce peasants,
Serfs of my county of Val di Marino,
Would do the bidding of their lord without
Distinguishing for love or hate his foes;
Alike to them Marcello or Cornaro,
A Gradenigo or a Foscari;
They are not used to start at those vain names,
Nor bow the knee before a civic senate;
A chief in armour is their Suzerain,
And not a thing in robes.
 Ber. F. We are enough;

* The Doge's family palace.

And for the dispositions of our clients
Against the senate I will answer.
  Doge.   Well,
The die is thrown; but for a warlike service,
Done in the field, commend me to my peasants:
They made the sun shine through the host of Huns
When sallow burghers slunk back to their tents,
And cower'd to hear their own victorious trumpet.
If there be small resistance, you will find
These citizens all lions, like their standard;
But if there's much to do, you'll wish with me,
A band of iron rustics at our backs.
  Ber. F. Thus thinking, I must marvel you resolve
To strike the blow so suddenly.
  Doge.   Such blows
Must be struck suddenly or never. When
I had o'ermaster'd the weak false remorse
Which yearn'd about my heart, too fondly yielding
A moment to the feelings of old days,
I was most fain to strike; and, firstly, that
I might not yield again to such emotions;
And, secondly, because of all these men,
Save Israel and Philip Calendaro,
I know not well the courage or the faith:
To-day might find 'mongst them a traitor to us,
As yesterday a thousand to the senate;
But once in, with their hilts hot in their hands,
They must *on* for their own sakes; one stroke struck,
And the mere instinct of the first-born Cain,
Which ever lurks somewhere in human hearts,
Though circumstance may keep it in abeyance,
Will urge the rest on like to wolves; the sight
Of blood to crowds begets the thirst of more,
As the first wine-cup leads to the long revel;
And you will find a harder task to quell
Than urge them when they *have* commenced, but till
That moment, a mere voice, a straw, a shadow,

Are capable of turning them aside.—
How goes the night?
    Ber. F.   Almost upon the dawn.
    Doge. Then it is time to strike upon the bell.
Are the men posted?
    Ber. F.   By this time they are;
But they have orders not to strike, until
They have command from you through me in person.
    Doge. 'Tis well.—Will the morn never put to rest
These stars which twinkle yet o'er all the heavens?
I am settled and bound up, and being so,
The very effort which it cost me to
Resolve to cleanse this commonwealth with fire,
Now leaves my mind more steady. I have wept,
And trembled at the thought of this dread duty;
But now I have put down all idle passion,
And look the growing tempest in the face,
As doth the pilot of an admiral galley:
Yet (wouldst thou think it, kinsman?) it hath been
A greater struggle to me, than when nations
Beheld their fate merged in the approaching fight,
Where I was leader of a phalanx, where
Thousands were sure to perish—Yes, to spill
The rank polluted current from the veins
Of a few bloated despots needed more
To steel me to a purpose such as made
Timoleon immortal, than to face
The toils and dangers of a life of war.
    Ber. F. It gladdens me to see your former wisdom
Subdue the furies which so wrung you ere
You were decided.
    Doge.   It was ever thus
With me; the hour of agitation came
In the first glimmerings of a purpose, when
Passion had too much room to sway; but in
The hour of action I have stood as calm
As were the dead who lay around me: this

They knew who made me what I am, and trusted
To the subduing power which I preserved
Over my mood, when its first burst was spent.
But they were not aware that there are things
Which make revenge a virtue by reflection,
And not an impulse of mere anger; though
The laws sleep, justice wakes, and injured souls
Oft do a public right with private wrong,
And justify their deeds unto themselves.—
Methinks the day breaks—is it not so? look,
Thine eyes are clear with youth;—the air puts on
A morning freshness, and, at least to me,
The sea looks greyer through the lattice.

Ber. F. True,
The morn is dappling in the sky.
Doge. Away then!
See that they strike without delay, and with
The first toll from St. Mark's, march on the palace
With all our house's strength; here I will meet you—
The Sixteen and their companies will move
In separate columns at the self-same moment—
Be sure you post yourself at the great gate:
I would not trust "the Ten" except to us—
The rest, the rabble of patricians, may
Glut the more careless swords of those leagued with us.
Remember that the cry is still "Saint Mark!
The Genoese are come—ho! to the rescue!
Saint Mark and Liberty!"—Now—now to action!

Ber. F. Farewell then, noble uncle! we will meet
In freedom and true sovereignty, or never!

Doge. Come hither, my Bertuccio—one embrace—
Speed, for the day grows broader—Send me soon
A messenger to tell me how all goes
When you rejoin our troops, and then sound—sound
The storm-bell from Saint Mark's!

[*Exit* BERTUCCIO FALIERO.

Doge (solus). He is gone,

And on each footstep moves a life. — 'Tis done.
Now the destroying angel hovers o'er
Venice, and pauses ere he pours the vial,
Even as the eagle overlooks his prey,
And for a moment, poised in middle air,
Suspends the motion of his mighty wings,
Then swoops with his unerring beak. — Thou day!
That slowly walk'st the waters! march — march on —
I would not smite i' the dark, but rather see
That no stroke errs. And you, ye blue sea-waves!
I have seen you dyed ere now, and deeply too,
With Genoese, Saracen, and Hunnish gore,
While that of Venice flow'd too, but victorious;
Now thou must wear an unmix'd crimson; no
Barbaric blood can reconcile us now
Unto that horrible incarnadine,
But friend or foe will roll in civic slaughter.
And have I lived to fourscore years for this?
I, who was named Preserver of the City?
I, at whose name the million's caps were flung
Into the air, and cries from tens of thousands
Rose up, imploring Heaven to send me blessings,
And fame, and length of days — to see this day?
But this day, black within the calendar,
Shall be succeeded by a bright millennium.
Doge Dandolo survived to ninety summers
To vanquish empires, and refuse their crown;
I will resign a crown, and make the state
Renew its freedom — but oh! by what means?
The noble end must justify them — What
Are a few drops of human blood? 'tis false,
The blood of tyrants is not human; they,
Like to incarnate Molochs, feed on ours,
Until 'tis time to give them to the tombs
Which they have made so populous. — Oh world!
Oh men! what are ye, and our best designs,
That we must work by crime to punish crime?

And slay as if Death had but this one gate,
When a few years would make the sword superfluous?
And I, upon the verge of th' unknown realm,
Yet send so many heralds on before me?—
I must not ponder this.

[*A pause.*

Hark! was there not
A murmur as of distant voices, and
The tramp of feet in martial unison?
What phantoms even of sound our wishes raise!
It cannot be—the signal hath not rung—
Why pauses it? My nephew's messenger
Should be upon his way to me, and he
Himself perhaps even now draws grating back
Upon its ponderous hinge the steep tower portal,
Where swings the sullen huge oracular bell,
Which never knells but for a princely death,
Or for a state in peril, pealing forth
Tremendous bodements; let it do its office,
And be this peal its awfullest and last
Sound till the strong tower rock!—What! silent still?
I would go forth, but that my post is here,
To be the centre of re-union to
The oft discordant elements which form
Leagues of this nature, and to keep compact
The wavering of the weak, in case of conflict;
For if they should do battle, 'twill be here,
Within the palace, that the strife will thicken:
Then here must be my station, as becomes
The master-mover.—Hark! he comes—he comes,
My nephew, brave Bertuccio's messenger.—
What tidings? Is he marching? hath he sped?—
They here!—all's lost—yet will I make an effort.

Enter a Signor of the Night, *with Guards, &c. &c.*

Sig. Doge, I arrest thee of high treason!
Doge. Me!

Thy prince, of treason? — Who are they that dare
Cloak their own treason under such an order?
    Sig. (*showing his order*). Behold my order from the as-
        sembled Ten.
    Doge. And *where* are they, and *why* assembled? no
Such council can be lawful, till the prince
Preside there, and that duty's mine: on thine
I charge thee, give me way, or marshal me
To the council chamber.
    Sig.   Duke! it may not be:
Nor are they in the wonted Hall of Council,
But sitting in the convent of Saint Saviour's.
    Doge. You dare to disobey me, then?
    Sig.   I serve
The state, and needs must serve it faithfully;
My warrant is the will of those who rule it.
    Doge. And till that warrant has my signature
It is illegal, and, as *now* applied,
Rebellious — Hast thou weigh'd well thy life's worth,
That thus you dare assume a lawless function?
    Sig. 'Tis not my office to reply, but act—
I am placed here as guard upon thy person,
And not as judge to hear or to decide.
    Doge (*aside*). I must gain time — So that the storm-bell
        sound
All may be well yet. — Kinsman, speed — speed — speed! —
Our fate is trembling in the balance, and
Woe to the vanquish'd! be they prince and people,
Or slaves and senate —
                [*The great bell of Saint Mark's tolls.*
                Lo! it sounds — it tolls!
    Doge (*aloud*). Hark, Signor of the Night! and you, ye
        hirelings,
Who wield your mercenary staves in fear,
It is your knell — Swell on, thou lusty peal!
Now, knaves, what ransom for your lives?
    Sig.   Confusion!

Stand to your arms, and guard the door—all's lost
Unless that fearful bell be silenced soon.
The officer hath miss'd his path or purpose,
Or met some unforeseen and hideous obstacle.
Anselmo, with thy company proceed
Straight to the tower; the rest remain with me.
[Exit part of the Guard.

Doge. Wretch! if thou wouldst have thy vile life, implore it;
It is not now a lease of sixty seconds.
Ay, send thy miserable ruffians forth;
They never shall return.
   Sig.   So let it be!
They die then in their duty, as will I.
   Doge. Fool! the high eagle flies at nobler game
Than thou and thy base myrmidons,—live on,
So thou provok'st not peril by resistance,
And learn (if souls so much obscured can bear
To gaze upon the sunbeams) to be free.
   Sig. And learn thou to be captive—It hath ceased,
[The bell ceases to toll.
The traitorous signal, which was to have set
The bloodhound mob on their patrician prey—
The knell hath rung, but it is not the senate's!
   Doge (after a pause). All's silent, and all's lost!
   Sig.   Now, Doge, denounce me
As rebel slave of a revolted council!
Have I not done my duty?
   Doge.   Peace, thou thing!
Thou hast done a worthy deed, and earn'd the price
Of blood, and they who use thee will reward thee.
But thou wert sent to watch, and not to prate,
As thou said'st even now—then do thine office,
But let it be in silence, as behoves thee,
Since, though thy prisoner, I am thy prince.
   Sig. I did not mean to fail in the respect
Due to your rank: in this I shall obey you.

ACT IV.   91

Doge (aside). There now is nothing left me save to die;
And yet how near success! I would have fallen,
And proudly, in the hour of triumph, but
To miss it thus! —

Enter other SIGNORS OF THE NIGHT, *with* BERTUCCIO FALIERO
prisoner.

2d Sig.   We took him in the act
Of issuing from the tower, where, at his order,
As delegated from the Doge, the signal
Had thus begun to sound.
   1st Sig.   Are all the passes
Which lead up to the palace well secured?
   2d Sig. They are — besides, it matters not; the chiefs
Are all in chains, and some even now on trial —
Their followers are dispersed, and many taken.
   Ber. F. Uncle!
   Doge.   It is in vain to war with Fortune;
The glory hath departed from our house.
   Ber. F. Who would have deem'd it? — Ah! one moment
       sooner!
   Doge. That moment would have changed the face of ages;
This gives us to eternity — We'll meet it
As men whose triumph is not in success,
But who can make their own minds all in all,
Equal to every fortune. Droop not, 'tis
But a brief passage — I would go alone,
Yet if they send us, as 'tis like, together,
Let us go worthy of our sires and selves.
   Ber. F. I shall not shame you, uncle.
   1st Sig.   Lords, our orders
Are to keep guard on both in separate chambers,
Until the council call ye to your trial.
   Doge. Our trial! will they keep their mockery up
Even to the last? but let them deal upon us,
As we had dealt on them, but with less pomp.
'Tis but a game of mutual homicides,

Who have cast lots for the first death, and they
Have won with false dice.—Who hath been our Judas?
    1st Sig. I am not warranted to answer that.
    Ber. F. I'll answer for thee—'tis a certain Bertram,
Even now deposing to the secret giunta.
    Doge. Bertram, the Bergamask! With what vile tools
We operate to slay or save! This creature,
Black with a double treason, now will earn
Rewards and honours, and be stamp'd in story
With the geese in the Capitol, which gabbled
Till Rome awoke, and had an annual triumph,
While Manlius, who hurl'd down the Gauls, was cast
From the Tarpeian.
    1st Sig.   He aspired to treason,
And sought to rule the state.
    Doge.   He saved the state,
And sought but to reform what he revived—
But this is idle—Come, sirs, do your work.
    1st Sig. Noble Bertuccio, we must now remove you
Into an inner chamber.
    Ber. F.   Farewell, uncle!
If we shall meet again in life I know not,
But they perhaps will let our ashes mingle.
    Doge. Yes, and our spirits, which shall yet go forth,
And do what our frail clay, thus clogg'd, hath fail'd in!
They cannot quench the memory of those
Who would have hurl'd them from their guilty thrones,
And such examples will find heirs, though distant.

ACT V.

SCENE I.

The Hall of the Council of Ten assembled with the additional Senators, who, on the Trials of the Conspirators for the Treason of MARINO FALIERO, *composed what was called the Giunta,— Guards, Officers, &c. &c. —* ISRAEL BERTUCCIO *and* PHILIP CALENDARO *as Prisoners. —* BERTRAM, LIONI, *and Witnesses, &c.*

The Chief of the Ten, BENINTENDE.

Ben. There now rests, after such conviction of
Their manifold and manifest offences,
But to pronounce on these obdurate men
The sentence of the law:— a grievous task
To those who hear, and those who speak. Alas!
That it should fall to me! and that my days
Of office should be stigmatised through all
The years of coming time, as bearing record
To this most foul and complicated treason
Against a just and free state, known to all
The earth as being the Christian bulwark 'gainst
The Saracen and the schismatic Greek,
The savage Hun, and not less barbarous Frank;
A city which has open'd India's wealth
To Europe; the last Roman refuge from
O'erwhelming Attila; the ocean's queen;
Proud Genoa's prouder rival! 'Tis to sap
The throne of such a city, these lost men
Have risk'd and forfeited their worthless lives —
So let them die the death.
　　I. Ber.　　　　　　We are prepared;
Your racks have done that for us. Let us die.
　　Ben. If ye have that to say which would obtain
Abatement of your punishment, the Giunta
Will hear you; if you have aught to confess,
Now is your time, perhaps it may avail ye.

 Ber. F. We stand to hear, and not to speak.
 Ben.   Your crimes
Are fully proved by your accomplices,
And all which circumstance can add to aid them;
Yet we would hear from your own lips complete
Avowal of your treason: on the verge
Of that dread gulf which none repass, the truth
Alone can profit you on earth or heaven—
Say, then, what was your motive?
 I. Ber.   Justice!
 Ben.   What
Your object?
 I. Ber. Freedom!
 Ben.   You are brief, sir.
 I. Ber. So my life grows: I
Was bred a soldier, not a senator.
 Ben. Perhaps you think by this blunt brevity
To brave your judges to postpone the sentence?
 I. Ber. Do you be brief as I am, and believe me,
I shall prefer that mercy to your pardon.
 Ben. Is this your sole reply to the tribunal?
 I. Ber. Go, ask your racks what they have wrung from us,
Or place us there again; we have still some blood left,
And some slight sense of pain in these wrench'd limbs:
But this ye dare not do; for if we die there —
And you have left us little life to spend
Upon your engines, gorged with pangs already —
Ye lose the public spectacle, with which
You would appal your slaves to further slavery!
Groans are not words, nor agony assent,
Nor affirmation truth, if nature's sense
Should overcome the soul into a lie,
For a short respite — must we bear or die?
 Ben. Say, who were your accomplices?
 I. Ber.   The Senate!
 Ben. What do you mean?

ACT V.

I. Ber.   Ask of the suffering people,
Whom your patrician crimes have driven to crime.
   Ben. You know the Doge?
   I. Ber.   I served with him at Zara
In the field, when *you* were pleading here your way
To present office; we exposed our lives,
While you but hazarded the lives of others,
Alike by accusation or defence;
And, for the rest, all Venice knows her Doge,
Through his great actions, and the Senate's insults.
   Ben. You have held conference with him?
   I. Ber.   I am weary—
Even wearier of your questions than your tortures:
I pray you pass to judgment.
   Ben.   It is coming.—
And you, too, Philip Calendaro, what
Have you to say why you should not be doom'd?
   Cal. I never was a man of many words,
And now have few left worth the utterance.
   Ben. A further application of yon engine
May change your tone.
   Cal.   Most true, it *will* do so;
A former application did so; but
It will not change my words, or, if it did—
   Ben. What then?
   Cal.   Will my avowal on yon rack
Stand good in law?
   Ben.   Assuredly.
   Cal.   Whoe'er
The culprit be whom I accuse of treason?
   Ben. Without doubt, he will be brought up to trial.
   Cal. And on this testimony would he perish?
   Ben. So your confession be detail'd and full,
He will stand here in peril of his life.
   Cal. Then look well to thy proud self, President!
For by the eternity which yawns before me,
I swear that *thou*, and only thou, shalt be

The traitor I denounce upon that rack,
If I be stretch'd there for the second time.
  One of the Giunta. Lord President, 'twere best proceed to
    judgment;
There is no more to be drawn from these men.
  Ben. Unhappy men! prepare for instant death.
The nature of your crime — our law — and peril
The state now stands in, leave not an hour's respite —
Guards! lead them forth, and upon the balcony
Of the red columns, where, on festal Thursday,*
The Doge stands to behold the chase of bulls,
Let them be justified: and leave exposed
Their wavering relics, in the place of judgment,
To the full view of the assembled people! —
And Heaven have mercy on their souls!
  The Giunta.   Amen!
  I. Ber. Signors, farewell! we shall not all again
Meet in one place.
  Ben.   And lest they should essay
To stir up the distracted multitude—
Guards! let their mouths be gagg'd** even in the act
Of execution. — Lead them hence!
  Cal.   What! must we
Not even say farewell to some fond friend,
Nor leave a last word with our confessor?
  Ben. A priest is waiting in the antechamber;
But, for your friends, such interviews would be
Painful to them, and useless all to you.
  Cal. I knew that we were gagg'd in life; at least
All those who had not heart to risk their lives
Upon their open thoughts; but still I deem'd
That in the last few moments, the same idle
Freedom of speech accorded to the dying,
Would not now be denied to us; but since —

---

* "Giovedì grasso," — "fat or greasy Thursday," — which I cannot literally translate in the text, was the day.
** Historical fact. See Sanuto, APPENDIX, Note (A).

ACT V.

I. Ber. Even let them have their way, brave Calendaro!
What matter a few syllables? let's die
Without the slightest show of favour from them;
So shall our blood more readily arise
To Heaven against them, and more testify
To their atrocities, than could a volume
Spoken or written of our dying words!
They tremble at our voices — nay, they dread
Our very silence — let them live in fear! —
Leave them unto their thoughts, and let us now
Address our own above! — Lead on; we are ready.

Cal. Israel, hadst thou but hearken'd unto me
It had not now been thus; and yon pale villain,
The coward Bertram, would —
   I. Ber.   Peace, Calendaro!
What brooks it now to ponder upon this?

Bert. Alas! I fain you died in peace with me:
I did not seek this task; 'twas forced upon me:
Say, you forgive me, though I never can
Retrieve my own forgiveness — frown not thus!

I. Ber. I die and pardon thee!

Cal. (spitting at him). I die and scorn thee!
      [*Exeunt* ISRAEL BERTUCCIO *and* PHILIP CALENDARO,
         Guards, &c.

Ben. Now that these criminals have been disposed of,
'Tis time that we proceed to pass our sentence
Upon the greatest traitor upon record
In any annals, the Doge Faliero!
The proofs and process are complete; the time
And crime require a quick procedure: shall
He now be call'd in to receive the award?

The Giunta. Ay, ay.

Ben. Avogadori, order that the Doge
Be brought before the council.

One of the Giunta.   And the rest,
When shall they be brought up?

Ben.   When all the chiefs

Have been disposed of. Some have fled to Chiozza;
But there are thousands in pursuit of them,
And such precaution ta'en on terra firma,
As well as in the islands, that we hope
None will escape to utter in strange lands
His libellous tale of treasons 'gainst the senate.

  Enter the Doge *as Prisoner, with Guards, &c. &c.*

 Ben. Doge — for such still you are, and by the law
Must be consider'd, till the hour shall come
When you must doff the ducal bonnet from
That head, which could not wear a crown more noble
Than empires can confer, in quiet honour,
But it must plot to overthrow your peers,
Who made you what you are, and quench in blood
A city's glory — we have laid already
Before you in your chamber at full length,
By the Avogadori, all the proofs
Which have appear'd against you; and more ample
Ne'er rear'd their sanguinary shadows to
Confront a traitor. What have you to say
In your defence?
 Doge. What shall I say to ye,
Since my defence must be your condemnation?
You are at once offenders and accusers,
Judges and executioners! — Proceed
Upon your power.
 Ben. Your chief accomplices
Having confess'd, there is no hope for you.
 Doge. And who be they?
 Ben.   In number many; but
The first now stands before you in the court,
Bertram, of Bergamo, — would you question him?
 Doge (looking at him contemptuously). No.
 Ben.   And two others, Israel Bertuccio,
And Philip Calendaro, have admitted
Their fellowship in treason with the Doge!

Doge. And where are they?
Ben. Gone to their place, and now
Answering to Heaven for what they did on earth.
Doge. Ah! the plebeian Brutus, is he gone?
And the quick Cassius of the arsenal?—
How did they meet their doom?
Ben. Think of your own:
It is approaching. You decline to plead, then?
Doge. I cannot plead to my inferiors, nor
Can recognise your legal power to try me.
Show me the law!
Ben. On great emergencies,
The law must be remodell'd or amended:
Our fathers had not fix'd the punishment
Of such a crime, as on the old Roman tables
The sentence against parricide was left
In pure forgetfulness: they could not render
That penal, which had neither name nor thought
In their great bosoms: who would have foreseen
That nature could be filed to such a crime
As sons 'gainst sires, and princes 'gainst their realms?
Your sin hath made us make a law which will
Become a precedent 'gainst such haught traitors,
As would with treason mount to tyranny:
Not even contented with a sceptre, till
They can convert it to a two-edged sword!
Was not the place of Doge sufficient for ye?
What's nobler than the signory of Venice?
Doge. The signory of Venice! You betray'd me—
You—*you*, who sit there, traitors as ye are!
From my equality with you in birth,
And my superiority in action,
You drew me from my honourable toils
In distant lands—on flood—in field—in cities—
You singled me out like a victim to
Stand crown'd, but bound and helpless, at the altar
Where you alone could minister. I knew not—

7*

I sought not—wish'd not—dream'd not the election,
Which reach'd me first at Rome, and I obey'd;
But found on my arrival, that, besides
The jealous vigilance which always led you
To mock and mar your sovereign's best intents,
You had, even in the interregnum of
My journey to the capital, curtail'd
And mutilated the few privileges
Yet left the duke: all this I bore, and would
Have borne, until my very hearth was stain'd
By the pollution of your ribaldry,
And he, the ribald, whom I see amongst you—
Fit judge in such tribunal!—

   Ben. (*interrupting him*).   Michel Steno
Is here in virtue of his office, as
One of the Forty; "the Ten" having craved
A Giunta of patricians from the senate
To aid our judgment in a trial arduous
And novel as the present: he was set
Free from the penalty pronounced upon him,
Because the Doge, who should protect the law,
Seeking to abrogate all law, can claim
No punishment of others by the statutes
Which he himself denies and violates!

   Doge. His PUNISHMENT! I rather see him *there*,
Where he now sits, to glut him with my death,
Than in the mockery of castigation,
Which your foul, outward, juggling show of justice
Decreed as sentence! Base as was his crime,
'Twas purity compared with your protection.

   Ben. And can it be, that the great Doge of Venice,
With three parts of a century of years
And honours on his head, could thus allow
His fury, like an angry boy's, to master
All feeling, wisdom, faith, and fear, on such
A provocation as a young man's petulance?

   Doge. A spark creates the flame—'tis the last drop

Which makes the cup run o'er, and mine was full
Already: you oppress'd the prince and people;
I would have freed both, and have fail'd in both:
The price of such success would have been glory,
Vengeance, and victory, and such a name
As would have made Venetian history
Rival to that of Greece and Syracuse
When they were freed, and flourish'd ages after,
And mine to Gelon and to Thrasybulus:—
Failing, I know the penalty of failure
Is present infamy and death—the future
Will judge, when Venice is no more, or free;
Till then, the truth is in abeyance. Pause not;
I would have shown no mercy, and I seek none;
My life was staked upon a mighty hazard,
And being lost, take what I would have taken!
I would have stood alone amidst your tombs:
Now you may flock round mine, and trample on it,
As you have done upon my heart while living.

   Ben. You do confess then, and admit the justice
Of our tribunal?

   Doge.   I confess to have fail'd;
Fortune is female: from my youth her favours
Were not withheld, the fault was mine to hope
Her former smiles again at this late hour.

   Ben. You do not then in aught arraign our equity?

   Doge. Noble Venetians! stir me not with questions.
I am resign'd to the worst; but in me still
Have something of the blood of brighter days,
And am not over-patient. Pray you, spare me
Further interrogation, which boots nothing,
Except to turn a trial to debate.
I shall but answer that which will offend you,
And please your enemies—a host already;
'Tis true, these sullen walls should yield no echo:
But walls have ears—nay, more, they have tongues; and if
There were no other way for truth to o'erleap them,

You who condemn me, you who fear and slay me,
Yet could not bear in silence to your graves
What you would hear from me of good or evil;
The secret were too mighty for your souls:
Then let it sleep in mine, unless you court
A danger which would double that you escape.
Such my defence would be, had I full scope
To make it famous; for true *words* are *things*,
And dying men's are things which long outlive,
And oftentimes avenge them; bury mine,
If ye would fain survive me: take this counsel,
And though too oft ye made me live in wrath,
Let me die calmly; you may grant me this;—
I deny nothing—defend nothing—nothing
I ask of you, but silence for myself,
And sentence from the court!

Ben. This full admission
Spares us the harsh necessity of ordering
The torture to elicit the whole truth.

Doge. The torture! you have put me there already,
Daily since I was Doge; but if you will
Add the corporeal rack, you may: these limbs
Will yield with age to crushing iron; but
There's that within my heart shall strain your engines.

Enter an OFFICER.

Officer. Noble Venetians! Duchess Faliero
Requests admission to the Giunta's presence.

Ben. Say, conscript fathers,* shall she be admitted?

One of the Giunta. She may have revelations of importance
Unto the state, to justify compliance
With her request.

Ben. Is this the general will?

All. It is.

Doge. Oh, admirable laws of Venice!

---

* The Venetian senate took the same title as the Roman, of "conscript fathers."

Which would admit the wife, in the full hope
That she might testify against the husband.
What glory to the chaste Venetian dames!
But such blasphemers 'gainst all honour, as
Sit here, do well to act in their vocation.
Now, villain Steno! if this woman fail,
I'll pardon thee thy lie, and thy escape,
And my own violent death, and thy vile life.

The DUCHESS *enters.*

    Ben. Lady! this just tribunal has resolved,
Though the request be strange, to grant it, and
Whatever be its purport, to accord
A patient hearing with the due respect
Which fits your ancestry, your rank, and virtues:
But you turn pale—ho! there, look to the lady!
Place a chair instantly.
    Ang.   A moment's faintness—
'Tis past; I pray you pardon me,—I sit not
In presence of my prince and of my husband,
While he is on his feet.
    Ben.   Your pleasure, lady?
    Ang. Strange rumours, but most true, if all I hear
And see be sooth, have reach'd me, and I come
To know the worst, even at the worst; forgive
The abruptness of my entrance and my bearing.
Is it—I cannot speak—I cannot shape
The question—but you answer it ere spoken,
With eyes averted, and with gloomy brows—
Oh God! this is the silence of the grave!
    Ben. (*after a pause*). Spare us, and spare thyself the re-
        petition
Of our most awful, but inexorable
Duty to heaven and man!
    Ang.   Yet speak; I cannot—
I cannot—no—even now believe these things.
Is *he* condemn'd?

Ben.   Alas!
Ang.   And was he guilty?
  Ben. Lady! the natural distraction of
Thy thoughts at such a moment makes the question
Merit forgiveness; else a doubt like this
Against a just and paramount tribunal
Were deep offence. But question even the Doge,
And if he can deny the proofs, believe him
Guiltless as thy own bosom.
  Ang.   Is it so?
My lord — my sovereign — my poor father's friend —
The mighty in the field, the sage in council;
Unsay the words of this man! — Thou art silent!
  Ben. He hath already own'd to his own guilt,
Nor, as thou see'st, doth he deny it now.
  Ang. Ay, but he must not die! Spare his few years,
Which grief and shame will soon cut down to days!
One day of baffled crime must not efface
Near sixteen lustres crowded with brave acts.
  Ben. His doom must be fulfill'd without remission
Of time or penalty — 'tis a decree.
  Ang. He hath been guilty, but there may be mercy.
  Ben. Not in this case with justice.
  Ang.   Alas! signor,
He who is only just is cruel; who
Upon the earth would live were all judged justly?
  Ben. His punishment is safety to the state.
  Ang. He was a subject, and hath served the state;
He was your general, and hath saved the state;
He is your sovereign, and hath ruled the state.
  One of the Council. He is a traitor, and betray'd the state.
  Ang. And, but for him, there now had been no state
To save or to destroy; and you, who sit
There to pronounce the death of your deliverer,
Had now been groaning at a Moslem oar,
Or digging in the Hunnish mines in fetters!

One of the Council. No, lady, there are others who would die
Rather than breathe in slavery!
 Ang.   If there are so
Within *these* walls, *thou* art not of the number:
The truly brave are generous to the fallen!—
Is there no hope?
 Ben.   Lady, it cannot be.
 Ang. (turning to the Doge). Then die, Faliero! since it
    must be so;
But with the spirit of my father's friend.
Thou hast been guilty of a great offence,
Half-cancell'd by the harshness of these men.
I would have sued to them—have pray'd to them—
Have begg'd as famish'd mendicants for bread—
Have wept as they will cry unto their God
For mercy, and be answer'd as they answer—
Had it been fitting for thy name or mine,
And if the cruelty in their cold eyes
Had not announced the heartless wrath within.
Then, as a prince, address thee to thy doom!
 Doge. I have lived too long not to know how to die!
Thy suing to these men were but the bleating
Of the lamb to the butcher, or the cry
Of seamen to the surge: I would not take
A life eternal, granted at the hands
Of wretches, from whose monstrous villanies
I sought to free the groaning nations!
 Michel Steno.   Doge,
A word with thee, and with this noble lady,
Whom I have grievously offended. Would
Sorrow, or shame, or penance on my part,
Could cancel the inexorable past!
But since that cannot be, as Christians let us
Say farewell, and in peace: with full contrition
I crave, not pardon, but compassion from you,
And give, however weak, my prayers for both.
 Ang. Sage Benintende, now chief judge of Venice,

I speak to thee in answer to yon signor.
Inform the ribald Steno, that his words
Ne'er weigh'd in mind with Loredano's daughter
Further than to create a moment's pity
For such as he is: would that others had
Despised him as I pity! I prefer
My honour to a thousand lives, could such
Be multiplied in mine, but would not have
A single life of others lost for that
Which nothing human can impugn—the sense
Of virtue, looking not to what is call'd
A good name for reward, but to itself.
To me the scorner's words were as the wind
Unto the rock: but as there are—alas!
Spirits more sensitive, on which such things
Light as the whirlwind on the waters; souls
To whom dishonour's shadow is a substance
More terrible than death, here and hereafter;
Men whose vice is to start at vice's scoffing,
And who, though proof against all blandishments
Of pleasure, and all pangs of pain, are feeble
When the proud name on which they pinnacled
Their hopes is breathed on, jealous as the eagle
Of her high aiery; let what we now
Behold, and feel, and suffer, be a lesson
To wretches how they tamper in their spleen
With beings of a higher order. Insects
Have made the lion mad ere now; a shaft
I' the heel o'erthrew the bravest of the brave;
A wife's dishonour was the bane of Troy;
A wife's dishonour unking'd Rome for ever;
An injured husband brought the Gauls to Clusium,
And thence to Rome, which perish'd for a time;
An obscene gesture cost Caligula
His life, while Earth yet bore his cruelties;
A virgin's wrong made Spain a Moorish province;
And Steno's lie, couch'd in two worthless lines,

Hath decimated Venice, put in peril
A senate which hath stood eight hundred years,
Discrown'd a prince, cut off his crownless head,
And forged new fetters for a groaning people!
Let the poor wretch, like to the courtesan
Who fired Persepolis, be proud of this,
If it so please him — 'twere a pride fit for him!
But let him not insult the last hours of
Him, who, whate'er he now is, *was* a hero,
By the intrusion of his very prayers;
Nothing of good can come from such a source,
Nor would we aught with him, nor now, nor ever:
We leave him to himself, that lowest depth
Of human baseness. Pardon is for men,
And not for reptiles — we have none for Steno,
And no resentment: things like him must sting,
And higher beings suffer; 'tis the charter
Of life. The man who dies by the adder's fang
May have the crawler crush'd, but feels no anger:
'Twas the worm's nature; and some men are worms
In soul, more than the living things of tombs.

 Doge (to Ben.). Signor! complete that which you deem
  your duty.

 Ben. Before we can proceed upon that duty,
We would request the princess to withdraw;
'Twill move her too much to be witness to it.

 Ang. I know it will, and yet I must endure it,
For 'tis a part of mine — I will not quit,
Except by force, my husband's side. — Proceed!
Nay, fear not either shriek, or sigh, or tear;
Though my heart burst, it shall be silent. — Speak!
I have that within which shall o'ermaster all.

 Ben. Marino Faliero, Doge of Venice,
Count of Val di Marino, Senator,
And some time General of the Fleet and Army,
Noble Venetian, many times and oft
Intrusted by the state with high employments,

Even to the highest, listen to the sentence.
Convict by many witnesses and proofs,
And by thine own confession, of the guilt
Of treachery and treason, yet unheard of
Until this trial—the decree is death.
Thy goods are confiscate unto the state,
Thy name is razed from out her records, save
Upon a public day of thanksgiving
For this our most miraculous deliverance,
When thou art noted in our calendars
With earthquakes, pestilence, and foreign foes,
And the great enemy of man, as subject
Of grateful masses for Heaven's grace in snatching
Our lives and country from thy wickedness.
The place wherein as Doge thou shouldst be painted,
With thine illustrious predecessors, is
To be left vacant, with a death-black veil
Flung over these dim words engraved beneath,—
"This place is of Marino Faliero,
Decapitated for his crimes."

 Doge.   "His crimes!"
But let it be so:—it will be in vain.
The veil which blackens o'er this blighted name,
And hides, or seems to hide, these lineaments,
Shall draw more gazers than the thousand portraits
Which glitter round it in their pictured trappings—
Your delegated slaves—the people's tyrants!
"Decapitated for his crimes!"—*What* crimes?
Were it not better to record the facts,
So that the contemplator might approve,
Or at the least learn *whence* the crimes arose?
When the beholder knows a Doge conspired,
Let him be told the cause—it is your history.

 Ben. Time must reply to that; our sons will judge
Their fathers' judgment, which I now pronounce.
As Doge, clad in the ducal robes and cap,
Thou shalt be led hence to the Giants' Staircase,

Where thou and all our princes are invested;
And there, the ducal crown being first resumed
Upon the spot where it was first assumed,
Thy head shall be struck off; and Heaven have mercy
Upon thy soul!
 Doge.   Is this the Giunta's sentence?
 Ben. It is.
 Doge.   I can endure it.—And the time?
 Ben. Must be immediate.—Make thy peace with God:
Within an hour thou must be in His presence.
 Doge. I am already; and my blood will rise
To Heaven before the souls of those who shed it.—
Are all my lands confiscated?
 Ben.   They are;
And goods, and jewels, and all kind of treasure,
Except two thousand ducats—these dispose of.
 Doge. That's harsh.—I would have fain reserved the lands
Near to Treviso, which I hold by investment
From Laurence the Count-bishop of Ceneda,
In fief perpetual to myself and heirs,
To portion them (leaving my city spoil,
My palace and my treasures, to your forfeit)
Between my consort and my kinsmen.
 Ben.   These
Lie under the state's ban; their chief, thy nephew,
In peril of his own life; but the council
Postpones his trial for the present. If
Thou will'st a state unto thy widow'd princess,
Fear not, for we will do her justice.
 Ang.   Signors,
I share not in your spoil! From henceforth, know
I am devoted unto God alone,
And take my refuge in the cloister.
 Doge.   Come!
The hour may be a hard one, but 'twill end.
Have I aught else to undergo save death?
 Ben. You have nought to do except confess and die.

The priest is robed, the scimitar is bare,
And both await without.—But, above all,
Think not to speak unto the people; they
Are now by thousands swarming at the gates,
But these are closed: the Ten, the Avogadori,
The Giunta, and the chief men of the Forty,
Alone will be beholders of thy doom,
And they are ready to attend the Doge.
    Doge. The Doge!
    Ben. Yes, Doge, thou hast lived and thou shalt die
A sovereign; till the moment which precedes
The separation of that head and trunk,
That ducal crown and head shall be united.
Thou hast forgot thy dignity in deigning
To plot with petty traitors; not so we,
Who in the very punishment acknowledge
The prince. Thy vile accomplices have died
The dog's death, and the wolf's; but thou shalt fall
As falls the lion by the hunters, girt
By those who feel a proud compassion for thee,
And mourn even the inevitable death
Provoked by thy wild wrath, and regal fierceness.
Now we remit thee to thy preparation:
Let it be brief, and we ourselves will be
Thy guides unto the place where first we were
United to thee as thy subjects, and
Thy senate; and must now be parted from thee
As such for ever, on the self-same spot.—
Guards! form the Doge's escort to his chamber.
                                            [*Exeunt.*

SCENE II.

The Doge's Apartment.

The DOGE *as Prisoner, and the* DUCHESS *attending him.*
    Doge. Now, that the priest is gone, 'twere useless all
To linger out the miserable minutes;
But one pang more, the pang of parting from thee,

And I will leave the few last grains of sand,
Which yet remain of the accorded hour,
Still falling—I have done with Time.
    Ang.   Alas!
And I have been the cause, the unconscious cause;
And for this funeral marriage, this black union,
Which thou, compliant with my father's wish,
Didst promise at *his* death, thou hast seal'd thine own.
    Doge. Not so: there was that in my spirit ever
Which shaped out for itself some great reverse;
The marvel is, it came not until now—
And yet it was foretold me.
    Ang.   How foretold you?
    Doge. Long years ago—so long, they are a doubt
In memory, and yet they live in annals:
When I was in my youth, and served the senate
And signory as podesta and captain
Of the town of Treviso, on a day
Of festival, the sluggish bishop who
Convey'd the Host aroused my rash young anger
By strange delay, and arrogant reply
To my reproof; I raised my hand and smote him
Until he reel'd beneath his holy burthen;
And as he rose from earth again, he raised
His tremulous hands in pious wrath towards Heaven.
Thence pointing to the Host, which had fallen from him,
He turn'd to me, and said, "The hour will come
When he thou hast o'erthrown shall overthrow thee:
The glory shall depart from out thy house,
The wisdom shall be shaken from thy soul,
And in thy best maturity of mind
A madness of the heart shall seize upon thee;
Passion shall tear thee when all passions cease
In other men, or mellow into virtues;
And majesty, which decks all other heads,
Shall crown to leave thee headless; honours shall
But prove to thee the heralds of destruction,

And hoary hairs of shame, and both of death,
But not such death as fits an aged man."
Thus saying, he pass'd on. — That hour is come.

Ang. And with this warning couldst thou not have striven
To avert the fatal moment, and atone,
By penitence for that which thou hadst done?

Doge. I own the words went to my heart, so much
That I remember'd them amid the maze
Of life, as if they form'd a spectral voice,
Which shook me in a supernatural dream;
And I repented; but 'twas not for me
To pull in resolution: what must be
I could not change, and would not fear. — Nay more,
Thou canst not have forgot, what all remember,
That on my day of landing here as Doge,
On my return from Rome, a mist of such
Unwonted density went on before
The bucentaur, like the columnar cloud
Which usher'd Israel out of Egypt, till
The pilot was misled, and disembark'd us
Between the pillars of Saint Mark's, where 'tis
The custom of the state to put to death
Its criminals, instead of touching at
The Riva della Paglia, as the wont is, —
So that all Venice shudder'd at the omen.

Ang. Ah! little boots it now to recollect
Such things.

Doge.   And yet I find a comfort in
The thought that these things are the work of Fate;
For I would rather yield to gods than men,
Or cling to any creed of destiny,
Rather than deem these mortals, most of whom
I know to be as worthless as the dust,
And weak as worthless, more than instruments
Of an o'er-ruling power; they in themselves
Were all incapable — they could not be
Victors of him who oft had conquer'd for them!

Ang. Employ the minutes left in aspirations
Of a more healing nature, and in peace
Even with these wretches take thy flight to Heaven.

Doge. I *am* at peace: the peace of certainty
That a sure hour will come, when their sons' sons,
And this proud city, and these azure waters,
And all which makes them eminent and bright,
Shall be a desolation and a curse,
A hissing and a scoff unto the nations,
A Carthage, and a Tyre, an Ocean Babel!

Ang. Speak not thus now; the surge of passion still
Sweeps o'er thee to the last; thou dost deceive
Thyself, and canst not injure them — be calmer.

Doge. I stand within eternity, and see
Into eternity, and I behold —
Ay, palpable as I see thy sweet face
For the last time — the days which I denounce
Unto all time against these wave-girt walls,
And they who are indwellers.

Guard (coming forward). Doge of Venice,
The Ten are in attendance on your highness.

Doge. Then farewell, Angiolina! — one embrace —
Forgive the old man who hath been to thee
A fond but fatal husband — love my memory —
I would not ask so much for me still living,
But thou canst judge of me more kindly now,
Seeing my evil feelings are at rest.
Besides, of all the fruit of these long years,
Glory, and wealth, and power, and fame, and name,
Which generally leave some flowers to bloom
Even o'er the grave, I have nothing left, not even
A little love, or friendship, or esteem,
No, not enough to extract an epitaph
From ostentatious kinsmen; in one hour
I have uprooted all my former life,
And outlived every thing, except thy heart,
The pure, the good, the gentle, which will oft

With unimpair'd but not a clamorous grief
Still keep—Thou turn'st so pale!—Alas! she faints,
She has no breath, no pulse!—Guards! lend your aid—
I cannot leave her thus, and yet 'tis better,
Since every lifeless moment spares a pang.
When she shakes off this temporary death,
I shall be with the Eternal.—Call her women—
One look!—how cold her hand!—as cold as mine
Shall be ere she recovers.—Gently tend her,
And take my last thanks—I am ready now.

[*The Attendants of* ANGIOLINA *enter and surround their mistress, who has fainted.—Exeunt the* DOGE, *Guards, &c. &c.*

SCENE III.

The Court of the Ducal Palace: the outer gates are shut against the people.—The DOGE *enters in his ducal robes, in procession with the Council of Ten and other Patricians, attended by the Guards, till they arrive at the top of the "Giants' Staircase" (where the Doges took the oaths); the Executioner is stationed there with his sword.—On arriving, a Chief of the Ten takes off the ducal cap from the Doge's head.*

Doge. So now the Doge is nothing, and at last
I am again Marino Faliero:
'Tis well to be so, though but for a moment.
Here was I crown'd, and here, bear witness, Heaven!
With how much more contentment I resign
That shining mockery, the ducal bauble,
Than I received the fatal ornament.
    One of the Ten. Thou tremblest, Faliero!
    Doge.   'Tis with age, then.*

---

* This was the actual reply of Bailli, maire of Paris, to a Frenchman who made him the same reproach on his way to execution, in the earliest part of their revolution. I find in reading over (since the completion of this tragedy), for the first time these six years, "Venice Preserved," a similar reply on a different occasion by Renault, and other coincidences arising from the subject. I need hardly remind the gentlest reader, that such coin-

Ben. Faliero! hast thou aught further to commend,
Compatible with justice, to the senate?
　Doge. I would commend my nephew to their mercy,
My consort to their justice; for methinks
My death, and such a death, might settle all
Between the state and me.
　Ben. 　　　　　　　　They shall be cared for;
Even notwithstanding thine unheard-of crime.
　Doge. Unheard of! ay, there's not a history
But shows a thousand crown'd conspirators
Against the people; but to set them free
One sovereign only died, and one is dying.
　Ben. And who were they who fell in such a cause?
　Doge. The King of Sparta, and the Doge of Venice —
Agis and Faliero!
　Ben. 　　　　　Hast thou more
To utter or to do?
　Doge. 　　　　May I speak?
　Ben. 　　　　　　　　　Thou may'st;
But recollect the people are without,
Beyond the compass of the human voice.
　Doge. I speak to Time and to Eternity,
Of which I grow a portion, not to man.
Ye elements! in which to be resolved
I hasten, let my voice be as a spirit
Upon you! Ye blue waves! which bore my banner,
Ye winds! which flutter'd o'er as if you loved it,
And fill'd my swelling sails as they were wafted
To many a triumph! Thou, my native earth,
Which I have bled for, and thou foreign earth,
Which drank this willing blood from many a wound!
Ye stones, in which my gore will not sink, but
Reek up to Heaven! Ye skies, which will receive it!
Thou sun! which shinest on these things, and Thou!

cidences must be accidental, from the very facility of their detection by reference to so popular a play on the stage and in the closet as Otway's chef-d'œuvre.

Who kindlest and who quenchest suns!—Attest!
I am not innocent—but are these guiltless?
I perish'd, but not unavenged; far ages
Float up from the abyss of time to be,
And show these eyes, before they close, the doom
Of this proud city, and I leave my curse
On her and hers for ever!—Yes, the hours
Are silently engendering of the day,
When she, who built 'gainst Attila a bulwark,
Shall yield, and bloodlessly and basely yield
Unto a bastard Attila, without
Shedding so much blood in her last defence
As these old veins, oft drain'd in shielding her,
Shall pour in sacrifice.—She shall be bought
And sold, and be an appanage to those
Who shall despise her!*—She shall stoop to be

* Should the dramatic picture seem harsh, let the reader look to the historical, of the period prophesied, or rather of the few years preceding that period. Voltaire calculated their "nostre bene morite Meretrici" at 12,000 of regulars, without including volunteers and local militia, on what authority I know not; but it is, perhaps, the only part of the population not decreased. Venice once contained two hundred thousand inhabitants: there are now about ninety thousand; and THESE!! few individuals can conceive, and none could describe, the actual state into which the more than infernal tyranny of Austria has plunged this unhappy city. From the present decay and degeneracy of Venice under the Barbarians, there are some honourable individual exceptions. There is Pasqualigo, the last, and, alas! posthumous son of the marriage of the Doges with the Adriatic, who fought his frigate with far greater gallantry than any of his French coadjutors in the memorable action off Lissa. I came home in the squadron with the prizes in 1811, and recollect to have heard Sir William Hoste, and the other officers engaged in that glorious conflict, speak in the highest terms of Pasqualigo's behaviour. There is the Abbate Morelli. There is Alvise Querini, who, after a long and honourable diplomatic career, finds some consolation for the wrongs of his country, in the pursuits of literature with his nephew, Vittor Benzon, the son of the celebrated beauty, the heroine of "La Biondina in Gondoletta." There are the patrician poet Morosini, and the poet Lamberti, the author of the "Biondina," &c. and many other estimable productions; and, not least in an Englishman's estimation, Madame Michelli, the translator of Shakspeare. There are the young Dandolo and the improvvisatore Carrer, and Giuseppe Albrizzi, the accomplished son of an accomplished mother. There is Aglietti, and, were

A province for an empire, petty town
In lieu of capital, with slaves for senates,
Beggars for nobles, panders for a people!
Then when the Hebrew's in thy palaces,*
The Hun in thy high places, and the Greek
Walks o'er thy mart, and smiles on it for his!
When thy patricians beg their bitter bread
In narrow streets, and in their shameful need
Make their nobility a plea for pity!
Then, when the few who still retain a wreck
Of their great fathers' heritage shall fawn
Round a barbarian Vice of Kings' Vice-gerent,
Even in the palace where they sway'd as sovereigns,
Even in the palace where they slew their sovereign,
Proud of some name they have disgraced, or sprung
From an adulteress boastful of her guilt
With some large gondolier or foreign soldier,
Shall bear about their bastardy in triumph
To the third spurious generation;—when
Thy sons are in the lowest scale of being,
Slaves turn'd o'er to the vanquish'd by the victors,
Despised by cowards for greater cowardice,
And scorn'd even by the vicious for such vices
As in the monstrous grasp of their conception
Defy all codes to image or to name them;
Then, when of Cyprus, now thy subject kingdom,
All thine inheritance shall be her shame
Entail'd on thy less virtuous daughters, grown
A wider proverb for worse prostitution;—
When all the ills of conquer'd states shall cling thee,

there nothing else, there is the immortality of Canova. Cicognara, Mustoxithi, Bucati, &c. &c. I do not reckon, because the one is a Greek, and the others were born at least a hundred miles off, which, throughout Italy, constitutes, if not a *foreigner*, at least a *stranger* (*forestiere*).

* The chief palaces on the Brenta now belong to the Jews; who in the earlier times of the republic were only allowed to inhabit Mestri, and not to enter the city of Venice. The whole commerce is in the hands of the Jews and Greeks, and the Huns form the garrison.

Vice without splendour, sin without relief
Even from the gloss of love to smooth it o'er,
But in its stead, coarse lusts of habitude,
Prurient yet passionless, cold studied lewdness,
Depraving nature's frailty to an art;—
When these and more are heavy on thee, when
Smiles without mirth, and pastimes without pleasure,
Youth without honour, age without respect,
Meanness and weakness, and a sense of woe
'Gainst which thou wilt not strive, and dar'st not murmur, *
Have made thee last and worst of peopled deserts,
Then, in the last gasp of thine agony,
Amidst thy many murders, think of *mine!*
Thou den of drunkards with the blood of princes!**

* If the Doge's prophecy seem remarkable, look to the following, made by Alamanni two hundred and seventy years ago:— "There is one very singular prophecy concerning Venice: 'If thou dost not change,' it says to that proud republic, 'thy liberty, which is already on the wing, will not reckon a century more than the thousandth year.' If we carry back the epocha of Venetian freedom to the establishment of the government under which the republic flourished, we shall find that the date of the election of the first Doge is 697; and if we add one century to a thousand, that is, eleven hundred years, we shall find the sense of the prediction to be literally this: 'Thy liberty will not last till 1797.' Recollect that Venice ceased to be free in the year 1796, the fifth year of the French republic; and you will perceive, that there never was prediction more pointed, or more exactly followed by the event. You will, therefore, note as very remarkable the three lines of Alamanni addressed to Venice; which, however, no one has pointed out:—

'Se non cangi pensier, un secol solo
Non conterà sopra 'l millesimo anno
Tua libertà, che va fuggendo a volo.'

Many prophecies have passed for such, and many men have been called prophets for much less."—GINGUENÉ, *Hist. Lit. de l'Italie*, t. ix. p. 144.

** Of the first fifty Doges, *five* abdicated—*five* were banished with their eyes put out—*five* were MASSACRED—and *nine* deposed; so that *nineteen* out of fifty lost the throne by violence, besides two who fell in battle: this occurred long previous to the reign of Marino Faliero. One of his more immediate predecessors, Andrea Dandolo, died of vexation. Marino Faliero himself perished as related. Amongst his successors, *Fuscari*, after seeing his son repeatedly tortured and banished, was deposed, and died of breaking a blood-vessel, on hearing the bell of Saint Mark's toll for the election

Gehenna of the waters! thou sea Sodom!
Thus I devote thee to the infernal gods!
Thee and thy serpent seed!

      [*Here the* DOGE *turns and addresses the Executioner.*
              Slave, do thine office!
Strike as I struck the foe! Strike as I would
Have struck those tyrants! Strike deep as my curse!
Strike—and but once!

      [*The* DOGE *throws himself upon his knees, and as the Executioner raises his sword the scene closes.*

SCENE IV.

The Piazza and Piazzetta of Saint Mark's.—*The People in crowds gathered round the grated gates of the Ducal Palace, which are shut.*

  First Citizen. I have gain'd the gate, and can discern the Ten,
Robed in their gowns of state, ranged round the Doge.
  Second Cit. I cannot reach thee with mine utmost effort.
How is it? let us hear at least, since sight
Is thus prohibited unto the people,
Except the occupiers of those bars.
  First Cit. One has approach'd the Doge, and now they strip
The ducal bonnet from his head—and now
He raises his keen eyes to Heaven; I see
Them glitter, and his lips move—Hush! hush!—no,
'Twas but a murmur—Curse upon the distance!
His words are inarticulate, but the voice
Swells up like mutter'd thunder; would we could
But gather a sole sentence!
  Second Cit. Hush! we perhaps may catch the sound.
  First Cit.   'Tis vain,
I cannot hear him.—How his hoary hair

---

of his successor. Morosini was impeached for the loss of Candia; but this was previous to his dukedom, during which he conquered the Morea, and was styled the Peloponnesian. Faliero might truly say,
    "Thou den of drunkards with the blood of princes!"

Streams on the wind like foam upon the wave!
Now — now — he kneels — and now they form a circle
Round him, and all is hidden — but I see
The lifted sword in air — Ah! hark! it falls!

                                        [*The People murmur.*

   Third Cit. Then they have murder'd him who would have
       freed us.
   Fourth Cit. He was a kind man to the commons ever.
   Fifth Cit. Wisely they did to keep their portals barr'd.
Would we had known the work they were preparing
Ere we were summon'd here — we would have brought
Weapons, and forced them!
   Sixth Cit.   Are you sure he's dead?
   First Cit. I saw the sword fall — Lo! what have we here?
Enter on the Balcony of the Palace which fronts Saint Mark's
   Place a CHIEF OF THE TEN,* *with a bloody sword. He waves*
   it thrice before the People, and exclaims,
"Justice hath dealt upon the mighty Traitor!"

              [*The gates are opened; the populace rush in towards*
               the "Giants' Staircase," where the execution has
               taken place. The foremost of them exclaims to
               those behind,
The gory head rolls down the Giants' Steps!

                                              [*The curtain falls.*

---

* "Un Capo de' Dieci!" are the words of Sanuto's Chronicle.

APPENDIX.

NOTE A.

[I AM obliged for the following excellent translation of the old Chronicle to Mr. F. Cohen, to whom the reader will find himself indebted for a version that I could not myself — though after many years' intercourse with Italian — have given by any means so purely and so faithfully.]

STORY OF MARINO FALIERO, DOGE XLIX. MCCCLIV.

On the eleventh day of September, in the year of our Lord 1354, Marino Faliero was elected and chosen to be the Duke of the Commonwealth of Venice. He was Count of Valdemarino, in the Marches of Treviso, and a Knight, and a wealthy man to boot. As soon as the election was completed, it was resolved in the Great Council, that a deputation of twelve should be despatched to Marino Faliero the Duke, who was then on his way from Rome; for when he was chosen, he was embassador at the court of the Holy Father, at Rome, — the Holy Father himself held his court at Avignon. When Messer Marino Faliero the Duke was about to land in this city, on the 5th day of October, 1354, a thick haze came on, and darkened the air; and he was enforced to land on the place of Saint Mark, between the two columns, on the spot where evil doers are put to death; and all thought that this was the worst of tokens. — Nor must I forget to write that which I have read in a chronicle. When Messer Marino Faliero was Podesta and Captain of Treviso, the Bishop delayed coming in with the holy sacrament, on a day when a procession was to take place. Now, the said Marino Faliero was so very proud and wrathful, that he buffeted the Bishop, and almost struck him to the ground: and, therefore, Heaven allowed Marino Faliero to go out of his right senses, in order that he might bring himself to an evil death.

When this Duke had held the dukedom during nine months and six days, he, being wicked and ambitious, sought to make himself Lord of Venice, in the manner which I have read in an ancient chronicle. When the Thursday arrived upon which they were wont to hunt the bull, the bull hunt took place as usual; and, according to the usage of those times, after the bull hunt had ended, they all proceeded unto the palace of the Duke, and assembled together in one of his halls; and they disported themselves with the women. And until the first bell tolled they danced, and then a banquet was served up. My Lord the Duke paid the expenses thereof, provided he had a Duchess, and after the banquet they all returned to their homes.

Now to this feast there came a certain Ser Michele Steno, a gentleman of poor estate and very young, but crafty and daring, and who loved one of the damsels of the Duchess. Ser Michele stood amongst the women upon the solajo; and he behaved indiscreotly, so that my Lord the Duke ordered that he should be kicked off the solajo; and the esquires of the Duke flung him down from the solajo accordingly. Ser Michele thought that such an affront was beyond all bearing; and when the feast was over, and all other persons had left the palace, he, continuing heated with anger, went to the hall of audience, and wrote certain unseemly words relating to the Duke and the Duchess upon the chair in which the Duke was used to sit; for in those days the Duke did not cover his chair with cloth of sendal, but he sat in a chair of wood. Ser Michele wrote thereon—"*Marin Falier, the husband of the fair wife; others kiss her, but he keeps her.*" In the morning the words were seen, and the matter was considered to be very scandalous; and the Senate commanded the Avogadori of the Commonwealth to proceed therein with the greatest diligence. A largess of great amount was immediately proffered by the Avogadori, in order to discover who had written these words. And at length it was known that Michele Steno had written them. It was resolved in the Council of Forty that he should be arrested; and he then confessed that in the fit of vexation and spite, occasioned by his being thrust off the solajo in the presence of his mistress, he had written the words. Therefore the Council debated thereon. And the Council took his youth into consideration, and that he was a lover; and therefore they adjudged that he should be kept in close confinement during two months, and that afterwards he should be banished from Venice and the state during one year. In consequence of this merciful sentence the Duke became exceedingly wroth, it appearing to him, that the Council had not acted in such a manner as was required by the respect due to his ducal dignity; and he said that they ought to have condemned Ser Michele to be hanged by the neck, or at least to be banished for life.

Now it was fated that my Lord Duke Marino was to have his head cut off. And as it is necessary when any effect is to be brought about, that the cause of such effect must happen, it therefore came to pass, that on the very day after sentence had been pronounced on Ser Michele Steno, being the first day of Lent, a gentleman of the house of Barbaro, a choleric gentleman, went to the arsenal, and required certain things of the masters of the galleys. This he did in the presence of the Admiral of the arsenal, and he, hearing the request, answered,—No, it cannot he done. High words arose between the gentleman and the Admiral, and the gentleman struck him with his fist just above the eye; and as he happened to have a ring on his finger, the ring cut the Admiral and drew blood. The Admiral, all bruised and bloody, ran straight to the Duke to complain, and with the intent of praying him to inflict some heavy punishment upon the gentleman of Cà Barbaro.—"What wouldst thou have me do for thee?" answered the Duke:—"think upon the shameful gibe which hath been written concerning me; and think on the manner in which they have punished that ribald Michele Steno, who wrote it; and see how the Council of Forty respect our person."—Upon this the Admiral answered,—"My Lord Duke, if you would wish to make yourself a prince, and to cut all those cuckoldy gentlemen to pieces, I have the heart, if you do but help me, to make you prince of all this state; and then you may punish them all."—Hearing this, the Duke said,—"How can such a matter be brought about?"—and so they discoursed thereon.

The Duke called for his nephew, Ser Bertuccio Faliero, who lived with him in the palace, and they communed about this plot. And without leaving the place, they sent for Philip Calendaro, a seaman of great repute, and for Bertuccio Israello, who was exceedingly wily and cunning. Then taking counsel amongst themselves, they agreed to call in some others; and so, for several nights successively, they met with the Duke at home in his palace. And the following men were called in singly; to wit;—Niccolo Fagiuolo, Giovanni da Corfu, Stefano Fagiono, Niccolo dalle Bende, Niccolo Biondo, and Stefano Trivisano.—It was concerted that sixteen or seventeen leaders should be stationed in various parts of the City, each being at the head of forty men, armed and prepared; but the followers were not to know their destination. On the appointed day they were to make affrays amongst themselves here and there, in order that the Duke might have a pretence for tolling the bells of San Marco; these bells are never rung but by the order of the Duke. And at the sound of the bells, these sixteen or seventeen, with their followers, were to come to San Marco, through the streets which open upon the Piazza. And when the noble and leading citizens should come into the Piazza, to know the cause of the riot, then the conspirators were to cut them in pieces; and this work being finished, my Lord Marino Faliero the Duke was to be proclaimed the Lord of Venice. Things having been thus settled, they agreed to fulfil their intent on Wednesday, the 15th day of April, in the year 1355. So covertly did they plot, that no one ever dreamt of their machinations.

But the Lord, who hath always helped this most glorious city, and who, loving its righteousness and holiness, hath never forsaken it, inspired one Beltramo Bergamasco to be the cause of bringing the plot to light, in the following manner. This Beltramo, who belonged to Ser Niccolo Lioni of Santo Stefano, had heard a word or two of what was to take place; and so, in the before-mentioned month of April, he went to the house of the aforesaid Ser Niccolo Lioni, and told him all the particulars of the plot. Ser Niccolo, when he heard all these things, was struck dead, as it were, with affright. He heard all the particulars; and Beltramo prayed him to keep it all secret; and if he told Ser Niccolo, it was in order that Ser Niccolo might stop at home on the 15th of April, and thus save his life. Beltramo was going, but Ser Niccolo ordered his servants to lay hands upon him, and lock him up. Ser Niccolo then went to the house of Messer Giovanni Gradonigo Nasoni, who afterwards became Duke, and who also lived at Santo Stefano, and told him all. The matter seemed to him to be of the very greatest importance, as indeed it was; and they two went to the house of Ser Marco Cornaro, who lived at San Felice; and, having spoken with him, they all three then determined to go back to the house of Ser Niccolo Lioni, to examine the said Beltramo; and having questioned him, and heard all that he had to say, they left him in confinement. And then they all three went into the sacristy of San Salvatore, and sent their men to summon the Councillors, the Avogadori, the Capi de' Dieci, and those of the Great Council.

When all were assembled, the whole story was told to them. They were struck dead, as it were, with affright. They determined to send for Beltramo. He was brought in before them. They examined him, and ascertained that the matter was true; and, although they were exceedingly troubled, yet they determined upon their measures. And they sent for the Capi de' Quarante, the Signori di Notte, the Capi do' Sestieri, and the Cinque della Pace; and they were ordered to associate to their men other good men and true, who were to proceed to the houses of the ringleaders of the conspiracy, and secure them. And they secured the foreman of the arsenal, in order that the conspirators might not do mischief. Towards nightfall they assembled in the palace. When they were assembled in the palace, they caused the gates of the quadrangle of the palace to be shut. And they sent to the keeper of the Bell-tower, and forbade the tolling of the bells. All this was carried into effect. The before-mentioned conspirators were secured, and they were brought to the palace; and, as the Council of Ten saw that the Duke was in the plot, they resolved that twenty of the leading men of the state should be associated to them, for the purpose of consultation and deliberation, but that they should not be allowed to ballot.

The counsellors were the following:— Ser Giovanni Mocenigo, of the Sestiero of Ssu Marco; Ser Almoro Veniero da Santa Marina, of the Sostioro of Castello; Ser Tomaso Viadro, of the Sestiero of Canareglo; Ser Giovanni Sanudo, of the Sestiero of Santa Croce; Ser Pietro Trivisano, of the Sestiero of San Paolo; Ser Pantalione Barbo il Grande, of the Sostiero of Ossoduro. The Avogadori of the Commonwealth were Zufredo Morosini, and Ser Orio Pasqualigo; and these did not ballot. Those of the Council of Ten were Ser Giovanni Marcello, Ser Tommaso Sanudo, and Ser Micheletto Dolfino, the heads of the aforesaid Council of Ten. Ser Luca da Leggo, and Ser Pietro da Mosto, inquisitors of the aforesaid Council. And Ser Marco Polani, Ser Marino Veniero, Ser Lando Lombardo and Ser Nicoletto Trivisano, of Sant' Angolo.

Late in the night, just before the dawning, they chose a junta of twenty noblemen of Venice from amongst the wisest, and the worthiest, and the oldest. They were to give counsel, but not to ballot. And they would not admit any one of Cà Faliero. And Niccolo Faliero, and another Niccolo Faliero, of San Tomaso, were expelled from the Council, because they belonged to the family of the Doge. And this resolution of creating the junta of twenty was much praised throughout the state. The following were the members of the junta of twenty:— Ser Marco Giustiniani, Procuratore, Ser Andrea Erizzo, Procuratore, Ser Lionardo Giustiniani, Procuratore, Ser Andrea Contarini, Ser Simone Dandolo, Ser Nicolo Volpe, Ser Giovanni Lorodano, Ser Marco Diedo, Ser Giovanni Gradenigo, Ser Andrea Cornaro, Cavaliero, Ser Marco Sorauzo, Ser Rinieri du Mosto, Ser Gazano Marcello, Ser Marino Morosini, Ser Stefano Belegno, Ser Nicolo Lioni, Ser Filippo Orio, Ser Marco Trivisano, Ser Jacopo Bragadino, Ser Giovanni Foscarini.

These twenty were accordingly called in to the Council of Ten; and they sent for my Lord Marino Faliero the Duke: and My Lord Marino was then consorting in the palace with people of great estate, gentlemen, and other good men, none of whom knew yet how the fact stood.

At the same time Bertucci Israello, who, as one of the ringleaders, was to head the conspirators in Santa Croce, was arrested and bound, and brought before the Council. Zanello del Brin, Nicoletto di Rosa, Nicoletto Alberto, and the Guardiaga, were also taken, together with several seamen, and people of various ranks. These were examined, and the truth of the plot was ascertained.

On the 16th of April judgment was given in the Council of Ten, that Filippo Calendaro and Bertuccio Israello should be hanged upon the red pillars of the balcony of the palace, from which the Duke is wont to look at the bull hunt: and they were hanged with gags in their mouths.

The next day the following were condemned:—Niccolo Zucuolo, Nicoletto Blondo, Nicoletto Doro, Marco Giuda, Jacomollo Dagolino, Nicoletto Fidelo, the son of Filippo Calendaro, Marco Torello, called Israello, Stofano Trivisano, the money changer of Santa Margherita, and Antonio dalle Bonde. These were all taken at Chiozza, for they were endeavouring to escape. Afterwards, by virtue of the sentence which was passed upon them in the Council of Ten, they were hanged on successive days; some singly and some in couples, upon the columns of the palace, beginning from the red columns, and so going onwards towards the canal. And other prisoners were discharged, because, although they had been involved in the conspiracy, yet they had not assisted in it: for they were given to understand by some of the heads of the plot, that they were to come armed and prepared for the service of the state, and in order to secure certain criminals; and they knew nothing else. Nicoletto Alberto, the Guardiaga, and Bartolommeo Ciricolo and his son, and several others, who were not guilty, were discharged.

On Friday, the 16th day of April, judgment was also given, in the aforesaid Council of Ten, that my Lord Marino Faliero, the Duke, should have his head cut off; and that the execution should be done on the landing-place of the stone staircase, where the Dukes take their oath when they first enter the palace. On the following day, the 17th of April, the doors of the palace being shut, the Duke had his head cut off, about the hour of noon. And the cap of estate was taken from the Duke's head before he came down stairs. When the execution was over, it is said that one of the Council of Ten went to the columns of the palace over against the place of St. Mark, and that he showed the bloody sword unto the people, crying out with a loud voice—"The terrible doom hath fallen upon the traitor!"—and the doors were opened, and the people all rushed in, to see the corpse of the Duke, who had been beheaded.

It must be known that Ser Giovanni Sanudo, the councillor, was not present when the aforesaid sentence was pronounced; because he was unwell and remained at home. So that only fourteen balloted; that is to say, five councillors, and nine of the Council of Ten. And it was adjudged, that all the lands and chattels of the Duke, as well as of the other traitors, should be forfeited to the state. And as a grace to the Duke, it was resolved in the Council of Ten, that he should be allowed to dispose of two thousand ducats out of his own property. And it was resolved, that all the councillors and all the Avogadori of the Commonwealth, those of the Council of Ten, and the members of the Junta, who had assisted in passing sentence on the Duke and the other traitors, should have the privilege of carrying arms both by day and by night in Venice, and from Grado to Cavazere. And they were also to be allowed two footmen carrying arms, the aforesaid footmen living and boarding with them in their own houses. And he who did not keep two footmen might transfer the privilege to his sons or his brothers; but only to two. Permission of carrying arms was also granted to the four Notaries of the Chancery, that is to say, of the Supreme Court, who took the depositions; and they were, Amedio, Nicoletto di Lorino, Steffanello, and Pietro de Compostolli, the secretaries of the Signori di Notte.

After the traitors had been hanged, and the Duke had had his head cut off, the state remained in great tranquillity and peace. And, as I have read in a Chronicle, the corpse of the Duke was removed in a barge, with eight torches, to his tomb in the church of San Giovanni e Paolo, where it was buried. The tomb is now in that aisle in the middle of the little church of Santa Maria della Pace, which was built by Bishop Gabriol of Bergamo. It is a coffin of stone, with these words engraven thereon: "*Hric jacet Dominus Marinus Faletro Dux.*" — And they did not paint his portrait in the hall of the Great Council; — but in the place where it ought to have been, you see these words — "*Hic est locus Marini Faletro, decupitati pro criminibus.*" — And it is thought that his house was granted to the church of Sant' Apostolo; it was that great one near the bridge. Yet this could not be the case, or else the family bought it back from the church; for it still belongs to Cà Faliero. I must not refrain from noting, that some wished to write the following words in the place where his portrait ong'it to have been, as aforesaid:—"*Marinus Fuletro Dux, temeritas me cepit. Pœnas lui, decapitatus pro criminibus.*" — Others, also, indited a couplet, worthy of being inscribed upon his tomb.

"*Dux Venetum jacet heic, patriam qui prodere tentans,
Sceptra, decus, censum perdidit, atque caput.*"

NOTE B.

PETRARCH ON THE CONSPIRACY OF MARINO FALIERO.

"Al giovane Doge Andrea Dandolo succedette un vecchio, il quale tardi si pose al timone della repubblica, ma sempre prima di quel, che facea d' uopo a lui, ed alla patria: egli è Marino Falidro, personaggio a me noto per antica dimestichezza. Falsa era l' opinione intorno a lui, giacchè egli si mostrò fornito più di corraggio, che di senno. Non pago della prima dignità, entrò con sinistro piede nel pubblico Palazzo: imperciocche questo Doge de Veneti, magistrato sacro in tutti i secoli, che dagli antichi fù sempre venerato qual nume in quella città, l' altr' jeri fù decollato nel vestibolo dell' istesso Palazzo. Discorrerei fin dal principio le cause di un tale evvento, e cosi vario, od ambiguo non ne fosse il grido. Nessuno però lo scusa, tutti affermano, che egli abbia voluto cangiar qualche cosa nell' ordine della repubblica a lui tramandato dai maggiori. Che desiderava egli di più? Io son d' avviso, che egli abbia ottenuto ciò, che non si concedetto a nessun altro: mentre adempiva gli uffici di legato presso il Pontefice, e sulle rive del Rodano trattava la pace, che io prima di lui avevo indarno tentato di conchiudere, gli fù conferito l'onore del Ducato, che ne chiedeva, ne s' aspettava. Tornato in patria, pensò a quello, cui nessuno non pose mente giammai, e soffrì quello, che a niuno accadde mai di soffrire: giacchè in quel luogo celeberrimo, e chiarissimo, e bellissimo infra tutti quelli, che io vidi, ove i suoi antenati avevano ricevuti grandissimi onori in mezzo alle pompe trionfali, ivi egli fù trascinato in modo servile, e spogliato delle insegne ducali, perdette la testa, e macchiò col proprio sangue le soglie del tempio, l'atrio del Palazzo, e le scale marmoree rendnte spesse volte illustri o dalle solenni festività, o dalle ostili spoglie. Hò notato il luogo, ora noto il tempo: è l'anno del Natale di Cristo 1355, fù il giorno 18 d' Aprile. Sì alto è il grido sparso, che se alcuno esaminerà la disciplina, e le costumanze di quella città, e quanto mutamento di cose venga minacciato dalla morte di un sol uomo (quantunque molti altri, come narrano, essendo complici, o subirono l' istesso supplicio, o lo aspettano) si accorgerà, che nulla di più grande avvenne ai nostri tempi nella Italia. Tu forse qui attendi il mio giudizio: assolvo il popolo, se credere alla fama, benchè abbia potuto e castigare più mitemente, e con maggior dolcezza vendicare il suo dolore: ma non così facilmente, si modera un' ira giusta insieme, e grande in un numeroso popolo principalmente, nel quale il precipitoso, ed instabile volgo aguzza gli stimoli dell' irracondia con rapidi, e sconsigliati clamori. Compatisco, e nell' istesso tempo mi adiro non quell' infelice uomo, il quale adorno di un' insolito onore, non so, che cosa si volesse negli estremi anni della sua vita: la calamità di lui diviene sempre più grave, perchè dalla sentenza contra di esso promulgata aperirà, che egli fù non solo misero, ma insano, e demente, e che con vane arti si usurpò per tanti anni una falsa fama di sapienza. Ammonisco i Dogi, i quali gli succederano, che questo e un' esempio posto inanzi ai loro occhj, quale specchio, nel quale veggano d' essere non Signori, ma Duci, anzi nemmeno Duci, ma onorati servi della Repubblica. Tu sta sano; e giacchè fluttuano le pubbliche cose, sforsiamosi di governar modestissimamente i privati nostri affari." — LEVATI, *Viaggi di Petrarca*, vol. iv. p. 323.

The above Italian translation from the Latin epistles of Petrarch proves—

1stly, That Marino Faliero was a personal friend of Petrarch's; "antica dimestichezza," old intimacy, is the phrase of the poet.

2dly, That Petrarch thought that he had more courage than conduct, "più di corraggio che di senno."

3dly, That there was some jealousy on the part of Petrarch; for he says that Marino Faliero was treating of the peace which he himself had "vainly attempted to conclude."

4thly, That the honour of the Dukedom was conferred upon him, which he neither sought nor expected, "che nè chiedeva nè aspettava," and which had never been granted to any other in like circumstances, "ciò che non si concedolte a nessun altro," a proof of the high esteem in which he must have been held.

5thly, That he had a reputation for *wisdom*, only forfeited by the last enterprise of his life, "si usurpò per tanti anni una falsa fama di sapienza." — "He had usurped for so many years a false fame of wisdom," rather a difficult task, I should think. People are generally found out before eighty years of age, at least in a republic.

From these, and the other historical notes which I have collected, it may be inferred, that Marino Faliero possessed many of the qualities, but not the success of a hero; and that his passions were too violent. The paltry and ignorant account of Dr. Moore falls to the ground. Petrarch says, "that there had been no greater event in his times" (*our times* literally), "nostri tempi," in Italy. He also differs from the historian in saying that Faliero was "on the banks of the Rhone," instead of at Rome, when elected; the other accounts say, that the deputation of the Venetian senate met him at Ravenna. How this may have been, it is not for me to decide, and is of no great importance. Had the man succeeded, he would have changed the face of Venice, and perhaps of Italy. As it is, what are they both?

NOTE C.

VENETIAN SOCIETY AND MANNERS.

"Vice without splendour, sin without relief
Even from the gloss of love to smooth it o'er;
But, in its stead, coarse lusts of habitude," &c.—(*See* p. 118.)

"To these attacks so frequently pointed by the government against the clergy, — to the continual struggles between the different constituted bodies, — to those enterprises carried on by the mass of the nobles against the depositaries of power, — to all those projects of innovation, which always ended by a stroke of state policy; we must add a cause not less fitted to spread contempt for ancient doctrines; *this was the excess of corruption*.

"That freedom of manners, which had been long boasted of as the principal charm of Venetian society, had degenerated into scandalous licentiousness: the tie of marriage was less sacred in that Catholic country, than among those nations where the laws and religion admit of its being dissolved. Because they could not break the contract, they feigned that it had not existed; and the ground of nullity, immodestly alleged by the married pair, was admitted with equal facility by priests and magistrates, alike corrupt. These divorces, veiled under another name, became so frequent, that the most important act of civil society was discovered to be amenable to a tribunal of exceptions; and to restrain the open scandal of such proceedings became the office of the police. In 1782, the Council of Ten decreed, that every woman who should sue for a dissolution of her marriage should be compelled to await the decision of the judges in some convent, to be named by the court.* Soon afterwards the same council summoned all causes of that nature before itself.** This infringement on ecclesiastical jurisdiction having occasioned some remonstrance from Rome, the council retained only the right of rejecting the petition of the married persons, and consented to refer such causes to the holy office as it should not previously have rejected.***

"There was a moment in which, doubtless, the destruction of private fortunes, the ruin of youth, the domestic discord occasioned by these abuses, determined the government to depart from its established maxims concerning the freedom of manners allowed the subject. All the courtesans were banished from Venice; but their absence was not enough to reclaim and bring back good morals to a whole people brought up in the most scandalous licentiousness. Depravity reached the very bosoms of private families, and even into the cloister; and they found themselves obliged to recall, and even to indemnify† women who sometimes gained possession of important secrets, and who might be usefully employed in the ruin of men whose fortunes might have rendered them dangerous. Since that time licentiousness has gone on increasing; and we have seen mothers, not only selling the innocence of their daughters, but selling it by a contract, authenticated by the signature of a public officer, and the performance of which was secured by the protection of the laws.††

"The parlours of the convents of noble ladies, and the houses of the courtesans, though the police carefully kept up a number of spies about them, were the only assemblies for society in Venice; and in these two places, so different from each other, there was equal freedom. Music, collations, gallantry, were not more forbidden in the parlours than at the casinos. There were a number of casinos for the purpose of public assemblies, where gaming was the principal pursuit of the company. It was a strange sight to see persons of either sex masked, or grave in their magisterial robes, round a table, invoking chance, and giving way at one instant to the agonies of despair, at the next to the illusions of hope, and that without uttering a single word.

"The rich had private casinos, but they lived *incognito* in them; and the wives whom they abandoned found compensation in the liberty they enjoyed. The corruption of morals had deprived them of their empire. We have just reviewed the whole history of Venice, and we have not once seen them exercise the slightest influence." — DARU: *Hist. de la Répub. de Venise*, vol. v. p. 95.

* Correspondence of M. Schlick, French chargé d'affaires. Despatch of 24th August, 1782.
** *Ibid.* Despatch, 31st August.
*** *Ibid.* Despatch of 3d September 1785.
† The decree for their recall designates them as *nostre benemerite meretrici*: a fund and some houses, called *case rumpane*, were assigned to them; hence the opprobrious appellation of *Carampane*.
†† Mayer, Description of Venice, vol. ii. and M. Archenholz, Picture of Italy, vol. i. ch. 2.

Note D
ACCOUNT OF THE ANCIENT VENETIAN NOBILITY, WITH THE CAUSES OF ITS DECAY.

> "She shall stoop to be
> A province for an empire, petty town
> In lieu of capital, with slaves for senates,
> Beggars for nobles, panders for a people!"
>
> Act V. Scene 3.

"The nobles of Venice, though all equal in the eye of the law, were fancifully divided into three classes; the first distinguished as that of the *sangue bid* or *sangue columbin*, i. e. blue blood or pigeon's blood; the second, as the division of the *morèl de mezo*, or the middle piece, and the poorest of all as *Bernaboti*, or Barnabites; from their inhabiting small and cheap houses in the parish of St. Barnabas.

"It will be easily conceived that the poor nobility must have been numerous in a state which considered all the legitimate sons of a patrician as noble; where commerce no longer offered a resource, and the only profession left was that of the law. This class, therefore, subsisting upon the employments of the republic, civil or military, at home and abroad, was necessarily ruined by the revolution. But the cause of the almost general havoc which involved the Venetian aristocracy is not so immediately visible; the less so, as the laws of the *fede-commesso*, which corresponds with our *entail*, were sufficiently rigorous in old Venice.

"I shall try, according to the information I have received, to explain how this was accomplished. The first and foremost cause was the excessive indolence and profusion of the last generations of the nobility, who appear to have resembled the ancestor of Sir Roger de Coverley; who, he tells us, 'would sign a deed for a mortgage covering one half his estate with his glove on:' with this difference, however, that the Venetian patrician could only mortgage his estate during his own natural life; a circumstance which, it appears at first sight, should have been the protection of the ancient houses of Venice. The protection was, however, in most instances, of no avail.

"In almost all countries the laws of honour often contravene the laws of the land, often mischievously; but they sometimes come in aid of sound morality. Such was their effect here. The law of the *fede-commesso* allowed a son to charge himself with the debts of a father, without prejudice to his successors; but it being considered as a point of honour to take up this burden, the son's son succeeded to it, and the debts of one generation were perpetuated through diverse succeeding ones.

"Things were in this state when the old government was overthrown, and the law of *fede-commesso* abolished here, as well as all over the countries revolutionised by France. The consequence was, the immediate seizure of property so encumbered. This was inevitable; and the creditor of the family of *Cornèr*, or any other Venetian house, seized upon his own.

"Thus one of the indirect consequences of the revolution was the destruction of an immense number of Venetian families of the *sangue blò* and *morél de mezo*. It was, however, more immediately destructive to those denominated the Barnabites, who were at once cut off from all the lucrative offices of the state. Nor was this all: the daughters of the indigent nobility had all of them pensions which they brought in dowry to their husbands; but place and pension, though bestowed for life, were annihilated, and, in the place of these, a miserable stipend of two Venetian livres a day (not quite ten-pence English) was bestowed on those who condescended to accept of it, by the mushroom municipality which flourished for its day out of the ruins of the aristocracy. Poor as this pittance was, even in this country where necessaries bear a price out of all proportion to luxuries, numbers *did* accept it, under the idea that it would be increased under happier circumstances; but the French, it will be easily believed, did not augment it, and (what could scarcely be believed but by those versed in the proceedings of the cabinet of Vienna) the Austrian government clipped this miserable mite, and clogged it with conditions which neither the revolutionary municipality nor the French were illiberal enough to impose.

"The municipality gave *their* compensation, and, the whole of the *terra ferma* being in possession of the enemy, perhaps they could give no more — the municipality gave it as unrestricted as the pensions it was to replace: the French made no alteration in the system; but the Austrians have not only limited it to persons not having two hundred ducats a year, (twenty-five pounds sterling), but have insisted upon its being spent in their own dominions. Of the rigour with which this condition is exacted, take the following example: — A lady, ignorant of the regulations which had been introduced, was absent two years in the south of France; she returned, and claimed the arrears of her pension, without having specified where she had been. The arrears were paid, after the usual difficulties; but her absence having been ascertained, she was ordered to disgorge her prey, under the threat of being excluded from all further provision.

"I have said, after the usual difficulties: I will now illustrate these. Another lady claimed *seven months*' arrears of pension, due during a residence in Lombardy and the Venetian state. Now, this was a claim verifiable by a single instrument, her passport, which ascertained the day of her arrival in every town, by the signature of accredited officers of the Austrian police. Notwithstanding this, she was *seven months* more before she could obtain her demand. These were spent in the presentation of petitions, always by order, always on stamped paper, and in the almost daily beat of half the official stairs of Venice, either in person or in proxy.*

---

* This is by no means a single case: A Venetian judge, displaced, but pensioned by the Austrians, neglected to receive his allowance according to the example of the others. At length he applied for his arrears, which were denied him. "What!" said he, "will you not give me what others have received?" "No!" was the answer, "and those others will be forced to refund." — Note that these pensions had been paid in virtue of a solemn and *printed* decree.

"But I willingly turn away my eyes from a picture, every detail of which is painful, and, having described the fortunes of the Venetian nobility, shall give some account of their honours. The patricians, as I said before, all equal in the eye of the law, had no titles as such, excepting that of *your Excellency;* though some bore them, as *Counts* &c. of *terra ferma,* before being enrolled in the nobility of Venice; and some had titles assigned them as compensations for, or rather as memorials of, fallen greatness. Thus the *Querini,* formerly lords of *Crema,* had the distinction continued to them, after *Crema* was absorbed in the Venetian state.

"These families, however, usually let their titles sleep, considering the quality of an untitled Venetian patrician as superior to any other distinction. Nor does this seem to have been an odd refinement, for the old republic sold titles for a pittance to whoever could pay for them, though such a person might not even have had the education of a gentleman.*
It was natural, therefore, that a lord of *Crema* should fear being confounded with this county *cusaylia,* and sink his having any thing in common with such a crew.

"The great political revolution that has taken place, destroying the splendour of the *libro d'oro,* has induced some to produce their *terra ferma* titles; but the majority content themselves with the style of *Cavaliere,*** which does not necessarily denote actual knighthood; and is often used almost as liberally in Italy, as the denomination of Squire now is in England. A striking proof, indeed, of good sense and dignity was given by the great body of the Venetian nobility, on being invited by Austria to claim nobility and title from her, on the verification of their rights; the great body of them merely desiring a recognition of their rank, without availing themselves of the offer held out to them. A few, indeed, have pursued a different line of conduct, and received patents of princes," &c.— ROSE: *Letters from the North of Italy,* vol. ii. p. 105.

* The qualification to be a Count was about what is supposed to qualify for knighthood in England, and the fee paid for the title, if I am rightly informed, 20 *l.* or 40 *l.*

** No order of knighthood was peculiar to Venice, and her citizens were precluded by law from becoming members of foreign orders.

THE TWO FOSCARI.

AN HISTORICAL TRAGEDY.

The father softens, but the governor's resolved. — CRITIC.

DRAMATIS PERSONÆ.

MEN.

FRANCIS FOSCARI, *Doge of Venice.*
JACOPO FOSCARI, *Son of the Doge.*
JAMES LOREDANO, *a Patrician.*
MARCO MEMMO, *a Chief of the Forty.*
BARBARIGO, *a Senator.*
Other Senators, The Council of Ten, Guards, Attendants, &c. &c.

WOMAN.

MARINA, *Wife of young* FOSCARI.

Scene — the Ducal Palace, Venice.

THE TWO FOSCARI.

ACT I.

SCENE I.

A Hall in the Ducal Palace.

Enter LOREDANO *and* BARBARIGO, *meeting.*

Lor. WHERE is the prisoner?
Bar.   Reposing from
The Question.
    Lor.   The hour's past—fix'd yesterday
For the resumption of his trial.— Let us
Rejoin our colleagues in the council, and
Urge his recall.
    Bar.   Nay, let him profit by
A few brief minutes for his tortured limbs;
He was o'erwrought by the Question yesterday,
And may die under it if now repeated.
    Lor. Well?
    Bar.   I yield not to you in love of justice,
Or hate of the ambitious Foscari,
Father and son, and all their noxious race;
But the poor wretch has suffer'd beyond nature's
Most stoical endurance.
    Lor.   Without owning
His crime?
    Bar.   Perhaps without committing any.
But he avow'd the letter to the Duke
Of Milan, and his sufferings half atone for
Such weakness.
    Lor.   We shall see.
    Bar.   You, Loredano,
Pursue hereditary hate too far.

Lor. How far?
Bar. To extermination.
Lor. When they are
Extinct, you may say this.— Let's in to council.
Bar. Yet pause— the number of our colleagues is not
Complete yet; two are wanting ere we can
Proceed.
Lor. And the chief judge, the Doge?
Bar. No— he,
With more than Roman fortitude, is ever
First at the board in this unhappy process
Against his last and only son.
Lor. True— true—
His *last*.
Bar. Will nothing move you?
Lor. *Feels he*, think you?
Bar. He shows it not.
Lor. I have mark'd *that*— the wretch!
Bar. But yesterday, I hear, on his return
To the ducal chambers, as he pass'd the threshold
The old man fainted.
Lor. It begins to work, then.
Bar. The work is half your own.
Lor. And should be *all* mine—
My father and my uncle are no more.
Bar. I have read their epitaph, which says they died
By poison.
Lor. When the Doge declared that he
Should never deem himself a sovereign till
The death of Peter Loredano, both
The brothers sicken'd shortly:— he *is* sovereign.
Bar. A wretched one.
Lor. What should they be who make
Orphans?
Bar. But *did* the Doge make you so?
Lor. Yes.
Bar. What solid proofs?

Lor. When princes set themselves
To work in secret, proofs and process are
Alike made difficult; but I have such
Of the first, as shall make the second needless.
    Bar. But you will move by law?
    Lor.   By all the laws
Which he would leave us.
    Bar.   They are such in this
Our state as render retribution easier
Than 'mongst remoter nations. Is it true
That you have written in your books of commerce,
(The wealthy practice of our highest nobles)
"Doge Foscari, my debtor for the deaths
Of Marco and Pietro Loredano,
My sire and uncle?"
    Lor.   It is written thus.
    Bar. And will you leave it unerased?
    Lor.   Till balanced.
    Bar. And how?
        [*Two Senators pass over the stage, as in their way to*
            "*the Hall of the Council of Ten.*"
    Lor.   You see the number is complete.
Follow me.   [*Exit* LOREDANO.
    Bar. (*solus*). Follow *thee!* I have follow'd long
Thy path of desolation, as the wave
Sweeps after that before it, alike whelming
The wreck that creaks to the wild winds, and wretch
Who shrieks within its riven ribs, as gush
The waters through them; but this son and sire
Might move the elements to pause, and yet
Must I on hardily like them—Oh! would
I could as blindly and remorselessly!—
Lo, where he comes!—Be still, my heart! they are
Thy foes, must be thy victims: wilt thou beat
For those who almost broke thee?

ACT I.

Enter Guards, with young FOSCARI *as prisoner, &c.*

   Guard.   Let him rest.
Signor, take time.
   Jac. Fos.   I thank thee, friend, I'm feeble;
But thou may'st stand reproved.
   Guard.   I'll stand the hazard.
   Jac. Fos. That's kind:—I meet some pity, but no mercy;
This is the first.
   Guard.   And might be last, did they
Who rule behold us.
   Bar. (advancing to the Guard). There is one who does:
Yet fear not; I will neither be thy judge
Nor thy accuser; though the hour is past,
Wait their last summons—I am of "the Ten,"
And waiting for that summons, sanction you
Even by my presence: when the last call sounds,
We'll in together.—Look well to the prisoner!
   Jac. Fos. What voice is that?—'Tis Barbarigo's! Ah!
Our house's foe, and one of my few judges.
   Bar. To balance such a foe, if such there be,
Thy father sits amongst thy judges.
   Jac. Fos.   True,
He judges.
   Bar.   Then deem not the laws too harsh
Which yield so much indulgence to a sire
As to allow his voice in such high matter
As the state's safety—
   Jac. Fos.   And his son's. I'm faint;
Let me approach, I pray you, for a breath
Of air, yon window which o'erlooks the waters.

Enter an Officer, who whispers BARBARIGO.

   Bar. (to the Guard). Let him approach. I must not speak
       with him
Further than thus: I have transgress'd my duty
In this brief parley, and must now redeem it
Within the Council Chamber.   [*Exit* BARBARIGO.
   [*Guard conducting* JACOPO FOSCARI *to the window.*

Guard. There, sir, 'tis
Open—How feel you?
Jac. Fos. Like a boy—Oh Venice!
Guard. And your limbs?
Jac. Fos. Limbs! how often have they borne me
Bounding o'er yon blue tide, as I have skimm'd
The gondola along in childish race,
And, masqued as a young gondolier, amidst
My gay competitors, noble as I,
Raced for our pleasure, in the pride of strength;
While the fair populace of crowding beauties,
Plebeian as patrician, cheer'd us on
With dazzling smiles, and wishes audible,
And waving kerchiefs, and applauding hands,
Even to the goal!—How many a time have I
Cloven with arm still lustier, breast more daring,
The wave all roughen'd; with a swimmer's stroke
Flinging the billows back from my drench'd hair,
And laughing from my lip the audacious brine,
Which kiss'd it like a wine-cup, rising o'er
The waves as they arose, and prouder still
The loftier they uplifted me; and oft,
In wantonness of spirit, plunging down
Into their green and glassy gulfs, and making
My way to shells and sea-weed, all unseen
By those above, till they wax'd fearful; then
Returning with my grasp full of such tokens
As show'd that I had search'd the deep: exulting,
With a far-dashing stroke, and drawing deep
The long-suspended breath, again I spurn'd
The foam which broke around me, and pursued
My track like a sea-bird.—I was a boy then.
Guard. Be a man now: there never was more need
Of manhood's strength.
Jac. Fos. (looking from the lattice). My beautiful, my own,
My only Venice—*this is breath!* Thy breeze,
Thine Adrian sea-breeze, how it fans my face!

Thy very winds feel native to my veins,
And cool them into calmness! How unlike
The hot gales of the horrid Cyclades,
Which howl'd about my Candiote dungeon, and
Made my heart sick.
    Guard.   I see the colour comes
Back to your cheek: Heaven send you strength to bear
What more may be imposed!—I dread to think on't.
    Jac. Fos. They will not banish me again?—No—no,
Let them wring on; I am strong yet.
    Guard.   Confess,
And the rack will be spared you.
    Jac. Fos.   I confess'd
Once—twice before: both times they exiled me.
    Guard. And the third time will slay you.
    Jac. Fos.   Let them do so,
So I be buried in my birth-place: better
Be ashes here than aught that lives elsewhere.
    Guard. And can you so much love the soil which hates
        you?
    Jac. Fos. The soil!—Oh no, it is the seed of the soil
Which persecutes me; but my native earth
Will take me as a mother to her arms.
I ask no more than a Venetian grave,
A dungeon, what they will, so it be here.

                Enter an Officer.

    Off. Bring in the prisoner!
    Guard.   Signor, you hear the order.
    Jac. Fos. Ay, I am used to such a summons; 'tis
The third time they have tortured me:—then lend me
Thine arm.   [*To the Guard.*
    Off.   Take mine, sir; 'tis my duty to
Be nearest to your person.
    Jac. Fos.   You!—you are he
Who yesterday presided o'er my pangs—
Away!—I'll walk alone.

Off.   As you please, signor;
The sentence was not of my signing, but
I dared not disobey the Council when
They—
    Jac. Fos. Bade thee stretch me on their horrid engine.
I pray thee touch me not—that is, just now;
The time will come they will renew that order,
But keep off from me till 'tis issued. As
I look upon thy hands my curdling limbs
Quiver with the anticipated wrenching,
And the cold drops strain through my brow, as if—
But onward—I have borne it—I can bear it.—
How looks my father?
    Off.   With his wonted aspect.
    Jac. Fos. So does the earth, and sky, the blue of ocean,
The brightness of our city, and her domes,
The mirth of her Piazza, even now
Its merry hum of nations pierces here,
Even here, into these chambers of the unknown
Who govern, and the unknown and the unnumber'd
Judged and destroy'd in silence,—all things wear
The self-same aspect, to my very sire!
Nothing can sympathise with Foscari,
Not even a Foscari.—Sir, I attend you.
            [*Exeunt* JACOPO FOSCARI, *Officer, &c.*

        Enter MEMMO *and another Senator.*

    Mem. He's gone—we are too late:—think you "the Ten"
Will sit for any length of time to-day?
    Sen. They say the prisoner is most obdurate,
Persisting in his first avowal; but
More I know not.
    Mem.   And that is much; the secrets
Of yon terrific chamber are as hidden
From us, the premier nobles of the state,
As from the people.
    Sen.   Save the wonted rumours,

Which—like the tales of spectres, that are rife
Near ruin'd buildings—never have been proved,
Nor wholly disbelieved: men know as little
Of the state's real acts as of the grave's
Unfathom'd mysteries.
 Mem.   But with length of time
We gain a step in knowledge, and I look
Forward to be one day of the decemvirs.
 Sen. Or Doge?
 Mem.   Why, no; not if I can avoid it.
 Sen. 'Tis the first station of the state, and may
Be lawfully desired, and lawfully
Attain'd by noble aspirants.
 Mem.   To such
I leave it; though born noble, my ambition
Is limited: I'd rather be an unit
Of an united and imperial "Ten,"
Than shine a lonely, though a gilded cipher.—
Whom have we here? the wife of Foscari?

   Enter MARINA, *with a female Attendant.*

 Mar. What, no one?—I am wrong, there still are two;
But they are senators.
 Mem.   Most noble lady,
Command us.
 Mar. *I command!*—Alas! my life
Has been one long entreaty, and a vain one.
 Mem. I understand thee, but I must not answer.
 Mar. (*fiercely*). True—none dare answer here save on
  the rack,
Or question save those—
 Mem. (*interrupting her*). High-born dame! bethink thee
Where thou now art.
 Mar.   Where I now am!—It was
My husband's father's palace.
 Mem.   The Duke's palace.
 Mar. And his son's prison;—true, I have not forgot it;

And if there were no other nearer, bitterer
Remembrances, would thank the illustrious Memmo
For pointing out the pleasures of the place.
    Mem. Be calm!
    Mar. (looking up towards heaven). I am; but oh, thou
        eternal God!
Canst *thou* continue so, with such a world?
    Mem. Thy husband yet may be absolved.
    Mar.   He is,
In heaven. I pray you, signor senator,
Speak not of that; you are a man of office,
So is the Doge; he has a son at stake
Now, at this moment, and I have a husband,
Or had; they are there within, or were at least
An hour since, face to face, as judge and culprit:
Will *he* condemn *him?*
    Mem.   I trust not.
    Mar.   But if
He does not, there are those will sentence both.
    Mem. They can.
    Mar.   And with them power and will are one
In wickedness:—my husband's lost!
    Mem.   Not so;
Justice is judge in Venice.
    Mar.   If it were so,
There now would be no Venice. But let it
Live on, so the good die not, till the hour
Of nature's summons; but "the Ten's" is quicker,
And we must wait on't. Ah! a voice of wail!
                                        [*A faint cry within.*
    Sen. Hark!
    Mem.   'Twas a cry of —
    Mar.   No, no; not my husband's —
Not Foscari's.
    Mem.   The voice was —
    Mar.   *Not his:* no.

He shriek! No; that should be his father's part,
Not his—not his—he'll die in silence.
                          [*A faint groan again within.*
    Mem.   What!
Again?
    Mar. His voice! it seem'd so: I will not
Believe it. Should he shrink, I cannot cease
To love; but—no—no—no—it must have been
A fearful pang, which wrung a groan from him.
    Sen. And, feeling for thy husband's wrongs, wouldst thou
Have him bear more than mortal pain, in silence?
    Mar. We all must bear our tortures. I have not
Left barren the great house of Foscari,
Though they sweep both the Doge and son from life;
I have endured as much in giving life
To those who will succeed them, as they can
In leaving it: but mine were joyful pangs:
And yet they wrung me till I *could* have shriek'd,
But did not; for my hope was to bring forth
Heroes, and would not welcome them with tears.
    Mem. All's silent now.
    Mar.   Perhaps all's over; but
I will not deem it: he hath nerved himself,
And now defies them.

              Enter an Officer hastily.
    Mem.   How now, friend, what seek you?
    Off. A leech. The prisoner has fainted.
                                      [*Exit Officer.*
    Mem.   Lady,
'Twere better to retire.
    Sen. (*offering to assist her*). I pray thee do so.
    Mar. Off! *I* will tend him.
    Mem.   You! Remember, lady!
Ingress is given to none within those chambers,
Except "the Ten," and their familiars.
    Mar.   Well,

I know that none who enter there return
As they have enter'd—many never; but
They shall not balk my entrance.
    Mem.   Alas! this
Is but to expose yourself to harsh repulse,
And worse suspense.
    Mar.   Who shall oppose me?
    Mem.   They
Whose duty 'tis to do so.
    Mar.   'Tis *their* duty
To trample on all human feelings, all
Ties which bind man to man, to emulate
The fiends who will one day requite them in
Variety of torturing! Yet I'll pass.
    Mem. It is impossible.
    Mar.   That shall be tried.
Despair defies even despotism: there is
That in my heart would make its way through hosts
With levell'd spears; and think you a few jailors,
Shall put me from my path? Give me, then, way;
This is the Doge's palace; I am wife
Of the Duke's son, the *innocent* Duke's son,
And they shall hear this!
    Mem.   It will only serve
More to exasperate his judges.
    Mar.   What
Are *judges* who give way to anger? they
Who do so are assassins. Give me way.
                                       [*Exit* MARINA.
    Sen. Poor lady!
    Mem.   'Tis mere desperation: she
Will not be admitted o'er the threshold.
    Sen.   And
Even if she be so, cannot save her husband.
But, see, the officer returns.
        [*The Officer passes over the stage with another person.*
    Mem.   I hardly

Thought that "the Ten" had even this touch of pity,
Or would permit assistance to this sufferer.
    Sen. Pity! Is't pity to recall to feeling
The wretch too happy to escape to death
By the compassionate trance, poor nature's last
Resource against the tyranny of pain?
    Mem. I marvel they condemn him not at once.
    Sen. That's not their policy: they'd have him live,
Because he fears not death; and banish him,
Because all earth, except his native land,
To him is one wide prison, and each breath
Of foreign air he draws seems a slow poison,
Consuming but not killing.
    Mem.   Circumstance
Confirms his crimes, but he avows them not.
    Sen. None, save the Letter, which he says was written,
Address'd to Milan's duke, in the full knowledge
That it would fall into the senate's hands,
And thus he should be re-convey'd to Venice.
    Mem. But as a culprit.
    Sen.   Yes, but to his country
And that was all he sought,—so he avouches.
    Mem. The accusation of the bribes was proved.
    Sen. Not clearly, and the charge of homicide
Has been annull'd by the death-bed confession
Of Nicolas Erizzo, who slew the late
Chief of "the Ten."
    Mem.   Then why not clear him?
    Sen.   That
They ought to answer; for it is well known
That Almoro Donato, as I said,
Was slain by Erizzo for private vengeance.
    Mem. There must be more in this strange process than
The apparent crimes of the accused disclose—
But here come two of "the Ten;" let us retire.
                             [*Exeunt* MEMMO *and Senator.*

Enter Loredano *and* Barbarigo.

Bar. (*addressing* Lor.) That were too much: believe me,
    'twas not meet
The trial should go further at this moment.
    Lor. And so the Council must break up, and Justice
Pause in her full career, because a woman
Breaks in on our deliberations?
    Bar.   No,
That's not the cause; you saw the prisoner's state.
    Lor. And had he not recover'd?
    Bar.   To relapse
Upon the least renewal.
    Lor.   'Twas not tried.
    Bar. 'Tis vain to murmur; the majority
In council were against you.
    Lor.   Thanks to you, sir,
And the old ducal dotard, who combined
The worthy voices which o'er-ruled my own.
    Bar. I am a judge; but must confess that part
Of our stern duty, which prescribes the Question,
And bids us sit and see its sharp infliction,
Makes me wish—
    Lor.   What?
    Bar.   That *you* would *sometimes* feel,
As I do always.
    Lor.   Go to, you're a child,
Infirm of feeling as of purpose, blown
About by every breath, shook by a sigh,
And melted by a tear—a precious judge
For Venice! and a worthy statesman to
Be partner in my policy.
    Bar.   He shed
No tears.
    Lor.   He cried out twice.
    Bar.   A saint had done so,
Even with the crown of glory in his eye,
At such inhuman artifice of pain

As was forced on him; but he did not cry
For pity; not a word nor groan escaped him,
And those two shrieks were not in supplication,
But wrung from pangs, and follow'd by no prayers.
　　Lor. He mutter'd many times between his teeth,
But inarticulately.
　　Bar. 　　　　　That I heard not;
You stood more near him.
　　Lor. 　　　　　I did so.
　　Bar. 　　　　　　　　Methought,
To my surprise too, you were touch'd with mercy,
And were the first to call out for assistance
When he was failing.
　　Lor. 　　　　　I believed that swoon
His last.
　　Bar. And have I not oft heard thee name
His and his father's death your nearest wish?
　　Lor. If he dies innocent, that is to say,
With his guilt unavow'd, he'll be lamented.
　　Bar. What, wouldst thou slay his memory?
　　Lor. 　　　　　　　　Wouldst thou have
His state descend to his children, as it must,
If he die unattainted?
　　Bar. 　　　　　War with *them* too?
　　Lor. With all their house, till theirs or mine are nothing.
　　Bar. And the deep agony of his pale wife,
And the repress'd convulsion of the high
And princely brow of his old father, which
Broke forth in a slight shuddering, though rarely,
Or in some clammy drops, soon wiped away
In stern serenity; these moved you not?

　　　　　　　　　　　　[*Exit* LOREDANO.

He's silent in his hate, as Foscari
Was in his suffering; and the poor wretch moved me
More by his silence than a thousand outcries
Could have effected. 'Twas a dreadful sight
When his distracted wife broke through into

The hall of our tribunal, and beheld
What we could scarcely look upon, long used
To such sights. I must think no more of this,
Lest I forget in this compassion for
Our foes their former injuries, and lose
The hold of vengeance Loredano plans
For him and me; but mine would be content
With lesser retribution than he thirsts for,
And I would mitigate his deeper hatred
To milder thoughts; but for the present, Foscari
Has a short hourly respite, granted at
The instance of the elders of the Council,
Moved doubtless by his wife's appearance in
The hall, and his own sufferings.—Lo! they come:
How feeble and forlorn! I cannot bear
To look on them again in this extremity:
I'll hence, and try to soften Loredano.
  [*Exit* BARBARIGO.

ACT II.

SCENE I.
A Hall in the DOGE'S *Palace.*

The DOGE *and a* SENATOR.

Sen. Is it your pleasure to sign the report
Now, or postpone it till to-morrow?
  Doge.   Now;
I overlook'd it yesterday: it wants
Merely the signature. Give me the pen—
  [*The* DOGE *sits down and signs the paper.*
There, signor.
  Sen. (*looking at the paper*). You have forgot; it is not sign'd.
  Doge. Not sign'd? Ah, I perceive my eyes begin
To wax more weak with age. I did not see
That I had dipp'd the pen without effect.

ACT II.

Sen. (*dipping the pen into the ink, and placing the paper be-
    fore the* Doge). Your hand, too, shakes, my lord:
    allow me, thus—
Doge. 'Tis done, I thank you.
Sen.   Thus the act confirm'd
By you and by "the Ten" gives peace to Venice.
Doge. 'Tis long since she enjoy'd it: may it be
As long ere she resume her arms!
Sen.   'Tis almost
Thirty-four years of nearly ceaseless warfare
With the Turk, or the powers of Italy;
The state had need of some repose.
Doge.   No doubt:
I found her Queen of Ocean, and I leave her
Lady of Lombardy; it is a comfort
That I have added to her diadem
The gems of Brescia and Ravenna; Crema
And Bergamo no less are hers; her realm
By land has grown by thus much in my reign,
While her sea-sway has not shrunk.
Sen.   'Tis most true,
And merits all our country's gratitude.
Doge. Perhaps so.
Sen.   Which should be made manifest.
Doge. I have not complain'd, sir.
Sen.   My good lord, forgive me.
Doge. For what?
Sen.   My heart bleeds for you.
Doge.   For me, signor?
Sen. And for your—
Doge.   Stop!
Sen.   It must have way, my lord:
I have too many duties towards you
And all your house, for past and present kindness,
Not to feel deeply for your son.
Doge.   Was this
In your commission?

Sen. What, my lord?
Doge. This prattle
Of things you know not: but the treaty's sign'd;
Return with it to them who sent you.
Sen. I
Obey. I had in charge, too, from the Council
That you would fix an hour for their re-union.
Doge. Say, when they will—now, even at this moment,
If it so please them: I am the state's servant.
Sen. They would accord some time for your repose.
Doge. I have no repose, that is, none which shall cause
The loss of an hour's time unto the state.
Let them meet when they will, I shall be found
Where I should be, and *what* I have been ever.
[*Exit* SENATOR.
[*The* DOGE *remains in silence.*

Enter an Attendant.

Att. Prince!
Doge. Say on.
Att. The illustrious lady Foscari
Requests an audience.
Doge. Bid her enter. Poor
Marina!
[*Exit Attendant.*
[*The* DOGE *remains in silence as before.*

Enter MARINA.

Mar. I have ventured, father, on
Your privacy.
Doge. I have none from you, my child.
Command my time, when not commanded by
The state.
Mar. I wish'd to speak to you of *him.*
Doge. Your husband?
Mar. And your son.
Doge. Proceed, my daughter!
Mar. I had obtain'd permission from "the Ten"

To attend my husband for a limited number
Of hours.
    Doge. You had so.
    Mar.   'Tis revoked.
    Doge.   By whom?
    Mar. "The Ten."—When we had reach'd "the Bridge
        of Sighs,"
Which I prepared to pass with Foscari,
The gloomy guardian of that passage first
Demurr'd: a messenger was sent back to
"The Ten;" but as the court no longer sate,
And no permission had been given in writing,
I was thrust back, with the assurance that
Until that high tribunal re-assembled
The dungeon walls must still divide us.
    Doge.   True,
The form has been omitted in the haste
With which the court adjourn'd; and till it meets,
'Tis dubious.
    Mar. Till it meets! and when it meets,
They'll torture him again; and he and *I*
Must purchase by renewal of the rack
The interview of husband and of wife,
The holiest tie beneath the heavens!—Oh God!
Dost thou see this?
    Doge.   Child—child—
    Mar. (abruptly).   Call *me* not "child!"
You soon will have no children—you deserve none—
You, who can talk thus calmly of a son
In circumstances which would call forth tears
Of blood from Spartans! Though these did not weep
Their boys who died in battle, is it written
That they beheld them perish piecemeal, nor
Stretch'd forth a hand to save them?
    Doge.   You behold me:
I cannot weep—I would I could; but if
Each white hair on this head were a young life,

This ducal cap the diadem of earth,
This ducal ring with which I wed the waves
A talisman to still them—I'd give all
For him.
    Mar. With less he surely might be saved.
    Doge. That answer only shows you know not Venice.
Alas! how should you? she knows not herself,
In all her mystery. Hear me—they who aim
At Foscari, aim no less at his father;
The sire's destruction would not save the son;
They work by different means to the same end,
And that is—but they have not conquer'd yet.
    Mar. But they have crush'd.
    Doge.   Nor crush'd as yet—I live.
    Mar. And your son,—how long will he live?
    Doge.   I trust,
For all that yet is past, as many years
And happier than his father. The rash boy,
With womanish impatience to return,
Hath ruin'd all by that detected letter:
A high crime, which I neither can deny
Nor palliate, as parent or as Duke:
Had he but borne a little, little longer
His Candiote exile, I had hopes—he has quench'd them—
He must return.
    Mar.   To exile?
    Doge.   I have said it.
    Mar. And can I not go with him?
    Doge.   You well know
This prayer of yours was twice denied before
By the assembled "Ten," and hardly now
Will be accorded to a third request,
Since aggravated errors on the part
Of your lord render them still more austere.
    Mar. Austere? Atrocious! The old human fiends,
With one foot in the grave, with dim eyes, strange
To tears save drops of dotage, with long white

And scanty hairs, and shaking hands, and heads
As palsied as their hearts are hard, they council,
Cabal, and put men's lives out, as if life
Were no more than the feelings long extinguish'd
In their accursed bosoms.
    Doge.   You know not —
    Mar. I do — I do — and so should you, methinks —
That these are demons: could it be else that
Men, who have been of women born and suckled —
Who have loved, or talk'd at least of love — have given
Their hands in sacred vows — have danced their babes
Upon their knees, perhaps have mourn'd above them —
In pain, in peril, or in death — who are,
Or were at least in seeming, human, could
Do as they have done by yours, and you yourself,
You, who abet them?
    Doge.   I forgive this, for
You know not what you say.
    Mar.   *You* know it well,
And feel it nothing.
    Doge.   I have borne so much,
That words have ceased to shake me.
    Mar.   Oh, no doubt!
You have seen your son's blood flow, and your flesh shook not:
And after that, what are a woman's words?
No more than woman's tears, that they should shake you.
    Doge. Woman, this clamorous grief of thine, I tell thee,
Is no more in the balance weigh'd with that
Which — but I pity thee, my poor Marina!
    Mar. Pity my husband, or I cast it from me;
Pity thy son! *Thou* pity! — 'tis a word
Strange to thy heart — how came it on thy lips?
    Doge. I must bear these reproaches, though they wrong me.
Couldst thou but read —
    Mar.   'Tis not upon thy brow,
Nor in thine eyes, nor in thine acts, — where then
Should I behold this sympathy? or shall?

Doge (*pointing downwards*). There.
Mar.   In the earth?
Doge.   To which I am tending: when
It lies upon this heart, far lightlier, though
Loaded with marble, than the thoughts which press it
Now, you will know me better.
    Mar.   Are you, then,
Indeed, thus to be pitied?
    Doge.   Pitied! None
Shall ever use that base word, with which men
Cloke their soul's hoarded triumph, as a fit one
To mingle with my name; that name shall be,
As far as *I* have borne it, what it was
When I received it.
    Mar.   But for the poor children
Of him thou canst not, or thou wilt not save,
You were the last to bear it.
    Doge.   Would it were so!
Better for him he never had been born;
Better for me.—I have seen our house dishonour'd.
    Mar. That's false! A truer, nobler, trustier heart,
More loving, or more loyal, never beat
Within a human breast. I would not change
My exiled, persecuted, mangled husband,
Oppress'd but not disgraced, crush'd, overwhelm'd,
Alive, or dead, for prince or paladin
In story or in fable, with a world
To back his suit. Dishonour'd!—*he* dishonour'd!
I tell thee, Doge, 'tis Venice is dishonour'd;
His name shall be her foulest, worst reproach,
For what he suffers, not for what he did.
'Tis ye who are all traitors, tyrant!—ye!
Did you but love your country like this victim
Who totters back in chains to tortures, and
Submits to all things rather than to exile,
You'd fling yourselves before him, and implore
His grace for your enormous guilt.

Doge.   He was
Indeed all you have said. I better bore
The deaths of the two sons Heaven took from me,
Than Jacopo's disgrace.
    Mar.   That word again?
    Doge. Has he not been condemn'd?
    Mar.   Is none but guilt so?
    Doge. Time may restore his memory—I would hope so.
He was my pride, my—but 'tis useless now—
I am not given to tears, but wept for joy
When he was born: those drops were ominous.
    Mar. I say he's innocent! And were he not so,
Is our own blood and kin to shrink from us
In fatal moments?
    Doge.   I shrank not from him:
But I have other duties than a father's;
The state would not dispense me from those duties;
Twice I demanded it, but was refused:
They must then be fulfill'd.

                    Enter an Attendant.

    Att.   A message from
"The Ten."
    Doge.   Who bears it?
    Att.   Noble Loredano.
    Doge. He!—but admit him.   [*Exit Attendant.*
    Mar.   Must I then retire?
    Doge. Perhaps it is not requisite, if this
Concerns your husband, and if not—Well, signor,
Your pleasure!   [*To* LOREDANO *entering.*
    Lor.   I bear that of "the Ten."
    Doge.   They
Have chosen well their envoy.
    Lor.   'Tis *their* choice
Which leads me here.
    Doge.   It does their wisdom honour,
And no less to their courtesy.—Proceed.

Lor. We have decided.
Doge.   We?
Lor.   "The Ten" in council.
Doge. What! have they met again, and met without
Apprising me?
Lor.   They wish'd to spare your feelings,
No less than age.
Doge.   That's new—when spared they either?
I thank them, notwithstanding.
Lor.   You know well
That they have power to act at their discretion,
With or without the presence of the Doge.
Doge. 'Tis some years since I learn'd this, long before
I became Doge, or dream'd of such advancement.
You need not school me, signor; I sate in
That council when you were a young patrician.
Lor. True, in my father's time; I have heard him and
The admiral, his brother, say as much.
Your highness may remember them; they both
Died suddenly.
Doge.   And if they did so, better
So die than live on lingeringly in pain.
Lor. No doubt; yet most men like to live their days out.
Doge. And did not they?
Lor.   The grave knows best: they died,
As I said, suddenly.
Doge.   Is that so strange,
That you repeat the word emphatically?
Lor. So far from strange, that never was there death
In my mind half so natural as theirs.
Think *you* not so?
Doge.   What should I think of mortals?
Lor. That they have mortal foes.
Doge.   I understand you;
Your sires were mine, and you are heir in all things.
Lor. You best know if I should be so.
Doge.   I do.

Your fathers were my foes, and I have heard
Foul rumours were abroad; I have also read
Their epitaph, attributing their deaths
To poison. 'Tis perhaps as true as most
Inscriptions upon tombs, and yet no less
A fable.
 Lor. Who dares say so?
 Doge.   I!—'Tis true
Your fathers were mine enemies, as bitter
As their son e'er can be, and I no less
Was theirs; but I was *openly* their foe:
I never work'd by plot in council, nor
Cabal in commonwealth, nor secret means
Of practice against life by steel or drug.
The proof is, your existence.
 Lor.   I fear not.
 Doge. You have no cause, being what I am; but were I
That you would have me thought, you long ere now
Were past the sense of fear. Hate on; I care not.
 Lor. I never yet knew that a noble's life
In Venice had to dread a Doge's frown,
That is, by open means.
 Doge.   But I, good signor,
Am, or at least *was*, more than a mere duke,
In blood, in mind, in means; and that they know
Who dreaded to elect me, and have since
Striven all they dare to weigh me down: be sure,
Before or since that period, had I held you
At so much price as to require your absence,
A word of mine had set such spirits to work
As would have made you nothing. But in all things
I have observed the strictest reverence;
Not for the laws alone, for those *you* have strain'd
(I do not speak of *you* but as a single
Voice of the many) somewhat beyond what
I could enforce for my authority,
Were I disposed to brawl; but, as I said,

I have observed with veneration, like
A priest's for the high altar, even unto
The sacrifice of my own blood and quiet,
Safety, and all save honour, the decrees,
The health, the pride, and welfare of the state.
And now, sir, to your business.
    Lor.   'Tis decreed,
That, without farther repetition of
The Question, or continuance of the trial,
Which only tends to show how stubborn guilt is,
("The Ten," dispensing with the stricter law
Which still prescribes the Question till a full
Confession, and the prisoner partly having
Avow'd his crime in not denying that
The letter to the Duke of Milan's his),
James Foscari return to banishment,
And sail in the same galley which convey'd him.
    Mar. Thank God! At least they will not drag him more
Before that horrible tribunal. Would he
But think so, to my mind the happiest doom,
Not he alone, but all who dwell here, could
Desire, were to escape from such a land.
    Doge. That is not a Venetian thought, my daughter.
    Mar. No, 'twas too human. May I share his exile?
    Lor. Of this "the Ten" said nothing.
    Mar.   So I thought:
That were too human, also. But it was not
Inhibited?
    Lor. It was not named
    Mar. (to the Doge).   Then, father,
Surely you can obtain or grant me thus much:
    [*To* LOREDANO.
And you, sir, not oppose my prayer to be
Permitted to accompany my husband.
    Doge. I will endeavour.
    Mar.   And you, signor?
    Lor.   Lady!

'Tis not for me to anticipate the pleasure
Of the tribunal.
    Mar.   Pleasure! what a word
To use for the decrees of—
    Doge.   Daughter, know you
In what a presence you pronounce these things?
    Mar. A prince's and his subject's.
    Lor.   Subject!
    Mar.   Oh!
It galls you:—well, you are his equal, as
You think; but that you are not, nor would be,
Were he a peasant:—well, then, you're a prince,
A princely noble; and what then am I?
    Lor. The offspring of a noble house.
    Mar.   And wedded
To one as noble. What, or whose, then, is
The presence that should silence my free thoughts?
    Lor. The presence of your husband's judges.
    Doge.   And
The deference due even to the lightest word
That falls from those who rule in Venice.
    Mar.   Keep
Those maxims for your mass of scared mechanics,
Your merchants, your Dalmatian and Greek slaves,
Your tributaries, your dumb citizens,
And mask'd nobility, your sbirri, and
Your spies, your galley and your other slaves,
To whom your midnight carryings off and drownings,
Your dungeons next the palace roofs, or under
The water's level; your mysterious meetings,
And unknown dooms, and sudden executions,
Your "Bridge of Sighs," your strangling chamber, and
Your torturing instruments, have made ye seem
The beings of another and worse world!
Keep such for them: I fear ye not. I know ye;
Have known and proved your worst, in the infernal
Process of my poor husband! Treat me as

Ye treated him:—you did so, in so dealing
With him. Then what have I to fear *from* you,
Even if I were of fearful nature, which
I trust I am not?
 Doge.   You hear, she speaks wildly.
 Mar. Not wisely, yet not wildly.
 Lor.   Lady! words
Utter'd within these walls I bear no further
Than to the threshold, saving such as pass
Between the Duke and me on the state's service.
Doge! have you aught in answer?
 Doge.   Something from
The Doge; it may be also from a parent.
 Lor. My mission *here* is to the *Doge.*
 Doge.   Then say
The Doge will choose his own embassador,
Or state in person what is meet; and for
The father—
 Lor. I remember *mine.*—Farewell!
I kiss the hands of the illustrious lady,
And bow me to the Duke. [*Exit* LOREDANO.
 Mar.   Are you content?
 Doge. I am what you behold.
 Mar.   And that's a mystery.
 Doge. All things are so to mortals; who can read them
Save he who made? or, if they can, the few
And gifted spirits, who have studied long
That loathsome volume—man, and pored upon
Those black and bloody leaves, his heart and brain,
But learn a magic which recoils upon
The adept who pursues it: all the sins
We find in others, nature made our own;
All our advantages are those of fortune;
Birth, wealth, health, beauty, are her accidents,
And when we cry out against Fate, 'twere well
We should remember Fortune can take nought

Save what she *gave* — the rest was nakedness,
And lusts, and appetites, and vanities,
The universal heritage, to battle
With as we may, and least in humblest stations,
Where hunger swallows all in one low want,
And the original ordinance, that man
Must sweat for his poor pittance, keeps all passions
Aloof, save fear of famine! All is low,
And false, and hollow — clay from first to last,
The prince's urn no less than potter's vessel.
Our fame is in men's breath, our lives upon
Less than their breath; our durance upon days,
Our days on seasons; our whole being on
Something which is not *us!* — So, we are slaves,
The greatest as the meanest — nothing rests
Upon our will; the will itself no less
Depends upon a straw than on a storm;
And when we think we lead, we are most led,
And still towards death, a thing which comes as much
Without our act or choice as birth, so that
Methinks we must have sinn'd in some old world,
And *this* is hell: the best is, that it is not
Eternal.

    Mar. These are things we cannot judge
On earth.

    Doge. And how then shall we judge each other,
Who are all earth, and I, who am call'd upon
To judge my son? I have administer'd
My country faithfully — victoriously —
I dare them to the proof, the *chart* of what
She was and is: my reign has doubled realms;
And, in reward, the gratitude of Venice
Has left, or is about to leave, *me* single

    Mar. And Foscari? I do not think of such things,
So I be left with him.

    Doge.   You shall be so;
Thus much they cannot well deny.

Mar.   And if
They should, I will fly with him.
    Doge.   That can ne'er be.
And whither would you fly?
    Mar.   I know not, reck not—
To Syria, Egypt, to the Ottoman—
Any where, where we might respire unfetter'd,
And live nor girt by spies, nor liable
To edicts of inquisitors of state.
    Doge. What, wouldst thou have a renegade for husband,
And turn him into traitor?
    Mar.   He is none!
The country is the traitress, which thrusts forth
Her best and bravest from her. Tyranny
Is far the worst of treasons. Dost thou deem
None rebels except subjects? The prince who
Neglects or violates his trust is more
A brigand than the robber-chief.
    Doge.   I cannot
Charge me with such a breach of faith.
    Mar.   No; thou
Observ'st, obey'st, such laws as make old Draco's
A code of mercy by comparison.
    Doge. I found the law; I did not make it. Were I
A subject, still I might find parts and portions
Fit for amendment; but as prince, I never
Would change, for the sake of my house, the charter
Left by our fathers.
    Mar.   Did they make it for
The ruin of their children?
    Doge.   Under such laws, Venice
Has risen to what she is—a state to rival
In deeds, and days, and sway, and, let me add,
In glory (for we have had Roman spirits
Amongst us), all that history has bequeath'd
Of Rome and Carthage in their best times, when
The people sway'd by senates.

ACT II.

Mar.   Rather say,
Groan'd under the stern oligarchs.
    Doge.   Perhaps so;
But yet subdued the world: in such a state
An individual, be he richest of
Such rank as is permitted, or the meanest,
Without a name, is alike nothing, when
The policy, irrevocably tending
To one great end, must be maintain'd in vigour.
    Mar. This means that you are more a Doge than father.
    Doge. It means, I am more citizen than either.
If we had not for many centuries
Had thousands of such citizens, and shall,
I trust, have still such, Venice were no city.
    Mar. Accursed be the city where the laws
Would stifle nature's!
    Doge.   Had I as many sons
As I have years, I would have given them all,
Not without feeling, but I would have given them
To the state's service, to fulfil her wishes
On the flood, in the field, or, if it must be,
As it, alas! has been, to ostracism,
Exile, or chains, or whatsoever worse
She might decree.
    Mar.   And this is patriotism?
To me it seems the worst barbarity.
Let me seek out my husband: the sage "Ten,"
With all its jealousy, will hardly war
So far with a weak woman as deny me
A moment's access to his dungeon.
    Doge.   I'll
So far take on myself, as order that
You may be admitted.
    Mar.   And what shall I say
To Foscari from his father?
    Doge.   That he obey
The laws.

Mar. And nothing more? Will you not see him
Ere he depart? It may be the last time.
  Doge. The last!—my boy!—the last time I shall see
My last of children! Tell him I will come.
                              [*Exeunt.*

ACT III.

SCENE I.

The Prison of JACOPO FOSCARI.

  Jac. Fos. (*solus*). No light, save yon faint gleam which
      shows me walls
Which never echo'd but to sorrow's sounds,
The sigh of long imprisonment, the step
Of feet on which the iron clank'd, the groan
Of death, the imprecation of despair!
And yet for this I have return'd to Venice,
With some faint hope, 'tis true, that time, which wears
The marble down, had worn away the hate
Of men's hearts; but I knew them not, and here
Must I consume my own, which never beat
For Venice but with such a yearning as
The dove has for her distant nest, when wheeling
High in the air on her return to greet
Her callow brood.   What letters are these which
                          [*Approaching the wall.*
Are scrawl'd along the inexorable wall?
Will the gleam let me trace them? Ah! the names
Of my sad predecessors in this place,
The dates of their despair, the brief words of
A grief too great for many.   This stone page
Holds like an epitaph their history;
And the poor captive's tale is graven on
His dungeon barrier, like the lover's record
Upon the bark of some tall tree, which bears
His own and his beloved's name.   Alas
I recognise some names familiar to me,

And blighted like to mine, which I will add,
Fittest for such a chronicle as this,
Which only can be read, as writ, by wretches.
[*He engraves his name.*

Enter a Familiar of "the Ten."

Fam. I bring you food.
Jac. Fos.   I pray you set it down;
I am past hunger: but my lips are parch'd—
The water!
    Fam.   There.
    Jac. Fos. (*after drinking*). I thank you: I am better.
    Fam. I am commanded to inform you that
Your further trial is postponed.
    Jac. Fos.   Till when?
    Fam. I know not.—It is also in my orders
That your illustrious lady be admitted.
    Jac. Fos. Ah! they relent, then—I had ceased to hope it:
'T was time.

Enter MARINA.

Mar.   My best beloved!
Jac. Fos. (*embracing her*). My true wife,
And only friend! What happiness!
    Mar.   We'll part
No more.
    Jac. Fos. How! would'st thou share a dungeon?
    Mar.   Ay,
The rack, the grave, all—any thing with thee,
But the tomb last of all, for there we shall
Be ignorant of each other, yet I will
Share that—all things except new separation;
It is too much to have survived the first.
How dost thou? How are those worn limbs? Alas!
Why do I ask? Thy paleness—
    Jac. Fos.   'Tis the joy
Of seeing thee again so soon, and so
Without expectancy, has sent the blood

Back to my heart, and left my cheeks like thine,
For thou art pale too, my Marina!
    Mar.   'Tis
The gloom of this eternal cell, which never
Knew sunbeam, and the sallow sullen glare
Of the familiar's torch, which seems akin
To darkness more than light, by lending to
The dungeon vapours its bituminous smoke,
Which cloud whate'er we gaze on, even thine eyes —
No, not thine eyes — they sparkle — how they sparkle!
    Jac. Fos. And thine! — but I am blinded by the torch.
    Mar. As I had been without it. Couldst thou see here?
    Jac. Fos. Nothing at first; but use and time had taught me
Familiarity with what was darkness;
And the grey twilight of such glimmerings as
Glide through the crevices made by the winds
Was kinder to mine eyes than the full sun,
When gorgeously o'ergilding any towers
Save those of Venice; but a moment ere
Thou camest hither I was busy writing.
    Mar. What?
    Jac. Fos. My name: look, 'tis there — recorded next
The name of him who here preceded me,
If dungeon dates say true.
    Mar.   And what of him?
    Jac. Fos. These walls are silent of men's ends; they only
Seem to hint shrewdly of them. Such stern walls
Were never piled on high save o'er the dead,
Or those who soon must be so. — *What of him?*
Thou askest. — What of me? may soon be ask'd,
With the like answer — doubt and dreadful surmise —
Unless thou tell'st my tale.
    Mar.   *I speak* of thee!
    Jac. Fos. And wherefore not? All then shall speak of me:
The tyranny of silence is not lasting,
And, though events be hidden, just men's groans
Will burst all cerement, even a living grave's!

I do not *doubt* my memory, but my life;
And neither do I fear.
    Mar.   Thy life is safe.
    Jac. Fos. And liberty?
    Mar.   The mind should make its own.
    Jac. Fos. That has a noble sound; but 'tis a sound,
A music most impressive, but too transient:
The mind is much, but is not all. The mind
Hath nerved me to endure the risk of death,
And torture positive, far worse than death
(If death be a deep sleep), without a groan,
Or with a cry which rather shamed my judges
Than me; but 'tis not all, for there are things
More woful—such as this small dungeon, where
I may breathe many years.
    Mar.   Alas! and this
Small dungeon is all that belongs to thee
Of this wide realm, of which thy sire is prince.
    Jac. Fos. That thought would scarcely aid me to endure it.
My doom is common, many are in dungeons,
But none like mine, so near their father's palace;
But then my heart is sometimes high, and hope
Will stream along those moted rays of light
Peopled with dusty atoms, which afford
Our only day; for, save the gaoler's torch,
And a strange firefly, which was quickly caught
Last night in yon enormous spider's net,
I ne'er saw aught here like a ray. Alas!
I know if mind may bear us up, or no,
For I have such, and shown it before men;
It sinks in solitude: my soul is social.
    Mar. I will be with thee.
    Jac. Fos.   Ah! if it were so!
But *that* they never granted—nor will grant,
And I shall be alone: no men—no books—
Those lying likenesses of lying men.
I ask'd for even those outlines of their kind,

Which they term annals, history, what you will,
Which men bequeath as portraits, and they were
Refused me,—so these walls have been my study,
More faithful pictures of Venetian story,
With all their blank, or dismal stains, than is
The Hall not far from hence, which bears on high
Hundreds of doges, and their deeds and dates.

  Mar. I come to tell thee the result of their
Last council on thy doom.

  Jac. Fos.   I know it—look!

[*He points to his limbs, as referring to the question which he had undergone.*]

  Mar. No—no—no more of that: even they relent
From that atrocity.

  Jac. Fos.   What then?

  Mar.   That you
Return to Candia.

  Jac. Fos.   Then my last hope's gone.
I could endure my dungeon, for 't was Venice;
I could support the torture, there was something
In my native air that buoy'd my spirits up
Like a ship on the ocean toss'd by storms,
But proudly still bestriding the high waves,
And holding on its course; but *there,* afar,
In that accursed isle of slaves and captives,
And unbelievers, like a stranded wreck,
My very soul seem'd mouldering in my bosom,
And piecemeal I shall perish, if remanded.

  Mar. And *here?*

  Jac. Fos. At once—by better means, as briefer.
What! would they even deny me my sire's sepulchre,
As well as home and heritage?

  Mar.   My husband!
I have sued to accompany thee hence,
And not so hopelessly. This love of thine
For an ungrateful and tyrannic soil
Is passion, and not patriotism; for me,

So I could see thee with a quiet aspect,
And the sweet freedom of the earth and air,
I would not cavil about climes or regions.
This crowd of palaces and prisons is not
A paradise; its first inhabitants
Were wretched exiles.
   Jac. Fos.   Well I know *how* wretched!
   Mar. And yet you see how from their banishment
Before the Tartar into these salt isles,
Their antique energy of mind, all that
Remain'd of Rome for their inheritance,
Created by degrees an ocean Rome;*
And shall an evil, which so often leads
To good, depress thee thus?
   Jac. Fos.   Had I gone forth
From my own land, like the old patriarchs, seeking
Another region, with their flocks and herds;
Had I been cast out like the Jews from Zion,
Or like our fathers, driven by Attila
From fertile Italy, to barren islets,
I would have given some tears to my late country,
And many thoughts; but afterwards address'd
Myself, with those about me, to create
A new home and fresh state: perhaps I could
Have borne this—though I know not.
   Mar.   Wherefore not?
It was the lot of millions, and must be
The fate of myriads more.
   Jac. Fos.   Ay—we but hear

* In Lady Morgan's fearless and excellent work upon Italy, I perceive the expression of "Rome of the Ocean" applied to Venice. The same phrase occurs in the "Two Foscari." My publisher can vouch for me, that the tragedy was written and sent to England some time before I had seen Lady Morgan's work, which I only received on the 16th of August. I hasten, however, to notice the coincidence, and to yield the originality of the phrase to her who first placed it before the public. I am the more anxious to do this, as I am informed (for I have seen but few of the specimens, and those accidentally,) that there have been lately brought against me charges of plagiarism.

Of the survivors' toil in their new lands,
Their numbers and success; but who can number
The hearts which broke in silence of that parting,
Or after their departure; of that malady
Which calls up green and native fields to view
From the rough deep, with such identity
To the poor exile's fever'd eye, that he
Can scarcely be restrained from treading them?
That melody, which out of tones and tunes
Collects such pasture for the longing sorrow
Of the sad mountaineer, when far away
From his snow canopy of cliffs and clouds,
That he feeds on the sweet, but poisonous thought,
And dies. You call this *weakness!* It is strength,
I say,—the parent of all honest feeling.
He who loves not his country, can love nothing.

 Mar. Obey her, then: 'tis she that puts thee forth.
 Jac. Fos. Ay, there it is; 'tis like a mother's curse
Upon my soul—the mark is set upon me.
The exiles you speak of went forth by nations,
Their hands upheld each other by the way,
Their tents were pitch'd together—I'm alone.

 Mar. You shall be so no more—I will go with thee
 Jac. Fos. My best Marina!—and our children?
 Mar.   They,
I fear, by the prevention of the state's
Abhorrent policy, (which holds all ties
As threads, which may be broken at her pleasure,)
Will not be suffer'd to proceed with us.

 Jac. Fos. And canst thou leave them?
 Mar.   Yes. With many a pang.
But—I *can* leave them, children as they are,
To teach you to be less a child. From this
Learn you to sway your feelings, when exacted
By duties paramount; and 'tis our first
On earth to bear.

 Jac. Fos.   Have I not borne?

Mar.   Too much
From tyrannous injustice, and enough
To teach you not to shrink now from a lot,
Which, as compared with what you have undergone
Of late, is mercy.
 Jac. Fos.   Ah! you never yet
Were far away from Venice, never saw
Her beautiful towers in the receding distance,
While every furrow of the vessel's track
Seem'd ploughing deep into your heart; you never
Saw day go down upon your native spires
So calmly with its gold and crimson glory,
And after dreaming a disturbed vision
Of them and theirs, awoke and found them not.
 Mar. I will divide this with you. Let us think
Of our departure from this much-loved city,
(Since you must *love* it, as it seems,) and this
Chamber of state, her gratitude allots you.
Our children will be cared for by the Doge,
And by my uncles: we must sail ere night.
 Jac. Fos. That's sudden. Shall I not behold my father?
 Mar. You will.
 Jac. Fos.   Where?
 Mar.   Here, or in the ducal chamber—
He said not which. I would that you could bear
Your exile as he bears it.
 Jac. Fos.   Blame him not.
I sometimes murmur for a moment; but
He could not now act otherwise. A show
Of feeling or compassion on his part
Would have but drawn upon his aged head
Suspicion from "the Ten," and upon mine
Accumulated ills.
 Mar.   Accumulated!
What pangs are those they have spared you?
 Jac. Fos.   That of leaving
Venice without beholding him or you,

Which might have been forbidden now, as 't was
Upon my former exile.
    Mar.   That is true,
And thus far I am also the state's debtor,
And shall be more so when I see us both
Floating on the free waves—away—away—
Be it to the earth's end, from this abhorr'd,
Unjust, and—
    Jac. Fos.   Curse it not. If I am silent,
Who dares accuse my country?
    Mar.   Men and angels!
The blood of myriads reeking up to heaven,
The groans of slaves in chains, and men in dungeons,
Mothers, and wives, and sons, and sires, and subjects,
Held in the bondage of ten bald-heads; and
Though last, not least, *thy silence.* Couldst thou say
Aught in its favour, who would praise like *thee?*
    Jac. Fos. Let us address us then, since so it must be,
To our departure. Who comes here?

         Enter LOREDANO, *attended by Familiars.*

    Lor. (to the Familiars).   Retire,
But leave the torch.   [*Exeunt the two Familiars.*
    Jac. Fos.   Most welcome, noble signor.
I did not deem this poor place could have drawn
Such presence hither.
    Lor.   'Tis not the first time
I have visited these places.
    Mar.   Nor would be
The last, were all men's merits well rewarded.
Came you here to insult us, or remain
As spy upon us, or as hostage for us?
    Lor. Neither are of my office, noble lady!
I am sent hither to your husband, to
Announce "the Ten's" decree.
    Mar.   That tenderness
Has been anticipated: it is known.

ACT III.

Lor. As how?
Mar. I have inform'd him, not so gently,
Doubtless, as your nice feelings would prescribe,
The indulgence of your colleagues; but he knew it.
If you come for our thanks, take them, and hence!
The dungeon gloom is deep enough without you,
And full of reptiles, not less loathsome, though
Their sting is honester.
   Jac. Fos. I pray you, calm you:
What can avail such words?
   Mar. To let him know
That he is known.
   Lor. Let the fair dame preserve
Her sex's privilege.
   Mar. I have some sons, sir,
Will one day thank you better.
   Lor. You do well
To nurse them wisely. Foscari—you know
Your sentence, then?
   Jac. Fos. Return to Candia?
   Lor. True—
For life.
   Jac. Fos. Not long.
   Lor. I said—for *life.*
   Jac. Fos. And I
Repeat—not long.
   Lor. A year's imprisonment
In Canea—afterwards the freedom of
The whole isle.
   Jac. Fos. Both the same to me: the after
Freedom as is the first imprisonment.
Is 't true my wife accompanies me?
   Lor. Yes,
If she so wills it.
   Mar. Who obtain'd that justice?
   Lor. One who wars not with women.
   Mar. But oppresses

Men: howsoever let him have *my* thanks
For the only boon I would have ask'd or taken
From him or such as he is.
    Lor.   He receives them
As they are offer'd.
    Mar.   May they thrive with him
So much!—no more.
    Jac. Fos.   Is this, sir, your whole mission?
Because we have brief time for preparation,
And you perceive your presence doth disquiet
This lady, of a house noble as yours.
    Mar. Nobler!
    Lor.   How nobler?
    Mar.   As more generous!
We say the "generous steed" to express the purity
Of his high blood. Thus much I've learnt, although
Venetian (who see few steeds save of bronze),
From those Venetians who have skimm'd the coasts
Of Egypt, and her neighbour Araby:
And why not say as soon the "*generous man!*"
If race be aught, it is in qualities
More than in years; and mine, which is as old
As yours, is better in its product, nay—
Look not so stern—but get you back, and pore
Upon your genealogic tree's most green
Of leaves and most mature of fruits, and there
Blush to find ancestors, who would have blush'd
For such a son—thou cold inveterate hater!
    Jac. Fos. Again, Marina!
    Mar.   Again! *still*, Marina.
See you not, he comes here to glut his hate
With a last look upon our misery?
Let him partake it!
    Jac. Fos.   That were difficult.
    Mar. Nothing more easy. He partakes it now —
Ay, he may veil beneath a marble brow
And sneering lip the pang, but he partakes it.

A few brief words of truth shame the devil's servants
No less than master; I have probed his soul
A moment, as the eternal fire, ere long,
Will reach it always. See how he shrinks from me!
With death, and chains, and exile in his hand
To scatter o'er his kind as he thinks fit;
They are his weapons, not his armour, for
I have pierced him to the core of his cold heart.
I care not for his frowns! We can but die,
And he but live, for him the very worst
Of destinies: each day secures him more
His tempter's.

  Jac. Fos.   This is mere insanity.
  Mar. It may be so; and *who* hath made us *mad?*
  Lor. Let her go on; it irks not me.
  Mar.   That's false!
You came here to enjoy a heartless triumph
Of cold looks upon manifold griefs! You came
To be sued to in vain—to mark our tears,
And hoard our groans—to gaze upon the wreck
Which you have made a prince's son—my husband;
In short, to trample on the fallen—an office
The hangman shrinks from, as all men from him!
How have you sped? We are wretched, signor, as
Your plots could make, and vengeance could desire us,
And how *feel you?*
  Lor.   As rocks.
  Mar.   By thunder blasted:
They feel not, but no less are shiver'd. Come,
Foscari; now let us go, and leave this felon,
The sole fit habitant of such a cell,
Which he has peopled often, but ne'er fitly
Till he himself shall brood in it alone.

      Enter the Doge.

  Jac. Fos. My father!
  Doge (embracing him). Jacopo! my son—my son!

Jac. Fos. My father still! How long it is since I
Have heard thee name my name—*our* name!
  Doge.   My boy!
Couldst thou but know—
  Jac. Fos.   I rarely, sir, have murmur'd.
  Doge. I feel too much thou hast not.
  Mar.   Doge, look there!
                          [*She points to* LOREDANO.
  Doge. I see the man—what mean'st thou?
  Mar.   Caution!
  Lor.   Being
The virtue which this noble lady most
May practise, she doth well to recommend it.
  Mar. Wretch! 'tis no virtue, but the policy
Of those who fain must deal perforce with vice:
As such I recommend it, as I would
To one whose foot was on an adder's path.
  Doge. Daughter, it is superfluous: I have long
Known Loredano.
  Lor.   You may know him better.
  Mar. Yes; *worse* he could not.
  Jac. Fos.   Father, let not these
Our parting hours be lost in listening to
Reproaches, which boot nothing. Is it—is it,
Indeed, our last of meetings?
  Doge.   You behold
These white hairs!
  Jac. Fos.   And I feel, besides, that mine
Will never be so white. Embrace me, father!
I loved you ever—never more than now.
Look to my children—to your last child's children:
Let them be all to you which he was once,
And never be to you what I am now.
May I not see *them* also?
  Mar.   No—not *here*.
  Jac. Fos. They might behold their parent anywhere.
  Mar. I would that they beheld their father in

A place which would not mingle fear with love,
To freeze their young blood in its natural current.
They have fed well, slept soft, and knew not that
Their sire was a mere hunted outlaw. Well,
I know his fate may one day be their heritage,
But let it only be their *heritage*,
And not their present fee. Their senses, though
Alive to love, are yet awake to terror;
And these vile damps, too, and yon *thick green* wave
Which floats above the place where we now stand—
A cell so far below the water's level,
Sending its pestilence through every crevice,
Might strike them: *this is not their* atmosphere,
However you—and you—and, most of all,
As worthiest—*you*, sir, noble Loredano!
May breathe it without prejudice.

  Jac. Fos.   I have not
Reflected upon this, but acquiesce.
I shall depart, then, without meeting them?
  Doge. Not so: they shall await you in my chamber.
  Jac. Fos. And must I leave them—*all?*
  Lor.   You must.
  Jac. Fos.   Not one?
  Lor. They are the state's.
  Mar.   I thought they had been mine.
  Lor. They are, in all maternal things.
  Mar.   That is,
In all things painful. If they're sick, they will
Be left to me to tend them; should they die,
To me to bury and to mourn; but if
They live, they'll make you soldiers, senators,
Slaves, exiles—what *you* will; or if they are
Females with portions, brides and *bribes* for nobles!
Behold the state's care for its sons and mothers!

  Lor. The hour approaches, and the wind is fair.
  Jac. Fos. How know you that here, where the genial wind
Ne'er blows in all its blustering freedom?

Lor.   'T was so
When I came here. The galley floats within
A bow-shot of the "Riva di Schiavoni."
  Jac. Fos. Father! I pray you to precede me, and
Prepare my children to behold their father.
  Doge. Be firm, my son!
  Jac. Fos.   I will do my endeavour.
  Mar. Farewell! at least to this detested dungeon,
And him to whose good offices you owe
In part your past imprisonment.
  Lor.   And present
Liberation.
  Doge.   He speaks truth.
  Jac. Fos.   No doubt! but 'tis
Exchange of chains for heavier chains I owe him.
He knows this, or he had not sought to change them.
But I reproach not.
  Lor.   The time narrows, signor.
  Jac. Fos. Alas! I little thought so lingeringly
To leave abodes like this : but when I feel
That every step I take, even from this cell,
Is one away from Venice, I look back
Even on these dull damp walls, and—
  Doge.   Boy! no tears.
  Mar. Let them flow on: he wept not on the rack
To shame him, and they cannot shame him now.
They will relieve his heart—that too kind heart—
And I will find an hour to wipe away
Those tears, or add my own. I could weep now,
But would not gratify yon wretch so far.
Let us proceed. Doge, lead the way.
  Lor. (to the Familiar).   The torch, there!
  Mar. Yes, light us on, as to a funeral pyre,
With Loredano mourning like an heir.
  Doge. My son, you are feeble; take this hand.
  Jac. Fos   Alas!

Must youth support itself on age, and I
Who ought to be the prop of yours?
 Lor.   Take mine.
 Mar. Touch it not, Foscari; 't will sting you. Signor,
Stand off! be sure, that if a grasp of yours
Would raise us from the gulf wherein we are plunged,
No hand of ours would stretch itself to meet it.
Come, Foscari, take the hand the altar gave you;
It could not save, but will support you ever.
               [*Exeunt.*

ACT IV.

SCENE I.

A Hall in the Ducal Palace.

Enter LOREDANO *and* BARBARIGO.

 Bar. And have you confidence in such a project?
 Lor. I have.
 Bar.   'Tis hard upon his years.
 Lor.   Say rather
Kind to relieve him from the cares of state.
 Bar. 'T will break his heart.
 Lor.   Age has no heart to break.
He has seen his son's half broken, and, except
A start of feeling in his dungeon, never
Swerved.
 Bar.   In his countenance, I grant you, never;
But I have seen him sometimes in a calm
So desolate, that the most clamorous grief
Had nought to envy him within. Where is he?
 Lor. In his own portion of the palace, with
His son, and the whole race of Foscaris.
 Bar. Bidding farewell.
 Lor.   A last. As soon he shall
Bid to his dukedom.
 Bar.   When embarks the son?

Lor. Forthwith—when this long leave is taken. 'Tis
Time to admonish them again.
  Bar.   Forbear;
Retrench not from their moments.
  Lor.   Not I, now
We have higher business for our own. This day
Shall be the last of the old Doge's reign,
As the first of his son's last banishment,
And that is vengeance.
  Bar.   In my mind, too deep.
  Lor. 'Tis moderate—not even life for life, the rule
Denounced of retribution from all time;
They owe me still my father's and my uncle's.
  Bar. Did not the Doge deny this strongly?
  Lor.   Doubtless.
  Bar. And did not this shake your suspicion?
  Lor.   No.
  Bar. But if this deposition should take place
By our united influence in the Council,
It must be done with all the deference
Due to his years, his station, and his deeds.
  Lor. As much of ceremony as you will,
So that the thing be done. You may, for aught
I care, depute the Council on their knees,
(Like Barbarossa to the Pope,) to beg him
To have the courtesy to abdicate.
  Bar. What, if he will not?
  Lor.   We 'll elect another,
And make him null.
  Bar.   But will the laws uphold us?
  Lor. What laws?—"The Ten" are laws; and if they
     were not,
I will be legislator in this business.
  Bar. At your own peril?
  Lor.   There is none, I tell you,
Our powers are such.
  Bar.   But he has twice already

Solicited permission to retire,
And twice it was refused.
  Lor.   The better reason
To grant it the third time.
  Bar.   Unask'd?
  Lor.   It shows
The impression of his former instances:
If they were from his heart, he may be thankful:
If not, 't will punish his hypocrisy.
Come, they are met by this time; let us join them,
And be *thou* fix'd in purpose for this once.
I have prepared such arguments as will not
Fail to move them, and to remove him: since
Their thoughts, their objects, have been sounded, do not
You, with your wonted scruples, teach us pause,
And all will prosper.
  Bar.   Could I but be certain
This is no prelude to such persecution
Of the sire as has fallen upon the son,
I would support you.
  Lor.   He is safe, I tell you;
His fourscore years and five may linger on
As long as he can drag them: 'tis his throne
Alone is aim'd at.
  Bar.   But discarded princes
Are seldom long of life.
  Lor.   And men of eighty
More seldom still.
  Bar.   And why not wait these few years?
  Lor. Because we have waited long enough, and he
Lived longer than enough. Hence! in to council!
      [*Exeunt* LOREDANO *and* BARBARIGO.

Enter MEMMO *and a Senator.*

  Sen. A summons to "the Ten!" Why so?
  Mem.   "The Ten"
Alone can answer; they are rarely wont

To let their thoughts anticipate their purpose
By previous proclamation. We are summon'd —
That is enough.
  Sen.   For them, but not for us;
I would know why.
  Mem.   You will know why anon,
If you obey; and, if not, you no less
Will know why you should have obey'd.
  Sen.   I mean not
To oppose them, *but*—
  Mem.   In Venice "*but*" 's a traitor.
But me no "*buts*," unless you would pass o'er
The Bridge which few repass.
  Sen.   I am silent.
  Mem.   Why
Thus hesitate? "The Ten" have call'd in aid
Of their deliberation five and twenty
Patricians of the senate — you are one,
And I another; and it seems to me
Both honour'd by the choice or chance which leads us
To mingle with a body so august.
  Sen. Most true. I say no more.
  Mem.   As we hope, signor,
And all may honestly, (that is, all those
Of noble blood may,) one day hope to be
Decemvir, it is surely for the senate's
Chosen delegates a school of wisdom, to
Be thus admitted, though as novices,
To view the mysteries.
  Sen.   Let us view them: they,
No doubt, are worth it.
  Mem.   Being worth our lives
If we divulge them, doubtless they are worth
Something, at least to you or me.
  Sen.   I sought not
A place within the sanctuary; but being

ACT IV.

Chosen, however reluctantly so chosen,
I shall fulfil my office.
   Mem.   Let us not
Be latest in obeying "the Ten's" summons.
   Sen. All are not met, but I am of your thought
So far—let 's in.
   Mem.   The earliest are most welcome
In earnest councils—we will not be least so.
                                                        [*Exeunt.*

        Enter the DOGE, JACOPO FOSCARI, *and* MARINA.

   Jac. Fos. Ah, father! though I must and will depart,
Yet—yet—I pray you to obtain for me
That I once more return unto my home,
Howe'er remote the period. Let there be
A point of time, as beacon to my heart,
With any penalty annex'd they please,
But let me still return.
   Doge.   Son Jacopo,
Go and obey our country's will: 'tis not
For us to look beyond.
   Jac. Fos.   But still I must
Look back. I pray you think of me.
   Doge.   Alas!
You ever were my dearest offspring, when
They were more numerous, nor can be less so
Now you are last; but did the state demand
The exile of the disinterred ashes
Of your three goodly brothers, now in earth,
And their desponding shades came flitting round
To impede the act, I must no less obey
A duty, paramount to every duty.
   Mar. My husband! let us on: this but prolongs
Our sorrow.
   Jac. Fos. But we are not summon'd yet;
The galley's sails are not unfurl'd:—who knows?
The wind may change.

Mar.   And if it do, it will not
Change *their* hearts, or your lot: the galley's oar
Will quickly clear the harbour.
   Jac. Fos.   O, ye elements!
Where are your storms?
   Mar.   In human breasts. Alas!
Will nothing calm you?
   Jac. Fos.   Never yet did mariner
Put up to patron saint such prayers for prosperous
And pleasant breezes, as I call upon you,
Ye tutelar saints of my own city! which
Ye love not with more holy love than I,
To lash up from the deep the Adrian waves,
And waken Auster, sovereign of the tempest!
Till the sea dash me back on my own shore
A broken corse upon the barren Lido,
Where I may mingle with the sands which skirt
The land I love, and never shall see more!
   Mar. And wish you this with *me* beside you?
   Jac. Fos.   No—
No—not for thee, too good, too kind! May'st thou
Live long to be a mother to those children
Thy fond fidelity for a time deprives
Of such support! But for myself alone,
May all the winds of heaven howl down the Gulf,
And tear the vessel, till the mariners,
Appall'd, turn their despairing eyes on me,
As the Phenicians did on Jonah, then
Cast me out from amongst them, as an offering
To appease the waves. The billow which destroys me
Will be more merciful than man, and bear me,
Dead, but *still bear* me to a native grave.
From fishers' hands upon the desolate strand,
Which, of its thousand wrecks, hath ne'er received
One lacerated like the heart which then
Will be—But wherefore breaks it not? why live I?
   Mar. To man thyself, I trust, with time, to master

Such useless passion. Until now thou wert
A sufferer, but not a loud one: why,
What is this to the things thou hast borne in silence—
Imprisonment and actual torture?

Jac. Fos.   Double,
Triple, and tenfold torture! But you are right,
It must be borne. Father, your blessing.

Doge.   Would
It could avail thee! but no less thou hast it.

Jac. Fos. Forgive—

Doge.   What?

Jac. Fos.   My poor mother, for my birth,
And me for having lived, and you yourself
(As I forgive you), for the gift of life,
Which you bestow'd upon me as my sire.

Mar. What hast thou done?

Jac. Fos.   Nothing. I cannot charge
My memory with much save sorrow: but
I have been so beyond the common lot
Chasten'd and visited, I needs must think
That I was wicked. If it be so, may
What I have undergone here keep me from
A like hereafter!

Mar.   Fear not: *that's* reserved
For your oppressors.

Jac. Fos.   Let me hope not.

Mar.   Hope not?

Jac. Fos. I cannot wish them *all* they have inflicted.

Mar. All! the consummate fiends! A thousandfold
May the worm which ne'er dieth feed upon them!

Jac. Fos. They may repent.

Mar.   And if they do, Heaven will not
Accept the tardy penitence of demons.

Enter an Officer and Guards.

Offi. Signor! the boat is at the shore—the wind
Is rising—we are ready to attend you.

Jac. Fos. And I to be attended. Once more, father,
Your hand!

Doge. Take it. Alas! how thine own trembles!

Jac. Fos. No—you mistake; 'tis yours that shakes, my
father.
Farewell!

Doge. Farewell! Is there aught else?

Jac. Fos. No—nothing.
[*To the Officer.*
Lend me your arm, good signor.

Offi. You turn pale—
Let me support you—paler—ho! some aid there!
Some water!

Mar. Ah, he is dying!

Jac. Fos. Now, I'm ready—
My eyes swim strangely—where's the door?

Mar. Away!
Let me support him—my best love! Oh, God!
How faintly beats this heart—this pulse!

Jac. Fos. The light!
Is it the light?—I am faint. [*Officer presents him with water.*

Offi. He will be better,
Perhaps, in the air.

Jac. Fos. I doubt not. Father—wife—
Your hands!

Mar. There's death in that damp clammy grasp,
Oh God!—My Foscari, how fare you?

Jac. Fos. Well! [*He dies.*

Offi. He's gone!

Doge. He's free.

Mar. No—no, he is not dead;
There must be life yet in that heart—he could not
Thus leave me.

Doge. Daughter!

Mar. Hold thy peace, old man!
I am no daughter now—thou hast no son.
Oh, Foscari!

Offi. We must remove the body.

Mar. Touch it not, dungeon miscreants! your base office
Ends with his life, and goes not beyond murder,
Even by your murderous laws. Leave his remains
To those who know to honour them.

Offi. I must
Inform the signory, and learn their pleasure.

Doge. Inform the signory, from *me*, the Doge,
They have no further power upon those ashes:
While he lived, he was theirs, as fits a subject—
Now he is *mine*—my broken-hearted boy! [*Exit Officer.*

Mar. And I must live!

Doge. Your children live, Marina.

Mar. My children! true—they live, and I must live
To bring them up to serve the state, and die
As died their father. Oh! what best of blessings
Were barrenness in Venice! Would my mother
Had been so!

Doge. My unhappy children!

Mar. What!
You feel it then at last—*you!*—Where is now
The stoic of the state?

Doge (*throwing himself down by the body*). Here!

Mar. Ay, weep on!
I thought you had no tears—you hoarded them
Until they are useless; but weep on! he never
Shall weep more—never, never more.

Enter LOREDANO *and* BARBARIGO.

Lor. What's here?

Mar. Ah! the devil come to insult the dead! Avaunt!
Incarnate Lucifer! 'tis holy ground.
A martyr's ashes now lie there, which make it
A shrine. Get thee back to thy place of torment!

Bar. Lady, we knew not of this sad event,
But pass'd here merely on our path from council.

Mar. Pass on.

Lor. We sought the Doge.

Mar. (*pointing to the Doge, who is still on the ground by his son's body*). He's busy, look,
About the business you provided for him.
Are ye content?
    Bar.   We will not interrupt
A parent's sorrows.
    Mar.   No, ye only make them,
Then leave them.
    Doge (*rising*). Sirs, I am ready.
    Bar.   No—not now.
    Lor. Yet 'twas important.
    Doge.   If 'twas so, I can
Only repeat—I am ready.
    Bar.   It shall not be
Just now, though Venice totter'd o'er the deep
Like a frail vessel. I respect your griefs.
    Doge. I thank you. If the tidings which you bring
Are evil, you may say them; nothing further
Can touch me more than him thou look'st on there;
If they be good, say on; you need not *fear*
That they can *comfort* me.
    Bar.   I would they could!
    Doge. I spoke not to *you*, but to Loredano.
He understands me.
    Mar.   Ah! I thought it would be so.
    Doge. What mean you?
    Mar.   Lo! there is the blood beginning
To flow through the dead lips of Foscari—
The body bleeds in presence of the assassin. [*To* LOREDANO.
Thou cowardly murderer by law, behold
How death itself bears witness to thy deeds!
    Doge. My child! this is a phantasy of grief.
Bear hence the body. [*To his attendants.*] Signors, if it please you,
Within an hour I'll hear you.
        [*Exeunt* DOGE, MARINA, *and attendants with the body.*
        Manent LOREDANO *and* BARBARIGO.

ACT IV.

Bar. He must not
Be troubled now.
Lor. He said himself that nought
Could give him trouble farther.
Bar. These are words;
But grief is lonely, and the breaking in
Upon it barbarous.
Lor. Sorrow preys upon
Its solitude, and nothing more diverts it
From its sad visions of the other world
Than calling it at moments back to this.
The busy have no time for tears.
Bar. And therefore
You would deprive this old man of all business?
Lor. The thing's decreed. The Giunta and "the Ten"
Have made it law — who shall oppose that law?
Bar. Humanity!
Lor. Because his son is dead?
Bar. And yet unburied.
Lor. Had we known this when
The act was passing, it might have suspended
Its passage, but impedes it not — once past.
Bar. I'll not consent.
Lor. You have consented to
All that's essential — leave the rest to me.
Bar. Why press his abdication now?
Lor. The feelings
Of private passion may not interrupt
The public benefit; and what the state
Decides to-day must not give way before
To-morrow for a natural accident.
Bar. You have a son.
Lor. I *have* — and *had* a father.
Bar. Still so inexorable?
Lor. Still.
Bar. But let him

Inter his son before we press upon him
This edict.
 Lor. Let him call up into life
My sire and uncle—I consent. Men may,
Even aged men, be, or appear to be,
Sires of a hundred sons, but cannot kindle
An atom of their ancestors from earth.
The victims are not equal; he has seen
His sons expire by natural deaths, and I
My sires by violent and mysterious maladies.
I used no poison, bribed no subtle master
Of the destructive art of healing, to
Shorten the path to the eternal cure.
His sons—and he had four—are dead, without
My dabbling in vile drugs.
 Bar.   And art thou sure
He dealt in such?
 Lor. Most sure.
 Bar.   And yet he seems
All openness.
 Lor. And so he seem'd not long
Ago to Carmagnuola.
 Bar.   The attainted
And foreign traitor?
 Lor.   Even so: when *he*,
After the very night in which "the Ten"
(Join'd with the Doge) decided his destruction,
Met the great Duke at daybreak with a jest,
Demanding whether he should augur him
"The good day or good night?" his Doge-ship answer'd,
"That he in truth had pass'd a night of vigil,
"In which (he added with a gracious smile),
"There often has been question about you."*
'Twas true; the question was the death resolved
Of Carmagnuola, eight months ere he died;
And the old Doge, who knew him doom'd, smiled on him

---

* An historical fact. See *Daru*, tom. ii.

With deadly cozenage, eight long months beforehand—
Eight months of such hypocrisy as is
Learnt but in eighty years. Brave Carmagnuola
Is dead; so is young Foscari and his brethren—
I never *smiled* on *them.*

   Bar.   Was Carmagnuola
Your friend?
   Lor.   He was the safeguard of the city.
In early life its foe, but in his manhood,
Its saviour first, then victim.
   Bar.   Ah! that seems
The penalty of saving cities. He
Whom we now act against not only saved
Our own, but added others to her sway.
   Lor. The Romans (and we ape them) gave a crown
To him who took a city; and they gave
A crown to him who saved a citizen
In battle: the rewards are equal. Now,
If we should measure forth the cities taken
By the Doge Foscari, with citizens
Destroy'd by him, or *through* him, the account
Were fearfully against him, although narrow'd
To private havoc, such as between him
And my dead father.
   Bar.   Are you then thus fix'd?
   Lor. Why, what should change me?
   Bar.   That which changes me:
But you, I know, are marble to retain
A feud. But when all is accomplish'd, when
The old man is deposed, his name degraded,
His sons all dead, his family depress'd,
And you and yours triumphant, shall you sleep?
   Lor. More soundly.
   Bar.   That's an error, and you'll find it
Ere you sleep with your fathers.
   Lor.   They sleep not
In their accelerated graves, nor will

Till Foscari fills his. Each night I see them
Stalk frowning round my couch, and, pointing towards
The ducal palace, marshal me to vengeance.
   Bar. Fancy's distemperature! There is no passion
More spectral or fantastical than Hate;
Not even its opposite, Love, so peoples air
With phantoms, as this madness of the heart.

              Enter an Officer.
   Lor. Where go you, sirrah?
   Offi.   By the ducal order
To forward the preparatory rites
For the late Foscari's interment.
   Bar.   Their
Vault has been often open'd of late years.
   Lor. 'Twill be full soon, and may be closed for ever.
   Offi. May I pass on?
   Lor.   You may.
   Bar.   How bears the Doge
This last calamity?
   Offi.   With desperate firmness.
In presence of another he says little,
But I perceive his lips move now and then;
And once or twice I heard him, from the adjoining
Apartment mutter forth the words—"My son!"
Scarce audibly. I must proceed.   [*Exit Officer.*
   Bar.   This stroke
Will move all Venice in his favour.
   Lor.   Right!
We must be speedy: let us call together
The delegates appointed to convey
The council's resolution.
   Bar.   I protest
Against it at this moment.
   Lor.   As you please —
I'll take their voices on it ne'ertheless,
And see whose most may sway them, yours or mine.
                  [*Exeunt* BARBARIGO *and* LOREDANO.

ACT V.

SCENE I.

The Doge's Apartment.

The Doge and Attendants.

Att. My lord, the deputation is in waiting;
But add, that if another hour would better
Accord with your will, they will make it theirs.
  Doge. To me all hours are like. Let them approach.
                                      [*Exit Attendant.*
  An Officer. Prince! I have done your bidding.
  Doge.   What command?
  Offi. A melancholy one—to call the attendance
Of—
  Doge. True—true—true: I crave your pardon. I
Begin to fail in apprehension, and
Wax very old—old almost as my years.
Till now I fought them off, but they begin
To overtake me.

Enter the Deputation, consisting of six of the Signory and the Chief of the Ten.

              Noble men, your pleasure!
  Chief of the Ten. In the first place, the Council doth condole
With the Doge on his late and private grief.
  Doge. No more—no more of that.
  Chief of the Ten.   Will not the Duke
Accept the homage of respect?
  Doge.   I do
Accept it as 'tis given—proceed.
  Chief of the Ten.   "The Ten,"
With a selected giunta from the senate
Of twenty-five of the best born patricians,
Having deliberated on the state
Of the republic, and the o'erwhelming cares

Which, at this moment, doubly must oppress
Your years, so long devoted to your country,
Have judged it fitting, with all reverence,
Now to solicit from your wisdom (which
Upon reflection must accord in this),
The resignation of the ducal ring,
Which you have worn so long and venerably:
And to prove that they are not ungrateful, nor
Cold to your years and services, they add
An appanage of twenty hundred golden
Ducats, to make retirement not less splendid
Than should become a sovereign's retreat.

 Doge. Did I hear rightly?
 Chief of the Ten.   Need I say again?
 Doge. No.—Have you done?
 Chief of the Ten. I have spoken. Twenty-four
Hours are accorded you to give an answer.
 Doge. I shall not need so many seconds.
 Chief of the Ten.   We
Will now retire.
 Doge.   Stay! Four and twenty hours
Will alter nothing which I have to say.
 Chief of the Ten. Speak!
 Doge.   When I twice before reiterated
My wish to abdicate, it was refused me:
And not alone refused, but ye exacted
An oath from me that I would never more
Renew this instance. I have sworn to die
In full exertion of the functions, which
My country call'd me here to exercise,
According to my honour and my conscience—
I cannot break *my* oath.
 Chief of the Ten.   Reduce us not
To the alternative of a decree,
Instead of your compliance.
 Doge.   Providence
Prolongs my days to prove and chasten me;

But ye have no right to reproach my length
Of days, since every hour has been the country's.
I am ready to lay down my life for her,
As I have laid down dearer things than life:
But for my dignity—I hold it of
The *whole* republic; when the *general* will
Is manifest, then you shall all be answer'd.
 Chief of the Ten. We grieve for such an answer; but it
   cannot
Avail you aught.
 Doge.   I can submit to all things,
But nothing will advance; no, not a moment.
What you decree—decree.
 Chief of the Ten. With this, then, must we
Return to those who sent us?
 Doge.   You have heard me.
 Chief of the Ten. With all due reverence we retire.
     [*Exeunt the Deputation, &c.*

   Enter an Attendant.
 Att.   My lord,
The noble dame Marina craves an audience.
 Doge. My time is hers.

   Enter MARINA.
 Mar.   My lord, if I intrude—
Perhaps you fain would be alone?
 Doge.   Alone!
Alone, come all the world around me, I
Am now and evermore. But we will bear it.
 Mar. We will, and for the sake of those who are,
Endeavour—Oh my husband!
 Doge.   Give it way;
I cannot comfort thee.
 Mar.   He might have lived,
So form'd for gentle privacy of life,
So loving, so beloved; the native of
Another land, and who so blest and blessing

As my poor Foscari? Nothing was wanting
Unto his happiness and mine save not
To be Venetian.
  Doge.   Or a prince's son.
  Mar. Yes; all things which conduce to other men's
Imperfect happiness or high ambition,
By some strange destiny, to him proved deadly.
The country and the people whom he loved,
The prince of whom he was the elder born,
And —
  Doge. Soon may be a prince no longer.
  Mar.   How?
  Doge. They have taken my son from me, and now aim
At my too long worn diadem and ring.
Let them resume the gewgaws!
  Mar.   Oh the tyrants!
In such an hour too!
  Doge.   'Tis the fittest time;
An hour ago I should have felt it.
  Mar.   And
Will you not now resent it? — Oh for vengeance!
But he, who, had he been enough protected,
Might have repaid protection in this moment,
Cannot assist his father.
  Doge.   Nor should do so
Against his country, had he a thousand lives
Instead of that —
  Mar.   They tortured from him. This
May be pure patriotism. I am a woman:
To me my husband and my children were
Country and home. I loved *him* — how I loved him!
I have seen him pass through such an ordeal as
The old martyrs would have shrunk from: he is gone,
And I, who would have given my blood for him,
Have nought to give but tears! But could I compass
The retribution of his wrongs! — Well, well;
I have sons, who shall be men.

Doge.   Your grief distracts you.
Mar. I thought I could have borne it, when I saw him
Bow'd down by such oppression; yes, I thought
That I would rather look upon his corse
Than his prolong'd captivity:—I am punish'd
For that thought now. Would I were in his grave!
Doge. I must look on him once more.
Mar.   Come with me!
Doge. Is he—
Mar.   Our bridal bed is now his bier.
Doge. And he is in his shroud!
Mar.   Come, come, old man!
[*Exeunt the* DOGE *and* MARINA

Enter BARBARIGO *and* LOREDANO.

Bar. (*to an Attendant*). Where is the Doge?
Att.   This instant retired hence
With the illustrious lady his son's widow.
Lor. Where?
Att.   To the chamber where the body lies.
Bar. Let us return, then.
Lor.   You forget, you cannot.
We have the implicit order of the Giunta
To await their coming here, and join them in
Their office: they'll be here soon after us.
Bar. And will they press their answer on the Doge?
Lor. 'Twas his own wish that all should be done promptly.
He answer'd quickly, and must so be answer'd;
His dignity is look'd to, his estate
Cared for—what would he more?
Bar.   Die in his robes:
He could not have lived long; but I have done
My best to save his honours, and opposed
This proposition to the last, though vainly.
Why would the general vote compel me hither?
Lor. 'Twas fit that some one of such different thoughts
From ours should be a witness, lest false tongues

Should whisper that a harsh majority
Dreaded to have its acts beheld by others.
 Bar. And not less, I must needs think, for the sake
Of humbling me for my vain opposition.
You are ingenious, Loredano, in
Your modes of vengeance, nay, poetical,
A very Ovid in the art of *hating;*
'Tis thus (although a secondary object,
Yet hate has microscopic eyes), to you
I owe, by way of foil to the more zealous,
This undesired association in
Your Giunta's duties.
 Lor.   How!—*my* Giunta!
 Bar.   *Yours!*
They speak your language, watch your nod, approve
Your plans, and do your work. Are they not *yours?*
 Lor. You talk unwarily. 'Twere best they hear not
This from you.
 Bar.   Oh! they'll hear as much one day
From louder tongues than mine; they have gone beyond
Even their exorbitance of power: and when
This happens in the most contemn'd and abject
States, stung humanity will rise to check it.
 Lor. You talk but idly.
 Bar.   That remains for proof.
Here come our colleagues.

    Enter the Deputation as before.

 Chief of the Ten. Is the Duke aware
We seek his presence?
 Att.   He shall be inform'd.
           [*Exit Attendant.*
 Bar. The Duke is with his son.
 Chief of the Ten.   If it be so,
We will remit him till the rites are over.
Let us return. 'Tis time enough to-morrow.
 Lor. (*aside to Bar.*) Now the rich man's hell-fire upon your
   tongue,

ACT V. 199

Unquench'd, unquenchable! I'll have it torn
From its vile babbling roots, till you shall utter
Nothing but sobs through blood, for this! Sage signors,
I pray ye be not hasty. [*Aloud to the others.*
    Bar.   But be human!
    Lor. See, the Duke comes!

Enter the DOGE.

    Doge.   I have obey'd your summons.
    Chief of the Ten. We come once more to urge our past
        request.
    Doge. And I to answer.
    Chief of the Ten.   What?
    Doge.   My only answer.
You have heard it.
    Chief of the Ten. Hear *you* then the last decree,
Definitive and absolute!
    Doge.   To the point—
To the point! I know of old the forms of office,
And gentle preludes to strong acts—Go on!
    Chief of the Ten. You are no longer Doge; you are released
From your imperial oath as sovereign;
Your ducal robes must be put off; but for
Your services, the state allots the appanage
Already mention'd in our former congress.
Three days are left you to remove from hence,
Under the penalty to see confiscated
All your own private fortune.
    Doge.   That last clause,
I am proud to say, would not enrich the treasury.
    Chief of the Ten. Your answer, Duke!
    Lor.   Your answer, Francis Foscari!
    Doge. If I could have foreseen that my old age
Was prejudicial to the state, the chief
Of the republic never would have shown
Himself so far ungrateful, as to place
His own high dignity before his country;

But this *life* having been so many years
Not useless to that country, I would fain
Have consecrated my last moments to her.
But the decree being rendered, I obey.
　　Chief of the Ten. If you would have the three days named
　　　　extended,
We willingly will lengthen them to eight,
As sign of our esteem.
　　Doge. 　　　　　　Not eight hours, signor,
Nor even eight minutes—There's the ducal ring,
　　　　　　[*Taking off his ring and cap.*
And there the ducal diadem. And so
The Adriatic's free to wed another.
　　Chief of the Ten. Yet go not forth so quickly.
　　Doge. 　　　　　　　　I am old, sir,
And even to move but slowly must begin
To move betimes. Methinks I see amongst you
A face I know not—Senator! your name,
You, by your garb, Chief of the Forty!
　　Mem. 　　　　　　　　Signor,
I am the son of Marco Memmo.
　　Doge. 　　　　　Ah!
Your father was my friend.—But *sons* and *fathers!*—
What, ho! my servants there!
　　Atten. 　　　　My prince!
　　Doge. 　　　　　　　　No prince—
There are the princes of the prince! [*Pointing to the Ten's
　　　Deputation.*]—Prepare
To part from hence upon the instant.
　　Chief of the Ten. 　　　Why
So rashly? 'twill give scandal.
　　Doge. 　　　　　Answer that; [*To the Ten.*
It is your province.—Sirs, bestir yourselves:
　　　　　　　　　　[*To the Servants.*
There is one burthen which I beg you bear
With care, although 'tis past all farther harm—
But I will look to that myself.

ACT V.

Bar.   He means
The body of his son.
    Doge.   And call Marina,
My daughter!
                 Enter MARINA.
    Doge.   Get thee ready, we must mourn
Elsewhere.
    Mar.   And everywhere.
    Doge.   True; but in freedom,
Without these jealous spies upon the great.
Signors, you may depart: what would you more?
We are going: do you fear that we shall bear
The palace with us? Its *old* walls, ten times
As *old* as I am, and I'm very old,
Have served you, so have I, and I and they
Could tell a tale; but I invoke them not
To fall upon you! else they would, as erst
The pillars of stone Dagon's temple on
The Israelite and his Philistine foes.
Such power I do believe there might exist
In such a curse as mine, provoked by such
As you; but I curse not. Adieu, good signors!
May the next duke be better than the present.
    Lor. The *present* duke is Paschal Malipiero.
    Doge. Not till I pass the threshold of these doors.
    Lor. Saint Mark's great bell is soon about to toll
For his inauguration.
    Doge.   Earth and heaven!
Ye will reverberate this peal; and I
Live to hear this!—the first doge who e'er heard
Such sound for his successor: Happier he,
My attainted predecessor, stern Faliero—
This insult at the least was spared him.
    Lor.   What!
Do you regret a traitor?
    Doge.   No—I merely
Envy the dead.

Chief of the Ten. My lord, if you indeed
Are bent upon this rash abandonment
Of the state's palace, at the least retire
By the private staircase, which conducts you towards
The landing-place of the canal.
  Doge.   No. I
Will now descend the stairs by which I mounted
To sovereignty—the Giants' Stairs, on whose
Broad eminence I was invested duke.
My services have called me up those steps,
The malice of my foes will drive me down them.
There five and thirty years ago was I
Install'd, and traversed these same halls, from which
I never thought to be divorced except
A corse—a corse, it might be, fighting for them—
But not push'd hence by fellow-citizens.
But come; my son and I will go together—
He to his grave, and I to pray for mine.
  Chief of the Ten. What! thus in public?
  Doge.   I was publicly
Elected, and so will I be deposed.
Marina! art thou willing?
  Mar.   Here's my arm!
  Doge. And here my *staff*: thus propp'd will I go forth.
  Chief of the Ten. It must not be—the people will perceive it.
  Doge. The people!—There's no people, you well know it,
Else you dare not deal thus by them or me.
There is a *populace*, perhaps, whose looks
May shame you; but they dare not groan nor curse you,
Save with their hearts and eyes.
  Chief of the Ten.   You speak in passion,
Else—
  Doge. You have reason. I have spoken much
More than my wont: it is a foible which
Was not of mine, but more excuses you,
Inasmuch as it shows that I approach

A dotage which may justify this deed
Of yours, although the law does not, nor will.
Farewell, sirs!

Bar. You shall not depart without
An escort fitting past and present rank.
We will accompany, with due respect,
The Doge unto his private palace. Say!
My brethren, will we not?

Different voices. Ay!—Ay!

Doge. You shall not
Stir—in my train, at least. I enter'd here
As sovereign—I go out as citizen
By the same portals, but as citizen.
All these vain ceremonies are base insults,
Which only ulcerate the heart the more,
Applying poisons there as antidotes.
Pomp is for princes—I am *none!*—That's false,
I *am*, but only to these gates.—Ah!

Lor. Hark!
[*The great bell of St. Mark's tolls.*

Bar. The bell!

Chief of the Ten. St. Mark's, which tolls for the election
Of Malipiero.

Doge. Well I recognise
The sound! I heard it once, but once before,
And that is five and thirty years ago;
Even *then I was not young.*

Bar. Sit down, my lord!
You tremble.

Doge. 'Tis the knell of my poor boy!
My heart aches bitterly.

Bar. I pray you sit.

Doge. No; my seat here has been a throne till now.
Marina! let us go.

Mar. Most readily.

Doge (*walks a few steps, then stops*). I feel athirst—will no one bring me here
A cup of water?
    Bar.   I—
    Mar.   And I—
    Lor.   And I—
    [*The* DOGE *takes a goblet from the hand of* LOREDANO.
    Doge. I take *yours*, Loredano, from the hand
Most fit for such an hour as this.
    Lor.   Why so?
    Doge. 'Tis said that our Venetian crystal has
Such pure antipathy to poisons as
To burst, if aught of venom touches it.
You bore this goblet, and it is not broken.
    Lor. Well, sir!
    Doge.   Then it is false, or you are true.
For my own part, I credit neither; 'tis
An idle legend.
    Mar.   You talk wildly, and
Had better now be seated, nor as yet
Depart. Ah! now you look as look'd my husband!
    Bar. He sinks!—support him!—quick—a chair—support him!
    Doge. The bell tolls on!—let's hence—my brain's on fire!
    Bar. I do beseech you, lean upon us!
    Doge.   No!
A sovereign should die standing. My poor boy!
Off with your arms!—*That bell!*
                      [*The* DOGE *drops down and dies.*
    Mar.   My God! My God!
    Bar. (*to Lor.*) Behold! your work's completed!
    Chief of the Ten.   Is there then
No aid? Call in assistance!
    Att.   'Tis all over.
    Chief of the Ten. If it be so, at least his obsequies
Shall be such as befits his name and nation,
His rank and his devotion to the duties

Of the realm, while his age permitted him
To do himself and them full justice. Brethren,
Say, shall it not be so?
  Bar.   He has not had
The misery to die a subject where
He reign'd: then let his funeral rites be princely.
 Chief of the Ten. We are agreed, then?
 All, except Lor. answer,   Yes.
 Chief of the Ten. Heaven's peace be with him!
 Mar. Signors, your pardon: this is mockery.
Juggle no more with that poor remnant, which,
A moment since, while yet it had a soul,
(A soul by whom you have increased your empire,
And made your power as proud as was his glory,)
You banish'd from his palace, and tore down
From his high place, with such relentless coldness;
And now, when he can neither know these honours,
Nor would accept them if he could, you, signors,
Purpose, with idle and superfluous pomp,
To make a pageant over what you trampled.
A princely funeral will be your reproach,
And not his honour.
 Chief of the Ten. Lady, we revoke not
Our purposes so readily.
 Mar.   I know it,
As far as touches torturing the living.
I thought the dead had been beyond even *you*,
Though (some, no doubt) consign'd to powers which may
Resemble that you exercise on earth.
Leave him to me; you would have done so for
His dregs of life, which you have kindly shorten'd:
It is my last of duties, and may prove
A dreary comfort in my desolation.
Grief is fantastical, and loves the dead,
And the apparel of the grave.
 Chief of the Ten.   Do you
Pretend still to this office?

Mar.   I do, signor.
Though his possessions have been all consumed
In the state's service, I have still my dowry,
Which shall be consecrated to his rites,
And those of—   [*She stops with agitation.*
   Chief of the Ten. Best retain it for your children.
   Mar. Ay, they are fatherless, I thank you.
   Chief of the Ten.   We
Cannot comply with your request. His relics
Shall be exposed with wonted pomp, and follow'd
Unto their home by the new Doge, not clad
As *Doge*, but simply as a senator.
   Mar. I have heard of murderers, who have interr'd
Their victims; but ne'er heard, until this hour,
Of so much splendour in hypocrisy
O'er those they slew.* I've heard of widows' tears—
Alas! I have shed some—always thanks to you!
I've heard of *heirs* in sables—you have left none
To the deceased, so you would act the part
Of such. Well, sirs, your will be done! as one day,
I trust, Heaven's will be done too!
   Chief of the Ten.   Know you, lady,
To whom ye speak, and perils of such speech?
   Mar. I know the former better than yourselves;
The latter—like yourselves: and can face both.
Wish you more funerals?

---

* The Venetians appear to have had a particular turn for breaking the hearts of their Doges. The following is another instance of the kind in the Doge Marco Barbarigo: he was succeeded by his brother Agostino Barbarigo, whose chief merit is here mentioned.—"Le doge, blessé de trouver constamment un contradicteur et un censeur si amer dans son frère, lui dit un jour en plein conseil: 'Messire Augustin, vous faites tout votre possible pour hâter ma mort; vous vous flattez de me succéder; mais, si les autres vous connaissent aussi-bien que je vous connais, ils n'auront garde de vous élire.' Là-dessus il se leva, ému de colère, rentra dans son appartement, et mourut quelques jours après. Ce frère, contre lequel il s'était emporté, fut précisément le successeur qu'on lui donna. C'était un mérite dont on aimait à tenir compte; surtout à un parent, de s'être mis en opposition avec le chef de la république."—DARU, *Hist. de Venise*, vol. ii. p. 533.

Bar.   Heed not her rash words;
Her circumstances must excuse her bearing.
Chief of the Ten. We will not note them down.
Bar. (turning to Lor. who is writing upon his tablets.) What
    art thou writing,
With such an earnest brow, upon thy tablets?
Lor. (pointing to the Doge's body). That *he* has paid me!*
Chief of the Ten. What debt did he owe you?
Lor. A long and just one; Nature's debt and *mine.*
                                        [*Curtain falls.*

* "*L'ha pagata.*" An historical fact. See *Hist. de Venise,* par P. Daru, t. ii. p. 411.—[Here the original MS. ends. The two lines which follow, were added by Mr. Gifford. In the margin of the MS., Lord Byron has written,—"If the last line should appear obscure to those who do not recollect the historical fact mentioned in the first act of Loredano's inscription in his book, of 'Doge Foscari, debtor for the deaths of my father and uncle,' you may add the following lines to the conclusion of the last act:—
    Chief of the Ten. For what has he repaid thee?
    Lor.   For my father's
    And father's brother's death—by his son's and own!
Ask Gifford about this."]

SARDANAPALUS,
A TRAGEDY.

TO

THE ILLUSTRIOUS GOETHE

A STRANGER

PRESUMES TO OFFER THE HOMAGE

OF A LITERARY VASSAL TO HIS LIEGE LORD,

THE FIRST OF EXISTING WRITERS,

WHO HAS CREATED

THE LITERATURE OF HIS OWN COUNTRY,

AND ILLUSTRATED THAT OF EUROPE.

THE UNWORTHY PRODUCTION

WHICH THE AUTHOR VENTURES TO INSCRIBE TO HIM

IS ENTITLED

SARDANAPALUS.

PREFACE.

In publishing the following Tragedies* I have only to repeat, that they were not composed with the most remote view to the stage. On the attempt made by the Managers in a former instance, the public opinion has been already expressed. With regard to my own private feelings, as it seems that they are to stand for nothing, I shall say nothing.

For the historical foundation of the following compositions the reader is referred to the Notes.

The Author has in one instance attempted to preserve, and in the other to approach, the "unities;" conceiving that with any very distant departure from them, there may be poetry, but can be no drama. He is aware of the unpopularity of this notion in present English literature; but it is not a system of his own, being merely an opinion, which, not very long ago, was the law of literature throughout the world, and is still so in the more civilised parts of it. But "nous avons changé tout cela," and are reaping the advantages of the change. The writer is far from conceiving that any thing he can adduce by personal precept or example can at all approach his regular, or even irregular predecessors: he is merely giving a reason why he preferred the more regular formation of a structure, however feeble, to an entire abandonment of all rules whatsoever. Where he has failed, the failure is in the architect,—and not in the art.

* "Sardanapalus" originally appeared in the same volume with "The Foscari" and "Cain."

DRAMATIS PERSONÆ.

MEN.

SARDANAPALUS, *King of Nineveh and Assyria, &c.*
ARBACES, *the Mede who aspired to the Throne.*
BELESES, *a Chaldean and Soothsayer.*
SALEMENES, *the King's Brother-in-law.*
ALTADA, *an Assyrian Officer of the Palace.*
PANIA.
ZAMES.
SPERO.
BALEA.

WOMEN.

ZARINA, *the Queen.*
MYRRHA, *an Ionian female Slave, and the Favourite of* SARDANAPALUS.
Women composing the Harem of SARDANAPALUS, *Guards, Attendants, Chaldean Priests, Medes, &c. &c.*

Scene—a Hall in the Royal Palace of Nineveh.

SARDANAPALUS.*

ACT I.

SCENE I.
A Hall in the Palace.

Salemenes (solus). He hath wrong'd his queen, but still he
    is her lord;
He hath wrong'd my sister, still he is my brother;
He hath wrong'd his people, still he is their sovereign,
And I must be his friend as well as subject:
He must not perish thus. I will not see
The blood of Nimrod and Semiramis
Sink in the earth, and thirteen hundred years
Of empire ending like a shepherd's tale;
He must be roused. In his effeminate heart
There is a careless courage which corruption
Has not all quench'd, and latent energies,
Repress'd by circumstance, but not destroy'd —
Steep'd, but not drown'd, in deep voluptuousness.
If born a peasant, he had been a man
To have reach'd an empire: to an empire born,
He will bequeath none; nothing but a name,
Which his sons will not prize in heritage:—
Yet, not all lost, even yet he may redeem
His sloth and shame, by only being that
Which he should be, as easily as the thing
He should not be and is. Were it less toil

---

* In this tragedy it has been my intention to follow the account of Diodorus Siculus; reducing it, however, to such dramatic regularity as I best could, and trying to approach the unities. I therefore suppose the rebellion to explode and succeed in one day by a sudden conspiracy, instead of the long war of the history.

To sway his nations than consume his life?
To head an army than to rule a harem?
He sweats in palling pleasures, dulls his soul,
And saps his goodly strength, in toils which yield not
Health like the chase, nor glory like the war—
He must be roused. Alas! there is no sound
          [*Sound of soft music heard from within.*
To rouse him short of thunder. Hark! the lute,
The lyre, the timbrel; the lascivious tinklings
Of lulling instruments, the softening voices
Of women, and of beings less than women,
Must chime in to the echo of his revel,
While the great king of all we know of earth
Lolls crown'd with roses, and his diadem
Lies negligently by to be caught up
By the first manly hand which dares to snatch it.
Lo, where they come! already I perceive
The reeking odours of the perfumed trains,
And see the bright gems of the glittering girls,
At once his chorus and his council, flash
Along the gallery, and amidst the damsels,
As femininely garb'd, and scarce less female,
The grandson of Semiramis, the man-queen.—
He comes! Shall I await him? yes, and front him,
And tell him what all good men tell each other,
Speaking of him and his. They come, the slaves
Led by the monarch subject to his slaves.

SCENE II.

Enter SARDANAPALUS *effeminately dressed, his Head crowned with Flowers, and his Robe negligently flowing, attended by a Train of Women and young Slaves.*

   Sar. (speaking to some of his attendants). Let the pavilion
          over the Euphrates
Be garlanded, and lit, and furnish'd forth
For an especial banquet; at the hour
Of midnight we will sup there: see nought wanting,

ACT I.

And bid the galley be prepared. There is
A cooling breeze which crisps the broad clear river:
We will embark anon. Fair nymphs, who deign
To share the soft hours of Sardanapalus,
We'll meet again in that the sweetest hour,
When we shall gather like the stars above us,
And you will form a heaven as bright as theirs;
Till then, let each be mistress of her time,
And thou, my own Ionian Myrrha,* choose,
Wilt thou along with them or me?
    Myr.   My lord—
    Sar. My lord, my life! why answerest thou so coldly?
It is the curse of kings to be so answer'd.
Rule thy own hours, thou rulest mine—say, would'st thou
Accompany our guests, or charm away
The moments from me?
    Myr.   The king's choice is mine.
    Sar. I pray thee say not so: my chiefest joy
Is to contribute to thine every wish.
I do not dare to breathe my own desire,
Lest it should clash with thine; for thou art still
Too prompt to sacrifice thy thoughts for others.
    Myr. I would remain: I have no happiness
Save in beholding thine; yet—
    Sar.   Yet! what YET?
Thy own sweet will shall be the only barrier
Which ever rises betwixt thee and me.
    Myr. I think the present is the wonted hour
Of council; it were better I retire.
    Sal. (*comes forward and says*) The Ionian slave says well: let
    Sar. Who answers? How now, brother?   [her retire.
    Sal.   The *queen*'s brother,
And your most faithful vassal, royal lord.

---

* "The Ionian name had been still more comprehensive, having included the Achaians and the Bœotians, who, together with those to whom it was afterwards confined, would make nearly the whole of the Greek nation; and among the orientals it was always the general name for the Greeks."—MITFORD's *Greece*, vol. i. p. 199.

Sar. (addressing his train). As I have said, let all dispose
  their hours
Till midnight, when again we pray your presence.
                                   [*The court retiring.*
(*To* MYRRHA, *who is going*) Myrrha! I thought *thou* wouldst
  remain.
  Myr.   Great king,
Thou didst not say so.
  Sar.   But *thou* lookedst it:
I know each glance of those Ionic eyes,
Which said thou wouldst not leave me.
  Myr.   Sire! your brother—
  Sal. His *consort's* brother, minion of Ionia!
How darest *thou* name *me* and not blush?
  Sar.   Not blush!
Thou hast no more eyes than heart to make her crimson
Like to the dying day on Caucasus,
Where sunset tints the snow with rosy shadows,
And then reproach her with thine own cold blindness,
Which will not see it. What, in tears, my Myrrha?
  Sal. Let them flow on; she weeps for more than one,
And is herself the cause of bitterer tears.
  Sar. Cursed be he who caused those tears to flow!
  Sal. Curse not thyself—millions do that already.
  Sar. Thou dost forget thee: make me not remember
I am a monarch.
  Sal.   Would thou couldst!
  Myr.   My sovereign,
I pray, and thou, too, prince, permit my absence.
  Sar. Since it must be so, and this churl has check'd
Thy gentle spirit, go; but recollect
That we must forthwith meet: I had rather lose
An empire than thy presence.   [*Exit* MYRRHA.
  Sal.   It may be,
Thou wilt lose both, and both for ever!
  Sar.   Brother,
I can at least command myself, who listen

To language such as this: yet urge me not
Beyond my easy nature.
   Sal.   'Tis beyond
That easy, far too easy, idle nature,
Which I would urge thee. O that I could rouse thee!
Though 'twere against myself.
   Sar.   By the god Baal!
The man would make me tyrant.
   Sal.   So thou art.
Think'st thou there is no tyranny but that
Of blood and chains? The despotism of vice—
The weakness and the wickedness of luxury—
The negligence—the apathy—the evils
Of sensual sloth—produce ten thousand tyrants,
Whose delegated cruelty surpasses
The worst acts of one energetic master,
However harsh and hard in his own bearing.
The false and fond examples of thy lusts
Corrupt no less than they oppress, and sap
In the same moment all thy pageant power
And those who should sustain it; so that whether
A foreign foe invade, or civil broil
Distract within, both will alike prove fatal:
The first thy subjects have no heart to conquer;
The last they rather would assist than vanquish.
   Sar. Why, what makes thee the mouth-piece of the people?
   Sal. Forgiveness of the queen, my sister's wrongs;
A natural love unto my infant nephews;
Faith to the king, a faith he may need shortly,
In more than words; respect for Nimrod's line;
Also, another thing thou knowest not.
   Sar. What's that?
   Sal.   To thee an unknown word.
   Sar.   Yet speak it;
I love to learn.
   Sal.   Virtue.
   Sar.   Not know the word!

Never was word yet rung so in my ears —
Worse than the rabble's shout, or splitting trumpet:
I've heard thy sister talk of nothing else.
    Sal. To change the irksome theme, then, hear of vice.
    Sar. From whom?
    Sal. Even from the winds, if thou couldst listen
Unto the echoes of the nation's voice.
    Sar. Come, I'm indulgent, as thou knowest, patient,
As thou hast often proved — speak out, what moves thee?
    Sal. Thy peril.
    Sar.   Say on.
    Sal.   Thus, then: all the nations,
For they are many, whom thy father left
In heritage, are loud in wrath against thee.
    Sar. 'Gainst *me!* What would the slaves?
    Sal.   A king.
    Sar.   And what
Am I then?
    Sal.   In their eyes a nothing; but
In mine a man who might be something still.
    Sar. The railing drunkards! why, what would they have?
Have they not peace and plenty?
    Sal.   Of the first
More than is glorious; of the last, far less
Than the king recks of.
    Sar.   Whose then is the crime,
But the false satraps', who provide no better?
    Sal. And somewhat in the monarch who ne'er looks
Beyond his palace walls, or if he stirs
Beyond them, 'tis but to some mountain palace,
Till summer heats wear down. O glorious Baal!
Who built up this vast empire, and wert made
A god, or at the least shinest like a god
Through the long centuries of thy renown,
This, thy presumed descendant, ne'er beheld
As king the kingdoms thou didst leave as hero,
Won with thy blood, and toil, and time, and peril!

For what? to furnish imposts for a revel,
Or multiplied extortions for a minion.
    Sar. I understand thee—thou wouldst have me go
Forth as a conqueror. By all the stars
Which the Chaldeans read—the restless slaves
Deserve that I should curse them with their wishes,
And lead them forth to glory.
    Sal.   Wherefore not?
Semiramis—a woman only—led
These our Assyrians to the solar shores
Of Ganges.
    Sar.   'Tis most true. And *how* return'd?
    Sal. Why, like a *man*—a hero; baffled, but
Not vanquish'd. With but twenty guards, she made
Good her retreat to Bactria.
    Sar.   And how many
Left she behind in India to the vultures?
    Sal. Our annals say not.
    Sar.   Then I will say for them—
That she had better woven within her palace
Some twenty garments, than with twenty guards
Have fled to Bactria, leaving to the ravens,
And wolves, and men—the fiercer of the three,
Her myriads of fond subjects. Is *this* glory?
Then let me live in ignominy ever.
    Sal. All warlike spirits have not the same fate.
Semiramis, the glorious parent of
A hundred kings, although she fail'd in India,
Brought Persia, Media, Bactria, to the realm
Which she once sway'd—and thou *might'st* sway.
    Sar.   I *sway* them—
She but subdued them.
    Sal.   It may be ere long
That they will need her sword more than your sceptre.
    Sar. There was a certain Bacchus, was there not?
I've heard my Greek girls speak of such—they say
He was a god, that is, a Grecian god,

An idol foreign to Assyria's worship,
Who conquer'd this same golden realm of Ind
Thou prat'st of, where Semiramis was vanquish'd.
  Sal. I have heard of such a man; and thou perceiv'st
That he is deem'd a god for what he did.
  Sar. And in his godship I will honour him—
Not much as man. What, ho! my cupbearer!
  Sal. What means the king?
  Sar.   To worship your new god
And ancient conqueror. Some wine, I say.

            Enter Cupbearer.
  Sar. (add·essing the Cupbearer). Bring me the golden goblet
        thick with gems,
Which bears the name of Nimrod's chalice. Hence,
Fill full, and bear it quickly.   [*Exit Cupbearer.*
  Sal.   Is this moment
A fitting one for the resumption of
Thy yet unslept-off revels?

          Re-enter Cupbearer, with wine.
  Sar. (taking the cup from him). Noble kinsman,
If these barbarian Greeks of the far shores
And skirts of these our realms lie not, this Bacchus
Conquer'd the whole of India, did he not?
  Sal. He did, and thence was deem'd a deity.
  Sar. Not so:—of all his conquests a few columns,
Which may be his, and might be mine, if I
Thought them worth purchase and conveyance, are
The landmarks of the seas of gore he shed,
The realms he wasted, and the hearts he broke.
But here, here in this goblet is his title
To immortality—the immortal grape
From which he first express'd the soul, and gave
To gladden that of man, as some atonement
For the victorious mischiefs he had done.
Had it not been for this, he would have been
A mortal still in name as in his grave;

And, like my ancestor Semiramis,
A sort of semi-glorious human monster.
Here's that which deified him—let it now
Humanise thee; my surly, chiding brother,
Pledge me to the Greek god!
    Sal.   For all thy realms
I would not so blaspheme our country's creed.
    Sar. That is to say, thou thinkest him a hero,
That he shed blood by oceans; and no god,
Because he turn'd a fruit to an enchantment,
Which cheers the sad, revives the old, inspires
The young, makes weariness forget his toil,
And fear her danger; opens a new world
When this, the present, palls. Well, then *I* pledge thee
And *him* as a true man, who did his utmost
In good or evil to surprise mankind.   [*Drinks.*
    Sal. Wilt thou resume a revel at this hour?
    Sar. And if I did, 'twere better than a trophy,
Being bought without a tear. But that is not
My present purpose: since thou wilt not pledge me,
Continue what thou pleasest.
(*To the Cupbearer*).   Boy, retire. [*Exit Cupbearer.*
    Sal. I would but have recall'd thee from thy dream;
Better by me awaken'd than rebellion.
    Sar. Who should rebel? or why? what cause? pretext?
I am the lawful king, descended from
A race of kings who knew no predecessors.
What have I done to thee, or to the people,
That thou shouldst rail, or they rise up against me?
    Sal. Of what thou hast done to me, I speak not.
    Sar.   But
Thou think'st that I have wrong'd the queen: is't not so?
    Sal. Think! Thou hast wrong'd her!
    Sar.   Patience, prince, and hear me.
She has all power and splendour of her station,
Respect, the tutelage of Assyria's heirs,
The homage and the appanage of sovereignty.

I married her as monarchs wed—for state,
And loved her as most husbands love their wives.
If she or thou supposedst I could link me
Like a Chaldean peasant to his mate,
Ye knew nor me, nor monarchs, nor mankind.
 Sal. I pray thee, change the theme: my blood disdains
Complaint, and Salemenes' sister seeks not
Reluctant love even from Assyria's lord!
Nor would she deign to accept divided passion
With foreign strumpets and Ionian slaves.
The queen is silent.
 Sar.   And why not her brother?
 Sal. I only echo thee the voice of empires,
Which he who long neglects not long will govern.
 Sar. The ungrateful and ungracious slaves! they murmur
Because I have not shed their blood, nor led them
To dry into the desert's dust by myriads,
Or whiten with their bones the banks of Ganges;
Nor decimated them with savage laws,
Nor sweated them to build up pyramids,
Or Babylonian walls.
 Sal.   Yet these are trophies
More worthy of a people and their prince
Than songs, and lutes, and feasts, and concubines,
And lavish'd treasures, and contemned virtues.
 Sar. Or for my trophies I have founded cities:
There's Tarsus and Anchialus, both built
In one day—what could that blood-loving beldame,
My martial grandam, chaste Semiramis,
Do more, except destroy them?
 Sal.   'Tis most true;
I own thy merit in those founded cities,
Built for a whim, recorded with a verse
Which shames both them and thee to coming ages.
 Sar. Shame me! By Baal, the cities, though well built,
Are not more goodly than the verse! Say what
Thou wilt 'gainst me, my mode of life or rule,

But nothing 'gainst the truth of that brief record.
Why, those few lines contain the history
Of all things human: hear—"Sardanapalus,
The king, and son of Anacyndaraxes,
In one day built Anchialus and Tarsus.
Eat, drink, and love; the rest's not worth a fillip."*

Sal. A worthy moral, and a wise inscription,
For a king to put up before his subjects!.

Sar. Oh, thou wouldst have me doubtless set up edicts—
"Obey the king—contribute to his treasure—
Recruit his phalanx—spill your blood at bidding—

* "For this expedition he took only a small chosen body of the phalanx, but all his light troops. In the first day's march he reached Anchialus, a town said to have been founded by the king of Assyria, Sardanapalus. The fortifications, in their magnitude and extent, still in Arrian's time, bore the character of greatness, which the Assyrians appear singularly to have affected in works of the kind. A monument representing Sardanapalus was found there, warranted by an inscription in Assyrian characters, of course in the old Assyrian language, which the Greeks, whether well or ill, interpreted thus: 'Sardanapalus, son of Anacyndaraxes, in one day founded Anchialus and Tarsus. Eat, drink, play: all other human joys are not worth a fillip.' Supposing this version nearly exact (for Arrian says it was not quite so), whether the purpose has not been to invite to civil order a people disposed to turbulence, rather than to recommend immoderate luxury, may perhaps reasonably be questioned. What, indeed, could be the object of a king of Assyria in founding such towns in a country so distant from his capital, and so divided from it by an immense extent of sandy deserts and lofty mountains, and, still more, how the inhabitants could be at once in circumstances to abandon themselves to the intemperate joys which their prince has been supposed to have recommended, is not obvious: but it may deserve observation that, in that line of coast, the southern of Lesser Asia, ruins of cities, evidently of an age after Alexander, yet barely named in history, at this day astonish the adventurous traveller by their magnificence and elegance. Amid the desolation which, under a singularly barbarian government, has for so many centuries been daily spreading in the finest countries of the globe, whether more from soil and climate, or from opportunities for commerce, extraordinary means must have been found for communities to flourish thero; whence it may seem that the measures of Sardanapalus were directed by juster views than have been commonly ascribed to him: but that monarch having been the last of a dynasty, ended by a revolution, obloquy on his memory would follow of course from the policy of his successors and their partisans. The inconsistency of traditions concerning Sardanapalus is striking in Diodorus's account of him."— MITFORD's *Greece*, vol. x. p. 311.

Fall down and worship, or get up and toil."
Or thus—"Sardanapalus on this spot
Slew fifty thousand of his enemies.
These are their sepulchres, and this his trophy."
I leave such things to conquerors; enough
For me, if I can make my subjects feel
The weight of human misery less, and glide
Ungroaning to the tomb: I take no license
Which I deny to them. We all are men.
 Sal. Thy sires have been revered as gods—
 Sar.   In dust
And death, where they are neither gods nor men.
Talk not of such to me! the worms are gods;
At least they banqueted upon your gods,
And died for lack of farther nutriment.
Those gods were merely men; look to their issue—
I feel a thousand mortal things about me,
But nothing godlike,—unless it may be
The thing which you condemn, a disposition
To love and to be merciful, to pardon
The follies of my species, and (that's human)
To be indulgent to my own.
 Sal.   Alas!
The doom of Nineveh is seal'd.—Woe—woe
To the unrivall'd city!
 Sar.   What dost dread?
 Sal. Thou art guarded by thy foes: in a few hours
The tempest may break out which overwhelms thee,
And thine and mine; and in another day
What *is* shall be the past of Belus' race.
 Sar. What must we dread?
 Sal.   Ambitious treachery,
Which has environ'd thee with snares; but yet
There is resource: empower me with thy signet
To quell the machinations, and I lay
The heads of thy chief foes before thy feet.
 Sar. The heads—how many?

Sal.   Must I stay to number
When even thine own's in peril? Let me go;
Give me thy signet—trust me with the rest.
   Sar. I will trust no man with unlimited lives.
When we take those from others, we nor know
What we have taken, nor the thing we give.
   Sal. Wouldst thou not take their lives who seek for thine?
   Sar. That's a hard question—But I answer, Yes.
Cannot the thing be done without? Who are they
Whom thou suspectest?—Let them be arrested.
   Sal. I would thou wouldst not ask me; the next moment
Will send my answer through thy babbling troop
Of paramours, and thence fly o'er the palace,
Even to the city, and so baffle all.—
Trust me.
   Sar.   Thou knowest I have done so ever:
Take thou the signet.   [*Gives the signet.*
   Sal.   I have one more request.—
   Sar. Name it.
   Sal. That thou this night forbear the banquet
In the pavilion over the Euphrates.
   Sar. Forbear the banquet! Not for all the plotters
That ever shook a kingdom! Let them come,
And do their worst: I shall not blench for them;
Nor rise the sooner; nor forbear the goblet;
Nor crown me with a single rose the less;
Nor lose one joyous hour.—I fear them not.
   Sal. But thou wouldst arm thee, wouldst thou not, if
        needful?
   Sar. Perhaps. I have the goodliest armour, and
A sword of such a temper; and a bow
And javelin, which might furnish Nimrod forth:
A little heavy, but yet not unwieldy.
And now I think on't, 'tis long since I've used them,
Even in the chase. Hast ever seen them, brother?
   Sal. Is this a time for such fantastic trifling?—
If need be, wilt thou wear them?

 Sar.   Will I not?
Oh! if it must be so, and these rash slaves
Will not be ruled with less, I'll use the sword
Till they shall wish it turn'd into a distaff.
 Sal. They say thy sceptre's turn'd to that already.
 Sar. That's false! but let them say so: the old Greeks,
Of whom our captives often sing, related
The same of their chief hero, Hercules,
Because he loved a Lydian queen: thou seest
The populace of all the nations seize
Each calumny they can to sink their sovereigns.
 Sal. They did not speak thus of thy fathers.
 Sar.   No;
They dared not. They were kept to toil and combat;
And never changed their chains but for their armour:
Now they have peace and pastime, and the license
To revel and to rail; it irks me not.
I would not give the smile of one fair girl
For all the popular breath that e'er divided
A name from nothing. What are the rank tongues
Of this vile herd, grown insolent with feeding,
That I should prize their noisy praise, or dread
Their noisome clamour?
 Sal.   You have said they are men;
As such their hearts are something.
 Sar.   -   So my dogs' are;
And better, as more faithful:—but, proceed;
Thou hast my signet:—since they are tumultuous,
Let them be temper'd, yet not roughly, till
Necessity enforce it. I hate all pain,
Given or received; we have enough within us,
The meanest vassal as the loftiest monarch,
Not to add to each other's natural burthen
Of mortal misery, but rather lessen,
By mild reciprocal alleviation,
The fatal penalties imposed on life:
But this they know not, or they will not know.

I have, by Baal! done all I could to soothe them:
I made no wars, I added no new imposts,
I interfered not with their civic lives,
I let them pass their days as best might suit them,
Passing my own as suited me.
    Sal.   Thou stopp'st
Short of the duties of a king; and therefore
They say thou art unfit to be a monarch.
    Sar. They lie.—Unhappily, I am unfit
To be aught save a monarch; else for me
The meanest Mede might be the king instead.
    Sal. There is one Mede, at least, who seeks to be so.
    Sar. What mean'st thou?—'tis thy secret; thou desirest
Few questions, and I'm not of curious nature.
Take the fit steps; and, since necessity
Requires, I sanction and support thee. Ne'er
Was man who more desired to rule in peace
The peaceful only: if they rouse me, better
They had conjured up stern Nimrod from his ashes,
"The mighty hunter." I will turn these realms
To one wide desert chase of brutes, who *were,*
But *would* no more, by their own choice, be human.
What they have found me, they belie; *that which*
They yet may find me—shall defy their wish
To speak it worse; and let them thank themselves.
    Sal. Then thou at last canst feel?
    Sar.   Feel! who feels not
Ingratitude?
    Sal.   I will not pause to answer
With words, but deeds. Keep thou awake that energy
Which sleeps at times, but is not dead within thee,
And thou may'st yet be glorious in thy reign,
As powerful in thy realm. Farewell!   [*Exit* SALEMENES.
    Sar. (*solus*).   Farewell!
He's gone; and on his finger bears my signet,
Which is to him a sceptre. He is stern
As I am heedless; and the slaves deserve

To feel a master. What may be the danger,
I know not: he hath found it, let him quell it
Must I consume my life—this little life—
In guarding against all may make it less?
It is not worth so much! It were to die
Before my hour, to live in dread of death,
Tracing revolt; suspecting all about me,
Because they are near; and all who are remote,
Because they are far. But if it should be so—
If they should sweep me off from earth and empire,
Why, what is earth or empire of the earth?
I have loved, and lived, and multiplied my image;
To die is no less natural than those
Acts of this clay! 'Tis true I have not shed
Blood as I might have done, in oceans, till
My name became the synonyme of death—
A terror and a trophy. But for this
I feel no penitence; my life is love:
If I must shed blood, it shall be by force.
Till now, no drop from an Assyrian vein
Hath flow'd for me, nor hath the smallest coin
Of Nineveh's vast treasures e'er been lavish'd
On objects which could cost her sons a tear:
If then they hate me, 'tis because I hate not.
If they rebel, 'tis because I oppress not.
Oh, men! ye must be ruled with scythes, not sceptres,
And mow'd down like the grass, else all we reap
Is rank abundance, and a rotten harvest
Of discontents infecting the fair soil,
Making a desert of fertility.—
I'll think no more.—Within there, ho!

Enter an ATTENDANT.

Sar.   Slave, tell
The Ionian Myrrha we would crave her presence.
  Attend. King, she is here.

MYRRHA *enters.*
  Sar. (apart to Attendant). Away!

(*Addressing* MYRRHA).   Beautiful being!
Thou dost almost anticipate my heart;
It throbb'd for thee, and here thou comest: let me
Deem that some unknown influence, some sweet oracle,
Communicates between us, though unseen,
In absence, and attracts us to each other.
    Myr. There doth.
    Sar.   I know there doth, but not its name:
What is it?
    Myr.   In my native land a God,
And in my heart a feeling like a God's,
Exalted; yet I own 'tis only mortal;
For what I feel is humble, and yet happy—
That is, it would be happy; but—   [MYRRHA *pauses.*
    Sar.   There comes
For ever something between us and what
We deem our happiness: let me remove
The barrier which that hesitating accent
Proclaims to thine, and mine is seal'd.
    Myr.   .   My lord!—
    Sar. My lord—my king—sire—sovereign; thus it is—
For ever thus, address'd with awe. I ne'er
Can see a smile, unless in some broad banquet's
Intoxicating glare, when the buffoons
Have gorged themselves up to equality,
Or I have quaff'd me down to their abasement.
Myrrha, I can hear all these things, these names,
Lord—king—sire—monarch—nay, time was I prized them;
That is, I suffer'd them—from slaves and nobles;
But when they falter from the lips I love,
The lips which have been press'd to mine, a chill
Comes o'er my heart, a cold sense of the falsehood
Of this my station, which represses feeling
In those for whom I have felt most, and makes me
Wish that I could lay down the dull tiara,
And share a cottage on the Caucasus
With thee, and wear no crowns but those of flowers.

Myr. Would that we could!
Sar. And dost *thou* feel this?—Why?
Myr. Then thou wouldst know what thou canst never
know.
Sar. And that is—
Myr. The true value of a heart;
At least, a woman's.
Sar. I have proved a thousand—
A thousand, and a thousand.
Myr. Hearts?
Sar. I think so.
Myr. Not one! the time may come thou may'st.
Sar. It will.
Hear, Myrrha; Salemenes has declared—
Or why or how he hath divined it, Belus,
Who founded our great realm, knows more than I—
But Salemenes hath declared my throne
In peril.
Myr. He did well.
Sar. And say'st *thou* so?
Thou whom he spurn'd so harshly, and now dared
Drive from our presence with his savage jeers,
And made thee weep and blush?
Myr. I should do both
More frequently, and he did well to call me
Back to my duty. But thou spakest of peril—
Peril to thee—
Sar. Ay, from dark plots and snares
From Medes—and discontented troops and nations.
I know not what—a labyrinth of things—
A maze of mutter'd threats and mysteries:
Thou know'st the man—it is his usual custom.
But he is honest. Come, we'll think no more on't—
But of the midnight festival.
Myr. 'Tis time
To think of aught save festivals. Thou hast not
Spurn'd his sage cautions?

ACT I.

Sar.   What?—and dost thou fear?
Myr. Fear?—I'm a Greek, and how should I fear death?
A slave, and wherefore should I dread my freedom?
Sar. Then wherefore dost thou turn so pale?
Myr.   I love.
Sar. And do not I? I love thee far—far more
Than either the brief life or the wide realm,
Which, it may be, are menaced;—yet I blench not.
Myr. That means thou lovest not thyself nor me;
For he who loves another loves himself,
Even for that other's sake. This is too rash:
Kingdoms and lives are not to be so lost.
Sar. Lost!—why, who is the aspiring chief who dared
Assume to win them?
Myr.   Who is he should dread
To try so much? When he who is their ruler
Forgets himself, will they remember him?
Sar. Myrrha!
Myr.   Frown not upon me: you have smiled
Too often on me not to make those frowns
Bitterer to bear than any punishment
Which they may augur.—King, I am your subject!
Master, I am your slave! Man, I have loved you!—
Loved you, I know not by what fatal weakness,
Although a Greek, and born a foe to monarchs—
A slave, and hating fetters— an Ionian,
And, therefore, when I love a stranger, more
Degraded by that passion than by chains!
Still I have loved you. If that love were strong
Enough to overcome all former nature,
Shall it not claim the privilege to save you?
Sar. Save me, my beauty! Thou art very fair,
And what I seek of thee is love—not safety.
Myr. And without love where dwells security?
Sar. I speak of woman's love.
Myr.   The very first
Of human life must spring from woman's breast,

Your first small words are taught you from her lips,
Your first tears quench'd by her, and your last sighs
Too often breathed out in a woman's hearing,
When men have shrunk from the ignoble care
Of watching the last hour of him who led them.
   Sar. My eloquent Ionian! thou speak'st music,
The very chorus of the tragic song
I have heard thee talk of as the favourite pastime
Of thy far father-land. Nay, weep not — calm thee.
   Myr. I weep not. — But I pray thee, do not speak
About my fathers or their land.
   Sar.   Yet oft
Thou speakest of them.
   Myr.   True — true: constant thought
Will overflow in words unconsciously;
But when another speaks of Greece, it wounds me.
   Sar. Well, then, how wouldst thou *save* me, as thou saidst?
   Myr. By teaching thee to save thyself, and not
Thyself alone, but these vast realms, from all
The rage of the worst war — the war of brethren.
   Sar. Why, child, I loathe all war, and warriors;
I live in peace and pleasure: what can man
Do more?
   Myr.   Alas! my lord, with common men
There needs too oft the show of war to keep
The substance of sweet peace; and, for a king,
'Tis sometimes better to be fear'd than loved.
   Sar. And I have never sought but for the last.
   Myr. And now art neither.
   Sar.   Dost *thou* say so, Myrrha?
   Myr. I speak of civic popular love, *self*-love,
Which means that men are kept in awe and law,
Yet not oppress'd — at least they must not think so;
Or if they think so, deem it necessary,
To ward off worse oppression, their own passions.
A king of feasts, and flowers, and wine, and revel,
And love, and mirth, was never king of glory.

Sar. Glory! what's that?
Myr. Ask of the gods thy fathers.
Sar. They cannot answer; when the priests speak for them,
'Tis for some small addition to the temple.
Myr. Look to the annals of thine empire's founders.
Ser. They are so blotted o'er with blood, I cannot.
But what wouldst have? the empire *has been* founded.
I cannot go on multiplying empires.
Myr. Preserve thine own.
Sar. At least, I will enjoy it.
Come, Myrrha, let us go on to the Euphrates:
The hour invites, the galley is prepared,
And the pavilion, deck'd for our return,
In fit adornment for the evening banquet,
Shall blaze with beauty and with light, until
It seems unto the stars which are above us
Itself an opposite star; and we will sit
Crown'd with fresh flowers like —
Myr. Victims.
Sar. No, like sovereigns,
The shepherd kings of patriarchal times,
Who knew no brighter gems than summer wreaths,
And none but tearless triumphs. Let us on.

Enter PANIA.

Pan. May the king live for ever!
Sar. Not an hour
Longer than he can love. How my soul hates
This language, which makes life itself a lie,
Flattering dust with eternity. Well, Pania!
Be brief.
Pan. I am charged by Salemenes to
Reiterate his prayer unto the king,
That for this day, at least, he will not quit
The palace: when the general returns,
He will adduce such reasons as will warrant

His daring, and perhaps obtain the pardon
Of his presumption.
 Sar.   What! am I then coop'd?
Already captive? can I not even breathe
The breath of heaven? Tell prince Salemenes,
Were all Assyria raging round the walls
In mutinous myriads, I would still go forth.
 Pan. I must obey, and yet—
 Myr.   Oh, monarch, listen.—
How many a day and moon thou hast reclined
Within these palace walls in silken dalliance,
And never shown thee to thy people's longing;
Leaving thy subjects' eyes ungratified,
The satraps uncontroll'd, the gods unworshipp'd,
And all things in the anarchy of sloth,
Till all, save evil, slumber'd through the realm!
And wilt thou not now tarry for a day,—
A day which may redeem thee? Wilt thou not
Yield to the few still faithful a few hours,
For them, for thee, for thy past father's race,
And for thy sons' inheritance?
 Pan.   'Tis true!
From the deep urgency with which the prince
Despatch'd me to your sacred presence, I
Must dare to add my feeble voice to that
Which now has spoken.
 Sar.   No, it must not be.
 Myr. For the sake of thy realm!
 Sar.   Away!
 Pan.   For that
Of all thy faithful subjects, who will rally
Round thee and thine.
 Sar.   These are mere fantasies;
There is no peril:—'tis a sullen scheme
Of Salemenes, to approve his zeal,
And show himself more necessary to us.
 Myr. By all that's good and glorious take this counsel.

Sar. Business to-morrow.
Myr.   Ay, or death to-night.
Sar. Why let it come then unexpectedly
'Midst joy and gentleness, and mirth and love;
So let me fall like the pluck'd rose!—far better
Thus than be wither'd.
Myr.   Then thou wilt not yield,
Even for the sake of all that ever stirr'd
A monarch into action, to forego
A trifling revel.
Sar.   No.
Myr.   Then yield for *mine;*
For my sake!
Sar.   Thine, my Myrrha!
Myr.   'Tis the first
Boon which I ever ask'd Assyria's king.
Sar. That's true, and wer't my kingdom must be granted.
Well, for thy sake, I yield me. Pania, hence!
Thou hear'st me.
Pan.   And obey.   [*Exit* PANIA.
Sar.   I marvel at thee.
What is thy motive, Myrrha, thus to urge me?
Myr. Thy safety; and the certainty that nought
Could urge the prince thy kinsman to require
Thus much from thee, but some impending danger.
Sar. And if I do not dread it, why shouldst thou?
Myr. Because *thou* dost not fear, I fear for *thee.*
Sar. To-morrow thou wilt smile at these vain fancies.
Myr. If the worst come, I shall be where none weep,
And that is better than the power to smile.
And thou?
Sar.   I shall be king, as heretofore.
Myr. Where?
Sar.   With Baal, Nimrod, and Semiramis,
Sole in Assyria, or with them elsewhere.
Fate made me what I am—may make me nothing—

But either that or nothing must I be:
I will not live degraded.
 Myr.   Hadst thou felt
Thus always, none would ever dare degrade thee.
 Sar. And who will do so now?
 Myr.   Dost thou suspect none?
 Sar. Suspect!—that's a spy's office. Oh! we lose
Ten thousand precious moments in vain words,
And vainer fears. Within there!—ye slaves, deck
The hall of Nimrod for the evening revel:
If I must make a prison of our palace,
At least we'll wear our fetters jocundly;
If the Euphrates be forbid us, and
The summer dwelling on its beauteous border,
Here we are still unmenaced. Ho! within there!
          [*Exit* SARDANAPALUS.
 Myr. (*sola*). Why do I love this man? My country's
    daughters
Love none but heroes. But I have no country!
The slave hath lost all save her bonds. I love him;
And that's the heaviest link of the long chain—
To love whom we esteem not. Be it so:
The hour is coming when he'll need all love,
And find none. To fall from him now were baser
Than to have stabb'd him on his throne when highest
Would have been noble in my country's creed:
I was not made for either. Could I save him,
I should not love *him* better, but myself;
And I have need of the last, for I have fallen
In my own thoughts, by loving this soft stranger:
And yet methinks I love him more, perceiving
That he is hated of his own barbarians,
The natural foes of all the blood of Greece.
Could I but wake a single thought like those
Which even the Phrygians felt when battling long
'Twixt Ilion and the sea, within his heart,
He would tread down the barbarous crowds, and triumph.

He loves me, and I love him; the slave loves
Her master, and would free him from his vices.
If not, I have a means of freedom still,
And if I cannot teach him how to reign,
May show him how alone a king can leave
His throne. I must not lose him from my sight. [*Exit.*

ACT II.

SCENE I.

The Portal of the same Hall of the Palace.

Beleses (solus). The sun goes down: methinks he sets
    more slowly,
Taking his last look of Assyria's empire.
How red he glares amongst those deepening clouds,
Like the blood he predicts. If not in vain,
Thou sun that sinkest, and ye stars which rise,
I have outwatch'd ye, reading ray by ray
The edicts of your orbs, which make Time tremble
For what he brings the nations, 'tis the furthest
Hour of Assyria's years. And yet how calm!
An earthquake should announce so great a fall —
A summer's sun discloses it. Yon disk,
To the star-read Chaldean, bears upon
Its everlasting page the end of what
Seem'd everlasting; but oh! thou true sun!
The burning oracle of all that live,
As fountain of all life, and symbol of
Him who bestows it, wherefore dost thou limit
Thy lore unto calamity? Why not
Unfold the rise of days more worthy thine
All-glorious burst from ocean? why not dart
A beam of hope athwart the future years,
As of wrath to its days? Hear me! oh, hear me!
I am thy worshipper, thy priest, thy servant—
I have gazed on thee at thy rise and fall,

And bow'd my head beneath thy mid-day beams,
When my eye dared not meet thee. I have watch'd
For thee, and after thee, and pray'd to thee,
And sacrificed to thee, and read, and fear'd thee,
And ask'd of thee, and thou hast answer'd — but
Only to thus much: while I speak, he sinks —
Is gone — and leaves his beauty, not his knowledge,
To the delighted west, which revels in
Its hues of dying glory. Yet what is
Death, so it be but glorious? 'Tis a sunset;
And mortals may be happy to resemble
The gods but in decay.

Enter ARBACES, *by an inner door.*

   Arb.   Beleses, why
So rapt in thy devotions? Dost thou stand
Gazing to trace thy disappearing god
Into some realm of undiscover'd day?
Our business is with night — 'tis come.
   Bel.   But not
Gone.
   Arb. Let it roll on — we are ready.
   Bel.   Yes.
Would it were over!
   Arb.   Does the prophet doubt
To whom the very stars shine victory?
   Bel. I do not doubt of victory — but the victor.
   Arb. Well, let thy science settle that. Meantime
I have prepared as many glittering spears
As will out-sparkle our allies — your planets.
There is no more to thwart us. The she-king,
That less than woman, is even now upon
The waters with his female mates. The order
Is issued for the feast in the pavilion.
The first cup which he drains will be the last
Quaff'd by the line of Nimrod.
   Bel.   'Twas a brave one.

Arb. And is a weak one—'tis worn out—we'll mend it.
Bel. Art sure of that?
Arb. Its founder was a hunter—
I am a soldier—what is there to fear?
Bel. The soldier.
Arb. And the priest, it may be: but
If you thought thus, or think, why not retain
Your king of concubines? why stir me up?
Why spur me to this enterprise? your own
No less than mine?
Bel. Look to the sky!
Arb. I look.
Bel. What seest thou?
Arb. A fair summer's twilight, and
The gathering of the stars.
Bel. And midst them, mark
Yon earliest, and the brightest, which so quivers,
As it would quit its place in the blue ether.
Arb. Well?
Bel. 'Tis thy natal ruler—thy birth planet.
Arb. (*touching his scabbard*). My star is in this scabbard:
when it shines,
It shall out-dazzle comets. Let us think
Of what is to be done to justify
Thy planets and their portents. When we conquer,
They shall have temples—ay, and priests—and thou
Shalt be the pontiff of—what gods thou wilt;
For I observe that they are ever just,
And own the bravest for the most devout.
Bel. Ay, and the most devout for brave—thou hast not
Seen me turn back from battle.
Arb. No; I own thee
As firm in fight as Babylonia's captain,
As skilful in Chaldea's worship: now,
Will it but please thee to forget the priest,
And be the warrior?
Bel. Why not both?

Arb.   The better;
And yet it almost shames me, we shall have
So little to effect. This woman's warfare
Degrades the very conqueror. To have pluck'd
A bold and bloody despot from his throne,
And grappled with him, clashing steel with steel,
That were heroic or to win or fall;
But to upraise my sword against this silkworm,
And hear him whine, it may be—
    Bel.   Do not deem it:
He has that in him which may make you strife yet;
And were he all you think, his guards are hardy,
And headed by the cool, stern Salemenes.
    Arb. They'll not resist.
    Bel.   Why not? they are soldiers.
    Arb.   True,
And therefore need a soldier to command them.
    Bel. That Salemenes is.
    Arb.   But not their king.
Besides, he hates the effeminate thing that governs,
For the queen's sake, his sister. Mark you not
He keeps aloof from all the revels?
    Bel.   But
Not from the council — there he is ever constant.
    Arb. And ever thwarted: what would you have more
To make a rebel out of? A fool reigning,
His blood dishonour'd, and himself disdain'd:
Why, it is *his* revenge we work for.
    Bel.   Could
He but be brought to think so: this I doubt of.
    Arb. What, if we sound him?
    Bel.   Yes — if the time served.
                    Enter BALEA.

    Bal. Satraps! The king commands your presence at
The feast to-night.
    Bel.   To hear is to obey.
In the pavilion?

Bal. No; here in the palace.
Arb. How! in the palace? it was not thus order'd.
Bal. It is so order'd now.
Arb. And why?
Bal. I know not.
May I retire?
Arb. Stay.
Bel. (to Arb. aside). Hush! let him go his way.
(*Alternately to Bal.*) Yes, Balea, thank the monarch, kiss the hem
Of his imperial robe, and say, his slaves
Will take the crums he deigns to scatter from
His royal table at the hour—was't midnight?
Bal. It was: the place, the hall of Nimrod. Lords,
I humble me before you, and depart.
[*Exit* BALEA.

Arb. I like not this same sudden change of place;
There is some mystery: wherefore should he change it?
Bel. Doth he not change a thousand times a day?
Sloth is of all things the most fanciful—
And moves more parasangs in its intents
Than generals in their marches, when they seek
To leave their foe at fault.—Why dost thou muse?
Arb. He loved that gay pavilion,—it was ever
His summer dotage.
Bel. And he loved his queen—
And thrice a thousand harlotry besides—
And he has loved all things by turns, except
Wisdom and glory.
Arb. Still—I like it not.
If he has changed—why, so must we: the attack
Were easy in the isolated bower,
Beset with drowsy guards and drunken courtiers;
But in the hall of Nimrod—
Bel. Is it so?
Methought the haughty soldier fear'd to mount
A throne too easily—does it disappoint thee

To find there is a slipperier step or two
Than what was counted on?
 Arb.   When the hour comes,
Thou shalt perceive how far I fear or no.
Thou hast seen my life at stake — and gaily play'd for:
But here is more upon the die — a kingdom.
 Bel. I have foretold already — thou wilt win it:
Then on, and prosper.
 Arb.   Now were I a soothsayer,
I would have boded so much to myself.
But be the stars obey'd — I cannot quarrel
With them, nor their interpreter. Who's here?

     Enter SALEMENES.

 Sal. Satraps!
 Bel. My prince!
 Sal.   Well met — I sought ye both,
But elsewhere than the palace.
 Arb.   Wherefore so?
 Sal. 'Tis not the hour.
 Arb.   The hour! — what hour?
 Sal.   Of midnight.
 Bel. Midnight, my lord!
 Sal.   What, are you not invited?
 Bel. Oh! yes — we had forgotten.
 Sal.   Is it usual
Thus to forget a sovereign's invitation?
 Arb. Why — we but now received it.
 Sal.   Then why here?
 Arb. On duty.
 Sal. On what duty?
 Bel.   On the state's.
We have the privilege to approach the presence;
But found the monarch absent.
 Sal.   And I too
Am upon duty.
 Arb. May we crave its purport?
 Sal. To arrest two traitors. Guards! Within there!

ACT II.

Enter Guards.

Sal. (continuing). Satraps,
Your swords.
    Bel. (delivering his). My lord, behold my scimitar.
    Arb. (drawing his sword). Take mine.
    Sal. (advancing). I will.
    Arb. But in your heart the blade—
The hilt quits not this hand.
    Sal. (drawing). How! dost thou brave me?
'Tis well—this saves a trial, and false mercy.
Soldiers, hew down the rebel!
    Arb. Soldiers! Ay—
Alone you dare not.
    Sal. Alone! foolish slave—
What is there in thee that a prince should shrink from
Of open force? We dread thy treason, not
Thy strength: thy tooth is nought without its venom—
The serpent's, not the lion's. Cut him down.
    Bel. (interposing). Arbaces! Are you mad? Have I not render'd
My sword? Then trust like me our sovereign's justice.
    Arb. No—I will sooner trust the stars thou prat'st of,
And this slight arm, and die a king at least
Of my own breath and body—so far that
None else shall chain them.
    Sal. (to the Guards). You hear *him* and *me*.
Take him not,—kill.

    [*The Guards attack* ARBACES, *who defends himself valiantly and dexterously till they waver.*

    Sal. Is it even so; and must
I do the hangman's office? Recreants! see
How you should fell a traitor.

    [SALEMENES *attacks* ARBACES.

Enter SARDANAPALUS *and Train.*

    Sar. Hold your hands—
Upon your lives, I say. What, deaf or drunken?

My sword! O fool, I wear no sword: here, fellow,
Give me thy weapon. [*To a Guard.*
    [SARDANAPALUS *snatches a sword from one of the soldiers,
    and rushes between the combatants—they separate.*
    Sar.   In my very palace!
What hinders me from cleaving you in twain,
Audacious brawlers?
    Bel.   Sire, your justice.
    Sal.   Or—
Your weakness.
    Sar. (*raising the sword*). How?
    Sal.   Strike! so the blow's repeated
Upon yon traitor—whom you spare a moment,
I trust, for torture—I'm content.
    Sar.   What—him!
Who dares assail Arbaces?
    Sal.   I!
    Sar.   Indeed!
Prince, you forget yourself. Upon what warrant?
    Sal. (*showing the signet*). Thine.
    Arb. (*confused*).   The king's!
    Sal.   Yes! and let the king confirm it.
    Sar. I parted not from this for such a purpose.
    Sal. You parted with it for your safety—I
Employ'd it for the best. Pronounce in person.
Here I am but your slave—a moment past
I was your representative.
    Sar.   Then sheathe
Your swords.
        [ARBACES *and* SALEMENES *return their swords to the
        scabbards.*
    Sal. Mine's sheathed: I pray you sheathe *not* yours:
'Tis the sole sceptre left you now with safety.
    Sar. A heavy one; the hilt, too, hurts my hand.
(*To a Guard.*) Here, fellow, take thy weapon back. Well, sirs,
What doth this mean?
    Bel.   The prince must answer that.

Sal. Truth upon my part, treason upon theirs.
Sar. Treason—Arbaces! treachery and Beleses!
That were an union I will not believe.
Bel. Where is the proof?
Sal.   I'll answer that, if once
The king demands your fellow-traitor's sword.
Arb. (*to Sal.*) A sword which hath been drawn as oft as
          thine
Against his foes.
Sal.   And now against his brother,
And in an hour or so against himself.
Sar. That is not possible: he dared not; no—
No—I'll not hear of such things. These vain bickerings
Are spawn'd in courts by base intrigues, and baser
Hirelings, who live by lies on good men's lives.
You must have been deceived, my brother.
Sal.   First
Let him deliver up his weapon, and
Proclaim himself your subject by that duty,
And I will answer all.
Sar.   Why, if I thought so—
But no, it cannot be: the Mede Arbaces—
The trusty, rough, true soldier—the best captain
Of all who discipline our nations—No,
I'll not insult him thus, to bid him render
The scimitar to me he never yielded
Unto our enemies. Chief, keep your weapon.
Sal. (*delivering back the signet*). Monarch, take back your
          signet.
Sar.   No, retain it;
But use it with more moderation.
Sal.   Sire,
I used it for your honour, and restore it
Because I cannot keep it with my own.
Bestow it on Arbaces.
Sar.   So I should:
He never ask'd it.

Sal.   Doubt not, he will have it,
Without that hollow semblance of respect.
    Bel. I know not what hath prejudiced the prince
So strongly 'gainst two subjects, than whom none
Have been more zealous for Assyria's weal.
    Sal. Peace, factious priest, and faithless soldier! thou
Unit'st in thy own person the worst vices
Of the most dangerous orders of mankind.
Keep thy smooth words and juggling homilies'
For those who know thee not. Thy fellow's sin
Is, at the least, a bold one, and not temper'd
By the tricks taught thee in Chaldea.
    Bel.   Hear him,
My liege—the son of Belus! he blasphemes
The worship of the land, which bows the knee
Before your fathers.
    Sar.   Oh! for that I pray you
Let him have absolution. I dispense with
The worship of dead men; feeling that I
Am mortal, and believing that the race
From whence I sprung are—what I see them—ashes.
    Bel. King! Do not deem so: they are with the stars,
And—
    Sar. You shall join them there ere they will rise,
If you preach farther—Why, *this* is rank treason.
    Sal. My lord!
    Sar.   To school me in the worship of
Assyria's idols! Let him be released—
Give him his sword.
    Sal.   My lord, and king, and brother,
I pray ye pause.
    Sar.   Yes, and be sermonised,
And dinn'd, and deafen'd with dead men and Baal,
And all Chaldea's starry mysteries.
    Bel. Monarch! respect them.
    Sar.   Oh! for that—I love them:
I love to watch them in the deep blue vault,

And to compare them with my Myrrha's eyes;
I love to see their rays redoubled in
The tremulous silver of Euphrates' wave,
As the light breeze of midnight crisps the broad
And rolling water, sighing through the sedges
Which fringe his banks: but whether they may be
Gods, as some say, or the abodes of gods,
As others hold, or simply lamps of night,
Worlds, or the lights of worlds, I know nor care not.
There's something sweet in my uncertainty
I would not change for your Chaldean lore;
Besides, I know of these all clay can know
Of aught above it, or below it—nothing.
I see their brilliancy and feel their beauty—
When they shine on my grave I shall know neither.

 Bel. For *neither*, sire, say *better.*
 Sar.   I will wait,
If it so please you, pontiff, for that knowledge.
In the mean time receive your sword, and know
That I prefer your service militant
Unto your ministry—not loving either.

 Sal. (aside). His lusts have made him mad. Then must I
  save him,
Spite of himself.
 Sar.   Please you to hear me, Satraps!
And chiefly thou, my priest, because I doubt thee
More than the soldier; and would doubt thee all
Wert thou not half a warrior: let us part
In peace—I'll not say pardon—which must be
Earn'd by the guilty; this I'll not pronounce ye,
Although upon this breath of mine depends
Your own; and, deadlier for ye, on my fears.
But fear not—for that I am soft, not fearful—
And so live on. Were I the thing some think me,
Your heads would now be dripping the last drops
Of their attainted gore from the high gates
Of this our palace, into the dry dust,

Their only portion of the coveted kingdom
They would be crown'd to reign o'er—let that pass.
As I have said, I will not *deem* ye guilty,
Nor *doom* ye guiltless. Albeit better men
Than ye or I stand ready to arraign you;
And should I leave your fate to sterner judges,
And proofs of all kinds, I might sacrifice
Two men, who, whatsoe'er they now are, were
Once honest. Ye are free, sirs.
  Arb.   Sire, this clemency—
  Bel. (interrupting him). Is worthy of yourself and, although
    innocent,
We thank—
  Sar. Priest! keep your thanksgivings for Belus;
His offspring needs none.
  Bel.   But being innocent—
  Sar. Be silent—Guilt is loud. If ye are loyal,
Ye are injured men, and should be sad, not grateful.
  Bel. So we should be, were justice always done
By earthly power omnipotent; but innocence
Must oft receive her right as a mere favour.
  Sar. That's a good sentence for a homily,
Though not for this occasion. Prithee keep it
To plead thy sovereign's cause before his people.
  Bel. I trust there is no cause.
  Sar.   No *cause*, perhaps;
But many causers:—if ye meet with such
In the exercise of your inquisitive function
On earth, or should you read of it in heaven
In some mysterious twinkle of the stars,
Which are your chronicles, I pray you note,
That there are worse things betwixt earth and heaven
Than him who ruleth many and slays none;
And, hating not himself, yet loves his fellows
Enough to spare even those who would not spare him
Were they once masters—but that's doubtful. Satraps!
Your swords and persons are at liberty

To use them as ye will—but from this hour
I have no call for either. Salemenes!
Follow me.
      [*Exeunt* SARDANAPALUS, SALEMENES, *and the Train, &c.
leaving* ARBACES *and* BELESES.

Arb.   Beleses!
Bel.   Now, what think you?
Arb. That we are lost.
Bel.   That we have won the kingdom.
  Arb. What? thus suspected—with the sword slung o'er us
But by a single hair, and that still wavering,
To be blown down by his imperious breath
Which spared us—why, I know not.
  Bel.   Seek not why;
But let us profit by the interval.
The hour is still our own—our power the same—
The night the same we destined. He hath changed
Nothing except our ignorance of all
Suspicion into such a certainty
As must make madness of delay.
  Arb.   And yet—
  Bel. What, doubting still?
  Arb.   He spared our lives, nay, more,
Saved them from Salemenes.
  Bel.   And how long
Will he so spare? till the first drunken minute.
  Arb. Or sober, rather. Yet he did it nobly;
Gave royally what we had forfeited
Basely—
  Bel. Say bravely.
  Arb.   Somewhat of both, perhaps.
But it has touch'd me, and, whate'er betide,
I will no further on.
  Bel.   And lose the world!
  Arb. Lose any thing except my own esteem.
  Bel. I blush that we should owe our lives to such
A king of distaffs!

Arb. But no less we owe them;
And I should blush far more to take the grantor's!

Bel. Thou may'st endure whate'er thou wilt—the stars
Have written otherwise.

Arb. Though they came down,
And marshall'd me the way in all their brightness,
I would not follow.

Bel. This is weakness—worse
Than a scared beldam's dreaming of the dead,
And waking in the dark.—Go to—go to.

Arb. Methought he look'd like Nimrod as he spoke,
Even as the proud imperial statue stands
Looking the monarch of the kings around it,
And sways, while they but ornament, the temple.

Bel. I told you that you had too much despised him,
And that there was some royalty within him—
What then? he is the nobler foe.

Arb. But we
The meaner.—Would he had not spared us!

Bel. So—
Wouldst thou be sacrificed thus readily?

Arb. No—but it had been better to have died
Than live ungrateful.

Bel. Oh, the souls of some men!
Thou wouldst digest what some call treason, and
Fools treachery—and, behold, upon the sudden,
Because for something or for nothing, this
Rash reveller steps, ostentatiously,
'Twixt thee and Salemenes, thou art turn'd
Into—what shall I say?—Sardanapalus!
I know no name more ignominious.

Arb. But
An hour ago, who dared to term me such
Had held his life but lightly —as it is,
I must forgive you, even as he forgave us—
Semiramis herself would not have done it.

Bel. No—the queen liked no sharers of the kingdom,
Not even a husband.
  Arb.   I must serve him truly—
  Bel. And humbly?
  Arb.   No, sir, proudly—being honest.
I shall be nearer thrones than you to heaven;
And if not quite so haughty, yet more lofty.
You may do your own deeming—you have codes,
And mysteries, and corollaries of
Right and wrong, which I lack for my direction,
And must pursue but what a plain heart teaches.
And now you know me.
  Bel.   Have you finish'd?
  Arb.   Yes—
With you.
  Bel. And would, perhaps, betray as well
As quit me?
  Arb. That's a sacerdotal thought
And not a soldier's.
  Bel.   Be it what you will—
Truce with these wranglings, and but hear me.
  Arb.   No—
There is more peril in your subtle spirit
Than in a phalanx.
  Bel.   If it must be so—
I'll on alone.
  Arb. Alone!
  Bel.   Thrones hold but one.
  Arb. But this is fill'd.
  Bel.   With worse than vacancy—
A despised monarch. Look to it, Arbaces:
I have still aided, cherish'd, loved, and urged you;
Was willing even to serve you, in the hope
To serve and save Assyria. Heaven itself
Seem'd to consent, and all events were friendly,
Even to the last, till that your spirit shrunk
Into a shallow softness; but now, rather

Than see my country languish, I will be
Her saviour or the victim of her tyrant,
Or one or both, for sometimes both are one;
And if I win, Arbaces is my servant.
 Arb. Your servant!
 Bel.   Why not? better than be slave,
The *pardon'd* slave of *she* Sardanapalus!

     Enter PANIA.

 Pan. My lords, I bear an order from the king.
 Arb. It is obey'd ere spoken.
 Bel.   Notwithstanding,
Let's hear it.
 Pan.   Forthwith, on this very night,
Repair to your respective satrapies
Of Babylon and Media.
 Bel.   With our troops?
 Pan. My order is unto the satraps and
Their household train.
 Arb.   But—
 Bel.   It must be obey'd:
Say, we depart.
 Pan.   My order is to see you
Depart, and not to bear your answer.
 Bel. (*aside*).   Ay!
Well, sir, we will accompany you hence.
 Pan. I will retire to marshal forth the guard
Of honour which befits your rank, and wait
Your leisure, so that it the hour exceeds not. [*Exit* PANIA.
 Bel. Now then obey!
 Arb.   Doubtless.
 Bel.   Yes, to the gates
That grate the palace, which is now our prison—
No further.
 Arb. Thou hast harp'd the truth indeed!
The realm itself, in all its wide extension,
Yawns dungeons at each step for thee and me.

Bel. Graves!
Arb. If I thought so, this good sword should dig
One more than mine.
Bel. It shall have work enough.
Let me hope better than thou augurest;
At present, let us hence as best we may.
Thou dost agree with me in understanding
This order as a sentence?
Arb. Why, what other
Interpretation should it bear? it is
The very policy of orient monarchs—
Pardon and poison—favours and a sword—
A distant voyage, and an eternal sleep.
How many satraps in his father's time—
For he I own is, or at least *was*, bloodless—
Bel. But *will* not, *can* not be so now.
Arb. I doubt it.
How many satraps have I seen set out
In his sire's day for mighty vice-royalties,
Whose tombs are on their path! I know not how,
But they all sicken'd by the way, it was
So long and heavy.
Bel. Let us but regain
The free air of the city, and we'll shorten
The journey.
Arb. 'Twill be shorten'd at the gates,
It may be.
Bel. No; they hardly will risk that.
They mean us to die privately, but not
Within the palace or the city walls,
Where we are known, and may have partisans:
If they had meant to slay us here, we were
No longer with the living. Let us hence.
Arb. If I but thought he did not mean my life—
Bel. Fool! hence—what else should despotism alarm'd
Mean? Let us but rejoin our troops, and march.
Arb. Towards our provinces?

Bel.   No; towards your kingdom.
There's time, there's heart, and hope, and power and means,
Which their half measures leave us in full scope.—
Away!
   Arb.   And I even yet repenting must
Relapse to guilt!
   Bel.   Self-defence is a virtue,
Sole bulwark of all right. Away, I say!
Let's leave this place, the air grows thick and choking,
And the walls have a scent of night-shade—hence!
Let us not leave them time for further council.
Our quick departure proves our civic zeal;
Our quick departure hinders our good escort,
The worthy Pania, from anticipating
The orders of some parasangs from hence:
Nay, there's no other choice, but—hence, I say.
          [*Exit with* ARBACES, *who follows reluctantly.*

          Enter SARDANAPALUS *and* SALEMENES.

   Sar. Well, all is remedied, and without bloodshed,
That worst of mockeries of a remedy;
We are now secure by these men's exile.
   Sal.   Yes,
As he who treads on flowers is from the adder
Twined round their roots.
   Sar.   Why, what wouldst have me do?
   Sal. Undo what you have done.
   Sar.   Revoke my pardon?
   Sal. Replace the crown now tottering on your temples.
   Sar. That were tyrannical.
   Sal.   But sure.
   Sar.   We are so.
What danger can they work upon the frontier?
   Sal. They are not there yet—never should they be so,
Were I well listen'd to.
   Sar.   Nay, I *have* listen'd
Impartially to thee—why not to them?

ACT II.

   Sal. You may know that hereafter; as it is,
I take my leave to order forth the guard.
   Sar. And you will join us at the banquet?
   Sal.   Sire,
Dispense with me — I am no wassailer:
Command me in all service save the Bacchant's.
   Sar. Nay, but 'tis fit to revel now and then.
   Sal. And fit that some should watch for those who revel
Too oft. Am I permitted to depart?
   Sar. Yes — Stay a moment, my good Salemenes,
My brother, my best subject, better prince
Than I am king. You should have been the monarch,
And I — I know not what, and care not; but
Think not I am insensible to all
Thine honest wisdom, and thy rough yet kind,
Though oft reproving, sufferance of my follies.
If I have spared these men against thy counsel,
That is, their lives — it is not that I doubt
The advice was sound; but, let them live: we will not
Cavil about their lives — so let them mend them.
Their banishment will leave me still sound sleep,
Which their death had not left me.
   Sal.   Thus you run
The risk to sleep for ever, to save traitors —
A moment's pang now changed for years of crime.
Still let them be made quiet.
   Sar.   Tempt me not:
My word is past.
   Sal.   But it may be recall'd.
   Sar. 'Tis royal.
   Sal.   And should therefore be decisive.
This half indulgence of an exile serves
But to provoke — a pardon should be full,
Or it is none.
   Sar.   And who persuaded me
After I had repeal'd them, or at least

Only dismiss'd them from our presence, who
Urged me to send them to their satrapies?
   Sal. True; that I had forgotten; that is, sire,
If they e'er reach'd their satrapies — why, then,
Reprove me more for my advice.
   Sar.   And if
They do not reach them — look to it! — in safety,
In safety, mark me — and security —
Look to thine own.
   Sal.   Permit me to depart;
Their *safety* shall be cared for.
   Sar.   Get thee hence, then;
And, prithee, think more gently of thy brother.
   Sal. Sire, I shall ever duly serve my sovereign.
                                      [*Exit* SALEMENES.
   Sar. (*solus*). That man is of a temper too severe;
Hard but as lofty as the rock, and free
From all the taints of common earth — while I
Am softer clay, impregnated with flowers:
But as our mould is, must the produce be.
If I have err'd this time, 'tis on the side
Where error sits most lightly on that sense
I know not what to call it: but it reckons
With me ofttimes for pain, and sometimes pleasure;
A spirit which seems placed about my heart
To count its throbs, not quicken them, and ask
Questions which mortal never dared to ask me,
Nor Baal, though an oracular deity —
Albeit his marble face majestical
Frowns as the shadows of the evening dim
His brows to changed expression, till at times
I think the statue looks in act to speak.
Away with these vain thoughts, I will be joyous —
And here comes Joy's true herald.
                       Enter MYRRHA.
   Myr.   King! the sky
Is overcast, and musters muttering thunder,

ACT II.   255

In clouds that seem approaching fast, and show
In forked flashes a commanding tempest.
Will you then quit the palace?
    Sar.   Tempest, say'st thou?
    Myr. Ay, my good lord.
    Sar.   For my own part, I should be
Not ill content to vary the smooth scene,
And watch the warring elements; but this
Would little suit the silken garments and
Smooth faces of our festive friends. Say, Myrrha,
Art thou of those who dread the roar of clouds?
    Myr. In my own country we respect their voices
As auguries of Jove.
    Sar.   Jove!—ay, your Baal—
Ours also has a property in thunder,
And ever and anon some falling bolt
Proves his divinity,—and yet sometimes
Strikes his own altars.
    Myr.   That were a dread omen.
    Sar. Yes—for the priests. Well, we will not go forth
Beyond the palace walls to-night, but make
Our feast within.
    Myr.   Now, Jove be praised! that he
Hath heard the prayer thou wouldst not hear. The gods
Are kinder to thee than thou to thyself,
And flash this storm between thee and thy foes,
To shield thee from them.
    Sar.   Child, if there be peril,
Methinks it is the same within these walls
As on the river's brink.
    Myr.   Not so; these walls
Are high and strong, and guarded. Treason has
To penetrate through many a winding way,
And massy portal; but in the pavilion
There is no bulwark.
    Sar.   No, nor in the palace,
Nor in the fortress, nor upon the top

Of cloud-fenced Caucasus, where the eagle sits
Nested in pathless clefts, if treachery be:
Even as the arrow finds the airy king,
The steel will reach the earthly. But be calm:
The men, or innocent or guilty, are
Banish'd, and far upon their way.

 Myr.   They live, then?
 Sar. So sanguinary? *Thou!*
 Myr.   I would not shrink
From just infliction of due punishment
On those who seek your life: wer't otherwise,
I should not merit mine. Besides, you heard
The princely Salemenes.
 Sar.   This is strange;
The gentle and the austere are both against me,
And urge me to revenge.
 Myr.   'Tis a Greek virtue.
 Sar. But not a kingly one—I'll none on't; or
If ever I indulge in't, it shall be
With kings—my equals.
 Myr.   These men sought to be so.
 Sar. Myrrha, this is too feminine, and springs
From fear—
 Myr.   For you.
 Sar.   No matter, still 'tis fear.
I have observed your sex, once roused to wrath,
Are timidly vindictive to a pitch
Of perseverance, which I would not copy.
I thought you were exempt from this, as from
The childish helplessness of Asian women.
 Myr. My lord, I am no boaster of my love,
Nor of my attributes; I have shared your splendour
And will partake your fortunes. You may live
To find one slave more true than subject myriads:
But this the gods avert! I am content
To be beloved on trust for what I feel,

Rather than prove it to you in your griefs,
Which might not yield to any cares of mine.
   Sar. Grief cannot come where perfect love exists,
Except to heighten it, and vanish from
That which it could not scare away. Let's in —
The hour approaches, and we must prepare
To meet the invited guests who grace our feast.
                                                      [*Exeunt.*

ACT III.

SCENE I.

The Hall of the Palace illuminated — SARDANAPALUS *and his Guests at Table. — A Storm without, and Thunder occasionally heard during the Banquet.*

   Sar. Fill full! why this is as it should be: here
Is my true realm, amidst bright eyes and faces
Happy as fair! Here sorrow cannot reach.
   Zam. Nor elsewhere — where the king is, pleasure sparkles.
   Sar. Is not this better now than Nimrod's huntings,
Or my wild grandam's chase in search of kingdoms
She could not keep when conquer'd?
   Alt.   Mighty though
They were, as all thy royal line have been,
Yet none of those who went before have reach'd
The acmé of Sardanapalus, who
Has placed his joy in peace — the sole true glory.
   Sar. And pleasure, good Altada, to which glory
Is but the path. What is it that we seek?
Enjoyment! We have cut the way short to it,
And not gone tracking it through human ashes,
Making a grave with every footstep.
   Zam.   No;
All hearts are happy, and all voices bless
The king of peace, who holds a world in jubilee.
   Sar. Art sure of that? I have heard otherwise;
Some say that there be traitors.

Zam.   Traitors they
Who dare to say so!—'Tis impossible.
What cause?
    Sar.   What cause? true,—fill the goblet up;
We will not think of them: there are none such,
Or if there be, they are gone.
    Alt.   Guests, to my pledge!
Down on your knees, and drink a measure to
The safety of the king—the monarch, say I?
The god Sardanapalus!
                       [ZAMES *and the Guests kneel and exclaim—*
                       Mightier than
His father Baal, the god Sardanapalus!
          [*It thunders as they kneel; some start up in confusion.*
    Zam. Why do you rise, my friends? in that strong peal
His father gods consented.
    Myr.   Menaced, rather.
King, wilt thou bear this mad impiety?
    Sar. Impiety!—nay, if the sires who reign'd
Before me can be gods, I'll not disgrace
Their lineage. But arise, my pious friends;
Hoard your devotion for the thunderer there:
I seek but to be loved, not worshipp'd.
    Alt.   Both—
Both you must ever be by all true subjects.
    Sar. Methinks the thunders still increase: it is
An awful night.
    Myr.   Oh yes, for those who have
No palace to protect their worshippers.
    Sar. That's true, my Myrrha; and could I convert
My realm to one wide shelter for the wretched,
I'd do it.
    Myr.   Thou'rt no god, then, not to be
Able to work a will so good and general,
As thy wish would imply.
    Sar.   And your gods, then,
Who can, and do not?

ACT III.

Myr.   Do not speak of that,
Lest we provoke them.
   Sar.   True, they love not censure
Better than mortals. Friends, a thought has struck me:
Were there no temples, would there, think ye, be
Air worshippers? that is, when it is angry,
And pelting as even now.
   Myr.   The Persian prays
Upon his mountain.
   Sar.   Yes, when the sun shines.
   Myr. And I would ask if this your palace were
Unroof'd and desolate, how many flatterers
Would lick the dust in which the king lay low?
   Alt. The fair Ionian is too sarcastic
Upon a nation whom she knows not well;
The Assyrians know no pleasure but their king's,
And homage is their pride.
   Sar.   Nay, pardon, guests,
The fair Greek's readiness of speech.
   Alt.   *Pardon!* sire:
We honour her of all things next to thee.
Hark! what was that?
   Zam.   That! nothing but the jar
Of distant portals shaken by the wind.
   Alt. It sounded like the clash of—hark again!
   Zam. The big rain pattering on the roof.
   Sar.   No more.
Myrrha, my love, hast thou thy shell in order?
Sing me a song of Sappho, her, thou know'st,
Who in thy country threw—

Enter PANIA, *with his sword and garments bloody, and disordered.*
The Guests rise in confusion.

   Pan. (*to the Guards*).   Look to the portals;
And with your best speed to the walls without.
Your arms! To arms! The king's in danger. Monarch!
Excuse this haste,—'tis faith.

17*

Sar. Speak on.
Pan. It is
As Salemenes fear'd; the faithless satraps—
   Sar. You are wounded—give some wine. Take breath,
       good Pania.
   Pan. 'Tis nothing—a mere flesh wound. I am worn
More with my speed to warn my sovereign,
Than hurt in his defence.
   Myr. Well, sir, the rebels?
   Pan. Soon as Arbaces and Beleses reach'd
Their stations in the city, they refused
To march; and on my attempt to use the power
Which I was delegated with, they call'd
Upon their troops, who rose in fierce defiance.
   Myr. All?
   Pan.   Too many.
   Sar. Spare not of thy free speech,
To spare mine ears the truth.
   Pan. My own slight guard
Were faithful, and what's left of it is still so.
   Myr. And are these all the force still faithful?
   Pan. No—
The Bactrians, now led on by Salemenes,
Who even then was on his way, still urged
By strong suspicion of the Median chiefs,
Are numerous, and make strong head against
The rebels, fighting inch by inch, and forming
An orb around the palace, where they mean
To centre all their force, and save the king.
(*He hesitates.*) I am charged to—
   Myr. 'Tis no time for hesitation.
   Pan. Prince Salemenes doth implore the king
To arm himself, although but for a moment,
And show himself unto the soldiers: his
Sole presence in this instant might do more
Than hosts can do in his behalf.

Sar.   What, ho!
My armour there.
   Myr.   And wilt thou?
   Sar.   Will I not?
Ho, there!—but seek not for the buckler: 'tis
Too heavy:—a light cuirass and my sword.
Where are the rebels?
   Pan.   Scarce a furlong's length
From the outward wall the fiercest conflict rages.
   Sar. Then I may charge on horseback. Sfero, ho!
Order my horse out.—There is space enough
Even in our courts, and by the outer gate,
To marshal half the horsemen of Arabia.
               [*Exit* SFERO *for the armour.*
   Myr. How I do love thee!
   Sar.   I ne'er doubted it.
   Myr. But now I know thee.
   Sar. (*to his Attendant*). Bring down my spear too.—
Where's Salemenes?
   Pan.   Where a soldier should be,
In the thick of the fight.
   Sar.   Then hasten to him—Is
The path still open, and communication
Left 'twixt the palace and the phalanx?
   Pan.   'Twas
When I late left him, and I have no fear:
Our troops were steady, and the phalanx form'd.
   Sar. Tell him to spare his person for the present,
And that I will not spare my own—and say,
I come.
   Pan. There's victory in the very word. [*Exit* PANIA.
   Sar. Altada—Zames—forth, and arm ye! There
Is all in readiness in the armoury.
See that the women are bestow'd in safety
In the remote apartments: let a guard
Be set before them, with strict charge to quit
The post but with their lives—command it, Zames.

Altada, arm yourself, and return here;
Your post is near our person.
    [Exeunt ZAMES, ALTADA, *and all save* MYRRHA.

    Enter SFERO *and others with the King's Arms*, &c.
    Sfe.   King! your armour.
    Sar. (*arming himself*). Give me the cuirass—so: my
        baldric; now
My sword: I had forgot the helm—where is it?
That's well—no, 'tis too heavy: you mistake, too—
It was not this I meant, but that which bears
A diadem around it.
    Sfe.   Sire, I deem'd
That too conspicuous from the precious stones
To risk your sacred brow beneath—and trust me,
This is of better metal, though less rich.
    Sar. You deem'd! Are you too turn'd a rebel? Fellow!
Your part is to obey: return, and—no—
It is too late—I will go forth without it.
    Sfe. At least, wear this.
    Sar.   Wear Caucasus! why, 'tis
A mountain on my temples.
    Sfe.   Sire, the meanest
Soldier goes not forth thus exposed to battle.
All men will recognise you—for the storm
Has ceased, and the moon breaks forth in her brightness.
    Sar. I go forth to be recognised, and thus
Shall be so sooner. Now—my spear! I'm arm'd.
        [*In going stops short, and turns to* SFERO.
Sfero—I had forgotten—bring the mirror.
    Sfe. The mirror, sire?
    Sar.   Yes, sir, of polish'd brass,
Brought from the spoils of India—but be speedy.
                [*Exit* SFERO.
    Sar. Myrrha, retire unto a place of safety.
Why went you not forth with the other damsels?
    Myr. Because my place is here.

ACT III.

Sar. And when I am gone—
Myr. I follow.
Sar. You! to battle?
Myr. If it were so,
'Twere not the first Greek girl had trod the path.
I will await here your *return*.
Sar. The place
Is spacious, and the first to be sought out,
If they prevail; and, if it be so,
And I return not—
Myr. Still we meet again.
Sar. How?
Myr. In the spot where all must meet at last—
In Hades! if there be, as I believe,
A shore beyond the Styx: and if there be not,
In ashes.
Sar. Darest thou so much?
Myr. I dare all things
Except survive what I have loved, to be
A rebel's booty: forth, and do your bravest.

Re-enter SFERO *with the mirror.*

Sar. (*looking at himself*). This cuirass fits me well, the baldric better,
And the helm not at all. Methinks I seem
    [*Flings away the helmet after trying it again.*
Passing well in these toys; and now to prove them.
Altada! Where's Altada?
Sfe. Waiting, sire,
Without: he has your shield in readiness.
Sar. True; I forgot he is my shield-bearer
By right of blood, derived from age to age.
Myrrha, embrace me;—yet once more—once more—
Love me, whate'er betide. My chiefest glory
Shall be to make me worthier of your love.
Myr. Go forth, and conquer!
    [*Exeunt* SARDANAPALUS *and* SFERO.

                              Now, I am alone.
All are gone forth, and of that all how few
Perhaps return. Let him but vanquish, and
Me perish! If he vanquish not, I perish;
For I will not outlive him. He has wound
About my heart, I know not how nor why.
Not for that he is king; for now his kingdom
Rocks underneath his throne, and the earth yawns
To yield him no more of it than a grave;
And yet I love him more. Oh, mighty Jove!
Forgive this monstrous love for a barbarian,
Who knows not of Olympus! yes, I love him
Now, now, far more than—Hark—to the war shout!
Methinks it nears me. If it should be so,
                    [*She draws forth a small vial.*
This cunning Colchian poison, which my father
Learn'd to compound on Euxine shores, and taught me
How to preserve, shall free me! It had freed me
Long ere this hour, but that I loved, until
I half forgot I was a slave:—where all
Are slaves save one, and proud of servitude,
So they are served in turn by something lower
In the degree of bondage, we forget
That shackles worn like ornaments no less
Are chains. Again that shout! and now the clash
Of arms—and now—and now—

                  Enter ALTADA.

  Alt.   Ho, Sfero, ho!
  Myr. He is not here; what wouldst thou with him? How
Goes on the conflict?
  Alt.   Dubiously and fiercely.
  Myr. And the king?
  Alt.   Like a king. I must find Sfero,
And bring him a new spear and his own helmet.
He fights till now bare-headed, and by far
Too much exposed. The soldiers knew his face,

And the foe too; and in the moon's broad light,
His silk tiara and his flowing hair
Make him a mark too royal. Every arrow
Is pointed at the fair hair and fair features,
And the broad fillet which crowns both.
 Myr.   Ye gods,
Who fulminate o'er my father's land, protect him!
Were you sent by the king?
 Alt.   By Salemenes,
Who sent me privily upon this charge,
Without the knowledge of the careless sovereign
The king! the king fights as he revels! ho!
What, Sfero! I will seek the armoury—
He must be there.   [*Exit* ALTADA.
 Myr.   'Tis no dishonour—no—
'Tis no dishonour to have loved this man.
I almost wish now, what I never wish'd
Before, that he were Grecian. If Alcides
Were shamed in wearing Lydian Omphale's
She-garb, and wielding her vile distaff; surely
He, who springs up a Hercules at once,
Nursed in effeminate arts from youth to manhood,
And rushes from the banquet to the battle,
As though it were a bed of love, deserves
That a Greek girl should be his paramour,
And a Greek bard his minstrel, a Greek tomb
His monument. How goes the strife, sir?
       Enter an Officer.
 Officer.   Lost,
Lost almost past recovery. Zames! Where
Is Zames?
 Myr. Posted with the guard appointed
To watch before the apartment of the women. [*Exit Officer.*
 Myr. (*sola*). He's gone; and told no more than that all's
    lost!
What need have I to know more? In those words,
Those little words, a kingdom and a king,

A line of thirteen ages, and the lives
Of thousands, and the fortune of all left
With life, are merged; and I, too, with the great,
Like a small bubble breaking with the wave
Which bore it, shall be nothing. At the least,
My fate is in my keeping: no proud victor
Shall count me with his spoils.

Enter PANIA.

Pan.   Away with me,
Myrrha, without delay; we must not lose
A moment — all that's left us now.
  Myr.   The king?
  Pan. Sent me here to conduct you hence, beyond
The river, by a secret passage.
  Myr.   Then
He lives —
  Pan.   And charged me to secure your life,
And beg you to live on for his sake, till
He can rejoin you.
  Myr.   Will he then give way?
  Pan. Not till the last. Still, still he does whate'er
Despair can do; and step by step disputes
The very palace.
  Myr.   They are here, then: — ay,
Their shouts come ringing through the ancient halls,
Never profaned by rebel echoes till
This fatal night. Farewell, Assyria's line!
Farewell to all of Nimrod! Even the name
Is now no more.
  Pan.   Away with me — away!
  Myr. No: I'll die here! — Away, and tell your king
I loved him to the last.

Enter SARDANAPALUS *and* SALEMENES *with Soldiers.* PANIA *quits*
       MYRRHA, *and ranges himself with them.*

  Sar.   Since it is thus,
We'll die where we were born — in our own halls.

Serry your ranks — stand firm. I have despatch'd
A trusty satrap for the guard of Zames,
All fresh and faithful; they'll be here anon.
All is not over. — Pania, look to Myrrha.
        [PANIA *returns towards* MYRRHA.
 Sal. We have breathing time; yet once more charge, my
    friends —
One for Assyria!
 Sar.   Rather say for Bactria!
My faithful Bactrians, I will henceforth be
King of your nation, and we'll hold together
This realm as province.
 Sal.   Hark! they come — they come.

   Enter BELESES *and* ARBACES *with the Rebels.*

 Arb. Set on, we have them in the toil. Charge! charge!
 Bel. On! on! — Heaven fights for us, and with us — On!
   [*They charge the King and* SALEMENES *with their Troops,
   who defend themselves till the Arrival of* ZAMES, *with
   the Guard before mentioned. The Rebels are then
   driven off, and pursued by* SALEMENES, &c. *As the
   King is going to join the pursuit,* BELESES *crosses him.*
 Bel. Ho! tyrant — *I* will end this war.
 Sar.   Even so,
My warlike priest, and precious prophet, and
Grateful and trusty subject: — yield, I pray thee.
I would reserve thee for a fitter doom,
Rather than dip my hands in holy blood.
 Bel. Thine hour is come.
 Sar.   No, thine. — I've lately read,
Though but a young astrologer, the stars;
And ranging round the zodiac, found thy fate
In the sign of the Scorpion, which proclaims
That thou wilt now be crush'd.
 Bel.   But not by thee.
   [*They fight;* BELESES *is wounded and disarmed.*

Sar. (raising his sword to despatch him, exclaims) —
Now call upon thy planets, will they shoot
From the sky to preserve their seer and credit?
> [*A party of Rebels enter and rescue* Beleses. *They assail the King, who, in turn, is rescued by a Party of his Soldiers, who drive the Rebels off.*

The villain was a prophet after all.
Upon them — ho! there — victory is ours.   [*Exit in pursuit.*
  Myr. (to Pan.) Pursue! Why stand'st thou here, and
    leavest the ranks
Of fellow-soldiers conquering without thee?
  Pan. The king's command was not to quit thee.
  Myr.   Me!
Think not of me — a single soldier's arm
Must not be wanting now. I ask no guard,
I need no guard: what, with a world at stake,
Keep watch upon a woman? Hence, I say,
Or thou art shamed! Nay, then, *I* will go forth,
A feeble female, 'midst their desperate strife,
And bid thee guard me *there* — where thou shouldst shield
Thy sovereign.   [*Exit* Myrrha.
  Pan.   Yet stay, damsel! She is gone.
If aught of ill betide her, better I
Had lost my life. Sardanapalus holds her
Far dearer than his kingdom, yet he fights
For that too; and can I do less than he,
Who never flash'd a scimitar till now?
Myrrha, return, and I obey you, though
In disobedience to the monarch.   [*Exit* Pania.

    Enter Altada *and* Sfero *by an opposite door.*
  Alt.   Myrrha!
What, gone? yet she was here when the fight raged
And Pania also. Can aught have befallen them?
  Sfe. I saw both safe, when late the rebels fled:
They probably are but retired to make
Their way back to the harem.

Alt.   If the king
Prove victor, as it seems even now he must,
And miss his own Ionian, we are doom'd
To worse than captive rebels.
    Sfe.   Let us trace them;
She cannot be fled far; and, found, she makes
A richer prize to our soft sovereign
Than his recover'd kingdom.
    Alt.   Baal himself
Ne'er fought more fiercely to win empire, than
His silken son to save it: he defies
All augury of foes or friends; and like
The close and sultry summer's day, which bodes
A twilight tempest, bursts forth in such thunder
As sweeps the air and deluges the earth.
The man's inscrutable.
    Sfe.   Not more than others.
All are the sons of circumstance: away—
Let's seek the slave out, or prepare to be
Tortured for his infatuation, and
Condemn'd without a crime.   [*Exeunt.*

         Enter SALEMENES *and Soldiers, &c.*

    Sal.   The triumph is
Flattering: they are beaten backward from the palace,
And we have open'd regular access
To the troops station'd on the other side
Euphrates, who may still be true; nay, must be,
When they hear of our victory. But where
Is the chief victor? where's the king?

     Enter SARDANAPALUS, *cum suis, &c. and* MYRRHA.

    Sar.   Here, brother.
    Sal. Unhurt, I hope.
    Sar.   Not quite; but let it pass.
We've clear'd the palace—
    Sal.   And I trust the city.

Our numbers gather: and I've ordered onward
A cloud of Parthians, hitherto reserved,
All fresh and fiery, to be pour'd upon them
In their retreat, which soon will be a flight.
 Sar. It is already, or at least they march'd
Faster than I could follow with my Bactrians,
Who spared no speed. I am spent: give me a seat.
 Sal. There stands the throne, sire.
 Sar.   'Tis no place to rest on,
For mind nor body: let me have a couch, [*They place a seat.*
A peasant's stool, I care not what: so—now
I breathe more freely.
 Sal.   This great hour has proved
The brightest and most glorious of your life.
 Sar. And the most tiresome. Where's my cupbearer?
Bring me some water.
 Sal. (*smiling*).   'Tis the first time he
Ever had such an order: even I,
Your most austere of counsellors, would now
Suggest a purpler beverage.
 Sar.   Blood—doubtless.
But there's enough of that shed; as for wine,
I have learn'd to-night the price of the pure element:
Thrice have I drank of it, and thrice renew'd,
With greater strength than the grape ever gave me,
My charge upon the rebels. Where's the soldier
Who gave me water in his helmet?
 One of the Guards.   Slain, sire!
An arrow pierced his brain, while, scattering
The last drops from his helm, he stood in act
To place it on his brows.
 Sar.   Slain! unrewarded!
And slain to serve my thirst: that's hard, poor slave!
Had he but lived, I would have gorged him with
Gold: all the gold of earth could ne'er repay
The pleasure of that draught; for I was parch'd
As I am now.   [*They bring water—he drinks.*

ACT III.

     I live again—from henceforth
The goblet I reserve for hours of love,
But war on water.
  Sal.   And that bandage, sire,
Which girds your arm?
  Sar.   A scratch from brave Beleses.
  Myr. Oh! he is wounded!
  Sar.   Not too much of that;
And yet it feels a little stiff and painful,
Now I am cooler.
  Myr.   You have bound it with—
  Sar. The fillet of my diadem: the first time
That ornament was ever aught to me,
Save an incumbrance.
  Myr. (to the Attendants). Summon speedily
A leech of the most skilful: pray, retire:
I will unbind your wound and tend it.
  Sar.   Do so,
For now it throbs sufficiently: but what
Know'st thou of wounds? yet wherefore do I ask?
Know'st thou, my brother, where I lighted on
This minion?
  Sal. Herding with the other females,
Like frighten'd antelopes.
  Sar.   No: like the dam
Of the young lion, femininely raging,
(And femininely meaneth furiously,
Because all passions in excess are female,)
Against the hunter flying with her cub,
She urged on with her voice and gesture, and
Her floating hair and flashing eyes, the soldiers,
In the pursuit.
  Sal. Indeed!
  Sar.   You see, this night
Made warriors of more than me. I paused
To look upon her, and her kindled cheek;

Her large black eyes, that flash'd through her long hair
As it stream'd o'er her; her blue veins that rose
Along her most transparent brow; her nostril
Dilated from its symmetry; her lips
Apart; her voice that clove through all the din,
As a lute's pierceth through the cymbal's clash,
Jarr'd but not drown'd by the loud brattling; her
Waved arms, more dazzling with their own born whiteness
Than the steel her hand held, which she caught up
From a dead soldier's grasp;—all these things made
Her seem unto the troops a prophetess
Of victory, or Victory herself,
Come down to hail us hers.

   Sal. (aside).   This is too much.
Again the love-fit's on him, and all's lost,
Unless we turn his thoughts.
                    (*Aloud.*) But pray thee, sire,
Think of your wound —you said even now 'twas painful.

   Sar. That's true, too; but I must not think of it.

   Sal. I have look'd to all things needful, and will now
Receive reports of progress made in such
Orders as I had given, and then return
To hear your further pleasure.

   Sar.   Be it so.

   Sal. (in retiring). Myrrha!
   Myr.   Prince!
   Sal.   You have shown a soul to-night,
Which, were he not my sister's lord—But now
I have no time: thou lovest the king?

   Myr.   I love
Sardanapalus.

   Sal.   But wouldst have him king still?

   Myr. I would not have him less than what he should be.

   Sal. Well then, to have him king, and yours, and all
He should, or should not be; to have him *live*,
Let him not sink back into luxury.
You have more power upon his spirit than

Wisdom within these walls, or fierce rebellion
Raging without: look well that he relapse not.
 Myr. There needed not the voice of Salemenes
To urge me on to this: I will not fail.
All that a woman's weakness can —
 Sal.   Is power
Omnipotent o'er such a heart as his:
Exert it wisely.   [*Exit* SALEMENES.
 Sar.   Myrrha! what, at whispers
With my stern brother? I shall soon be jealous.
 Myr. (*smiling*). You have cause, sire; for on the earth
   there breathes not
A man more worthy of a woman's love —
A soldier's trust — a subject's reverence —
A king's esteem — the whole world's admiration!
 Sar. Praise him, but not so warmly. I must not
Hear those sweet lips grow eloquent in aught
That throws me into shade; yet you speak truth.
 Myr. And now retire, to have your wound look'd to.
Pray, lean on me.
 Sar.   Yes, love! but not from pain.
           [*Exeunt omnes.*

ACT IV.

SCENE I.

SARDANAPALUS *discovered sleeping upon a Couch, and occasionally disturbed in his Slumbers, with* MYRRHA *watching.*

 Myr. (*sola, gazing*). I have stolen upon his rest, if rest
   it be,
Which thus convulses slumber: shall I wake him?
No, he seems calmer. Oh, thou God of Quiet!
Whose reign is o'er seal'd eyelids and soft dreams,
Or deep, deep sleep, so as to be unfathom'd,
Look like thy brother, Death, — so still — so stirless —
For then we are happiest, as it may be, we
Are happiest of all within the realm

Of thy stern, silent, and unwakening twin.
Again he moves — again the play of pain
Shoots o'er his features, as the sudden gust
Crisps the reluctant lake that lay so calm
Beneath the mountain shadow; or the blast
Ruffles the autumn leaves, that drooping cling
Faintly and motionless to their loved boughs.
I must awake him — yet not yet: who knows
From what I rouse him? It seems pain; but if
I quicken him to heavier pain? The fever
Of this tumultuous night, the grief too of
His wound, though slight, may cause all this, and shake
Me more to see than him to suffer. No:
Let Nature use her own maternal means,—
And I await to second, not disturb her.

    Sar. (*awakening*). Not so — although ye multiplied the stars,
And gave them to me as a realm to share
From you and with you! I would not so purchase
The empire of eternity. Hence — hence —
Old hunter of the earliest brutes! and ye,
Who hunted fellow-creatures as if brutes!
Once bloody mortals — and now bloodier idols,
If your priests lie not! And thou, ghastly beldame!
Dripping with dusky gore, and trampling on
The carcasses of Inde — away! away!
Where am I? Where the spectres? Where — No — that
Is no false phantom: I should know it 'midst
All that the dead dare gloomily raise up
From their black gulf to daunt the living. Myrrha!

    Myr. Alas! thou art pale, and on thy brow the drops
Gather like night dew. My beloved, hush —
Calm thee. Thy speech seems of another world,
And thou art lord of this. Be of good cheer;
All will go well.

    Sar.   Thy *hand* — so — 'tis thy hand;
'Tis flesh; grasp — clasp — yet closer, till I feel
Myself that which I was.

Myr.   At least know me
For what I am, and ever must be — thine.
   Sar. I know it now. I know this life again.
Ah, Myrrha! I have been where we shall be.
   Myr. My lord!
   Sar. I've been i' the grave — where worms are lords,
And kings are — But I did not deem it so;
I thought 'twas nothing.
   Myr.   So it is; except
Unto the timid, who anticipate
That which may never be.
   Sar.   Oh, Myrrha! if
Sleep shows such things, what may not death disclose?
   Myr. I know no evil death can show, which life
Has not already shown to those who live
Embodied longest. If there be indeed
A shore where mind survives, 'twill be as mind,
All unincorporate: or if there flits
A shadow of this cumbrous clog of clay,
Which stalks, methinks, between our souls and heaven,
And fetters us to earth — at least the phantom,
Whate'er it have to fear, will not fear death.
   Sar. I fear it not; but I have felt — have seen —
A legion of the dead.
   Myr.   And so have I.
The dust we tread upon was once alive,
And wretched. But proceed: what hast thou seen?
Speak it, 'twill lighten thy dimm'd mind.
   Sar.   Methought —
   Myr. Yet pause, thou art tired — in pain — exhausted; all
Which can impair both strength and spirit: seek
Rather to sleep again.
   Sar.   Not now — I would not
Dream; though I know it now to be a dream
What I have dreamt: — and canst thou bear to hear it?
   Myr. I can bear all things, dreams of life or death,

Which I participate with you in semblance
Or full reality.
 Sar.   And this look'd real,
I tell you: after that these eyes were open,
I saw them in their flight—for then they fled.
 Myr. Say on.
 Sar.   I saw, that is, I dream'd myself
Here—here—even where we are, guests as we were,
Myself a host that deem'd himself but guest,
Willing to equal all in social freedom;
But, on my right hand and my left, instead
Of thee and Zames, and our custom'd meeting,
Was ranged on my left hand a haughty, dark,
And deadly face—I could not recognise it,
Yet I had seen it, though I knew not where:
The features were a giant's, and the eye
Was still, yet lighted; his long locks curl'd down
On his vast bust, whence a huge quiver rose
With shaft-heads feather'd from the eagle's wing,
That peep'd up bristling through his serpent hair.
I invited him to fill the cup which stood
Between us, but he answer'd not—I fill'd it—
He took it not, but stared upon me, till
I trembled at the fix'd glare of his eye:
I frown'd upon him as a king should frown—
He frown'd not in his turn, but look'd upon me
With the same aspect, which appall'd me more,
Because it changed not; and I turn'd for refuge
To milder guests, and sought them on the right,
Where thou wert wont to be. But— [*He pauses.*
 Myr.   What instead?
 Sar. In thy own chair—thy own place in the banquet—
I sought thy sweet face in the circle—but
Instead—a grey-hair'd, wither'd, bloody-eyed,
And bloody-handed, ghastly, ghostly thing,
Female in garb, and crown'd upon the brow,
Furrow'd with years, yet sneering with the passion

Of vengeance, leering too with that of lust,
Sate:—my veins curdled.
    Myr.   Is this all?
    Sar.   Upon
Her right hand—her lank, bird-like right hand—stood
A goblet, bubbling o'er with blood; and on
Her left, another, fill'd with—what I saw not,
But turn'd from it and her. But all along
The table sate a range of crowned wretches,
Of various aspects, but of one expression.
    Myr. And felt you not this a mere vision?
    Sar.   No:
It was so palpable, I could have touch'd them.
I turn'd from one face to another, in
The hope to find at last one which I knew
Ere I saw theirs: but no—all turn'd upon me,
And stared, but neither ate nor drank, but stared,
Till I grew stone, as they seem'd half to be,
Yet breathing stone, for I felt life in them,
And life in me: there was a horrid kind
Of sympathy between us, as if they
Had lost a part of death to come to me,
And I the half of life to sit by them.
We were in an existence all apart
From heaven or earth—And rather let me see
Death all than such a being!
    Myr.   And the end?
    Sar. At last I sate, marble, as they, when rose
The hunter and the crone; and smiling on me—
Yes, the enlarged but noble aspect of
The hunter smiled upon me—I should say,
His lips, for his eyes moved not—and the woman's
Thin lips relax'd to something like a smile.
Both rose, and the crown'd figures on each hand
Rose also, as if aping their chief shades—
Mere mimics even in death—but I sate still:
A desperate courage crept through every limb,

And at the last I fear'd them not, but laugh'd
Full in their phantom faces. But then—then
The hunter laid his hand on mine: I took it,
And grasp'd it—but it melted from my own;
While he too vanish'd, and left nothing but
The memory of a hero, for he look'd so.
   Myr. And was: the ancestor of heroes, too,
And thine no less.
   Sar.   Ay, Myrrha, but the woman,
The female who remain'd, she flew upon me,
And burnt my lips up with her noisome kisses;
And, flinging down the goblets on each hand,
Methought their poisons flow'd around us, till
Each form'd a hideous river. Still she clung;
The other phantoms, like a row of statues,
Stood dull as in our temples, but she still
Embraced me, while I shrunk from her, as if,
In lieu of her remote descendant, I
Had been the son who slew her for her incest.
Then—then—a chaos of all loathsome things
Throng'd thick and shapeless: I was dead, yet feeling—
Buried, and raised again—consumed by worms,
Purged by the flames, and wither'd in the air!
I can fix nothing further of my thoughts,
Save that I long'd for thee, and sought for thee,
In all these agonies,—and woke and found thee.
   Myr. So shalt thou find me ever at thy side,
Here and hereafter, if the last may be.
But think not of these things—the mere creations
Of late events, acting upon a frame
Unused to toil, yet over-wrought by toil
Such as might try the sternest.
   Sar.   I am better.
Now that I see *thee once* more, *what was seen*
Seems nothing.
              Enter SALEMENES.
   Sal.   Is the king so soon awake?

ACT IV.   279

    Sar. Yes, brother, and I would I had not slept;
For all the predecessors of our line
Rose up, methought, to drag me down to them.
My father was amongst them, too; but he,
I know not why, kept from me, leaving me
Between the hunter-founder of our race,
And her, the homicide and husband-killer,
Whom you call glorious.
    Sal.   So I term you also,
Now you have shown a spirit like to hers.
By day-break I propose that we set forth,
And charge once more the rebel crew, who still
Keep gathering head, repulsed, but not quite quell'd.
    Sar. How wears the night?
    Sal.   There yet remain some hours
Of darkness: use them for your further rest.
    Sar. No, not to-night, if 'tis not gone: methought
I pass'd hours in that vision.
    Myr.   Scarcely one;
I watch'd by you: it was a heavy hour,
But an hour only.
    Sar.   Let us then hold council;
To-morrow we set forth.
    Sal.   But ere that time,
I had a grace to seek.
    Sar.   'Tis granted.
    Sal.   Hear it
Ere you reply too readily; and 'tis
For *your* ear only.
    Myr.   Prince, I take my leave.
                                      [*Exit* MYRRHA.
    Sal. That slave deserves her freedom.
    Sar.   Freedom only!
That slave deserves to share a throne.
    Sal.   Your patience—
'Tis not yet vacant, and 'tis of its partner
I come to speak with you.

Sar. How! of the queen?
Sal. Even so. I judged it fitting for their safety,
That, ere the dawn, she sets forth with her children
For Paphlagonia, where our kinsman Cotta
Governs; and there at all events secure
My nephews and your sons their lives, and with them
Their just pretensions to the crown in case —
Sar. I perish — as is probable: well thought —
Let them set forth with a sure escort.
Sal. That
Is all provided, and the galley ready
To drop down the Euphrates; but ere they
Depart, will you not see —
Sar. My sons? It may
Unman my heart, and the poor boys will weep;
And what can I reply to comfort them,
Save with some hollow hopes, and ill-worn smiles?
You know I cannot feign.
Sal. But you can feel
At least, I trust so: in a word, the queen
Requests to see you ere you part — for ever.
Sar. Unto what end? what purpose? I will grant
Aught — all that she can ask — but such a meeting.
Sal. You know, or ought to know, enough of women,
Since you have studied them so steadily,
That what they ask in aught that touches on
The heart, is dearer to their feelings or
Their fancy, than the whole external world.
I think as you do of my sister's wish;
But 'twas her wish — she is my sister — you
Her husband — will you grant it?
Sar. 'Twill be useless:
But let her come.
Sal. I go. [*Exit* SALEMENES.
Sar. We have lived asunder
Too long to meet again — and *now* to meet!
Have I not cares enow, and pangs enow,

To bear alone, that we must mingle sorrows,
Who have ceased to mingle love?

Re-enter SALEMENES *and* ZARINA.

Sal. My sister! Courage:
Shame not our blood with trembling, but remember
From whence we sprung. The queen is present, sire.
Zar. I pray thee, brother, leave me.
Sal. Since you ask it.
[*Exit* SALEMENES.
Zar. Alone with him! How many a year has pass'd,
Though we are still so young, since we have met,
Which I have worn in widowhood of heart.
He loved me not: yet he seems little changed—
Changed to me only—would the change were mutual!
He speaks not—scarce regards me—not a word—
Nor look—yet he *was* soft of voice and aspect,
Indifferent, not austere. My lord!
Sar. Zarina!
Zar. No, *not* Zarina—do not say Zarina.
That tone—that word—annihilate long years,
And things which make them longer.
Sar. 'Tis too late
To think of these past dreams. Let's not reproach—
That is, reproach me not—for the *last* time—
Zar. And *first.* I ne'er reproach'd you.
Sar. 'Tis most true;
And that reproof comes heavier on my heart
Than—But our hearts are not in our own power.
Zar. Nor hands; but I gave both.
Sar. Your brother said
It was your will to see me, ere you went
From Nineveh with—(*He hesitates*).
Zar. Our children: it is true.
I wish'd to thank you that you have not divided
My heart from all that's left it now to love—
Those who are yours and mine, who look like you,

And look upon me as you look'd upon me
Once — But they have not changed.
 Sar.   Nor ever will.
I fain would have them dutiful.
 Zar.   I cherish
Those infants, not alone from the blind love
Of a fond mother, but as a fond woman.
They are now the only tie between us.
 Sar.   Deem not
I have not done you justice: rather make them
Resemble your own line than their own sire.
I trust them with you—to you: fit them for
A throne, or, if that be denied—You have heard
Of this night's tumults?
 Zar.   I had half forgotten,
And could have welcomed any grief save yours,
Which gave me to behold your face again.
 Sar. The throne—I say it not in fear—but 'tis
In peril; they perhaps may never mount it:
But let them not for this lose sight of it.
I will dare all things to bequeath it them;
But if I fail, then they must win it back
Bravely—and, won, wear it wisely, not as I
Have wasted down my royalty.
 Zar.   They ne'er
Shall know from me of aught but what may honour
Their father's memory.
 Sar.   Rather let them hear
The truth from you than from a trampling world.
If they be in adversity, they'll learn
Too soon the scorn of crowds for crownless princes,
And find that all their father's sins are theirs.
My boys!—I could have borne it were I childless.
 Zar. Oh! do not say so—do not poison all
My peace left, by unwishing that thou wert
A father. If thou conquerest, they shall reign,

And honour him who saved the realm for them,
So little cared for as his own; and if—

Sar. 'Tis lost, all earth will cry out thank your father!
And they will swell the echo with a curse.

Zar. That they shall never do; but rather honour
The name of him, who, dying like a king,
In his last hours did more for his own memory
Than many monarchs in a length of days,
Which date the flight of time, but make no annals.

Sar. Our annals draw perchance unto their close;
But at the least, whate'er the past, their end
Shall be like their beginning—memorable.

Zar. Yet, be not rash—be careful of your life,
Live but for those who love.

Sar. And who are they?
A slave, who loves from passion—I'll not say
Ambition—she has seen thrones shake, and loves;
A few friends who have revell'd till we are
As one, for they are nothing if I fall;
A brother I have injured—children whom
I have neglected, and a spouse—

Zar. Who loves.

Sar. And pardons?

Zar. I have never thought of this,
And cannot pardon till I have condemn'd.

Sar. My wife!

Zar. Now blessings on thee for that word!
I never thought to hear it more—from thee.

Sar. Oh! thou wilt hear it from my subjects. Yes—
These slaves whom I have nurtured, pamper'd, fed,
And swoln with peace, and gorged with plenty, till
They reign themselves—all monarchs in their mansions—
Now swarm forth in rebellion, and demand
His death, who made their lives a jubilee;
While the few upon whom I have no claim
Are faithful! This is true, yet monstrous.

Zar. 'Tis

Perhaps too natural; for benefits
Turn poison in bad minds.
  Sar.   And good ones make
Good out of evil. Happier than the bee,
Which hives not but from wholesome flowers.
  Zar.   Then reap
The honey, nor enquire whence 'tis derived.
Be satisfied—you are not all abandon'd.
  Sar. My life insures me that. How long, bethink you,
Were not I yet a king, should I be mortal;
That is, where mortals *are*, not where they must be?
  Zar. I know not. But yet live for my—that is,
Your children's sake!
  Sar.   My gentle, wrong'd Zarina!
I am the very slave of circumstance
And impulse—borne away with every breath!
Misplaced upon the throne—misplaced in life.
I know not what I could have been, but feel
I am not what I should be—let it end.
But take this with thee: if I was not form'd
To prize a love like thine, a mind like thine,
Nor dote even on thy beauty—as I've doted
On lesser charms, for no cause save that such
Devotion was a duty, and I hated
All that look'd like a chain for me or others
(This even rebellion must avouch); yet hear
These words, perhaps among my last—that none
E'er valued more thy virtues, though he knew not
To profit by them—as the miner lights
Upon a vein of virgin ore, discovering
That which avails him nothing: he hath found it,
But 'tis not his—but some superior's, who
Placed him to dig, but not divide the wealth
Which sparkles at his feet; nor dare he lift
Nor poise it, but must grovel on, upturning
The sullen earth.
  Zar.   Oh! if thou hast at length

Discover'd that my love is worth esteem,
I ask no more—but let us hence together,
And *I*—let me say *we*—shall yet be happy.
Assyria is not all the earth—we'll find
A world out of our own—and be more bless'd
Than I have ever been, or thou, with all
An empire to indulge thee.

Enter SALEMENES.

  Sal.   I must part ye—
The moments, which must not be lost, are passing.
  Zar. Inhuman brother! wilt thou thus weigh out
Instants so high and blest?
  Sal.   Blest!
  Zar.   He hath been
So gentle with me, that I cannot think
Of quitting.
  Sal.   So—this feminine farewell
Ends as such partings end, in *no* departure.
I thought as much, and yielded against all
My better bodings. But it must not be.
  Zar. Not be?
  Sal.   Remain, and perish—
  Zar.   With my husband—
  Sal. And children.
  Zar.   Alas!
  Sal.   Hear me, sister, like
My sister:—all's prepared to make your safety
Certain, and of the boys too, our last hopes;
'Tis not a single question of mere feeling,
Though that were much—but 'tis a point of state:
The rebels would do more to seize upon
The offspring of their sovereign, and so crush—
  Zar. Ah! do not name it.
  Sal.   Well, then, mark me: when
They are safe beyond the Median's grasp, the rebels
Have miss'd their chief aim—the extinction of

The line of Nimrod. Though the present king
Fall, his sons live for victory and vengeance.
 Zar. But could not I remain, alone?
 Sal.   What! leave
Your children, with two parents and yet orphans—
In a strange land—so young, so distant?
 Zar.   No—
My heart will break.
 Sal.   Now you know all—decide.
 Sar. Zarina, he hath spoken well, and we
Must yield awhile to this necessity.
Remaining here, you may lose all; departing,
You save the better part of what is left
To both of us, and to such loyal hearts
As yet beat in these kingdoms.
 Sal.   The time presses.
 Sar. Go, then. If e'er we meet again, perhaps
I may be worthier of you—and, if not,
Remember that my faults, though not atoned for,
Are *ended*. Yet, I dread thy nature will
Grieve more above the blighted name and ashes
Which once were mightiest in Assyria—than—
But I grow womanish again, and must not;
I must learn sternness now. My sins have all
Been of the softer order—*hide* thy tears—
I do not bid thee *not* to shed them—'twere
Easier to stop Euphrates at its source
Than one tear of a true and tender heart—
But let me not behold them; they unman me
Here when I had remann'd myself. My brother,
Lead her away.
 Zar.   Oh, God! I never shall
Behold him more!
 Sal. (*striving to conduct her*). Nay, sister, I *must* be obey'd.
 Zar. I must remain—away! you shall not hold me.
What, shall he die alone?—*I* live alone?

Sal. He shall *not die alone;* but lonely you
Have lived for years.
  Zar.   That's false! I knew *he* lived,
And lived upon his image—let me go!
  Sal. (conducting her off the stage). Nay, then, I must use
    some fraternal force,
Which you will pardon.
  Zar.   Never. Help me! Oh!
Sardanapalus, wilt thou thus behold me
Torn from thee?
  Sal.   Nay—then all is lost again,
If that this moment is not gain'd.
  Zar.   My brain turns—
My eyes fail—where is he?   [*She faints.*
  Sar. (advancing.)   No—set her down—
She's dead—and you have slain her.
  Sal.   'Tis the mere
Faintness of o'erwrought passion: in the air
She will recover. Pray, keep back.—[*Aside.*] I must
Avail myself of this sole moment to
Bear her to where her children are embark'd,
I' the royal galley on the river. [SALEMENES *bears her off.*
  Sar. (solus).   This, too—
And this too must I suffer—I, who never
Inflicted purposely on human hearts
A voluntary pang! But that is false—
She loved me, and I loved her.—Fatal passion!
Why dost thou not expire *at once* in hearts
Which thou hast lighted up at once? Zarina!
I must pay dearly for the desolation
Now brought upon thee. Had I never loved
But thee, I should have been an unopposed
Monarch of honouring nations. To what gulfs
A single deviation from the track
Of human duties leads even those who claim
The homage of mankind as their born due,
And find it, till they forfeit it themselves!

Enter MYRRHA.

  Sar. You here! Who call'd you?
  Myr.   No one — but I heard
Far off a voice of wail and lamentation,
And thought —
  Sar.   It forms no portion of your duties
To enter here till sought for.
  Myr.   Though I might,
Perhaps, recal some softer words of yours
(Although they *too were chiding*), which reproved me,
Because I ever dreaded to intrude;
Resisting my own wish and your injunction
To heed no time nor presence, but approach you
Uncall'd for: — I retire.
  Sar.   Yet stay — being here.
I pray you pardon me: events have sour'd me
Till I wax peevish — heed it not: I shall
Soon be myself again.
  Myr.   I wait with patience,
What I shall see with pleasure.
  Sar.   Scarce a moment
Before your entrance in this hall, Zarina,
Queen of Assyria, departed hence.
  Myr. Ah!
  Sar.   Wherefore do you start?
  Myr.   Did I do so?
  Sar. 'Twas well you enter'd by another portal,
Else you had met. That pang at least is spared her.
  Myr. I know to feel for her.
  Sar.   That is too much,
And beyond nature — 'tis nor mutual
Nor possible. You cannot pity her,
Nor she aught but —
  Myr.   Despise the favourite slave?
Not more than I have ever scorn'd myself.
  Sar. Scorn'd! what, to be the envy of your sex,
And lord it o'er the heart of the world's lord?

Myr. Were you the lord of twice ten thousand worlds—
As you are like to lose the one you sway'd—
I did abase myself as much in being
Your paramour, as though you were a peasant—
Nay, more, if that the peasant were a Greek.
   Sar. You talk it well—
   Myr.   And truly.
   Sar.   In the hour
Of man's adversity all things grow daring
Against the falling; but as I am not
Quite fall'n, nor now disposed to bear reproaches,
Perhaps because I merit them too often,
Let us then part while peace is still between us.
   Myr. Part!
   Sar.   Have not all past human beings parted,
And must not all the present one day part?
   Myr. Why?
   Sar.   For your safety, which I will have look'd to,
With a strong escort to your native land;
And such gifts, as, if you had not been all
A queen, shall make your dowry worth a kingdom.
   Myr. I pray you talk not thus.
   Sar.   The queen is gone:
You need not shame to follow. I would fall
Alone—I seek no partners but in pleasure.
   Myr. And I no pleasure but in parting not.
You shall not force me from you.
   Sar.   Think well of it—
It soon may be too late.
   Myr.   So let it be;
For then you cannot separate me from you.
   Sar. And will not; but I thought you wish'd it.
   Myr.   I!
   Sar. You spoke of your abasement.
   Myr.   And I feel it
Deeply—more deeply than all things but love.
   Sar. Then fly from it.

Myr. 'Twill not recal the past—
'Twill not restore my honour, nor my heart.
No—here I stand or fall. If that you conquer,
I live to joy in your great triumph: should
Your lot be different, I'll not weep, but share it.
You did not doubt me a few hours ago.
    Sar. Your courage never—nor your love till now;
And none could make me doubt it save yourself.
Those words—
    Myr. Were words. I pray you, let the proofs
Be in the past acts you were pleased to praise
This very night, and in my further bearing,
Beside, wherever you are borne by fate.
    Sar. I am content: and, trusting in my cause,
Think we may yet be victors and return
To peace—the only victory I covet.
To me war is no glory—conquest no
Renown. To be forced thus to uphold my right
Sits heavier on my heart than all the wrongs
These men would bow me down with. Never, never
Can I forget this night, even should I live
To add it to the memory of others.
I thought to have made mine inoffensive rule
An era of sweet peace 'midst bloody annals,
A green spot amidst desert centuries,
On which the future would turn back and smile,
And cultivate, or sigh when it could not
Recal Sardanapalus' golden reign.
I thought to have made my realm a paradise,
And every moon an epoch of new pleasures.
I took the rabble's shouts for love—the breath
Of friends for truth—the lips of woman for
My only guerdon—so they are, my Myrrha: [*He kisses her.*
Kiss me. Now let them take my realm and life!
They shall have both, but never thee!
    Myr. No, never!
Man may despoil his brother man of all

That's great or glittering—kingdoms fall—hosts yield—
Friends fail—slaves fly—and all betray—and, more
Than all, the most indebted—but a heart
That loves without self-love! 'Tis here—now prove it.

Enter SALEMENES.

Sal. I sought you—How! *she* here again?
Sar. Return not
Now to reproof: methinks your aspect speaks
Of higher matter than a woman's presence.
Sal. The only woman whom it much imports me
At such a moment now is safe in absence—
The queen's embark'd.
Sar. And well? say that much.
Sal. Yes.
Her transient weakness has pass'd o'er; at least,
It settled into tearless silence: her
Pale face and glittering eye, after a glance
Upon her sleeping children, were still fix'd
Upon the palace towers as the swift galley
Stole down the hurrying stream beneath the starlight;
But she said nothing.
Sar. Would I felt no more
Than she has said!
Sal. 'Tis now too late to feel!
Your feelings cannot cancel a sole pang:
To change them, my advices bring sure tidings
That the rebellious Medes and Chaldees, marshall'd
By their two leaders, are already up
In arms again; and, scrrying their ranks,
Prepare to attack: they have apparently
Been join'd by other satraps.
Sar. What! more rebels?
Let us be first, then.
Sal. That were hardly prudent
Now, though it was our first intention. If
By noon to-morrow we are join'd by those

I've sent for by sure messengers, we shall be
In strength enough to venture an attack,
Ay, and pursuit too; but till then, my voice
Is to await the onset.
  Sar.   I detest
That waiting; though it seems so safe to fight
Behind high walls, and hurl down foes into
Deep fosses, or behold them sprawl on spikes
Strew'd to receive them, still I like it not—
My soul seems lukewarm; but when I set on them,
Though they were piled on mountains, I would have
A pluck at them, or perish in hot blood!—
Let me then charge.
  Sal.   You talk like a young soldier.
  Sar. I am no soldier, but a man: speak not
Of soldiership, I loathe the word, and those
Who pride themselves upon it; but direct me
Where I may pour upon them.
  Sal.   You must spare
To expose your life too hastily; 'tis not
Like mine or any other subject's breath:
The whole war turns upon it—with it; this
Alone creates it, kindles, and may quench it—
Prolong it—end it.
  Sar.   Then let us end both!
'Twere better thus, perhaps, than prolong either;
I'm sick of one, perchance of both.
        [*A trumpet sounds without.*
  Sal.   Hark!
  Sar.   Let us
Reply, not listen.
  Sal. And your wound!
  Sar.   'Tis bound—
'Tis heal'd—I had forgotten it. Away!
A leech's lancet would have scratch'd me deeper;
The slave that gave it might be well ashamed
To have struck so weakly.

Sal.   Now, may none this hour
Strike with a better aim!
    Sar.   Ay, if we conquer;
But if not, they will only leave to me
A task they might have spared their king. Upon them!
                                 [*Trumpet sounds again.*
    Sal. I am with you.
    Sar.   Ho, my arms! again, my arms!
                                       [*Exeunt.*

ACT V.

SCENE I.

The same Hall in the Palace.

MYRRHA *and* BALEA.

    Myr. (*at a window*). The day at last has broken. What a night
Hath usher'd it! How beautiful in heaven!
Though varied with a transitory storm,
More beautiful in that variety!
How hideous upon earth! where peace and hope,
And love and revel, in an hour were trampled
By human passions to a human chaos,
Not yet resolved to separate elements—
'Tis warring still! And can the sun so rise,
So bright, so rolling back the clouds into
Vapours more lovely than the unclouded sky,
With golden pinnacles, and snowy mountains,
And billows purpler than the ocean's, making
In heaven a glorious mockery of the earth,
So like we almost deem it permanent;
So fleeting, we can scarcely call it aught
Beyond a vision, 'tis so transiently
Scatter'd along the eternal vault: and yet
It dwells upon the soul, and soothes the soul,
And blends itself into the soul, until

Sunrise and sunset form the haunted epoch
Of sorrow and of love; which they who mark not,
Know not the realms where those twin genii
(Who chasten and who purify our hearts,
So that we would not change their sweet rebukes
For all the boisterous joys that ever shook
The air with clamour) build the palaces
Where their fond votaries repose and breathe
Briefly;—but in that brief cool calm inhale
Enough of heaven to enable them to bear
The rest of common, heavy, human hours,
And dream them through in placid sufferance;
Though seemingly employ'd like all the rest
Of toiling breathers in allotted tasks
Of pain or pleasure, *two* names for *one* feeling,
Which our internal, restless agony
Would vary in the sound, although the sense
Escapes our highest efforts to be happy.

 Bal. You muse right calmly: and can you so watch
The sunrise which may be our last?
 Myr.   It is
Therefore that I so watch it, and reproach
Those eyes, which never may behold it more,
For having look'd upon it oft, too oft,
Without the reverence and the rapture due
To that which keeps all earth from being as fragile
As I am in this form. Come, look upon it,
The Chaldee's god, which, when I gaze upon,
I grow almost a convert to your Baal.

 Bal. As now he reigns in heaven, so once on earth
He sway'd.

 Myr.   He sways it now far more, then; never
Had earthly monarch half the power and glory
Which centres in a single ray of his.

 Bal. Surely he is a god!

 Myr.   So we Greeks deem too;
And yet I sometimes think that gorgeous orb

Must rather be the abode of gods than one
Of the immortal sovereigns. Now he breaks
Through all the clouds, and fills my eyes with light
That shuts the world out. I can look no more.
 Bal. Hark! heard you not a sound?
 Myr.   No, 'twas mere fancy;
They battle it beyond the wall, and not
As in late midnight conflict in the very
Chambers: the palace has become a fortress
Since that insidious hour; and here, within
The very centre, girded by vast courts
And regal halls of pyramid proportions,
Which must be carried one by one before
They penetrate to where they then arrived,
We are as much shut in even from the sound
Of peril as from glory.
 Bal.   But they reach'd
Thus far before.
 Myr.   Yes, by surprise, and were
Beat back by valour: now at once we have
Courage and vigilance to guard us.
 Bal.   May they
Prosper!
 Myr. That is the prayer of many, and
The dread of more: it is an anxious hour;
I strive to keep it from my thoughts. Alas!
How vainly!
 Bal.   It is said the king's demeanour
In the late action scarcely more appall'd
The rebels than astonish'd his true subjects.
 Myr. 'Tis easy to astonish or appal
The vulgar mass which moulds a horde of slaves;
But he did bravely.
 Bal.   Slew he not Beleses?
I heard the soldiers say he struck him down.
 Myr. The wretch was overthrown, but rescued to
Triumph, perhaps, o'er one who vanquish'd him

In fight, as he had spared him in his peril;
And by that heedless pity risk'd a crown.
  Bal. Hark!
  Myr. You are right; some steps approach, but slowly.

Enter Soldiers, bearing in SALEMENES *wounded, with a broken Javelin in his Side: they seat him upon one of the Couches which furnish the Apartment.*

  Myr. Oh, Jove!
  Bal.   Then all is over.
  Sal.   That is false.
Hew down the slave who says so, if a soldier.
  Myr. Spare him — he's none: a mere court butterfly,
That flutters in the pageant of a monarch.
  Sal. Let him live on, then.
  Myr.   So wilt thou, I trust.
  Sal. I fain would live this hour out, and the event,
But doubt it. Wherefore did ye bear me here?
  Sol. By the king's order. When the javelin struck you,
You fell and fainted: 'twas his strict command
To bear you to this hall.
  Sal.   'Twas not ill done:
For seeming slain in that cold dizzy trance,
The sight might shake our soldiers — but — 'tis vain,
I feel it ebbing!
  Myr.   Let me see the wound;
I am not quite skilless: in my native land
'Tis part of our instruction. War being constant,
We are nerved to look on such things.
  Sol.   Best extract
The javelin.
  Myr.   Hold! no, no, it cannot be.
  Sal. I am sped, then!
  Myr.   With the blood that fast must follow
The extracted weapon, I do fear thy life.
  Sal. And I *not* death. Where was the king when you
Convey'd me from the spot where I was stricken?

Sol. Upon the same ground, and encouraging
With voice and gesture the dispirited troops
Who had seen you fall, and falter'd back.
    Sal.   Whom heard ye
Named next to the command?
    Sol.   I did not hear.
    Sal. Fly, then, and tell him, 'twas my last request
That Zames take my post until the junction,
So hoped for, yet delay'd, of Ofratanes,
Satrap of Susa. Leave me here: our troops
Are not so numerous as to spare your absence.
    Sol. But, prince—
    Sal.   Hence, I say! Here's a courtier and
A woman, the best chamber company.
As you would not permit me to expire
Upon the field, I'll have no idle soldiers
About my sick couch. Hence! and do my bidding!
                             [*Exeunt the Soldiers.*
    Myr. Gallant and glorious spirit! must the earth
So soon resign thee?
    Sal.   Gentle Myrrha, 'tis
The end I would have chosen, had I saved
The monarch or the monarchy by this;
As 'tis, I have not outlived them.
    Myr.   You wax paler.
    Sal. Your hand; this broken weapon but prolongs
My pangs, without sustaining life enough
To make me useful: I would draw it forth
And my life with it, could I but hear how
The fight goes.
             Enter SARDANAPALUS *and Soldiers.*
    Sar.   My best brother!
    Sal.   And the battle
Is lost?
    Sar. (*despondingly*). You see *me here.*
    Sal.   I'd rather see you *thus!*
        [*He draws out the weapon from the wound, and dies.*

Sar. And *thus* I will be seen; unless the succour,
The last frail reed of our beleaguer'd hopes,
Arrive with Ofratanes.
 Myr. Did you not
Receive a token from your dying brother,
Appointing Zames chief?
 Sar. I did.
 Myr. Where's Zames?
 Sar. Dead.
 Myr. And Altada?
 Sar. Dying.
 Myr. Pania? Sfero?
 Sar. Pania yet lives; but Sfero's fled or captive.
I am alone.
 Myr. And is all lost?
 Sar. Our walls,
Though thinly mann'd, may still hold out against
Their present force, or aught save treachery:
But i' the field—
 Myr. I thought 'twas the intent
Of Salemenes not to risk a sally
Till ye were strengthen'd by the expected succours.
 Sar. *I* over-ruled him.
 Myr. Well, the fault's a brave one.
 Sar. But fatal. Oh, my brother! I would give
These realms, of which thou wert the ornament,
The sword and shield, the sole-redeeming honour,
To call back—But I will not weep for thee;
Thou shalt be mourn'd for as thou wouldst be mourn'd.
It grieves me most that thou couldst quit this life
Believing that I could survive what thou
Hast died for—our long royalty of race.
If I redeem it, I will give thee blood
Of thousands, tears of millions, for atonement
(The tears of all the good are thine already).
If not, we meet again soon,—if the spirit
Within us lives beyond:—thou readest mine,

And dost me justice now. Let me once clasp
That yet warm hand, and fold that throbless heart
                    [*Embraces the body.*
To this which beats so bitterly   Now, bear
The body hence.
  Soldier.   Where?
  Sar.   To my proper chamber.
Place it beneath my canopy, as though
The king lay there: when this is done, we will
Speak further of the rites due to such ashes.
          [*Exeunt Soldiers with the body of* SALEMENES.

              Enter PANIA.

  Sar. Well, Pania! have you placed the guards, and issued
The orders fix'd on?
  Pan.   Sire, I have obey'd.
  Sar. And do the soldiers keep their hearts up?
  Pan.   Sire?
  Sar. I'm answer'd! When a king asks twice, and has
A question as an answer to *his* question,
It is a portent. What! they are dishearten'd?
  Pan. The death of Salemenes, and the shouts
Of the exulting rebels on his fall,
Have made them —
  Sar.   *Rage* — not droop — it should have been.
We'll find the means to rouse them.
  Pan.   Such a loss
Might sadden even a victory.
  Sar.   Alas!
Who can so feel it as I feel? but yet,
Though coop'd within these walls, they are strong, and we
Have those without will break their way through hosts,
To make their sovereign's dwelling what it was —
A palace; not a prison, nor a fortress.

          Enter an Officer, hastily.

  Sar. Thy face seems ominous. Speak!
  Offi.   I dare not.

Sar.   Dare not?
While millions dare revolt with sword in hand!
That's strange. I pray thee break that loyal silence
Which loathes to shock its sovereign; we can hear
Worse than thou hast to tell.
  Pan.   Proceed, thou hearest.
  Offi. The wall which skirted near the river's brink
Is thrown down by the sudden inundation
Of the Euphrates, which now rolling, swoln
From the enormous mountains where it rises,
By the late rains of that tempestuous region,
O'erfloods its banks, and hath destroy'd the bulwark.
  Pan. That's a black augury! it has been said
For ages, "That the city ne'er should yield
"To man, until the river grew its foe."
  Sar. I can forgive the omen, not the ravage.
How much is swept down of the wall?
  Offi.   About
Some twenty stadii.*
  Sar.   And all this is left
Pervious to the assailants?
  Offi.   For the present
The river's fury must impede the assault;
But when he shrinks into his wonted channel,
And may be cross'd by the accustom'd barks,
The palace is their own.
  Sar.   That shall be never.
Though men, and gods, and elements, and omens,
Have risen up 'gainst one who ne'er provoked them,
My father's house shall never be a cave
For wolves to horde and howl in.
  Pan.   With your sanction,
I will proceed to the spot, and take such measures
For the assurance of the vacant space
As time and means permit.
  Sar.   About it straight,

* About two miles and a half.

And bring me back, as speedily as full
And fair investigation may permit,
Report of the true state of this irruption
Of waters.   [*Exeunt* Pania *and the Officer.*
  Myr.   Thus the very waves rise up
Against you.
  Sar.   They are not my subjects, girl,
And may be pardon'd, since they can't be punish'd.
  Myr. I joy to see this portent shakes you not.
  Sar. I am past the fear of portents: they can tell me
Nothing I have not told myself since midnight:
Despair anticipates such things.
  Myr.   Despair!
  Sar. No; not despair precisely. When we know
All that can come, and how to meet it, our
Resolves, if firm, may merit a more noble
Word than this is to give it utterance.
But what are words to us? we have well nigh done
With them and all things.
  Myr.   Save *one deed*—the last
And greatest to all mortals; crowning act
Of all that was—or is—or is to be—
The only thing common to all mankind,
So different in their births, tongues, sexes, natures,
Hues, features, climes, times, feelings, intellects,
Without one point of union save in this,
To which we tend, for which we're born, and thread
The labyrinth of mystery, call'd life.
  Sar. Our clew being well nigh wound out, let's be cheer-
        ful.
They who have nothing more to fear may well
Indulge a smile at that which once appall'd;
As children at discover'd bugbears.
              Re-enter Pania.
  Pan.   'Tis
As was reported: I have order'd there
A double guard, withdrawing from the wall

Where it was strongest the required addition
To watch the breach occasion'd by the waters.
    Sar. You have done your duty faithfully, and as
My worthy Pania! further ties between us
Draw near a close. I pray you take this key: [*Gives a key.*
It opens to a secret chamber, placed
Behind the couch in my own chamber. (Now
Press'd by a nobler weight than e'er it bore—
Though a long line of sovereigns have lain down
Along its golden frame—as bearing for
A time what late was Salemenes). Search
The secret covert to which this will lead you;
'Tis full of treasure; take it for yourself
And your companions: there's enough to load ye
Though ye be many. Let the slaves be freed, too;
And all the inmates of the palace, of
Whatever sex, now quit it in an hour.
Thence launch the regal barks, once form'd for pleasure,
And now to serve for safety, and embark.
The river's broad and swoln, and uncommanded
(More potent than a king) by these besiegers.
Fly! and be happy!
    Pan.   Under your protection!
So you accompany your faithful guard.
    Sar. No, Pania! that must not be; get thee hence,
And leave me to my fate.
    Pan.   'Tis the first time
I ever disobey'd: but now—
    Sar.   So all men
Dare beard me now, and Insolence within
Apes Treason from without. Question no further;
'Tis my command, my last command. Wilt *thou*
Oppose it? *thou!*
    Pan.   But yet—not yet.
    Sar.   Well, then,
Swear that you will obey when I shall give
The signal.

Pan.   With a heavy but true heart,
I promise.
    Sar.   'Tis enough. Now order here
Faggots, pine-nuts, and wither'd leaves, and such
Things as catch fire and blaze with one sole spark;
Bring cedar, too, and precious drugs, and spices,
And mighty planks, to nourish a tall pile;
Bring frankincense and myrrh, too, for it is
For a great sacrifice I build the pyre;
And heap them round yon throne.
    Pan.   My lord!
    Sar.   I have said it,
And *you* have *sworn*.
    Pan.   And could keep my faith
Without a vow.   [*Exit* PANIA.
    Myr.   What mean you?
    Sar.   You shall know
Anon—what the whole earth shall ne'er forget.

        PANIA, *returning with a Herald.*

    Pan. My king, in going forth upon my duty,
This herald has been brought before me, craving
An audience.
    Sar.   Let him speak.
    Her.   The *King* Arbaces—
    Sar. What, crown'd already—But, proceed.
    Her.   Beleses,
The anointed high-priest—
    Sar.   Of what god or demon?
With new kings rise new altars. But, proceed;
You are sent to prate your master's will, and not
Reply to mine.
    Her.   And Satrap Ofratanes—
    Sar. Why, *he is ours*.
    Her. (*showing a ring*). Be sure that he is now
In the camp of the conquerors; behold
His signet ring.

Sar.   'Tis his. A worthy triad!
Poor Salemenes! thou hast died in time
To see one treachery the less: this man
Was thy true friend and my most trusted subject.
Proceed.
    Her.   They offer thee thy life, and freedom
Of choice to single out a residence
In any of the further provinces,
Guarded and watch'd, but not confined in person,
Where thou shalt pass thy days in peace; but on
Condition that the three young princes are
Given up as hostages.
    Sar. (*ironically*).   The generous victors!
    Her. I wait the answer.
    Sar.   Answer, slave! How long
Have slaves decided on the doom of kings?
    Her. Since they were free.
    Sar.   Mouthpiece of mutiny!
Thou at the least shalt learn the penalty
Of treason, though its proxy only. Pania!
Let his head be thrown from our walls within
The rebels' lines, his carcass down the river.
Away with him!   [PANIA *and the Guards seizing him.*
    Pan.   I never yet obey'd
Your orders with more pleasure than the present.
Hence with him, soldiers! do not soil this hall
Of royalty with treasonable gore;
Put him to rest without.
    Her.   A single word:
My office, king, is sacred.
    Sar.   And what's *mine?*
That thou shouldst come and dare to ask of me
To lay it down?
    Her.   I but obey'd my orders,
At the same peril if refused, as now
Incurr'd by my obedience.
    Sar.   So there are

ACT V.

New monarchs of an hour's growth as despotic
As sovereigns swathed in purple, and enthroned
From birth to manhood!
    Her.   My life waits your breath.
Yours (I speak humbly)—but it may be—yours
May also be in danger scarce less imminent:
Would it then suit the last hours of a line
Such as is that of Nimrod, to destroy
A peaceful herald, unarm'd, in his office;
And violate not only all that man
Holds sacred between man and man—but that
More holy tie which links us with the gods?
    Sar. He's right.—Let him go free.—My life's last act
Shall not be one of wrath. Here, fellow, take
              [*Gives him a golden cup from a table near.*
This golden goblet, let it hold your wine,
And think of *me;* or melt it into ingots,
And think of nothing but their weight and value.
    Her. I thank you doubly for my life, and this
Most gorgeous gift, which renders it more precious.
But must I bear no answer?
    Sar.   Yes,—I ask
An hour's truce to consider.
    Her.   But an hour's?
    Sar. An hour's: if at the expiration of
That time your masters hear no further from me,
They are to deem that I reject their terms,
And act befittingly.
    Her.   I shall not fail
To be a faithful legate of your pleasure.
    Sar. And hark! a word more.
    Her.   I shall not forget it,
Whate'er it be.
    Sar.   Commend me to Beleses;
And tell him, ere a year expire, I summon
Him hence to meet me.
    Her.   Where?

  Sar.   At Babylon.
At least from thence he will depart to meet me.
  Her. I shall obey you to the letter.   [*Exit Herald.*
  Sar.   Pania!—
Now, my good Pania!—quick—with what I order'd.
  Pan. My lord,—the soldiers are already charged.
And see! they enter.
    [*Soldiers enter, and form a Pile about the Throne, &c.*
  Sar.   Higher, my good soldiers,
And thicker yet; and see that the foundation
Be such as will not speedily exhaust
Its own too subtle flame; nor yet be quench'd
With aught officious aid would bring to quell it.
Let the throne form the *core* of it; I would not
Leave that, save fraught with fire unquenchable,
To the new comers. Frame the whole as if
'Twere to enkindle the strong tower of our
Inveterate enemies. Now it bears an aspect!
How say you, Pania, will this pile suffice
For a king's obsequies?
  Pan.   Ay, for a kingdom's.
I understand you, now.
  Sar.   And blame me?
  Pan.   No—
Let me but fire the pile, and share it with you.
  Myr. That duty's mine.
  Pan.   A woman's!
  Myr.   'Tis the soldier's
Part to die *for* his sovereign, and why not
The woman's with her lover?
  Pan.   'Tis most strange!
  Myr. But not so rare, my Pania, as thou think'st it.
In the mean time, live thou.—Farewell! the pile
Is ready.
  Pan. I should shame to leave my sovereign
With but a single female to partake
His death.

Sar.   Too many far have heralded
Me to the dust, already. Get thee hence;
Enrich thee.
    Pan.   And live wretched!
    Sar.   Think upon
Thy vow:—'tis sacred and irrevocable.
    Pan. Since it is so, farewell.
    Sar.   Search well my chamber,
Feel no remorse at bearing off the gold;
Remember, what you leave you leave the slaves
Who slew me: and when you have borne away
All safe off to your boats, blow one long blast
Upon the trumpet as you quit the palace.
The river's brink is too remote, its stream
Too loud at present to permit the echo
To reach distinctly from its banks. Then fly,—
And as you sail, turn back; but still keep on
Your way along the Euphrates: if you reach
The land of Paphlagonia, where the queen
Is safe with my three sons in Cotta's court,
Say, what you *saw* at parting, and request
That she remember what I *said* at one
Parting more mournful still.
    Pan.   That royal hand!
Let me then once more press it to my lips;
And these poor soldiers who throng round you, and
Would fain die with you!
        [*The Soldiers and* PANIA *throng round him, kissing
        his hand and the hem of his robe.*
    Sar.   My best! my last friends!
Let's not unman each other: part at once:
All farewells should be sudden, when for ever,
Else they make an eternity of moments,
And clog the last sad sands of life with tears.
Hence, and be happy: trust me, I am not
Now to be pitied; or far more for what
Is past than present;—for the future, 'tis

In the hands of the deities, if such
There be: I shall know soon.   Farewell—Farewell.
                        [*Exeunt* PANIA *and Soldiers.*
    Myr. These men were honest: it is comfort still
That our last looks should be on loving faces.
    Sar. And *lovely* ones, my beautiful!—but hear me!
If at this moment,—for we now are on
The brink,—thou feel'st an inward shrinking from
This leap through flame into the future, say it:
I shall not love thee less; nay, perhaps more,
For yielding to thy nature: and there's time
Yet for thee to escape hence.
    Myr.   Shall I light
One of the torches which lie heap'd beneath
The ever-burning lamp that burns without,
Before Baal's shrine, in the adjoining hall?
    Sar. Do so. Is that thy answer?
    Myr.   Thou shalt see.
                                [*Exit* MYRRHA.
    Sar. (*solus*). She's firm. My fathers! whom I will rejoin,
It may be, purified by death from some
Of the gross stains of too material being,
I would not leave your ancient first abode
To the defilement of usurping bondmen;
If I have not kept your inheritance
As ye bequeath'd it, this bright part of it,
Your treasure, your abode, your sacred relics
Of arms, and records, monuments, and spoils,
In which *they* would have revell'd, I bear with me
To you in that absorbing element,
Which most personifies the soul as leaving
The least of matter unconsumed before
Its fiery workings:—and the light of this
Most royal of funereal pyres shall be
Not a mere pillar form'd of cloud and flame,
A beacon in the horizon for a day,
And then a mount of ashes, but a light

To lesson ages, rebel nations, and
Voluptuous princes. Time shall quench full many
A people's records, and a hero's acts;
Sweep empire after empire, like this first
Of empires, into nothing; but even then
Shall spare this deed of mine, and hold it up
A problem few dare imitate, and none
Despise—but, it may be, avoid the life
Which led to such a consummation.

MYRRHA *returns with a lighted Torch in one Hand, and a Cup
in the other.*

Myr. Lo!
I've lit the lamp which lights us to the stars.
 Sar. And the cup?
 Myr. 'Tis my country's custom to
Make a libation to the gods.
 Sar. And mine
To make libations amongst men. I've not
Forgot the custom; and although alone,
Will drain one draught in memory of many
A joyous banquet past.
 [SARDANAPALUS *takes the cup, and after drinking and
 tinkling the reversed cup, as a drop falls, exclaims—*
 And this libation
Is for the excellent Beleses.
 Myr. Why
Dwells thy mind rather upon that man's name
Than on his mate's in villany?
 Sar. The one
Is a mere soldier, a mere tool, a kind
Of human sword in a friend's hand; the other
Is master-mover of his warlike puppet:
But I dismiss them from my mind.—Yet pause,
My Myrrha! dost thou truly follow me,
Freely and fearlessly?
 Myr. And dost thou think

A Greek girl dare not do for love, that which
An Indian widow braves for custom?
  Sar.   Then
We but await the signal.
  Myr.   It is long
In sounding.
  Sar. Now, farewell; one last embrace.
  Myr. Embrace, but *not* the last; there is one more.
  Sar. True, the commingling fire will mix our ashes.
  Myr. And pure as is my love to thee, shall they,
Purged from the dross of earth, and earthly passion,
Mix pale with thine. A single thought yet irks me.
  Sar. Say it.
  Myr.   It is that no kind hand will gather
The dust of both into one urn.
  Sar.   The better:
Rather let them be borne abroad upon
The winds of heaven, and scatter'd into air,
Than be polluted more by human hands
Of slaves and traitors. In this blazing palace,
And its enormous walls of reeking ruin,
We leave a nobler monument than Egypt
Hath piled in her brick mountains, o'er dead kings,
Or *kine*, for none know whether those proud piles
Be for their monarch, or their ox-god Apis:
So much for monuments that have forgotten
Their very record!
  Myr.   Then farewell, thou earth!
And loveliest spot of earth! farewell, Ionia!
Be thou still free and beautiful, and far
Aloof from desolation! My last prayer
Was for thee, my last thoughts, save *one*, were of thee!
  Sar. And that?
  Myr.   Is yours.
      [*The trumpet of* PANIA *sounds without.*
  Sar.   Hark!
  Myr.   *Now!*

ACT V.

Sar. Adieu, Assyria!
I loved thee well, my own, my fathers' land,
And better as my country than my kingdom.
I sated thee with peace and joys; and this
Is my reward! and now I owe thee nothing,
Not even a grave. [*He mounts the pile.*
 Now, Myrrha!
 Myr. Art thou ready?
Sar. As the torch in thy grasp.
 [MYRRHA *fires the pile.*
 Myr. 'Tis fired! I come.
 [*As* MYRRHA *springs forward to throw herself into the flames, the Curtain falls.*

WERNER;
OR,
THE INHERITANCE.
A TRAGEDY.

PREFACE.

THE following drama is taken entirely from the "*German's Tale, Kruitzner,*" published many years ago in *Lee's Canterbury Tales;* written (I believe) by two sisters, of whom one furnished only this story and another, both of which are considered superior to the remainder of the collection.* I have adopted the characters, plan, and even the language, of many parts of this story. Some of the characters are modified or altered, a few of the names changed, and one character (Ida of Stralenheim) added by myself: but in the rest the original is chiefly followed. When I was young (about fourteen, I think,) I first read this tale, which made a deep impression upon me; and may, indeed, be said to contain the germ of much that I have since written. I am not sure that it ever was very popular; or, at any rate, its popularity has since been eclipsed by that of other great writers in the same department. But I have generally found that those who *had* read it, agreed with me in their estimate

---

* This is not correct. "The Young Lady's Tale, or the Two Emily's," and "the Clergyman's Tale, or Pembroke," were contributed by Sophia Lee, the author of "The Recess," the comedy of "The Chapter of Accidents," and "Almoyda, a Tragedy," who died in 1824. The "German's Tale," and all the others in the Canterbury Collection, were written by Harriet, the younger of the sisters.

of the singular power of mind and conception which it developes. I should also add *conception*, rather than execution; for the story might, perhaps, have been developed with greater advantage. Amongst those whose opinions agreed with mine upon this story, I could mention some very high names: but it is not necessary, nor indeed of any use; for every one must judge according to his own feelings. I merely refer the reader to the original story, that he may see to what extent I have borrowed from it; and am not unwilling that he should find much greater pleasure in perusing it than the drama which is founded upon its contents.

I had begun a drama upon this tale so far back as 1815, (the first I ever attempted, except one at thirteen years old, called "*Ulric and Ilvina*," which I had sense enough to burn,) and had nearly completed an act, when I was interrupted by circumstances. This is somewhere amongst my papers in England; but as it has not been found, I have rewritten the first, and added the subsequent acts.

The whole is neither intended, nor in any shape adapted, for the stage.

Pisa, February, 1822.

TO
THE ILLUSTRIOUS GOETHE,
BY ONE OF HIS HUMBLEST ADMIRERS,

THIS TRAGEDY

IS DEDICATED.

DRAMATIS PERSONÆ.

MEN.

WERNER.	GABOR.	ARNHEIM.
ULRIC.	FRITZ.	MEISTER.
STRALENHEIM.	HENRICK.	RODOLPH.
IDENSTEIN.	ERIC.	LUDWIG.

WOMEN.

JOSEPHINE.   IDA STRALENHEIM.

Scene—Partly on the Frontier of Silesia, and partly in Siegendorf Castle, near Prague.

Time—the Close of the Thirty Years' War.

WERNER.

ACT I.

SCENE I.

The Hall of a decayed Palace near a small Town on the Northern Frontier of Silesia—the Night tempestuous.

WERNER *and* JOSEPHINE *his wife.*

Jos. My love, be calmer!
Wer. I am calm.
Jos. To me—
Yes, but not to thyself: thy pace is hurried,
And no one walks a chamber like to ours
With steps like thine when his heart is at rest.
Were it a garden, I should deem thee happy,
And stepping with the bee from flower to flower;
But *here!*
Wer. 'Tis chill; the tapestry lets through
The wind to which it waves: my blood is frozen.
Jos. Ah, no!
Wer. (smiling). Why! wouldst thou have it so?
Jos. I would
Have it a healthful current.
Wer. Let it flow
Until 'tis spilt or check'd—how soon, I care not.
Jos. And am I nothing in thy heart?
Wer. All—all.
Jos. Then canst thou wish for that which must break mine?
Wer. (approaching her slowly). But for *thee* I had been—
no matter what,
But much of good and evil; what I am,

Thou knowest; what I might or should have been,
Thou knowest not: but still I love thee, nor
Shall aught divide us.
    [WERNER *walks on abruptly, and then approaches*
    JOSEPHINE.
        The storm of the night
Perhaps affects me; I'm a thing of feelings,
And have of late been sickly, as, alas!
Thou know'st by sufferings more than mine, my love!
In watching me.
 Jos.   To see thee well is much—
To see thee happy—
 Wer.   Where hast thou seen such?
Let me be wretched with the rest!
 Jos.   But think
How many in this hour of tempest shiver
Beneath the biting wind and heavy rain,
Whose every drop bows them down nearer earth,
Which hath no chamber for them save beneath
Her surface.
 Wer. And that's not the worst: who cares
For chambers? rest is all. The wretches whom
Thou namest—ay, the wind howls round them, and
The dull and dropping rain saps in their bones
The creeping marrow. I have been a soldier,
A hunter, and a traveller, and am
A beggar, and should know the thing thou talk'st of.
 Jos. And art thou not now shelter'd from them all?
 Wer. Yes. And from these alone.
 Jos.   And that is something.
 Wer. True—to a peasant.
 Jos.   Should the nobly born
Be thankless for that refuge which their habits
Of early delicacy render more
Needful than to the peasant, when the ebb
Of fortune leaves them on the shoals of life?
 Wer. It is not that, thou know'st it is not; we

Have borne all this, I'll not say patiently,
Except in thee—but we have borne it.
  Jos.   Well?
  Wer. Something beyond our outward sufferings (though
These were enough to gnaw into our souls)
Hath stung me oft, and, more than ever, *now*.
When, but for this untoward sickness, which
Seized me upon this desolate frontier, and
Hath wasted, not alone my strength, but means,
And leaves us—no! this is beyond me!—but
For this I had been happy—*thou* been happy—
The splendour of my rank sustain'd—my name—
My father's name—been still upheld; and, more
Than those—
  Jos. (abruptly). My son—our son—our Ulric,
Been clasp'd again in these long-empty arms,
And all a mother's hunger satisfied.
Twelve years! he was but eight then:—beautiful
He was, and beautiful he must be now,
My Ulric! my adored!
  Wer.   I have been full oft
The chase of Fortune; now she hath o'ertaken
My spirit where it cannot turn at bay,—
Sick, poor, and lonely.
  Jos.   Lonely! my dear husband?
  Wer. Or worse—involving all I love, in this
Far worse than solitude. *Alone*, I had died,
And all been over in a nameless grave.
  Jos. And I had not outlived thee; but pray take
Comfort! We have struggled long; and they who strive
With Fortune win or weary her at last,
So that they find the goal or cease to feel
Further. Take comfort,—we shall find our boy.
  Wer. We were in sight of him, of every thing
Which could bring compensation for past sorrow—
And to be baffled thus!
  Jos.   We are not baffled.

Wer. Are we not penniless?
Jos. We ne'er were wealthy.
Wer. But I was born to wealth, and rank, and power;
Enjoy'd them, loved them, and, alas! abused them,
And forfeited them by my father's wrath,
In my o'er-fervent youth; but for the abuse
Long sufferings have atoned. My father's death
Left the path open, yet not without snares.
This cold and creeping kinsman, who so long
Kept his eye on me, as the snake upon
The fluttering bird, hath ere this time outstept me,
Become the master of my rights, and lord
Of that which lifts him up to princes in
Dominion and domain.
Jos. Who knows? our son
May have return'd back to his grandsire, and
Even now uphold thy rights for thee?
Wer. 'Tis hopeless.
Since his strange disappearance from my father's,
Entailing, as it were, my sins upon
Himself, no tidings have reveal'd his course.
I parted with him to his grandsire, on
The promise that his anger would stop short
Of the third generation; but Heaven seems
To claim her stern prerogative, and visit
Upon my boy his father's faults and follies.
Jos. I must hope better still,—at least we have yet
Baffled the long pursuit of Stralenheim.
Wer. We should have done, but for this fatal sickness;
More fatal than a mortal malady,
Because it takes not life, but life's sole solace:
Even now I feel my spirit girt about
By the snares of this avaricious fiend;—
How do I know he hath not track'd us here?
Jos. He does not know thy person; and his spies,
Who so long watch'd thee, have been left at Hamburgh.
Our unexpected journey, and this change

Of name, leaves all discovery far behind:
None hold us here for aught save what we seem.
    Wer. Save what we seem! save what we *are*—sick beg-
        gars,
Even to our very hopes.—Ha! ha!
    Jos.   Alas!
That bitter laugh!
    Wer.   Who would read in this form
The high soul of the son of a long line?
Who, in this garb, the heir of princely lands?
Who, in this sunken, sickly eye, the pride
Of rank and ancestry? In this worn cheek
And famine-hollow'd brow, the lord of halls
Which daily feast a thousand vassals?
    Jos.   You
Ponder'd not thus upon these worldly things,
My Werner! when you deign'd to choose for bride
The foreign daughter of a wandering exile.
    Wer. An exile's daughter with an outcast son
Were a fit marriage; but I still had hopes
To lift thee to the state we both were born for.
Your father's house was noble, though decay'd;
And worthy by its birth to match with ours.
    Jos. Your father did not think so, though 't was noble;
But had my birth been all my claim to match
With thee, I should have deem'd it what it is.
    Wer. And what is that in thine eyes?
    Jos.   All which it
Has done in our behalf,—nothing.
    Wer.   How,—nothing?
    Jos. Or worse; for it has been a canker in
Thy heart from the beginning: but for this,
We had not felt our poverty but as
Millions of myriads feel it, cheerfully;
But for these phantoms of thy feudal fathers,
Thou mightst have earn'd thy bread, as thousands earn it;

Or, if that seem too humble, tried by commerce,
Or other civic means, to amend thy fortunes.

   Wer. (*ironically*). And been an Hanseatic burgher? Excellent!

   Jos. Whate'er thou mightst have been, to me thou art
What no state high or low can ever change,
My heart's first choice;—which chose thee, knowing neither
Thy birth, thy hopes, thy pride; nought, save thy sorrows;
While they last, let me comfort or divide them;
When they end, let mine end with them, or thee!

   Wer. My better angel! such I have ever found thee;
This rashness, or this weakness of my temper,
Ne'er raised a thought to injure thee or thine.
Thou didst not mar my fortunes: my own nature
In youth was such as to unmake an empire,
Had such been my inheritance; but now,
Chasten'd, subdued, out-worn, and taught to know
Myself,—to lose this for our son and thee!
Trust me, when, in my two-and-twentieth spring,
My father barr'd me from my father's house,
The last sole scion of a thousand sires
(For I was then the last,) it hurt me less
Than to behold my boy and my boy's mother
Excluded in their innocence from what
My faults deserved—exclusion; although then
My passions were all living serpents, and
Twined like the gorgon's round me.

                              [*A loud knocking is heard.*
   Jos.   Hark!
   Wer.   A knocking!
   Jos. Who can it be at this lone hour? We have
Few visiters.

   Wer.   And poverty hath none,
Save those who come to make it poorer still.
Well, I am prepared.

            [WERNER *puts his hand into his bosom, as if to search for some weapon.*

Jos.   Oh! do not look so. I
Will to the door. It cannot be of import
In this lone spot of wintry desolation:—
The very desert saves man from mankind.
                    [*She goes to the door.*

                Enter IDENSTEIN.

   Iden. A fair good evening to my fairer hostess
And worthy—What's your name, my friend?
   Wer.   Are you
Not afraid to demand it?
   Iden.   Not afraid?
Egad! I am afraid. You look as if
I ask'd for something better than your name,
By the face you put on it.
   Wer.   Better, sir!
   Iden. Better or worse, like matrimony: what
Shall I say more? You have been a guest this month
Here in the prince's palace—(to be sure,
His highness had resign'd it to the ghosts
And rats these twelve years—but 'tis still a palace)—
I say you have been our lodger, and as yet
We do not know your name.
   Wer.   My name is Werner.
   Iden. A goodly name, a very worthy name
As e'er was gilt upon a trader's board:
I have a cousin in the lazaretto
Of Hamburgh, who has got a wife who bore
The same. He is an officer of trust,
Surgeon's assistant (hoping to be surgeon),
And has done miracles i' the way of business.
Perhaps you are related to my relative?
   Wer. To yours?
   Jos.   Oh, yes; we are, but distantly.
                    [*Aside to* WERNER.
Cannot you humour the dull gossip till
We learn his purpose?

Iden.   Well, I'm glad of that;
I thought so all along, such natural yearnings
Play'd round my heart:—blood is not water, cousin;
And so let's have some wine, and drink unto
Our better acquaintance: relatives should be
Friends.
    Wer. You appear to have drank enough already;
And if you had not, I've no wine to offer,
Else it were yours: but this you know, or should know:
You see I am poor, and sick, and will not see
That I would be alone; but to your business!
What brings you here?
    Iden.   Why, what should bring me here?
    Wer. I know not, though I think that I could guess
That which will send you hence.
    Jos. (aside).   Patience, dear Werner!
    Iden. You don't know what has happen'd, then?
    Jos.   How should we?
    Iden. The river has o'erflow'd.
    Jos.   Alas! we have known
That to our sorrow for these five days; since
It keeps us here.
    Iden.   But what you don't know is,
That a great personage, who fain would cross
Against the stream and three postilions' wishes,
Is drown'd below the ford, with five post-horses,
A monkey, and a mastiff, and a valet.
    Jos. Poor creatures! are you sure?
    Iden.   Yes, of the monkey,
And the valet, and the cattle; but as yet
We know not if his excellency's dead
Or no; your noblemen are hard to drown,
As it is fit that men in office should be;
But what is certain is, that he has swallow'd
Enough of the Oder to have burst two peasants;
And now a Saxon and Hungarian traveller,
Who, at their proper peril, snatch'd him from

The whirling river, have sent on to crave
A lodging, or a grave, according as
It may turn out with the live or dead body.
   Jos. And where will you receive him? here, I hope,
If we can be of service — say the word.
   Iden. Here? no; but in the prince's own apartment,
As fits a noble guest: — 'tis damp, no doubt,
Not having been inhabited these twelve years;
But then he comes from a much damper place,
So scarcely will catch cold in't, if he be
Still liable to cold — and if not, why
He'll be worse lodged to-morrow: ne'ertheless,
I have order'd fire and all appliances
To be got ready for the worst — that is,
In case he should survive.
   Jos.   Poor gentleman!
I hope he will, with all my heart.
   Wer.   Intendant,
Have you not learn'd his name? My Josephine,
                              [*Aside to his wife.*
Retire: I'll sift this fool.   [*Exit* JOSEPHINE.
   Iden.   His name? oh Lord!
Who knows if he hath now a name or no?
'Tis time enough to ask it when he's able
To give an answer; or if not, to put
His heir's upon his epitaph. Methought
Just now you chid me for demanding names?
   Wer. True, true, I did so; you say well and wisely.

              Enter GABOR.

   Gab. If I intrude, I crave —
   Iden.   Oh, no intrusion!
This is the palace; this a stranger like
Yourself; I pray you make yourself at home:
But where's his excellency? and how fares he?
   Gab. Wetly and wearily, but out of peril:
He paused to change his garments in a cottage,

21*

(Where I doff'd mine for these, and came on hither)
And has almost recover'd from his drenching.
He will be here anon.
 Iden.   What ho, there! bustle!
Without there, Herman, Weilburg, Peter, Conrad!
    [*Gives directions to different servants who enter.*
A nobleman sleeps here to-night—see that
All is in order in the damask chamber—
Keep up the stove—I will myself to the cellar—
And Madame Idenstein (my consort, stranger,)
Shall furnish forth the bed-apparel; for,
To say the truth, they are marvellous scant of this
Within the palace precincts, since his highness
Left it some dozen years ago. And then
His excellency will sup, doubtless?
 Gab.   Faith!
I cannot tell; but I should think the pillow
Would please him better than the table after
His soaking in your river: but for fear
Your viands should be thrown away, I mean
To sup myself, and have a friend without
Who will do honour to your good cheer with
A traveller's appetite.
 Iden.   But are you sure
His excellency—But his name: what is it?
 Gab. I do not know.
 Iden.   And yet you saved his life.
 Gab. I help'd my friend to do so.
 Iden.   Well, that's strange,
To save a man's life whom you do not know.
 Gab. Not so; for there are some I know so well,
I scarce should give myself the trouble.
 Iden.   Pray,
Good friend, and who may you be?
 Gab.   By my family,
Hungarian.
 Iden. Which is call'd?

Gab.   It matters little.

Iden. (aside). I think that all the world are grown anonymous,
Since no one cares to tell me what he's call'd!
Pray, has his excellency a large suite?
Gab.   Sufficient.
Iden. How many?
Gab.   I did not count them.
We came up by mere accident, and just
In time to drag him through his carriage window.

Iden. Well, what would I give to save a great man!
No doubt you'll have a swinging sum as recompense.
Gab. Perhaps.
Iden.   Now, how much do you reckon on?
Gab. I have not yet put up myself to sale:
In the mean time, my best reward would be
A glass of your Hochheimer — a *green* glass,
Wreath'd with rich grapes and Bacchanal devices,
O'erflowing with the oldest of your vintage;
For which I promise you, in case you e'er
Run hazard of being drown'd, (although I own
It seems, of all deaths, the least likely for you,)
I'll pull you out for nothing. Quick, my friend,
And think, for every bumper I shall quaff,
A wave the less may roll above your head.

Iden. (aside). I don't much like this fellow — close and dry
He seems, two things which suit me not; however
Wine he shall have; if that unlocks him not,
I shall not sleep to-night for curiosity.   [*Exit* IDENSTEIN.

Gab. (to WERNER). This master of the ceremonies is
The intendant of the palace, I presume:
'Tis a fine building, but decay'd.
Wer.   The apartment
Design'd for him you rescued will be found
In fitter order for a sickly guest.
Gab. I wonder then you occupied it not,
For you seem delicate in health.

Wer. (*quickly*). Sir!
Gab. Pray
Excuse me: have I said aught to offend you?
Wer. Nothing: but we are strangers to each other.
Gab. And that's the reason I would have us less so:
I thought our bustling guest without had said
You were a chance and passing guest, the counterpart
Of me and my companions.
Wer. Very true.
Gab. Then, as we never met before, and never,
It may be, may again encounter, why,
I thought to cheer up this old dungeon here
(At least to me) by asking you to share
The fare of my companions and myself.
Wer. Pray, pardon me; my health—
Gab. Even as you please.
I have been a soldier, and perhaps am blunt
In bearing.
Wer. I have also served, and can
Requite a soldier's greeting.
Gab. In what service?
The Imperial?
Wer. (*quickly, and then interrupting himself*). I commanded
—no—I mean
I served; but it is many years ago,
When first Bohemia raised her banner 'gainst
The Austrian.
Gab. Well, that's over now, and peace
Has turn'd some thousand gallant hearts adrift
To live as they best may; and, to say truth,
Some take the shortest.
Wer. What is that?
Gab. Whate'er
They lay their hands on. All Silesia and
Lusatia's woods are tenanted by bands
Of the late troops, who levy on the country
Their maintenance: the Chatelains must keep

Their castle walls—beyond them 'tis but doubtful
Travel for your rich count or full-blown baron.
My comfort is that, wander where I may,
I've little left to lose now.
 Wer.   And I—nothing.
 Gab. That's harder still. You say you were a soldier.
 Wer. I was.
 Gab.   You look one still. All soldiers are
Or should be comrades, even though enemies.
Our swords when drawn must cross, our engines aim
(While levell'd) at each other's hearts; but when
A truce, a peace, or what you will, remits
The steel into its scabbard, and lets sleep
The spark which lights the matchlock, we are brethren.
You are poor and sickly—I am not rich but healthy;
I want for nothing which I cannot want;
You seem devoid of this—wilt share it?
         [GABOR *pulls out his purse.*
 Wer.   Who
Told you I was a beggar?
 Gab.   You yourself,
In saying you were a soldier during peace-time.
 Wer. (*looking at him with suspicion*). You know me not?
 Gab.   I know no man, not even
Myself: how should I then know one I ne'er
Beheld till half an hour since?
 Wer.   Sir, I thank you.
Your offer's noble were it to a friend,
And not unkind as to an unknown stranger,
Though scarcely prudent; but no less I thank you.
I am a beggar in all save his trade;
And when I beg of any one, it shall be
Of him who was the first to offer what
Few can obtain by asking. Pardon me. [*Exit* WER.
 Gab. (*solus*). A goodly fellow by his looks, though worn,
As most good fellows are, by pain or pleasure,
Which tear life out of us before our time;

I scarce know which most quickly: but he seems
To have seen better days, as who has not
Who has seen yesterday?—But here approaches
Our sage intendant, with the wine: however,
For the cup's sake I'll bear the cupbearer.

Enter IDENSTEIN.

 Iden. 'Tis here! the supernaculum! twenty years
Of age, if 'tis a day.
 Gab.   Which epoch makes
Young women and old wine; and 'tis great pity,
Of two such excellent things, increase of years,
Which still improves the one, should spoil the other.
Fill full—Here's to our hostess!—your fair wife!
          [*Takes the glass.*
 Iden. Fair!—Well, I trust your taste in wine is equal
To that you show for beauty; but I pledge you
Nevertheless.
 Gab. Is not the lovely woman
I met in the adjacent hall, who, with
An air, and port, and eye, which would have better
Beseem'd this palace in its brightest days
('Though in a garb adapted to its present
Abandonment), return'd my salutation—
Is not the same your spouse?
 Iden.   I would she were!
But you're mistaken:—that's the stranger's wife.
 Gab. And by her aspect she might be a prince's:
Though time hath touch'd her too, she still retains
Much beauty, and more majesty.
 Iden.   And that
Is more than I can say for Madame Idenstein,
At least in beauty: as for majesty,
She has some of its properties which might
Be spared—but never mind!
 Gab.   I don't. But who

May be this stranger? He too hath a bearing
Above his outward fortunes.
  Iden.   There I differ.
He's poor as Job, and not so patient; but
Who he may be, or what, or aught of him,
Except his name (and that I only learn'd
To-night), I know not.
  Gab.   But how came he here?
  Iden. In a most miserable old caleche,
About a month since, and immediately
Fell sick, almost to death. He should have died.
  Gab. Tender and true!—but why?
  Iden.   Why, what is life
Without a living? He has not a stiver.
  Gab. In that case, I much wonder that a person
Of your apparent prudence should admit
Guests so forlorn into this noble mansion.
  Iden. That's true; but pity, as you know, *does* make
One's heart commit these follies; and besides,
They had some valuables left at that time,
Which paid their way up to the present hour;
And so I thought they might as well be lodged
Here as at the small tavern, and I gave them
The run of some of the oldest palace rooms.
They served to air them, at the least as long
As they could pay for fire-wood.
  Gab.   Poor souls!
  Iden.   Ay,
Exceeding poor.
  Gab.   And yet unused to poverty,
If I mistake not. Whither were they going?
  Iden. Oh! Heaven knows where, unless to heaven itself.
Some days ago that look'd the likeliest journey
For Werner.
  Gab.   Werner! I have heard the name:
But it may be a feign'd one.
  Iden.   Like enough!

But hark! a noise of wheels and voices, and
A blaze of torches from without. As sure
As destiny, his excellency's come.
I must be at my post: will you not join me,
To help him from his carriage, and present
Your humble duty at the door?
  Gab.   I dragg'd him
From out that carriage when he would have given
His barony or county to repel
The rushing river from his gurgling throat.
He has valets now enough: they stood aloof then,
Shaking their dripping ears upon the shore,
All roaring "Help!" but offering none; and as
For *duty* (as you call it)—I did mine *then*,
Now do *yours*. Hence, and bow and cringe him here!
  Iden. *I* cringe!—but I shall lose the opportunity—
Plague take it! he'll be *here*, and I *not there!*
        [*Exit* IDENSTEIN *hastily.*

    Re-enter WERNER.

  Wer. (*to himself*). I heard a noise of wheels and voices. How
All sounds now jar me!
      Still here! Is he not
        [*Perceiving* GABOR.
A spy of my pursuer's? His frank offer
So suddenly, and to a stranger, wore
The aspect of a secret enemy;
For friends are slow at such.
  Gab.   Sir, you seem rapt;
And yet the time is not akin to thought.
These old walls will be noisy soon. The baron,
Or count (or whatsoe'er this half-drown'd noble
May be), for whom this desolate village and
Its lone inhabitants show more respect
Than did the elements, is come.
  Iden.(*without*).   This way—
This way, your excellency:—have a care,
The staircase is a little gloomy, and

Somewhat decay'd; but if we had expected
So high a guest—Pray take my arm, my lord!

Enter STRALENHEIM, IDENSTEIN, *and Attendants — partly his own, and partly Retainers of the Domain of which* IDENSTEIN *is Intendant.*

 Stral. I'll rest me here a moment.
 Iden. (*to the servants*).   Ho! a chair!
Instantly, knaves!   [STRALENHEIM *sits down.*
 Wer. (*aside*). 'Tis he!
 Stral.   I'm better now.
Who are these strangers?
 Iden.   Please you, my good lord,
One says he is no stranger.
 Wer. (*aloud and hastily*). Who says that?
      [*They look at him with surprise.*
 Iden. Why, no one spoke *of you*, or *to you!*—but
Here's one his excellency may be pleased
To recognise.   [*Pointing to* GABOR.
 Gab. I seek not to disturb
His noble memory.
 Stral.   I apprehend
This is one of the strangers to whose aid
I owe my rescue. Is not that the other?
      [*Pointing to* WERNER.
My state when I was succour'd must excuse
My uncertainty to whom I owe so much.
 Iden. He!—no, my lord! he rather wants for rescue
Than can afford it. 'Tis a poor sick man,
Travel-tired, and lately risen from a bed
From whence he never dream'd to rise.
 Stral.   Methought
That there were two.
 Gab.   There were, in company;
But, in the service render'd to your lordship,
I needs must say but *one*, and he is absent.
The chief part of whatever aid was render'd

Was *his:* it was his fortune to be first.
My will was not inferior, but his strength
And youth outstripp'd me; therefore do not waste
Your thanks on me. I was but a glad second
Unto a nobler principal.
  Stral.   Where is he?
  An Atten. My lord, he tarried in the cottage where
Your excellency rested for an hour,
And said he would be here to-morrow.
  Stral.   Till
That hour arrives, I can but offer thanks,
And then—
  Gab. I seek no more, and scarce deserve
So much. My comrade may speak for himself.
  Stral. (fixing his eyes upon WERNER: *then aside).*
It cannot be! and yet he must be look'd to.
'Tis twenty years since I beheld him with
These eyes; and, though my agents still have kept
Theirs on him, policy has held aloof
My own from his, not to alarm him into
Suspicion of my plan. Why did I leave
At Hamburgh those who would have made assurance
If this be he or no? I thought, ere now,
To have been lord of Siegendorf, and parted
In haste, though even the elements appear
To fight against me, and this sudden flood
May keep me prisoner here till—
   [*He pauses, and looks at* WERNER; *then resumes.*
         This man must
Be watch'd. If it is he, he is so changed,
His father, rising from his grave again,
Would pass him by unknown. I must be wary:
An error would spoil all.
  Iden.   Your lordship seems
Pensive. Will it not please you to pass on?
  Stral. 'Tis past fatigue which gives my weigh'd-down spirit
An outward show of thought. I will to rest.

Iden. The prince's chamber is prepared, with all
The very furniture the prince used when
Last here, in its full splendour.
                    (*Aside*). Somewhat tatter'd,
And devilish damp, but fine enough by torch-light;
And that's enough for your right noble blood
Of twenty quarterings upon a hatchment;
So let their bearer sleep 'neath something like one
Now, as he one day will for ever lie.
    Stral. (*rising and turning to* GABOR). Good night, good
            people! Sir, I trust to-morrow
Will find me apter to requite your service.
In the mean time I crave your company
A moment in my chamber.
    Gab.   I attend you.
    Stral. (*after a few steps, pauses, and calls* WERNER.) Friend!
    Wer.   Sir!
    Iden. Sir! Lord—oh Lord! Why don't you say
His lordship, or his excellency? Pray
My lord, excuse this poor man's want of breeding:
He hath not been accustom'd to admission
To such a presence.
    Stral. (*to* IDENSTEIN). Peace, intendant!
    Iden.   Oh!
I am dumb.
    Stral. (*to* WERNER). Have you been long here?
    Wer.   Long?
    Stral.   I sought
An answer, not an echo.
    Wer.   You may seek
Both from the walls. I am not used to answer
Those whom I know not.
    Stral.   Indeed! Ne'er the less,
You might reply with courtesy to what
Is ask'd in kindness.
    Wer.   When I know it such,
I will requite—that is, *reply*—in unison.

Stral. The intendant said, you had been detain'd by
            sickness —
If I could aid you — journeying the same way?
    Wer. (quickly). I am not journeying the same way!
    Stral.   How know ye
That, ere you know my route?
    Wer.   Because there is
But one way that the rich and poor must tread
Together. You diverged from that dread path
Some hours ago, and I some days: henceforth
Our roads must lie asunder, though they tend
All to one home.
    Stral.   Your language is above
Your station.
    Wer. (bitterly). Is it?
    Stral.   Or, at least, beyond
Your garb.
    Wer.   'Tis well that it is not beneath it,
As sometimes happens to the better clad.
But, in a word, what would you with me?
    Stral. (startled).   I?
    Wer. Yes — you! You know me not, and question me,
And wonder that I answer not — not knowing
My inquisitor. Explain what you would have,
And then I'll satisfy yourself, or me.
    Stral. I knew not that you had reasons for reserve.
    Wer. Many have such: — Have you none?
    Stral.   None which can
Interest a mere stranger.
    Wer.   Then forgive
The same unknown and humble stranger, if
He wishes to remain so to the man
Who can have nought in common with him.
    Stral.   Sir,
I will not balk your humour, though untoward:
I only meant you service — but good night!

Intendant, show the way! (*to* GABOR). Sir, you will with me?

[*Exeunt* STRALENHEIM *and attendants;* IDENSTEIN *and* GABOR.

Wer. (*solus*). 'Tis he! I am taken in the toils. Before
I quitted Hamburgh, Giulio, his late steward,
Inform'd me that he had obtain'd an order
From Brandenburg's elector, for the arrest
Of Kruitzner (such the name I then bore) when
I came upon the frontier; the free city
Alone preserved my freedom—till I left
Its walls—fool that I was to quit them! But
I deem'd this humble garb, and route obscure,
Had baffled the slow hounds in their pursuit.
What's to be done? He knows me not by person;
Nor could aught, save the eye of apprehension,
Have recognised *him*, after twenty years,
We met so rarely and so coldly in
Our youth. But those about him! Now I can
Divine the frankness of the Hungarian, who
No doubt is a mere tool and spy of Stralenheim's,
To sound and to secure me. Without means!
Sick, poor—begirt too with the flooding rivers,
Impassable even to the wealthy, with
All the appliances which purchase modes
Of overpowering peril with men's lives,—
How can I hope! An hour ago methought
My state beyond despair; and now, 'tis such,
The past seems paradise. Another day,
And I'm detected,—on the very eve
Of honours, rights, and my inheritance,
When a few drops of gold might save me still
In favouring an escape.

Enter IDENSTEIN *and* FRITZ *in conversation.*

Fritz. Immediately.
Iden. I tell you, 'tis impossible.

Fritz. It must
Be tried, however; and if one express
Fail, you must send on others, till the answer
Arrives from Frankfort, from the commandant.
   Iden. I will do what I can.
   Fritz. And recollect
To spare no trouble; you will be repaid
Tenfold.
   Iden. The baron is retired to rest?
   Fritz. He hath thrown himself into an easy chair
Beside the fire, and slumbers; and has order'd
He may not be disturb'd until eleven,
When he will take himself to bed.
   Iden. Before
An hour is past I'll do my best to serve him.
   Fritz. Remember! [*Exit* Fritz.
   Iden. The devil take these great men! they
Think all things made for them. Now here must I
Rouse up some half a dozen shivering vassals
From their scant pallets, and, at peril of
Their lives, despatch them o'er the river towards
Frankfort. Methinks the baron's own experience
Some hours ago might teach him fellow-feeling:
But no, "it *must*," and there's an end. How now?
Are you there, Mynheer Werner?
   Wer. You have left
Your noble guest right quickly.
   Iden. Yes — he's dozing,
And seems to like that none should sleep besides.
Here is a packet for the commandant
Of Frankfort, at all risks and all expenses;
But I must not lose time: Good night! [*Exit* Iden.
   Wer. "To Frankfort!"
So, so, it thickens! Ay, "the commandant."
This tallies well with all the prior steps
Of this cool, calculating fiend, who walks
Between me and my father's house. No doubt

He writes for a detachment to convey me
Into some secret fortress. — Sooner than
This—
   [WERNER *looks around, and snatches up a knife ly-
   ing on a table in a recess.*
  Now I am master of myself at least.
Hark,—footsteps! How do I know that Stralenheim
Will wait for even the show of that authority
Which is to overshadow usurpation?
That he suspects me's certain. I'm alone;
He with a numerous train. I weak; he strong
In gold, in numbers, rank, authority.
I nameless, or involving in my name
Destruction, till I reach my own domain;
He full-blown with his titles, which impose
Still further on these obscure petty burghers
Than they could do elsewhere. Hark! nearer still!
I'll to the secret passage, which communicates
With the—No! all is silent—'twas my fancy!—
Still as the breathless interval between
The flash and thunder:—I must hush my soul
Amidst its perils. Yet I will retire,
To see if still be unexplored the passage
I wot of: it will serve me as a den
Of secrecy for some hours, at the worst.
  [WERNER *draws a panel, and exit, closing it after him.*
   Enter GABOR *and* JOSEPHINE.
 Gab. Where is your husband?
 Jos.   *Here*, I thought: I left him
Not long since in his chamber. But these rooms
Have many outlets, and he may be gone
To accompany the intendant.
 Gab.   Baron Stralenheim
Put many questions to the intendant on
The subject of your lord, and, to be plain,
I have my doubts if he means well.
 Jos.   Alas!

What can there be in common with the proud
And wealthy baron, and the unknown Werner?
   Gab. That you know best.
   Jos.   Or, if it were so, how
Come you to stir yourself in his behalf,
Rather than that of him whose life you saved?
   Gab. I help'd to save him, as in peril; but
I did not pledge myself to serve him in
Oppression. I know well these nobles, and
Their thousand modes of trampling on the poor.
I have proved them; and my spirit boils up when
I find them practising against the weak:—
This is my only motive.
   Jos.   It would be
Not easy to persuade my consort of
Your good intentions.
   Gab.   Is he so suspicious?
   Jos. He was not once; but time and troubles have
Made him what you beheld.
   Gab.   I'm sorry for it.
Suspicion is a heavy armour, and
With its own weight impedes more than protects.
Good night! I trust to meet with him at daybreak.
                                  [*Exit* GABOR.

   Re-enter IDENSTEIN *and some Peasants.* JOSEPHINE *retires up the Hall.*

   First Peasant. But if I'm drown'd?
   Iden. Why, you will be well paid for 't,
And have risk'd more than drowning for as much,
I doubt not.
   Second Peasant. But our wives and families?
   Iden. Cannot be worse off than they are, and may
Be better.
   Third Peasant. I have neither, and will venture.
   Iden. That's right. A gallant carle, and fit to be
A soldier. I'll promote you to the ranks

In the prince's body-guard—if you succeed;
And you shall have besides, in sparkling coin,
Two thalers.
   Third Peasant. No more!
   Iden.   Out upon your avarice!
Can that low vice alloy so much ambition?
I tell thee, fellow, that two thalers in
Small change will subdivide into a treasure.
Do not five hundred thousand heroes daily
Risk lives and souls for the tithe of one thaler?
When had you half the sum?
   Third Peasant.   Never—but ne'er
The less I must have three.
   Iden.   Have you forgot
Whose vassal you were born, knave?
   Third Peasant.   No—the prince's,
And not the stranger's.
   Iden.   Sirrah! in the prince's
Absence, I'm sovereign; and the baron is
My intimate connection;—"Cousin Idenstein!
(Quoth he) you'll order out a dozen villains."
And so, you villains! troop—march—march, I say;
And if a single dog's-ear of this packet
Be sprinkled by the Oder—look to it!
For every page of paper, shall a hide
Of yours be stretch'd as parchment on a drum,
Like Ziska's skin, to beat alarm to all
Refractory vassals, who can not effect
Impossibilities—Away, ye earth-worms!
                            [*Exit, driving them out.*
   Jos. (*coming forward*). I fain would shun these scenes,
        too oft repeated,
Of feudal tyranny o'er petty victims;
I cannot aid, and will not witness such.
Even here, in this remote, unnamed, dull spot,
The dimmest in the district's map, exist
The insolence of wealth in poverty

O'er something poorer still—the pride of rank
In servitude, o'er something still more servile;
And vice in misery affecting still
A tatter'd splendour. What a state of being!
In Tuscany, my own dear sunny land,
Our nobles were but citizens and merchants,
Like Cosmo. We had evils, but not such
As these; and our all-ripe and gushing valleys
Made poverty more cheerful, where each herb
Was in itself a meal, and every vine
Rain'd, as it were, the beverage which makes glad
The heart of man; and the ne'er unfelt sun
(But rarely clouded, and when clouded, leaving
His warmth behind in memory of his beams)
Makes the worn mantle, and the thin robe, less
Oppressive than an emperor's jewell'd purple.
But, here! the despots of the north appear
To imitate the ice-wind of their clime,
Searching the shivering vassal through his rags,
To wring his soul—as the bleak elements
His form. And 'tis to be amongst these sovereigns
My husband pants! and such his pride of birth—
That twenty years of usage, such as no
Father born in a humble state could nerve
His soul to persecute a son withal,
Hath changed no atom of his early nature;
But I, born nobly also, from my father's
Kindness was taught a different lesson. Father!
May thy long-tried and now rewarded spirit
Look down on us and our so long desired
Ulric! I love my son, as thou didst me!
What's that? Thou, Werner! can it be? and thus?

Enter WERNER *hastily, with the knife in his hand, by the secret panel, which he closes hurriedly after him.*

Wer. (*not at first recognising her*). Discover'd! then I'll
    stab—(*recognising her.*)

Ah! Josephine,
Why art thou not at rest?
   Jos.   What rest? My God!
What doth this mean?
   Wer. (*showing a rouleau*). Here's *gold—gold*, Josephine,
Will rescue us from this detested dungeon.
   Jos. And how obtain'd?—that knife!
   Wer.   'Tis bloodless—*yet.*
Away—we must to our chamber.
   Jos.   But whence comest thou?
   Wer. Ask not! but let us think where we shall go—
This—this will make us way—(*showing the gold*)—I'll fit
      them now.
   Jos. I dare not think thee guilty of dishonour.
   Wer. Dishonour!
   Jos.   I have said it.
   Wer.   Let us hence:
'Tis the last night, I trust, that we need pass here.
   Jos. And not the worst, I hope.
   Wer.   Hope! I make *sure.*
But let us to our chamber.
   Jos.   Yet one question—
What hast thou *done?*
   Wer. (*fiercely*).   Left one thing *undone*, which
Had made all well: let me not think of it!
Away!
   Jos. Alas, that I should doubt of thee!   [*Exeunt.*

ACT II.

SCENE I.

A Hall in the same Palace.

Enter IDENSTEIN *and Others.*

   Iden. Fine doings! goodly doings! honest doings!
A baron pillaged in a prince's palace!
Where, till this hour, such a sin ne'er was heard of.

Fritz. It hardly could, unless the rats despoil'd
The mice of a few shreds of tapestry.
 Iden. Oh! that I e'er should live to see this day!
The honour of our city's gone for ever.
 Fritz. Well, but now to discover the delinquent:
The baron is determined not to lose
This sum without a search.
 Iden. And so am I.
 Fritz. But whom do you suspect?
 Iden. Suspect! all people
Without—within—above—below—Heaven help me!
 Fritz. Is there no other entrance to the chamber?
 Iden. None whatsoever.
 Fritz. Are you sure of that?
 Iden. Certain. I have lived and served here since my birth,
And if there were such, must have heard of such,
Or seen it.
 Fritz. Then it must be some one who
Had access to the antechamber.
 Iden. Doubtless.
 Fritz. The man call'd *Werner*'s poor!
 Iden. Poor as a miser.
But lodged so far off, in the other wing,
By which there's no communication with
The baron's chamber, that it can't be he.
Besides, I bade him "good night" in the hall,
Almost a mile off, and which only leads
To his own apartment, about the same time
When this burglarious, larcenous felony
Appears to have been committed.
 Fritz. There's another,
The stranger—
 Iden. The Hungarian?
 Fritz. He who help'd
To fish the baron from the Oder.
 Iden. Not

Unlikely. But, hold—might it not have been
One of the suite?
  Fritz.   How? *We*, sir!
  Iden.   No—not *you*,
But some of the inferior knaves. You say
The baron was asleep in the great chair—
The velvet chair—in his embroider'd night-gown;
His toilet spread before him, and upon it
A cabinet with letters, papers, and
Several rouleaux of gold; of which *one* only
Has disappear'd:—the door unbolted, with
No difficult access to any.
  Fritz.   Good sir,
Be not so quick; the honour of the corps
Which forms the baron's household's unimpeach'd
From steward to scullion, save in the fair way
Of peculation; such as in accompts,
Weights, measures, larder, cellar, buttery,
Where all men take their prey; as also in
Postage of letters, gathering of rents,
Purveying feasts, and understanding with
The honest trades who furnish noble masters:
But for your petty, picking, downright thievery,
We scorn it as we do board-wages. Then
Had one of our folks done it, he would not
Have been so poor a spirit as to hazard
His neck for *one* rouleau, but have swoop'd all;
Also the cabinet, if portable.
  Iden. There is some sense in that—
  Fritz.   No, sir, be sure
'Twas none of our corps; but some petty, trivial
Picker and stealer, without art or genius.
The only question is—Who else could have
Access, save the Hungarian and yourself?
  Iden. You don't mean me?
  Fritz.   No, sir; I honour more
Your talents—

Iden.   And my principles, I hope.
Fritz. Of course. But to the point: What's to be done?
Iden. Nothing — but there's a good deal to be said.
We'll offer a reward; move heaven and earth,
And the police (though there's none nearer than
Frankfort); post notices in manuscript
(For we've no printer); and set by my clerk
To read them (for few can, save he and I).
We'll send out villains to strip beggars, and
Search empty pockets; also, to arrest
All gipsies, and ill-clothed and sallow people.
Prisoners we'll have at least, if not the culprit;
And for the baron's gold — if 'tis not found,
At least he shall have the full satisfaction
Of melting twice its substance in the raising
The ghost of this rouleau. Here's alchymy
For your lord's losses!
  Fritz.   He hath found a better.
  Iden. Where?
  Fritz.   In a most immense inheritance.
The late Count Siegendorf, his distant kinsman,
Is dead near Prague, in his castle, and my lord
Is on his way to take possession.
  Iden.   Was there
No heir?
  Fritz. Oh, yes; but he has disappear'd
Long from the world's eye, and perhaps the world.
A prodigal son, beneath his father's ban
For the last twenty years; for whom his sire
Refused to kill the fatted calf; and, therefore,
If living, he must chew the husks still. But
The baron would find means to silence him,
Were he to re-appear: he's politic,
And has much influence with a certain court.
  Iden. He's fortunate.
  Fritz.   'Tis true, there is a grandson,
Whom the late count reclaim'd from his son's hands

And educated as his heir; but then
His birth is doubtful.
  Iden.   How so?
  Fritz.   His sire made
A left-hand, love, imprudent sort of marriage,
With an Italian exile's dark-eyed daughter:
Noble, they say, too; but no match for such
A house as Siegendorf's. The grandsire ill
Could brook the alliance; and could ne'er be brought
To see the parents, though he took the son.
  Iden. If he's a lad of mettle, he may yet
Dispute your claim, and weave a web that may
Puzzle your baron to unravel.
  Fritz.   Why,
For mettle, he has quite enough: they say,
He forms a happy mixture of his sire
And grandsire's qualities,—impetuous as
The former, and deep as the latter; but
The strangest is, that he too disappear'd
Some months ago.
  Iden.   The devil he did!
  Fritz.   Why, yes:
It must have been at his suggestion, at
An hour so critical as was the eve
Of the old man's death, whose heart was broken by it.
  Iden. Was there no cause assign'd?
  Fritz.   Plenty, no doubt,
And none perhaps the true one. Some averr'd
It was to seek his parents; some because
The old man held his spirit in so strictly
(But that could scarce be, for he doted on him);
A third believed he wish'd to serve in war,
But peace being made soon after his departure,
He might have since return'd, were that the motive;
A fourth set charitably have surmised,
As there was something strange and mystic in him,
That in the wild exuberance of his nature

He had join'd the black bands, who lay waste Lusatia,
The mountains of Bohemia and Silesia,
Since the last years of war had dwindled into
A kind of general condotticro system
Of bandit warfare; each troop with its chief,
And all against mankind.
  Iden.   That cannot be.
A young heir, bred to wealth and luxury,
To risk his life and honours with disbanded
Soldiers and desperadoes!
  Fritz.   Heaven best knows!
But there are human natures so allied
Unto the savage love of enterprise,
That they will seek for peril as a pleasure.
I've heard that nothing can reclaim your Indian,
Or tame the tiger, though their infancy
Were fed on milk and honey. After all,
Your Wallenstein, your Tilly and Gustavus,
Your Bannier, and your Torstenson and Weimar,
Were but the same thing upon a grand scale;
And now that they are gone, and peace proclaim'd,
They who would follow the same pastime must
Pursue it on their own account. Here comes
The baron, and the Saxon stranger, who
Was his chief aid in yesterday's escape,
But did not leave the cottage by the Oder
Until this morning.
     Enter STRALENHEIM *and* ULRIC.
  Stral.   Since you have refused
All compensation, gentle stranger, save
Inadequate thanks, you almost check even them,
Making me feel the worthlessness of words,
And blush at my own barren gratitude,
They seem so niggardly, compared with what
Your courteous courage did in my behalf—
  Ulr. I pray you press the theme no further.
  Stral.   But

Can I not serve you? You are young, and of
That mould which throws out heroes; fair in favour;
Brave, I know, by my living now to say so;
And doubtlessly, with such a form and heart,
Would look into the fiery eyes of war,
As ardently for glory as you dared
An obscure death to save an unknown stranger
In an as perilous, but opposite, element.
You are made for the service: I have served;
Have rank by birth and soldiership, and friends,
Who shall be yours. 'Tis true this pause of peace
Favours such views at present scantily;
But 't will not last, men's spirits are too stirring;
And, after thirty years of conflict, peace
Is but a petty war, as the times show us
In every forest, or a mere arm'd truce.
War will reclaim his own; and, in the meantime,
You might obtain a post, which would ensure
A higher soon, and, by my influence, fail not
To rise. I speak of Brandenburg, wherein
I stand well with the elector; in Bohemia,
Like you, I am a stranger, and we are now
Upon its frontier.
 Ulr.   You perceive my garb
Is Saxon, and of course my service due
To my own sovereign. If I must decline
Your offer, 'tis with the same feeling which
Induced it.
 Stral. Why, this is mere usury!
I owe my life to you, and you refuse
The acquaintance of the interest of the debt,
To heap more obligations on me, till
I bow beneath them.
 Ulr.   You shall say so when
I claim the payment.
 Stral. Well, sir, since you will not—
You are nobly born?

Ulr.   I have heard my kinsmen say so.
Stral. Your actions show it. Might I ask your name?
Ulr. Ulric.
Stral.   Your house's?
Ulr.   When I'm worthy of it,
I'll answer you.
 Stral. (aside). Most probably an Austrian,
Whom these unsettled times forbid to boast
His lineage on these wild and dangerous frontiers,
Where the name of his country is abhorr'd.
        [*Aloud to* Fritz *and* Idenstein.
So, sirs! how have ye sped in your researches?
 Iden. Indifferent well, your excellency.
 Stral.   Then
I am to deem the plunderer is caught?
 Iden. Humph!—not exactly.
 Stral.   Or at least suspected?
 Iden. Oh! for that matter, very much suspected.
 Stral. Who may he be?
 Iden.   Why, don't *you* know, my lord?
 Stral. How should I? I was fast asleep.
 Iden.   And so
Was I, and that's the cause I know no more
Than does your excellency.
 Stral.   Dolt!
 Iden.   Why, if
Your lordship, being robb'd, don't recognise
The rogue; how should I, not being robb'd, identify
The thief among so many? In the crowd,
May it please your excellency, your thief looks
Exactly like the rest, or rather better:
'Tis only at the bar and in the dungeon
That wise men know your felon by his features;
But I'll engage, that if seen there but once,
Whether he be found criminal or no,
His face shall be so.

Stral. (to Fritz*).* Prithee, Fritz, inform me
What hath been done to trace the fellow?
Fritz. Faith!
My lord, not much as yet, except conjecture.
Stral. Besides the loss (which, I must own, affects me
Just now materially), I needs would find
The villain out of public motives; for
So dexterous a spoiler, who could creep
Through my attendants, and so many peopled
And lighted chambers, on my rest, and snatch
The gold before my scarce-closed eyes, would soon
Leave bare your borough, Sir Intendant!
Iden. True;
If there were aught to carry off, my lord.
Ulr. What is all this?
Stral. You join'd us but this morning,
And have not heard that I was robb'd last night.
Ulr. Some rumour of it reach'd me as I pass'd
The outer chambers of the palace, but
I know no further.
Stral. It is a strange business;
The intendant can inform you of the facts.
Iden. Most willingly. You see—
Stral. (impatiently). Defer your tale,
Till certain of the hearer's patience.
Iden. That
Can only be approved by proofs. You see—
Stral. (again interrupting him, and addressing Ulric*).*
In short, I was asleep upon a chair,
My cabinet before me, with some gold
Upon it (more than I much like to lose,
Though in part only): some ingenious person
Contrived to glide through all my own attendants,
Besides those of the place, and bore away
A hundred golden ducats, which to find
I would be fain, and there's an end. Perhaps
You (as I still am rather faint) would add

To yesterday's great obligation, this,
Though slighter, not yet slight, to aid these men
(Who seem but lukewarm) in recovering it?

Ulr. Most willingly, and without loss of time —
(*To* IDENSTEIN.) Come hither, mynheer!

Iden. But so much haste bodes
Right little speed, and —

Ulr. Standing motionless
None; so let's march: we'll talk as we go on.

Iden. But —

Ulr. Show the spot, and then I'll answer you.

Fritz. I will, sir, with his excellency's leave.

Stral. Do so, and take yon old ass with you.

Fritz. Hence!

Ulr. Come on, old oracle, expound thy riddle!

[*Exit with* IDENSTEIN *and* FRITZ.

Stral. (*solus*). A stalwart, active, soldier-looking stripling,
Handsome as Hercules ere his first labour,
And with a brow of thought beyond his years
When in repose, till his eye kindles up
In answering yours. I wish I could engage him:
I have need of some such spirits near me now,
For this inheritance is worth a struggle.
And though I am not the man to yield without one,
Neither are they who now rise up between me
And my desire. The boy, they say, 's a bold one;
But he hath play'd the truant in some hour
Of freakish folly, leaving fortune to
Champion his claims. That's well. The father, whom
For years I've track'd, as does the blood-hound, never
In sight, but constantly in scent, had put me
To fault; but *here* I *have* him, and that's better.
It must be he! All circumstance proclaims it;
And careless voices, knowing not the cause
Of my enquiries, still confirm it.— Yes!
The man, his bearing, and the mystery
Of his arrival, and the time; the account, too,

The intendant gave (for I have not beheld her)
Of his wife's dignified but foreign aspect;
Besides the antipathy with which we met,
As snakes and lions shrink back from each other
By secret instinct that both must be foes
Deadly, without being natural prey to either;
All—all—confirm it to my mind. However,
We'll grapple, ne'ertheless. In a few hours
The order comes from Frankfort, if these waters
Rise not the higher (and the weather favours
Their quick abatement), and I'll have him safe
Within a dungeon, where he may avouch
His real estate and name; and there's no harm done,
Should he prove other than I deem. This robbery
(Save for the actual loss) is lucky also:
He's poor, and that's suspicious—he's unknown,
And that's defenceless.—True, we have no proofs
Of guilt,—but what hath he of innocence?
Were he a man indifferent to my prospects,
In other bearings, I should rather lay
The inculpation on the Hungarian, who
Hath something which I like not; and alone
Of all around, except the intendant, and
The prince's household and my own, had ingress
Familiar to the chamber.

Enter GABOR.

      Friend, how fare you?

 Gab. As those who fare well everywhere, when they
Have supp'd and slumber'd, no great matter how—
And you, my lord?

 Stral.   Better in rest than purse:
Mine inn is like to cost me dear.

 Gab.   I heard
Of your late loss; but 'tis a trifle to
One of your order.

 Stral.   You would hardly think so,
Were the loss yours.

Gab.   I never had so much
(At once) in my whole life, and therefore am not
Fit to decide. But I came here to seek you.
Your couriers are turn'd back—I have outstripp'd them,
In my return.
    Stral.   You!—Why?
    Gab.   I went at daybreak,
To watch for the abatement of the river,
As being anxious to resume my journey.
Your messengers were all check'd like myself;
And, seeing the case hopeless, I await
The current's pleasure.
    Stral.   Would the dogs were in it!
Why did they not, at least, attempt the passage?
I order'd this at all risks.
    Gab.   Could you order
The Oder to divide, as Moses did
The Red Sea (scarcely redder than the flood
Of the swoln stream), and be obey'd, perhaps
They might have ventured.
    Stral.   I must see to it:
The knaves! the slaves!—but they shall smart for this.
                    [*Exit* STRALENHEIM.

    Gab.(*solus*). There goes my noble, feudal, self-will'd baron!
Epitome of what brave chivalry
The preux chevaliers of the good old times
Have left us. Yesterday he would have given
His lands (if he hath any), and, still dearer,
His sixteen quarterings, for as much fresh air
As would have fill'd a bladder, while he lay
Gurgling and foaming half way through the window
Of his o'erset and water-logg'd conveyance;
And now he storms at half a dozen wretches
Because they love their lives too! Yet, he's right:
'Tis strange they should, when such as he may put them
To hazard at his pleasure. Oh! thou world!
Thou art indeed a melancholy jest!   [*Exit* GABOR.

SCENE II.

The Apartment of WERNER, *in the Palace.*

Enter JOSEPHINE *and* ULRIC.

Jos. Stand back, and let me look on thee again!
My Ulric!—my beloved!—can it be—
After twelve years?
    Ulr.   My dearest mother!
    Jos.   Yes!
My dream is realised—how beautiful!—
How more than all I sigh'd for! Heaven receive
A mother's thanks!—a mother's tears of joy!
This is indeed thy work!—At such an hour, too,
He comes not only as a son, but saviour.
    Ulr. If such a joy await me, it must double
What I now feel, and lighten from my heart
A part of the long debt of duty, not
Of love (for that was ne'er withheld)—forgive me!
This long delay was not my fault.
    Jos.   I know it,
But cannot think of sorrow now, and doubt
If I e'er felt it, 'tis so dazzled from
My memory by this oblivious transport!—
My son!

Enter WERNER.

    Wer. What have we here,—more strangers?
    Jos.   No!
Look upon him! What do you see?
    Wer.   A stripling,
For the first time—
    Ulr. (*kneeling*). For twelve long years, my father!
    Wer. Oh, God!
    Jos.   He faints!
    Wer.   No—I am better now—
Ulric! (*Embraces him.*)
    Ulr. My father, Siegendorf!

Wer. (starting). Hush! boy —
The walls may hear that name!
Ulr. What then?
Wer. Why, then —
But we will talk of that anon. Remember,
I must be known here but as Werner. Come!
Come to my arms again! Why, thou look'st all
I should have been, and was not. Josephine!
Sure 'tis no father's fondness dazzles me;
But, had I seen that form amid ten thousand
Youth of the choicest, my heart would have chosen
This for my son!
Ulr. And yet you knew me not!
Wer. Alas! I have had that upon my soul
Which makes me look on all men with an eye
That only knows the evil at first glance.
Ulr. My memory served me far more fondly: I
Have not forgotten aught; and oft-times in
The proud and princely halls of—(I'll not name them,
As you say that 'tis perilous)—but i' the pomp
Of your sire's feudal mansion, I look'd back
To the Bohemian mountains many a sunset,
And wept to see another day go down
O'er thee and me, with those huge hills between us.
They shall not part us more.
Wer. I know not that.
Are you aware my father is no more?
Ulr. Oh, heavens! I left him in a green old age,
And looking like the oak, worn, but still steady
Amidst the elements, whilst younger trees
Fell fast around him. 'Twas scarce three months since.
Wer. Why did you leave him?
Jos. (embracing Ulric). Can you ask that question?
Is he not *here?*
Wer. True; he hath sought his parents,
And found them; but, oh! *how,* and in what state!
Ulr. All shall be better'd. What we have to do

Is to proceed, and to assert our rights,
Or rather yours; for I wave all, unless
Your father has disposed in such a sort
Of his broad lands as to make mine the foremost,
So that I must prefer my claim for form:
But I trust better, and that all is yours.
 Wer. Have you not heard of Stralenheim?
 Ulr.   I saved
His life but yesterday: he's here.
 Wer.   You saved
The serpent who will sting us all!
 Ulr.   You speak
Riddles: what is this *Stralenheim* to us?
 Wer. Every thing. One who claims our father's lands;
Our distant kinsman, and our nearest foe.
 Ulr. I never heard his name till now. The count,
Indeed, spoke sometimes of a kinsman, who,
If his own line should fail, might be remotely
Involved in the succession; but his titles
Were never named before me — and what then?
His right must yield to ours.
 Wer.   Ay, if at Prague:
But here he is all-powerful; and has spread
Snares for thy father, which, if hitherto
He hath escaped them, is by fortune, not
By favour.
 Ulr. Doth he personally know you?
 Wer. No; but he guesses shrewdly at my person,
As he betray'd last night; and I, perhaps,
But owe my temporary liberty
To his uncertainty.
 Ulr.   I think you wrong him
(Excuse me for the phrase); but Stralenheim
Is not what you prejudge him, or, if so,
He owes me something both for past and present.
I saved his life, he therefore trusts in me.
He hath been plunder'd too, since he came hither:

Is sick; a stranger; and as such not now
Able to trace the villain who hath robb'd him:
I have pledged myself to do so; and the business
Which brought me here was chiefly that: but I
Have found, in searching for another's dross,
My own whole treasure—you, my parents!

   Wer. (*agitatedly*).   Who
Taught you to mouth that name of "villain?"
   Ulr.   What
More noble name belongs to common thieves?
   Wer. Who taught you thus to brand an unknown being
With an infernal stigma?
   Ulr.   My own feelings
Taught me to name a ruffian from his deeds.
   Wer. Who taught you, long-sought and ill-found boy!
             that
It would be safe for my own son to insult me?
   Ulr. I named a villain. What is there in common
With such a being and my father?
   Wer.   Every thing!
That ruffian is thy father!
   Jos.   Oh, my son!
Believe him not—and yet!—(*her voice falters.*)
   Ulr. (*starts, looks earnestly at* WERNER, *and then says slowly,*)
                         And you avow it?
   Wer. Ulric, before you dare despise your father,
Learn to divine and judge his actions. Young,
Rash, new to life, and rear'd in luxury's lap,
Is it for you to measure passion's force,
Or misery's temptation? Wait—(not long,
It cometh like the night, and quickly)—Wait!—
Wait till, like me, your hopes are blighted—till
Sorrow and shame are handmaids of your cabin;
Famine and poverty your guests at table;
Despair your bed-fellow—then rise, but not
From sleep, and judge! Should that day e'er arrive—
Should you see then the serpent, who hath coil'd

Himself around all that is dear and noble
Of you and yours, lie slumbering in your path,
With but *his* folds between your steps and happiness,
When *he*, who lives but to tear from you name,
Lands, life itself, lies at your mercy, with
Chance your conductor; midnight for your mantle;
The bare knife in your hand, and earth asleep,
Even to your deadliest foe; and he as 't were
Inviting death, by looking like it, while
His death alone can save you:— Thank your God!
If then, like me, content with petty plunder,
You turn aside—I did so.
    Ulr.   But—
    Wer. (abruptly).   Hear me
I will not brook a human voice—scarce dare
Listen to my own (if that be human still)—
Hear me! you do not know this man—I do.
He's mean, deceitful, avaricious. You
Deem yourself safe, as young and brave; but learn
None are secure from desperation, few
From subtilty. My worst foe, Stralenheim,
Housed in a prince's palace, couch'd within
A prince's chamber, lay below my knife!
An instant—a mere motion—the least impulse—
Had swept him and all fears of mine from earth.
He was within my power—my knife was raised—
Withdrawn—and I'm in his:—are you not so?
Who tells you that he knows you *not?* Who says
He hath not lured you here to end you? or
To plunge you, with your parents, in a dungeon?
                                           [*He pauses.*
    Ulr. Proceed—proceed!
    Wer.   *Me* he hath ever known,
And hunted through each change of time—name—fortune—
And why not *you?* Are you more versed in men?
He wound snares round me; flung along my path
Reptiles, whom, in my youth, I would have spurn'd

Even from my presence; but, in spurning now,
Fill only with fresh venom. Will you be
More patient? Ulric!—Ulric!—there are crimes
Made venial by the occasion, and temptations
Which nature cannot master or forbear.
  Ulr. (*looks first at him, and then at* JOSEPHINE).
My mother!
  Wer.   Ay! I thought so: you have now
Only one parent. I have lost alike
Father and son, and stand alone.
  Ulr.   But stay!
        [WERNER *rushes out of the chamber*.
  Jos. (*to* ULRIC). Follow him not, until this storm of passion
Abates. Think'st thou, that were it well for him,
I had not follow'd?
  Ulr.   I obey you, mother,
Although reluctantly. My first act shall not
Be one of disobedience.
  Jos.   Oh! he is good!
Condemn him not from his own mouth, but trust
To me, who have borne so much with him, and for him,
That this is but the surface of his soul,
And that the depth is rich in better things.
  Ulr. These then are but my father's principles?
My mother thinks not with him?
  Jos.   Nor doth he
Think as he speaks. Alas! long years of grief
Have made him sometimes thus.
  Ulr.   Explain to me
More clearly, then, these claims of Stralenheim,
That, when I see the subject in its bearings,
I may prepare to face him, or at least
To extricate you from your present perils.
I pledge myself to accomplish this—but would
I had arrived a few hours sooner!
  Jos.   Ay!
Hadst thou but done so!

Enter Gabor *and* Idenstein, *with Attendants.*

Gab. (*to* Ulric). I have sought you, comrade.
So this is my reward!
   Ulr.   What do you mean?
   Gab. 'Sdeath! have I lived to these years, and for this!
(*To* Idenstein). But for your age and folly, I would—
   Iden.   Help!
Hands off! Touch an intendant!
   Gab.   Do not think
I'll honour you so much as save your throat
From the Ravenstone* by choking you myself.
   Iden. I thank you for the respite: but there are
Those who have greater need of it than me.
   Ulr. Unriddle this vile wrangling, or—
   Gab.   At once, then,
The baron has been robb'd, and upon me
This worthy personage has deign'd to fix
His kind suspicions—me! whom he ne'er saw
Till yester' evening.
   Iden.   Wouldst have me suspect
My own acquaintances? You have to learn
That I keep better company.
   Gab.   You shall
Keep the best shortly, and the last for all men,
The worms! you hound of malice!   [Gabor *seizes on him.*
   Ulr. (*interfering*).   Nay, no violence:
He's old, unarm'd—be temperate, Gabor!
   Gab. (*letting go* Idenstein).   True:
I am a fool to lose myself because
Fools deem me knave: it is their homage.
   Ulr. (*to* Idenstein).   How
Fare you?
   Iden.   Help!
   Ulr.   I *have* help'd you.

---

* The Ravenstone, "Rabenstein," is the *stone gibbet* of Germany, and so called from the ravens perching on it.

   Iden.   Kill him! then
I'll say so.
   Gab.   I am calm — live on!
   Iden.   That's more
Than you shall do, if there be judge or judgment
In Germany. The baron shall decide!
   Gab. Does *he* abet you in your accusation?
   Iden. Does he not?
   Gab.   Then next time let him go sink
Ere I go hang for snatching him from drowning.
But here he comes!

               Enter STRALENHEIM.

   Gab. (*goes up to him*). My noble lord, I'm here!
   Stral. Well, sir!
   Gab.   Have you aught with me?
   Stral.   What should I
Have with you?
   Gab.   You know best, if yesterday's
Flood has not wash'd away your memory;
But that's a trifle. I stand here accused,
In phrases not equivocal, by yon
Intendant, of the pillage of your person
Or chamber: — is the charge your own or his?
   Stral. I accuse no man.
   Gab.   Then you acquit me, baron?
   Stral. I know not whom to accuse, or to acquit,
Or scarcely to suspect.
   Gab.   But you at least
Should know whom *not* to suspect. I am insulted —
Oppress'd here by these menials, and I look
To you for remedy — teach them their duty!
To look for thieves at home were part of it,
If duly taught; but, in one word, if I
Have an accuser, let it be a man
Worthy to be so of a man like me.
I am your equal.
   Stral.   You!

Gab.   Ay, sir; and, for
Aught that you know, superior; but proceed—
I do not ask for hints, and surmises,
And circumstance, and proofs; I know enough
Of what I have done for you, and what you owe me,
To have at least waited your payment rather
Than paid myself, had I been eager of
Your gold. I also know, that were I even
The villain I am deem'd, the service render'd
So recently would not permit you to
Pursue me to the death, except through shame,
Such as would leave your scutcheon but a blank.
But this is nothing: I demand of you
Justice upon your unjust servants, and
From your own lips a disavowal of
All sanction of their insolence: thus much
You owe to the unknown, who asks no more,
And never thought to have ask'd so much.
  Stral.   This tone
May be of innocence.
  Gab.   'Sdeath! who dare doubt it
Except such villains as ne'er had it?
  Stral.   You
Are hot, sir.
  Gab.   Must I turn an icicle
Before the breath of menials, and their master?
  Stral. Ulric! you know this man; I found him in
Your company.
  Gab.   We found *you* in the Oder;
Would we had left you there!
  Stral.   I give you thanks, sir.
  Gab. I've earn'd them; but might have earn'd more from
        others,
Perchance, if I had left you to your fate.
  Stral. Ulric! you know this man?
  Gab.   No more than you do,
If he avouches not my honour.

Ulr.   I
Can vouch your courage, and, as far as my
Own brief connection led me, honour.
    Stral.   Then
I'm satisfied.
    Gab. (*ironically*). Right easily, methinks.
What is the spell in his asseveration
More than in mine?
    Stral.   I merely said that *I*
Was satisfied — not that you are absolved.
    Gab. Again! Am I accused or no?
    Stral.   Go to!
You wax too insolent. If circumstance
And general suspicion be against you,
Is the fault mine? Is't not enough that I
Decline all question of your guilt or innocence?
    Gab. My lord, my lord, this is mere cozenage,
A vile equivocation; you well know
Your doubts are certainties to all around you —
Your looks a voice — your frowns a sentence; you
Are practising your power on me — because
You have it; but beware! you know not whom
You strive to tread on.
    Stral.   Threat'st thou?
    Gab.   Not so much
As you accuse. You hint the basest injury,
And I retort it with an open warning.
    Stral. As you have said, 'tis true I owe you something,
For which you seem disposed to pay yourself.
    Gab. Not with your gold.
    Stral.   With bootless insolence.
                  [*To his Attendants and* IDENSTEIN
You need not further to molest this man,
But let him go his way. Ulric, good morrow!
            [*Exit* STRALENHEIM, IDENSTEIN, *and Attendants.*
    Gab. (*following*). I'll after him and —
    Ulr. (*stopping him*).   Not a step.

Gab.   Who shall
Oppose me?
   Ulr.   Your own reason, with a moment's
Thought.
   Gab.   Must I bear this?
   Ulr.   Pshaw! we all must bear
The arrogance of something higher than
Ourselves—the highest cannot temper Satan,
Nor the lowest his vicegerents upon earth.
I've seen you brave the elements, and bear
Things which had made this silkworm cast his skin—
And shrink you from a few sharp sneers and words?
   Gab. Must I bear to be deem'd a thief? If 't were
A bandit of the woods, I could have borne it—
There's something daring in it;—but to steal
The moneys of a slumbering man!—
   Ulr.   It seems, then,
You are *not* guilty?
   Gab.   Do I hear aright?
You too!
   Ulr.   I merely ask'd a simple question.
   Gab. If the judge ask'd me, I would answer "No"—
To you I answer *thus.* (*He draws*).
   Ulr. (*drawing*).   With all my heart!
   Jos. Without there! Ho! help! help!—Oh, God! here's
         murder!

                           [*Exit* JOSEPHINE, *shrieking.*

GABOR *and* ULRIC *fight.* GABOR *is disarmed just as* STRALEN-
    HEIM, JOSEPHINE, IDENSTEIN, *&c. re-enter.*

   Jos. Oh! glorious heaven! He's safe!
   Stral. (*to* JOSEPHINE). *Who's* safe?
   Jos.   My—
   Ulr. (*interrupting her with a stern look, and turning after-
        wards to* STRALENHEIM).   Both!
Here's no great harm done.
   Stral.   What hath caused all this?

Ulr. You, baron, I believe; but as the effect
Is harmless, let it not disturb you.—Gabor!
There is your sword; and when you bare it next,
Let it not be against your *friends.*
　　　　　[ULRIC *pronounces the last words slowly and emphatically in a low voice to* GABOR.
　Gab.　　　　　　　　　I thank you
Less for my life than for your counsel.
　Stral.　　　　　　　　　These
Brawls must end here.
　Gab. (*taking his sword*). They shall.　You have wrong'd me, Ulric,
More with your unkind thoughts than sword: I would
The last were in my bosom rather than
The first in yours.　I could have borne yon noble's
Absurd insinuations—ignorance
And dull suspicion are a part of his
Entail will last him longer than his lands.—
But I may fit *him* yet:—you have vanquish'd me.
I was the fool of passion to conceive
That I could cope with you, whom I had seen
Already proved by greater perils than
Rest in this arm.　We way meet by and by,
However—but in friendship.　　　　　[*Exit* GABOR.
　Stral.　　　　　　　I will brook
No more!　This outrage following up his insults,
Perhaps his guilt, has cancell'd all the little
I owed him heretofore for the so-vaunted
Aid which he added to your abler succour.
Ulric, you are not hurt?—
　Ulr.　　　　　Not even by a scratch.
　Stral. (*to* IDENSTEIN). Intendant! take your measures to secure
Yon fellow: I revoke my former lenity.
He shall be sent to Frankfort with an escort
The instant that the waters have abated.
　Iden. Secure him! He hath got his sword again—

And seems to know the use on't; 'tis his trade,
Belike;—I'm a civilian.
   Stral.   Fool! are not
Yon score of vassals dogging at your heels
Enough to seize a dozen such? Hence! after him!
   Ulr. Baron, I do beseech you!
   Stral.   I must be
Obey'd. No words!
   Iden.   Well, if it must be so—
March, vassals! I'm your leader, and will bring
The rear up: a wise general never should
Expose his precious life—on which all rests.
I like that article of war.
                     [*Exit* IDENSTEIN *and Attendants.*
   Stral.   Come hither,
Ulric: what does that woman here? Oh! now
I recognise her, 'tis the stranger's wife
Whom they *name* "Werner."
   Ulr.   'Tis his name.
   Stral.   Indeed!
Is not your husband visible, fair dame?—
   Jos. Who seeks him?
   Stral.   No one—for the present: but
I fain would parley, Ulric, with yourself
Alone.
   Ulr. I will retire with you.
   Jos.   Not so:
You are the latest stranger, and command
All places here.
(*Aside to* ULRIC, *as she goes out*). O Ulric! have a care—
Remember what depends on a rash word!
   Ulr. (*to* JOSEPHINE).   Fear not!—
                            [*Exit* JOSEPHINE.

   Stral. Ulric, I think that I may trust you:
You saved my life—and acts like these beget
Unbounded confidence.
   Ulr.   Say on.

Stral.   Mysterious
And long-engender'd circumstances (not
To be now fully enter'd on) have made
This man obnoxious—perhaps fatal to me.
   Ulr. Who? Gabor, the Hungarian?
   Stral.   No—this "Werner"—
With the false name and habit.
   Ulr.   How can this be?
He is the poorest of the poor—and yellow
Sickness sits cavern'd in his hollow eye:
The man is helpless.
   Stral.   He is—'tis no matter;—
But if he be the man I deem (and that
He is so, all around us here—and much
That is not here—confirm my apprehension)
He must be made secure ere twelve hours further.
   Ulr. And what have I to do with this?
   Stral.   I have sent
To Frankfort, to the governor, my friend
(I have the authority to do so by
An order of the house of Brandenburg),
For a fit escort—but this cursed flood
Bars all access, and may do for some hours.
   Ulr. It is abating.
   Stral.   That is well.
   Ulr.   But how
Am I concern'd?
   Stral.   As one who did so much
For me, you cannot be indifferent to
That which is of more import to me than
The life you rescued.—Keep your eye on *him!*
The man avoids me, knows that I now know him.—
Watch him!—as you would watch the wild boar when
He makes against you in the hunter's gap—
Like him he must be spear'd.
   Ulr.   Why so?
   Stral.   He stands

Between me and a brave inheritance!
Oh! could you see it! But you shall.
   Ulr.   I hope so.
   Stral. It is the richest of the rich Bohemia,
Unscathed by scorching war. It lies so near
The strongest city, Prague, that fire and sword
Have skimm'd it lightly: so that now, besides
Its own exuberance, it bears double value
Confronted with whole realms far and near
Made deserts.
   Ulr.   You describe it faithfully.
   Stral. Ay—could you see it, you would say so—but,
As I have said, you shall.
   Ulr.   I accept the omen.
   Stral. Then claim a recompense from it and me,
Such as *both* may make worthy your acceptance
And services to me and mine for ever.
   Ulr. And this sole, sick, and miserable wretch —
This way-worn stranger—stands between you and
This Paradise?—(As Adam did between
The devil and his)—[*Aside.*]
   Stral.   He doth.
   Ulr.   Hath he no right?
   Stral. Right! none. A disinherited prodigal,
Who for these twenty years disgraced his lineage
In all his acts—but chiefly by his marriage,
And living amidst commerce-fetching burghers,
And dabbling merchants, in a mart of Jews.
   Ulr. He has a wife, then?
   Stral.   You'd be sorry to
Call such your mother. You have seen the woman
He *calls* his wife.
   Ulr.   Is she not so?
   Stral.   No more
Than he's your father:—an Italian girl,
The daughter of a banish'd man, who lives
On love and poverty with this same Werner.

Ulr. They are childless, then?
Stral.   There is or was a bastard,
Whom the old man — the grandsire (as old age
Is ever doting) took to warm his bosom,
As it went chilly downward to the grave:
But the imp stands not in my path — he has fled,
No one knows whither; and if he had not,
His claims alone were too contemptible
To stand. — Why do you smile?
Ulr.   At your vain fears:
A poor man almost in his grasp — a child
Of doubtless birth — can startle a grandee!
   Stral. All's to be fear'd, where all is to be gain'd.
   Ulr. True; and aught done to save or to obtain it.
   Stral. You have harp'd the very string next to my heart.
I may depend upon you?
   Ulr.   'T were too late
To doubt it.
   Stral.   Let no foolish pity shake
Your bosom (for the appearance of the man
Is pitiful) — he is a wretch, as likely
To have robb'd me as the fellow more suspected,
Except that circumstance is less against him;
He being lodged far off, and in a chamber
Without approach to mine: and, to say truth,
I think too well of blood allied to mine,
To deem he would descend to such an act:
Besides, he was a soldier, and a brave one
Once — though too rash.
   Ulr.   And they, my lord, we know
By our experience, never plunder till
They knock the brains out first — which makes them heirs,
Not thieves. The dead, who feel nought, can lose nothing,
Nor e'er be robb'd: their spoils are a bequest —
No more.
   Stral. Go to! you are a wag. But say
I may be sure you'll keep an eye on this man,

And let me know his slightest movement towards
Concealment or escape?
　Ulr.　　　　　　You may be sure
You yourself could not watch him more than I
Will be his sentinel.
　Stral.　　　　　By this you make me
Yours, and for ever.
　Ulr.　　　　Such is my intention.　　　[*Exeunt.*

ACT III.

SCENE I.

A Hall in the same Palace, from whence the secret Passage leads.

　　　　Enter WERNER *and* GABOR.
　Gab. Sir, I have told my tale: if it so please you
To give me refuge for a few hours, well—
If not, I'll try my fortune elsewhere.
　Wer.　　　　　　　　　　How
Can I, so wretched, give to Misery
A shelter?—wanting such myself as much
As e'er the hunted deer a covert—
　Gab.　　　　　　　　Or
The wounded lion his cool cave. Methinks
You rather look like one would turn at bay,
And rip the hunter's entrails.
　Wer.　　　　　Ah!
　Gab.　　　　　　　　I care not
If it be so, being much disposed to do
The same myself. But will you shelter me?
I am oppress'd like you—and poor like you—
Disgraced—
　Wer. (*abruptly*). Who told you that I was disgraced?
　Gab. No one; nor did I say you were so: with
Your poverty my likeness ended; but
I said *I* was so—and would add, with truth,
As undeservedly as *you.*

Wer. Again!
As I?
  Gab. Or any other honest man.
What the devil would you have? You don't believe me
Guilty of this base theft?
  Wer.   No, no — I cannot.
  Gab. Why that's my heart of honour! you young gallant —
Your miserly intendant and dense noble —
All — all suspected me; and why? because
I am the worst-clothed, and least named amongst them;
Although, were Momus' lattice in your breasts,
My soul might brook to open it more widely
Than theirs: but thus it is — you poor and helpless —
Both still more than myself.
  Wer.   How know you that?
  Gab. You're right: I ask for shelter at the hand
Which I call helpless; if you now deny it,
I were well paid. But you, who seem to have proved
The wholesome bitterness of life, know well,
By sympathy, that all the outspread gold
Of the New World the Spaniard boasts about
Could never tempt the man who knows its worth,
Weigh'd at its proper value in the balance,
Save in such guise (and there I grant its power,
Because I feel it,) as may leave no nightmare
Upon his heart o' nights.
  Wer.   What do you mean?
  Gab. Just what I say; I thought my speech was plain:
You are no thief — nor I — and, as true men,
Should aid each other.
  Wer.   It is a damn'd world, sir.
  Gab. So is the nearest of the two next, as
The priests say (and no doubt they should know best),
Therefore I'll stick by this — as being loth
To suffer martyrdom, at least with such
An epitaph as larceny upon my tomb.
It is but a night's lodging which I crave;

To-morrow I will try the waters, as
The dove did, trusting that they have abated.
 Wer. Abated? Is there hope of that?
 Gab.   There was
At noontide.
 Wer.   Then we may be safe.
 Gab.   Are *you*
In peril?
 Wer.   Poverty is ever so.
 Gab. That I know by long practice. Will you not
Promise to make mine less?
 Wer.   Your poverty?
 Gab. No — you don't look a leech for that disorder;
I meant my peril only: you've a roof,
And I have none; I merely seek a covert.
 Wer. Rightly; for how should such a wretch as I
Have gold?
 Gab.   Scarce honestly, to say the truth on't,
Although I almost wish you had the baron's.
 Wer. Dare you insinuate?
 Gab.   What?
 Wer.   Are you aware
To whom you speak?
 Gab.   No; and I am not used
Greatly to care. (*A noise heard without.*) But hark! they come!
 Wer.   Who come?
 Gab. The intendant and his man-hounds after me:
I'd face them — but it were in vain to expect
Justice at hands like theirs. Where shall I go?
But show me any place. I do assure you,
If there be faith in man, I am most guiltless:
Think if it were your own case!
 Wer. (*Aside*).   Oh, just God!
Thy hell is not hereafter! Am I dust still?
 Gab. I see you're moved; and it shows well in you:
I may live to requite it.

Wer.   Are you not
A spy of Stralenheim's?
   Gab.   Not I! and if
I were, what is there to espy in you?
Although I recollect his frequent question
About you and your spouse might lead to some
Suspicion; but you best know—what—and why
I am his deadliest foe.
   Wer.   *You?*
   Gab.   After such
A treatment for the service which in part
I render'd him, I am his enemy:
If you are not his friend, you will assist me.
   Wer. I will.
   Gab.   But how?
   Wer. (*showing the panel*). There is a secret spring
Remember, I discover'd it by chance,
And used it but for safety.
   Gab.   Open it,
And I will use it for the same.
   Wer.   I found it,
As I have said: it leads through winding walls,
(So thick as to bear paths within their ribs,
Yet lose no jot of strength or stateliness,)
And hollow cells, and obscure niches, to
I know not whither; you must not advance:
Give me your word.
   Gab.   It is unnecessary:
How should I make my way in darkness through
A Gothic labyrinth of unknown windings?
   Wer. Yes, but who knows to what place it may lead?
I know not—(mark you!)—but who knows it might not
Lead even into the chamber of your foe?
So strangely were contrived these galleries
By our Teutonic fathers in old days,
When man built less against the elements
Than his next neighbour. You must not advance

Beyond the two first windings; if you do
(Albeit I never pass'd them), I'll not answer
For what you may be led to.
  Gab.   But I will.
A thousand thanks!
  Wer.   You'll find the spring more obvious
On the other side; and, when you would return,
It yields to the least touch.
  Gab.   I'll in—farewell!
      [GABOR *goes in by the secret panel.*
  Wer. (*solus*). What have I done? Alas! what *had* I done
Before to make this fearful? Let it be
Still some atonement that I save the man,
Whose sacrifice had saved perhaps my own—
They come! to seek elsewhere what is before them!

    Enter IDENSTEIN *and Others.*

  Iden. Is he not here? He must have vanish'd then
Through the dim Gothic glass by pious aid
Of pictured saints upon the red and yellow
Casements, through which the sunset streams like sunrise
On long pearl-colour'd beards and crimson crosses,
And gilded crosiers, and cross'd arms, and cowls,
And helms, and twisted armour, and long swords,
All the fantastic furniture of windows
Dim with brave knights and holy hermits, whose
Likeness and fame alike rest in some panes
Of crystal, which each rattling wind proclaims
As frail as any other life or glory.
He's gone, however.
  Wer.   Whom do you seek?
  Iden.   A villain.
  Wer. Why need you come so far, then?
  Iden.   In the search
Of him who robb'd the baron.
  Wer.   Are you sure
You have divined the man?

Iden.   As sure as you
Stand there: but where's he gone?
Wer.   Who?
Iden.   He we sought.
Wer. You see he is not here.
Iden.   And yet we traced him
Up to this hall. Are you accomplices?
Or deal you in the black art?
Wer.   I deal plainly,
To many men the blackest.
Iden.   It may be
I have a question or two for yourself
Hereafter; but we must continue now
Our search for t' other.
Wer.   You had best begin
Your inquisition now: I may not be
So patient always.
Iden.   I should like to know,
In good sooth, if you really are the man
That Stralenheim's in quest of.
Wer.   Insolent!
Said you not that he was not here?
Iden.   Yes, one;
But there's another whom he tracks more keenly,
And soon, it may be, with authority
Both paramount to his and mine. But, come!
Bustle, my boys! we are at fault.
     [*Exit* IDENSTEIN *and Attendants.*
Wer.   In what
A maze hath my dim destiny involved me!
And one base sin hath done me less ill than
The leaving undone one far greater. Down,
Thou busy devil, rising in my heart!
Thou art too late! I'll nought to do with blood.

Enter ULRIC.

Ulr. I sought you, father.

Wer.   Is't not dangerous?
Ulr. No; Stralenheim is ignorant of all
Or any of the ties between us: more —
He sends me here a spy upon your actions,
Deeming me wholly his.
    Wer.   I cannot think it:
'Tis but a snare he winds about us both,
To swoop the sire and son at once.
    Ulr.   I cannot
Pause in each petty fear, and stumble at
The doubts that rise like briers in our path,
But must break through them, as an unarm'd carle
Would, though with naked limbs, were the wolf rustling
In the same thicket where he hew'd for bread.
Nets are for thrushes, eagles are not caught so:
We'll overfly or rend them.
    Wer.   Show me *how?*
    Ulr. Can you not guess?
    Wer.   I cannot.
    Ulr.   That is strange.
Came the thought ne'er into your mind *last night?*
    Wer. I understand you not.
    Ulr.   Then we shall never
More understand each other. But to change
The topic —
    Wer.   You mean to *pursue* it, as
'Tis of our safety.
    Ulr.   Right; I stand corrected.
I see the subject now more clearly, and
Our general situation in its bearings.
The waters are abating; a few hours
Will bring his summon'd myrmidons from Frankfort,
When you will be a prisoner, perhaps worse,
And I an outcast, bastardised by practice
Of this same baron to make way for him.
    Wer. And now your remedy! I thought to escape
By means of this accursed gold; but now

I dare not use it, show it, scarce look on it.
Methinks it wears upon its face my guilt
For motto, not the mintage of the state;
And, for the sovereign's head, my own begirt
With hissing snakes, which curl around my temples,
And cry to all beholders, Lo! a villain!
  Ulr. You must not use it, at least now; but take
This ring.   [*He gives* Werner *a jewel.*
  Wer. A gem! It was my father's!
  Ulr.   And
As such is now your own. With this you must
Bribe the intendant for his old caleche
And horses to pursue your route at sunrise,
Together with my mother.
  Wer.   And leave you,
So lately found, in peril too?
  Ulr.   Fear nothing!
The only fear were if we fled together,
For that would make our ties beyond all doubt.
The waters only lie in flood between
This burgh and Frankfort; so far's in our favour.
The route on to Bohemia, though encumber'd,
Is not impassable; and when you gain
A few hours' start, the difficulties will be
The same to your pursuers. Once beyond
The frontier, and you're safe.
  Wer.   My noble boy!
  Ulr. Hush! hush! no transports: we'll indulge in them
In Castle Siegendorf! Display no gold:
Show Idenstein the gem (I know the man,
And have look'd through him): it will answer thus
A double purpose. Stralenheim lost *gold*—
No jewel: therefore it could *not* be his;
And then the man who was possest of this
Can hardly be suspected of abstracting
The baron's coin, when he could thus convert
This ring to more than Stralenheim has lost

By his last night's slumber. Be not over timid
In your address, nor yet too arrogant,
And Idenstein will serve you.
 Wer.   I will follow
In all things your direction.
 Ulr.   I would have
Spared you the trouble; but had I appear'd
To take an interest in you, and still more
By dabbling with a jewel in your favour,
All had been known at once.
 Wer.   My guardian angel!
This overpays the past. But how wilt thou
Fare in our absence?
 Ulr.   Stralenheim knows nothing
Of me as aught of kindred with yourself.
I will but wait a day or two with him
To lull all doubts, and then rejoin my father.
 Wer. To part no more!
 Ulr.   I know not that; but at
The least we'll meet again once more.
 Wer.   My boy!
My friend! my only child, and sole preserver!
Oh, do not hate me!
 Ulr.   Hate my father!
 Wer.   Ay,
My father hated me. Why not my son?
 Ulr. Your father knew you not as I do.
 Wer.   Scorpions
Are in thy words! Thou know me? in this guise
Thou canst not know me, I am not myself;
Yet (hate me not) I will be soon.
 Ulr.   I'll *wait!*
In the mean time be sure that all a son
Can do for parents shall be done for mine.
 Wer. I see it, and I feel it; yet I feel
Further—that you despise me.
 Ulr.   Wherefore should I?

  Wer. Must I repeat my humiliation?
  Ulr.   No!
I have fathom'd it and you. But let us talk
Of this no more. Or if it must be ever,
Not *now*. Your error has redoubled all
The present difficulties of our house,
At secret war with that of Stralenheim:
All we have now to think of is to baffle
Him. I have shown *one* way.
  Wer.   The only one,
And I embrace it, as I did my son,
Who show'd *himself* and father's *safety* in
One day.
  Ulr. You *shall* be safe; let that suffice.
Would Stralenheim's appearance in Bohemia
Disturb your right, or mine, if once we were
Admitted to our lands?
  Wer.   Assuredly,
Situate as we are now, although the first
Possessor might, as usual, prove the strongest,
Especially the next in blood.
  Ulr.   *Blood!* 'tis
A word of many meanings; in the veins,
And out of them, it is a different thing —
And so it should be, when the same in blood
(As it is call'd) are aliens to each other,
Like Theban brethren: when a part is bad,
A few spilt ounces purify the rest.
  Wer. I do not apprehend you.
  Ulr.   That may be —
And should, perhaps — and yet — but get ye ready;
You and my mother must away to-night.
Here comes the intendant: sound him with the gem;
'Twill sink into his venal soul like lead
Into the deep, and bring up slime and mud,
And ooze too, from the bottom, as the lead doth
With its greased understratum; but no less

Will serve to warn our vessels through these shoals.
The freight is rich, so heave the line in time!
Farewell! I scarce have time, but yet your *hand*,
My father!—
  Wer. Let me embrace thee!
  Ulr. We may be
Observed: subdue your nature to the hour!
Keep off from me as from your foe!
  Wer. Accursed
Be he who is the stifling cause which smothers
The best and sweetest feeling of our hearts;
At such an hour too!
  Ulr. Yes, curse—it will ease you!
Here is the intendant.

Enter IDENSTEIN.

   Master Idenstein,
How fare you in your purpose? Have you caught
The rogue?
  Iden. No, faith!
  Ulr. Well, there are plenty more:
You may have better luck another chase.
Where is the baron?
  Iden. Gone back to his chamber:
And now I think on't, asking after you
With nobly-born impatience.
  Ulr. Your great men
Must be answer'd on the instant, as the bound
Of the stung steed replies unto the spur:
'Tis well they have horses, too; for if they had not,
I fear that men must draw their chariots, as
They say kings did Sesostris.
  Iden. Who was he?
  Ulr. An old Bohemian—an imperial gipsy.
  Iden. A gipsy or Bohemian, 'tis the same,
For they pass by both names. And was he one?
  Ulr. I've heard so; but I must take leave. Intendant,

Your servant!— Werner (*to* Werner *slightly*), if that be :
          name,
Yours.   [*Exit* U
     Iden. A well-spoken, pretty-faced young man!
And prettily behaved! He knows his station,
You see, sir: how he gave to each his due
Precedence!
     Wer.   I perceived it, and applaud
His just discernment and your own.
     Iden.   That's well—
That's very well. You also know your place, too;
And yet I don't know that I know your place.
     Wer. (*showing the ring*). Would this assist your k:
          ledge?
     Iden.   How!—What!—Eh!
A jewel!
     Wer. 'Tis your own on one condition.
     Iden. Mine!—Name it!
     Wer.   That hereafter you permit
At thrice its value to redeem it: 'tis
A family ring.
     Iden.   A family!—*yours!*—a gem!
I'm breathless!
     Wer.   You must also furnish me
An hour ere daybreak with all means to quit
This place.
     Iden.   But is it real? Let me look on it:
Diamond, by all that's glorious!
     Wer.   Come, I'll trust you.
You have guess'd, no doubt, that I was born above
My present seeming.
     Iden.   I can't say I did,
Though this looks like it: this is the true breeding
Of gentle blood!
     Wer.   I have important reasons
For wishing to continue privily
My journey hence.

Iden.   So then *you are* the man
Whom Stralenheim's in quest of?
   Wer.   I am not;
But being taken for him might conduct
So much embarrassment to me just now,
And to the baron's self hereafter—'tis
To spare both that I would avoid all bustle.
   Iden. Be you the man or no, 'tis not my business;
Besides, I never should obtain the half
From this proud, niggardly noble, who would raise
The country for some missing bits of coin,
And never offer a precise reward—
But *this!*—another look!
   Wer.   Gaze on it freely;
At day-dawn it is yours.
   Iden.   Oh, thou sweet sparkler!
Thou more than stone of the philosopher!
Thou touchstone of Philosophy herself!
Thou bright eye of the Mine! thou loadstar of
The soul! the true magnetic Pole to which
All hearts point duly north, like trembling needles!
Thou flaming Spirit of the Earth! which, sitting
High on the monarch's diadem, attractest
More worship than the majesty who sweats
Beneath the crown which makes his head ache, like
Millions of hearts which bleed to lend it lustre!
Shalt thou be mine? I am, methinks, already
A little king, a lucky alchymist!—
A wise magician, who has bound the devil
Without the forfeit of his soul. But come,
Werner, or what else?
   Wer.   Call me Werner still;
You may yet know me by a loftier title.
   Iden. I do believe in thee! thou art the spirit
Of whom I long have dream'd in a low garb.—
But come, I'll serve thee; thou shalt be as free
As air, despite the waters; let us hence:

I'll show thee I am honest—(oh, thou jewel!)
Thou shalt be furnish'd, Werner, with such means
Of flight, that if thou wert a snail, not birds
Should overtake thee.—Let me gaze again!
I have a foster-brother in the mart
Of Hamburgh skill'd in precious stones. How many
Carats may it weigh?—Come, Werner, I will wing thee.
[*Exeunt.*

SCENE II.

STRALENHEIM's *Chamber.*

STRALENHEIM *and* FRITZ.

Fritz. All's ready, my good lord!
Stral.   I am not sleepy,
And yet I must to bed; I fain would say
To rest, but something heavy on my spirit,
Too dull for wakefulness, too quick for slumber,
Sits on me as a cloud along the sky,
Which will not let the sunbeams through, nor yet
Descend in rain and end, but spreads itself
'Twixt earth and heaven, like envy between man
And man, an everlasting mist;—I will
Unto my pillow.
    Fritz.   May you rest there well!
    Stral. I feel, and fear, I shall.
    Fritz.   And wherefore fear?
    Stral. I know not why, and therefore do fear more,
Because an undescribable—but 'tis
All folly. Were the locks (as I desired)
Changed, to-day, of this chamber? for last night's
Adventure makes it needful.
    Fritz.   Certainly,
According to your order, and beneath
The inspection of myself and the young Saxon
Who saved your life. I think they call him "Ulric."
    Stral. You *think!* you supercilious slave! what right

Have you to *tax your* memory, which should be
Quick, proud, and happy to retain the *name*
Of him who saved your master, as a litany
Whose daily repetition marks your duty.—
Get hence! "*You think*," indeed! you who stood still
Howling and dripping on the bank, whilst I
Lay dying, and the stranger dash'd aside
The roaring torrent, and restored me to
Thank him—and despise you. "*You think!*" and scarce
Can recollect his name! I will not waste
More words on you. Call me betimes.
   Fritz.   Good night!
I trust to-morrow will restore your lordship
To renovated strength and temper.   [*The scene closes.*

SCENE III.

The secret Passage.

   Gab. (solus).   Four—
Five—six hours have I counted, like the guard
Of outposts, on the never-merry clock:
That hollow tongue of time, which, even when
It sounds for joy, takes something from enjoyment
With every clang. 'Tis a perpetual knell,
Though for a marriage-feast it rings: each stroke
Peals for a hope the less; the funeral note
Of Love deep-buried without resurrection
In the grave of Possession; while the knoll
Of long-lived parents finds a jovial echo
To triple Time in the son's ear.
                             I'm cold—
I'm dark;—I've blown my fingers—number'd o'er
And o'er my steps—and knock'd my head against
Some fifty buttresses—and roused the rats
And bats in general insurrection, till
Their cursed pattering feet and whirling wings

Leave me scarce hearing for another sound.
A light! It is at distance (if I can
Measure in darkness distance): but it blinks
As through a crevice or a key-hole, in
The inhibited direction: I must on,
Nevertheless, from curiosity.
A distant lamp-light is an incident
In such a den as this. Pray Heaven it lead me
To nothing that may tempt me! Else—Heaven aid me
To obtain or to escape it! Shining still!
Were it the star of Lucifer himself,
Or he himself girt with its beams, I could
Contain no longer. Softly! mighty well!
That corner's turn'd—so—ah! no;—right! it draws
Nearer. Here is a darksome angle—so,
That's weather'd.—Let me pause.—Suppose it leads
Into some greater danger than that which
I have escaped—no matter, 'tis a new one;
And novel perils, like fresh mistresses,
Wear more magnetic aspects:—I will on,
And be it where it may—I have my dagger,
Which may protect me at a pinch.—Burn still,
Thou little light! Thou art my *ignis fatuus!*
My stationary Will-o'-the-wisp!—So! so!
He hears my invocation, and fails not. [*The scene closes.*

SCENE IV.

A Garden.

Enter WERNER.

I could not sleep—and now the hour's at hand;
All's ready. Idenstein has kept his word;
And station'd in the outskirts of the town,
Upon the forest's edge, the vehicle
Awaits us. Now the dwindling stars begin
To pale in heaven; and for the last time I

Look on these horrible walls. Oh! never, never
Shall I forget them. Here I came most poor,
But not dishonour'd: and I leave them with
A stain,—if not upon my name, yet in
My heart!—a never-dying canker-worm,
Which all the coming splendour of the lands,
And rights, and sovereignty of Siegendorf
Can scarcely lull a moment. I must find
Some means of restitution, which would ease
My soul in part; but how without discovery?—
It must be done, however; and I'll pause
Upon the method the first hour of safety.
The madness of my misery led to this
Base infamy; repentance must retrieve it:
I will have nought of Stralenheim's upon
My spirit, though he would grasp all of mine;
Lands, freedom, life,—and yet he sleeps! as soundly,
Perhaps, as infancy, with gorgeous curtains
Spread for his canopy, o'er silken pillows,
Such as when—Hark! what noise is that? Again!
The branches shake; and some loose stones have fallen
From yonder terrace.
     [ULRIC *leaps down from the terrace.*
    Ulric! ever welcome!
Thrice welcome now! this filial—
 Ulr.   Stop! before
We approach, tell me—
 Wer.   Why look you so?
 Ulr.   Do I
Behold my father, or—
 Wer.   What?
 Ulr.   An assassin?
 Wer. Insane or insolent!
 Ulr.   Reply, sir, as
You prize your life, or mine!
 Wer.   To what must I
Answer?

Ulr.   Are you or are you not the assassin
Of Stralenheim?
    Wer.   I never was as yet
The murderer of any man.   What mean you?
    Ulr.   Did not you *this* night (as the night before)
Retrace the secret passage?   Did you not
Again revisit Stralenheim's chamber? and —   [ULRIC *pauses.*
    Wer.   Proceed.
    Ulr.   *Died* he not by your hand?
    Wer.   Great God!
    Ulr.   You are innocent, then! my father's innocent!
Embrace me! Yes, — your tone — your look — yes, yes, —
Yet *say* so.
    Wer.   If I e'er, in heart or mind,
Conceived deliberately such a thought,
But rather strove to trample back to hell
Such thoughts — if e'er they glared a moment through
The irritation of my oppressed spirit —
May heaven be shut for ever from my hopes
As from mine eyes!
    Ulr.   But Stralenheim is dead.
    Wer   'Tis horrible! 'tis hideous, as 'tis hateful! —
But what have I to do with this?
    Ulr.   No bolt
Is forced; no violence can be detected,
Save on his body.   Part of his own household
Have been alarm'd; but as the intendant is
Absent, I took upon myself the care
Of mustering the police.   His chamber has,
Past doubt, been enter'd secretly.   Excuse me,
If nature —
    Wer.   Oh, my boy! what unknown woes
Of dark fatality, like clouds, are gathering
Above our house!
    Ulr.   My father! I acquit you!
But will the world do so? will even the judge,
If — But you must away this instant.

Wer.   No!
I'll face it. Who shall dare suspect me?
    Ulr.   Yet
You had *no* guests—*no* visiters—no life
Breathing around you, save my mother's?
    Wer.   Ah!
The Hungarian!
    Ulr.   He is gone! he disappear'd
Ere sunset.
    Wer.   No; I hid him in that very
Conceal'd and fatal gallery.
    Ulr.   *There* I'll find him.
                                                    [ULRIC *is going.*
    Wer. It is too late: he had left the palace ere
I quitted it. I found the secret panel
Open, and the doors which lead from that hall
Which masks it: I but thought he had snatch'd the silent
And favourable moment to escape
The myrmidons of Idenstein, who were
Dogging him yester-even.
    Ulr.   You reclosed
The panel?
    Wer.   Yes; and not without reproach
(And inner trembling for the avoided peril)
At his dull heedlessness, in leaving thus
His shelterer's asylum to the risk
Of a discovery.
    Ulr.   You are sure you closed it?
    Wer. Certain.
    Ulr.   That's well; but had been better, if
You ne'er had turn'd it to a den for—
                                                   [*He pauses.*
    Wer.   Thieves!
Thou wouldst say: I must bear it and deserve it;
But not—
    Ulr.   No, father; do not speak of this:
This is no hour to think of petty crimes,

But to prevent the consequence of great ones.
Why would you shelter this man?
  Wer.   Could I shun it?
A man pursued by my chief foe; disgraced
For my own crime; a victim to *my* safety,
Imploring a few hours' concealment from
The very wretch who was the cause he needed
Such refuge. Had he been a wolf, I could not
Have in such circumstances thrust him forth.

  Ulr. And like the wolf he hath repaid you. But
It is too late to ponder thus:—you must
Set out ere dawn. I will remain here to
Trace the murderer, if 'tis possible.

  Wer. But this my sudden flight will give the Moloch
Suspicion: two new victims in the lieu
Of one, if I remain. The fled Hungarian,
Who seems the culprit, and—

  Ulr.   Who *seems?* Who else
Can be so?

  Wer. Not *I*, though just now you doubted—
You, my *son!*—doubted—

  Ulr.   And do you doubt of him
The fugitive?

  Wer. Boy! since I fell into
The abyss of crime (though not of *such* crime), I,
Having seen the innocent oppress'd for me,
May doubt even of the guilty's guilt. Your heart
Is free, and quick with virtuous wrath to accuse
Appearances; and views a criminal
In Innocence's shadow, it may be,
Because 'tis dusky.

  Ulr.   And if I do so,
What will mankind, who know you not, or knew
But to oppress? You must not stand the hazard.
Away!—I'll make all easy. Idenstein
Will for his own sake and his jewel's hold

His peace—he also is a partner in
Your flight—moreover—
    Wer.   Fly! and leave my name
Link'd with the Hungarian's, or preferr'd as poorest,
To bear the brand of bloodshed?
    Ulr.   Pshaw! leave any thing
Except our father's sovereignty and castles,
For which you have so long panted and in vain!
What *name?* You have *no name*, since that you bear
Is feign'd.
    Wer.   Most true; but still I would not have it
Engraved in crimson in men's memories,
Though in this most obscure abode of men—
Besides the search—
    Ulr.   I will provide against
Aught that can touch you. No one knows you here
As heir of Siegendorf: if Idenstein
Suspects, 'tis *but suspicion*, and he is
A fool: his folly shall have such employment,
Too, that the unknown Werner shall give way
To nearer thoughts of self. The laws (if e'er
Laws reach'd this village) are all in abeyance
With the late general war of thirty years,
Or crush'd, or rising slowly from the dust,
To which the march of armies trampled them.
Stralenheim, although noble, is unheeded
Here, save as *such*—without lands, influence,
Save what hath perish'd with him. Few prolong
A week beyond their funeral rites their sway
O'er men, unless by relatives, whose interest
Is roused: such is not here the case; he died
Alone, unknown,—a solitary grave,
Obscure as his deserts, without a scutcheon,
Is all he'll have, or wants. If *I* discover
The assassin, 'twill be well—if not, believe me
None else; though all the full-fed train of menials
May howl above his ashes (as they did

Around him in his danger on the Oder),
Will no more stir a finger *now* than *then*.
Hence! hence! I must not hear your answer.—Look!
The stars are almost faded, and the grey
Begins to grizzle the black hair of night.
You shall not answer:—Pardon me that I
Am peremptory; 'tis your son that speaks,
Your long-lost, late-found son.—Let's call my mother!
Softly and swiftly step, and leave the rest
To me: I'll answer for the event as far
As regards *you*, and that is the chief point,
As my first duty, which shall be observed.
We'll meet in Castle Siegendorf—once more
Our banners shall be glorious! Think of that
Alone, and leave all other thoughts to me,
Whose youth may better battle with them.—Hence!
And may your age be happy!—I will kiss
My mother once more, then Heaven's speed be with you!
    Wer. This counsel's safe—but is it honourable?
    Ulr. To save a father is a child's chief honour. [*Exeunt.*

ACT IV.

SCENE I.

A Gothic Hall in the Castle of Siegendorf, near Prague.

Enter ERIC *and* HENRICK, *Retainers of the Count.*

    Eric. So better times are come at last; to these
Old walls new masters and high wassail—both
A long desideratum.
    Hen.   Yes, for *masters*,
It might be unto those who long for novelty,
Though made by a new grave: but as for wassail,
Methinks the old Count Siegendorf maintain'd
His feudal hospitality as high
As e'er another prince of the empire.

ACT IV.

Eric.   Why,
For the mere cup and trencher, we no doubt
Fared passing well; but as for merriment
And sport, without which salt and sauces season
The cheer but scantily, our sizings were
Even of the narrowest.
    Hen.   The old count loved not
The roar of revel; are you sure that *this* does?
    Eric. As yet he hath been courteous as he's bounteous,
And we all love him.
    Hen.   His reign is as yet
Hardly a year o'erpast its honey-moon,
And the first year of sovereigns is bridal:
Anon, we shall perceive his real sway
And moods of mind.
    Eric.   Pray Heaven he keep the present!
Then his brave son, Count Ulric—there's a knight!
Pity the wars are o'er!
    Hen.   Why so?
    Eric.   Look on him!
And answer that yourself.
    Hen.   He's very youthful,
And strong and beautiful as a young tiger.
    Eric. That's not a faithful vassal's likeness.
    Hen.   But
Perhaps a true one.
    Eric.   Pity, as I said,
The wars are over: in the hall, who like
Count Ulric for a well-supported pride,
Which awes, but yet offends not? in the field,
Who like him with his spear in hand, when, gnashing
His tusks, and ripping up from right to left
The howling hounds, the boar makes for the thicket?
Who backs a horse, or bears a hawk, or wears
A sword like him? Whose plume nods knightlier?
    Hen. No one's, I grant you. Do not fear, if war
Be long in coming, he is of that kind

Will make it for himself, if he hath not
Already done as much.
    Eric.   What do you mean?
    Hen. You can't deny his train of followers
(But few our native fellow vassals born
On the domain) are such a sort of knaves
As— (*Pauses.*)
    Eric.   What?
    Hen. The war (you love so much) leaves living.
Like other parents, she spoils her worst children.
    Eric. Nonsense! they are all brave iron-visaged fellows,
Such as old Tilly loved.
    Hen.   And who loved Tilly?
Ask that at Magdeburg—or for that matter
Wallenstein either;—they are gone to—
    Eric.   Rest;
But what beyond 'tis not ours to pronounce.
    Hen. I wish they had left us something of their rest:
The country (nominally now at peace)
Is over-run with—God knows who: they fly
By night, and disappear with sunrise; but
Leave us no less desolation, nay, even more,
Than the most *open* warfare.
    Eric.   But Count Ulric—
What has all this to do with him?
    Hen.   With *him!*
He—might prevent it. As you say he's fond
Of war, why makes he it not on those marauders?
    Eric. You'd better ask himself.
    Hen.   I would as soon
Ask the lion why he laps not milk.
    Eric. And here he comes!
    Hen.   The devil! you'll hold your tongue?
    Eric. Why do you turn so pale?
    Hen.   'Tis nothing—but
Be silent.
    Eric. I will, upon what you have said.

Hen. I assure you I meant nothing,— a mere sport
Of words, no more; besides, had it been otherwise,
He is to espouse the gentle Baroness
Ida of Stralenheim, the late baron's heiress;
And she, no doubt, will soften whatsoever
Of fierceness the late long intestine wars
Have given all natures, and most unto those
Who were born in them, and bred up upon
The knees of Homicide; sprinkled, as it were,
With blood even at their baptism. Prithee, peace
On all that I have said!

Enter ULRIC *and* RODOLPH.

Good morrow, count.
   Ulr. Good morrow, worthy Henrick. Eric, is
All ready for the chase?
   Eric. The dogs are order'd
Down to the forest, and the vassals out
To beat the bushes, and the day looks promising.
Shall I call forth your excellency's suite?
What courser will you please to mount?
   Ulr. The dun,
Walstein.
   Eric. I fear he scarcely has recover'd
The toils of Monday: 'twas a noble chase:
You spear'd *four* with your own hand.
   Ulr. True, good Eric;
I had forgotten — let it be the grey, then,
Old Ziska: he has not been out this fortnight.
   Eric. He shall be straight caparison'd. How many
Of your immediate retainers shall
Escort you?
   Ulr. I leave that to Weilburgh, our
Master of the horse. [*Exit* ERIC.
Rodolph!
   Rod. My lord!
   Ulr. The news

Is awkward from the — (Rodolph *points to* Henrick.)
                        How now, Henrick? why
Loiter you here?
   Hen.   For your commands, my lord.
   Ulr. Go to my father, and present my duty,
And learn if he would aught with me before
I mount.   [*Exit* Henrick.
           Rodolph, our friends have had a check
Upon the frontiers of Franconia, and
'Tis rumour'd that the column sent against them
Is to be strengthen'd. I must join them soon.
   Rod. Best wait for further and more sure advices.
   Ulr. I mean it — and indeed it could not well
Have fallen out at a time more opposite
To all my plans.
   Rod.   It will be difficult
To excuse your absence to the count your father.
   Ulr. Yes, but the unsettled state of our domain
In high Silesia will permit and cover
My journey. In the mean time, when we are
Engaged in the chase, draw off the eighty men
Whom Wolffe leads — keep the forests on your route:
You know it well?
   Rod.   As well as on that night
When we —
   Ulr.   We will not speak of that until
We can repeat the same with like success:
And when you have join'd, give Rosenberg this letter.
                                [*Gives a letter.*
Add further, that I have sent this slight addition
To our force with you and Wolffe, as herald of
My coming, though I could but spare them ill
At this time, as my father loves to keep
Full numbers of retainers round the castle,
Until this marriage, and its feasts and fooleries,
Are rung out with its peal of nuptial nonsense.
   Rod. I thought you loved the lady Ida?

Ulr.   Why,
I do so—but it follows not from that
I would bind in my youth and glorious years,
So brief and burning, with a lady's zone,
Although 'twere that of Venus;—but I love her,
As woman should be loved, fairly and solely.
   Rod. And constantly?
   Ulr.   I think so; for I love
Nought else.—But I have not the time to pause
Upon these gewgaws of the heart. Great things
We have to do ere long. Speed! speed! good Rodolph!
   Rod. On my return, however, I shall find
The Baroness Ida lost in Countess Siegendorf?
   Ulr. Perhaps my father wishes it; and sooth
'Tis no bad policy: this union with
The last bud of the rival branch at once
Unites the future and destroys the past.
   Rod. Adieu.
   Ulr.   Yet hold—we had better keep together
Until the chase begins; then draw thou off,
And do as I have said.
   Rod.   I will. But to
Return—'twas a most kind act in the count
Your father to send up to Königsberg
For this fair orphan of the baron, and
To hail her as his daughter.
   Ulr.   Wondrous kind!
Especially as little kindness till
Then grew between them.
   Rod.   The late baron died
Of a fever, did he not?
   Ulr.   How should I know?
   Rod. I have heard it whisper'd there was something
       strange
About his death—and even the place of it
Is scarcely known.

Ulr.   Some obscure village on
The Saxon or Silesian frontier.
    Rod.   He
Has left no testament—no farewell words?
    Ulr. I am neither confessor nor notary,
So cannot say.
    Rod.   Ah! here's the lady Ida.
                Enter IDA STRALENHEIM.
    Ulr. You are early, my sweet cousin!
    Ida.   Not *too* early,
Dear Ulric, if I do not interrupt you.
Why do you call me "*cousin?*"
    Ulr. (*smiling*).   Are we not so?
    Ida. Yes, but I do not like the name; methinks
It sounds so cold, as if you thought upon
Our pedigree, and only weigh'd our blood.
    Ulr. (*starting*).   Blood!
    Ida. Why does yours start from your cheeks?
    Ulr.   Ay! doth it?
    Ida. It doth—but no! it rushes like a torrent
Even to your brow again.
    Ulr. (*recovering himself*). And if it fled,
It only was because your presence sent it
Back to my heart, which beats for you, sweet cousin!
    Ida. "Cousin" again.
    Ulr.   Nay, then I'll call you sister.
    Ida. I like that name still worse.—Would we had ne'er
Been aught of kindred!
    Ulr. (*gloomily*).   Would we never had!
    Ida. Oh heavens! and can *you wish that?*
    Ulr.   Dearest Ida!
Did I not echo your own wish?
    Ida.   Yes, Ulric,
But then I wish'd it not with such a glance,
And scarce knew what I said; but let me be
Sister, or cousin, what you will, so that
I still to you am something.

Ulr. You shall be
All — all —
Ida. And you to *me are* so already;
But I can wait.
Ulr. Dear Ida!
Ida. Call me Ida,
Your Ida, for I would be yours, none else's —
Indeed I have none else left, since my poor father —
[*She pauses.*

Ulr. You have *mine* — you have *me.*
Ida. Dear Ulric, how I wish
My father could but view my happiness,
Which wants but this!
Ulr. Indeed!
Ida. You would have loved him,
He you; for the brave ever love each other:
His manner was a little cold, his spirit
Proud (as is birth's prerogative); but under
This grave exterior — Would you had known each other!
Had such as you been near him on his journey,
He had not died without a friend to soothe
His last and lonely moments.
Ulr. Who says *that?*
Ida. What?
Ulr. That he *died alone.*
Ida. The general rumour,
And disappearance of his servants, who
Have ne'er return'd: that fever was most deadly
Which swept them all away.
Ulr. If they were near him,
He could not die neglected or alone.
Ida. Alas! what is a menial to a deathbed,
When the dim eye rolls vainly round for what
It loves? — They say he died of a fever.
Ulr. *Say!*
It *was* so.
Ida. I sometimes dream otherwise.

Ulr. All dreams are false.
Ida. And yet I see him as
I see you.
Ulr. Where?
Ida. In sleep — I see him lie
Pale, bleeding, and a man with a raised knife
Beside him.
Ulr. But you do not see his *face?*
Ida (looking at him). No! Oh, my God! do *you?*
Ulr. Why do you ask?
Ida. Because you look as if you saw a murderer!
Ulr. (agitatedly). Ida, this is mere childishness; your weakness
Infects me, to my shame; but as all feelings
Of yours are common to me, it affects me.
Prithee, sweet child, change—
Ida. Child, indeed! I have
Full fifteen summers! [*A bugle sounds.*
Rod. Hark, my lord, the bugle!
Ida (peevishly to RODOLPH). Why need you tell him that?
Can he not hear it
Without your echo?
Rod. Pardon me, fair baroness!
Ida. I will not pardon you, unless you earn it
By aiding me in my dissuasion of
Count Ulric from the chase to-day.
Rod. You will not,
Lady, need aid of mine.
Ulr. I must not now
Forego it.
Ida. But you shall!
Ulr. Shall!
Ida. Yes, or be
No true knight.—Come, dear Ulric! yield to me
In this, for this one day: the day looks heavy,
And you are turn'd so pale and ill.
Ulr. You jest.

Ida. Indeed I do not:—ask of Rodolph.
Rod. Truly,
My lord, within this quarter of an hour
You have changed more than e'er I saw you change
In years.
Ulr. 'Tis nothing; but if 'twere, the air
Would soon restore me. I'm the true chameleon,
And live but on the atmosphere; your feasts
In castle halls, and social banquets, nurse not
My spirit—I'm a forester and breather
Of the steep mountain-tops, where I love all
The eagle loves.
Ida. Except his prey, I hope.
Ulr. Sweet Ida, wish me a fair chase, and I
Will bring you six boars' heads for trophies home.
Ida. And will you not stay, then? You shall not go!
Come! I will sing to you.
Ulr. Ida, you scarcely
Will make a soldier's wife.
Ida. I do not wish
To be so; for I trust these wars are over,
And you will live in peace on your domains.

Enter WERNER *as* COUNT SIEGENDORF.

Ulr. My father, I salute you, and it grieves me
With such brief greeting.—You have heard our bugle;
The vassals wait.
Sieg. So let them.—You forget
To-morrow is the appointed festival
In Prague for peace restored. You are apt to follow
The chase with such an ardour as will scarce
Permit you to return to-day, or if
Return'd, too much fatigued to join to-morrow
The nobles in our marshall'd ranks.
Ulr. You, count,
Will well supply the place of both—I am not
A lover of these pageantries.

    Sieg.   No, Ulric:
It were not well that you alone of all
Our young nobility—
    Ida.   And far the noblest
In aspect and demeanour.
    Sieg. (*to* IDA).   True, dear child,
Though somewhat frankly said for a fair damsel.—
But, Ulric, recollect too our position,
So lately reinstated in our honours.
Believe me, 'twould be mark'd in any house,
But most in *ours*, that one should be found wanting
At such a time and place. Besides, the Heaven
Which gave us back our own, in the same moment
It spread its peace o'er all, hath double claims
On us for thanksgiving: first, for our country;
And next, that we are here to share its blessings.
    Ulr. (*aside*). Devout, too! Well, sir, I obey at once.
                     (*Then aloud to a Servant.*)
Ludwig, dismiss the train without!   [*Exit* LUDWIG
    Ida.   And so
You yield at once to him what I for hours
Might supplicate in vain.
    Sieg. (*smiling*).   You are not jealous
Of me, I trust, my pretty rebel! who
Would sanction disobedience against all
Except thyself? But fear not; thou shalt rule him
Hereafter with a fonder sway and firmer.
    Ida. But I should like to govern *now*.
    Sieg.   You shall,
Your *harp*, which by the way awaits you with
The countess in her chamber. She complains
That you are a sad truant to your music:
She attends you.
    Ida.   Then good morrow, my kind kinsmen!
Ulric, you'll come and hear me?
    Ulr.   By and by.
    Ida. Be sure I'll sound it better than your bugles;

Then pray you be as punctual to its notes:
I'll play you King Gustavus' march.
 Ulr.   And why not
Old Tilly's?
 Ida. Not that monster's! I should think
My harp-strings rang with groans, and not with music,
Could aught of *his* sound on it:—but come quickly;
Your mother will be eager to receive you.
             [*Exit* IDA.

 Sieg. Ulric, I wish to speak with you alone.
 Ulr. My time's your vassal.
(*Aside to* RODOLPH.) Rodolph, hence! and do
As I directed: and by his best speed
And readiest means let Rosenberg reply.
 Rod. Count Siegendorf, command you aught? I am bound
Upon a journey past the frontier.
 Sieg. (*starts.*)   Ah!—
Where? on *what* frontier?
 Rod.   The Silesian, on
My way—(*Aside to* ULRIC.)— *Where* shall I say?
 Ulr. (*aside to* RODOLPH). To Hamburgh.
      (*Aside to himself.*) That
Word will, I think, put a firm padlock on
His further inquisition.
 Rod.   Count, to Hamburgh.
 Sieg. (*agitated*). Hamburgh! No, I have nought to do
  there, nor
Am aught connected with that city. Then
God speed you!
 Rod.   Fare ye well, Count Siegendorf!
            [*Exit* RODOLPH.
 Sieg. Ulric, this man, who has just departed, is
One of those strange companions whom I fain
Would reason with you on.
 Ulr.   My lord, he is
Noble by birth, of one of the first houses
In Saxony.

Sieg.   I talk not of his birth,
But of his bearing. Men speak lightly of him.
    Ulr. So they will do of most men. Even the monarch
Is not fenced from his chamberlain's slander, or
The sneer of the last courtier whom he has made
Great and ungrateful.
    Sieg.   If I must be plain,
The world speaks more than lightly of this Rodolph:
They say he is leagued with the "black bands" who still
Ravage the frontier.
    Ulr.   And will you believe
The world?
    Sieg.   In this case—yes.
    Ulr.   In *any* case,
I thought you knew it better than to take
An accusation for a sentence.
    Sieg.   Son!
I understand you: you refer to—but
My Destiny has so involved about me
Her spider web, that I can only flutter
Like the poor fly, but break it not. Take heed,
Ulric; you have seen to what the passions led me:
Twenty long years of misery and famine
Quench'd them not—twenty thousand more, perchance,
Hereafter (or even here in *moments* which
Might date for years, did Anguish make the dial)
May not obliterate or expiate
The madness and dishonour of an instant.
Ulric, be warn'd by a father!—I was not
By mine, and you behold me!
    Ulr.   I behold
The prosperous and beloved Siegendorf,
Lord of a prince's appanage, and honour'd
By those he rules and those he ranks with.
    Sieg.   Ah!
Why wilt thou call me prosperous, while I fear
For thee? Beloved, when thou lovest me not!

All hearts but one may beat in kindness for me —
But if my son's is cold! —
    Ulr.   Who *dare* say that?
    Sieg. None else but I, who see it — *feel* it — keener
Than would your adversary, who dared say so,
Your sabre in his heart! But mine survives
The wound.
    Ulr.   You err. My nature is not given
To outward fondling: how should it be so,
After twelve years' divorcement from my parents?
    Sieg. And did not *I* too pass those twelve torn years
In a like absence? But 'tis vain to urge you —
Nature was never call'd back by remonstrance.
Let's change the theme. I wish you to consider
That these young violent nobles of high name,
But dark deeds (ay, the darkest, if all Rumour
Reports be true), with whom thou consortest,
Will lead thee —
    Ulr. (*impatiently*). I'll be *led* by no man.
    Sieg.   Nor
Be leader of such, I would hope: at once
To wean thee from the perils of thy youth
And haughty spirit, I have thought it well
That thou shouldst wed the lady Ida — more
As thou appear'st to love her.
    Ulr.   I have said
I will obey your orders, were they to
Unite with Hecate — can a son say more?
    Sieg. He says too much in saying this. It is not
The nature of thine age, nor of thy blood,
Nor of thy temperament, to talk so coolly,
Or act so carelessly, in that which is
The bloom or blight of all men's happiness,
(For Glory's pillow is but restless if
Love lay not down his cheek there): some strong bias,
Some master fiend is in thy service to
Misrule the mortal who believes him slave,

And makes his every thought subservient; else
Thou'dst say at once—"I love young Ida, and
Will wed her;" or, "I love her not, and all
The powers of earth shall never make me."—So
Would I have answer'd.
      Ulr.   Sir, *you wed* for love.
    Sieg. I did, and it has been my only refuge
In many miseries.
      Ulr.   Which miseries
Had never been but for this love-match.
    Sieg.   Still
Against your age and nature! Who at twenty
E'er answer'd thus till now?
    Ulr.   Did you not warn me
Against your own example?
    Sieg.   Boyish sophist!
In a word, do you love, or love not, Ida?
    Ulr. What matters it, if I am ready to
Obey you in espousing her?
    Sieg.   As far
As you feel, nothing, but all life for her.
She's young—all beautiful—adores you—is
Endow'd with qualities to give happiness,
Such as rounds common life into a dream
Of something which your poets cannot paint,
And (if it were not wisdom to love virtue)
For which Philosophy might barter Wisdom;
And giving so much happiness, deserves
A little in return. I would not have her
Break her heart for a man who has none to break;
Or wither on her stalk like some pale rose
Deserted by the bird she thought a nightingale,
According to the Orient tale. She is—
    Ulr. The daughter of dead Stralenheim, your foe:
I'll wed her, ne'ertheless; though, to say truth,
Just now I am not violently transported
In favour of such unions.

Sieg. But she loves you.
Ulr. And I love her, and therefore would think *twice*.
Sieg. Alas! Love never *did* so.
Ulr. Then 'tis time
He should begin, and take the bandage from
His eyes, and look before he leaps: till now
He hath ta'en a jump i' the dark.
Sieg. But you consent?
Ulr. I did, and do.
Sieg. Then fix the day.
Ulr. 'Tis usual,
And certes courteous, to leave that to the lady.
Sieg. I will engage for *her*.
Ulr. So will not *I*
For any woman; and as what I fix,
I fain would see unshaken, when she gives
Her answer, I'll give mine.
Sieg. But 'tis your office
To woo.
Ulr. Count, 'tis a marriage of your making,
So be it of your wooing; but to please you
I will now pay my duty to my mother,
With whom, you know, the lady Ida is.—
What would you have? You have forbid my stirring
For manly sports beyond the castle walls,
And I obey; you bid me turn a chamberer,
To pick up gloves, and fans, and knitting-needles,
And list to songs and tunes, and watch for smiles,
And smile at pretty prattle, and look into
The eyes of feminine, as though they were
The stars receding early to our wish
Upon the dawn of a world-winning battle—
What can a son or man do more? [*Exit* ULRIC.
Sieg. (*solus*). Too much!—
Too much of duty and too little love!
He pays me in the coin he owes me not:
For such hath been my wayward fate, I could not

Fulfil a parent's duties by his side
Till now; but love he owes me, for my thoughts
Ne'er left him, nor my eyes long'd without tears
To see my child again, and now I have found him!
But how!—obedient, but with coldness; duteous
In my sight, but with carelessness; mysterious—
Abstracted—distant—much given to long absence,
And where—none know—in league with the most riotous
Of our young nobles; though, to do him justice,
He never stoops down to their vulgar pleasures;
Yet there's some tie between them which I cannot
Unravel. They look up to him—consult him—
Throng round him as a leader: but with me
He hath no confidence! Ah! can I hope it
After—what! doth my father's curse descend
Even to my child? Or is the Hungarian near
To shed more blood? or—Oh! if it should be!
Spirit of Stralenheim, dost thou walk these walls
To wither him and his—who, though they slew not,
Unlatch'd the door of death for thee? 'Twas not
Our fault, nor is our sin: thou wert our foe,
And yet I spared thee when my own destruction
Slept with thee, to awake with thine awakening!
And only took—Accursed gold! thou liest
Like poison in my hands; I dare not use thee,
Nor part from thee; thou camest in such a guise,
Methinks thou wouldst contaminate all hands
Like mine. Yet I have done, to atone for thee,
Thou villanous gold! and thy dead master's doom,
Though he died not by me or mine, as much
As if he were my brother! I have ta'en
His orphan Ida—cherish'd her as one
Who will be mine.

Enter an ATTENDANT.

Atten. The abbot, if it please
Your excellency, whom you sent for, waits
Upon you. [*Exit* ATTENDANT.

ACT IV.

Enter the PRIOR ALBERT.

Prior.   Peace be with these walls, and all
Within them!
Sieg.   Welcome, welcome, holy father!
And may thy prayer be heard!—all men have need
Of such, and I—
Prior.   Have the first claim to all
The prayers of our community. Our convent,
Erected by your ancestors, is still
Protected by their children.
Sieg.   Yes, good father;
Continue daily orisons for us
In these dim days of heresies and blood,
Though the schismatic Swede, Gustavus, is
Gone home.
Prior.   To the endless home of unbelievers,
Where there is everlasting wail and woe,
Gnashing of teeth, and tears of blood, and fire
Eternal, and the worm which dieth not!
Sieg. True, father: and to avert those pangs from one,
Who, though of our most faultless holy church,
Yet died without its last and dearest offices,
Which smooth the soul through purgatorial pains,
I have to offer humbly this donation
In masses for his spirit.

[SIEGENDORF *offers the gold which he had taken from* STRALENHEIM.

Prior.   Count, if I
Receive it, 'tis because I know too well
Refusal would offend you. Be assured
The largess shall be only dealt in alms,
And every mass no less sung for the dead.
Our house needs no donations, thanks to yours,
Which has of old endow'd it; but from you
And yours in all meet things 'tis fit we obey.
For whom shall mass be said?
Sieg. (faltering).   For—for—the dead.

Prior. His name?
Sieg. 'Tis from a soul, and not a name,
I would avert perdition.
Prior. I meant not
To pry into your secret. We will pray
For one unknown, the same as for the proudest.
Sieg. Secret! I have none; but, father, he who's gone
Might *have* one; or, in short, he did bequeath—
No, not bequeath—but I bestow this sum
For pious purposes.
Prior. A proper deed
In the behalf of our departed friends.
Sieg. But he who's gone was not my friend, but foe,
The deadliest and the stanchest.
Prior. Better still!
To employ our means to obtain heaven for the souls
Of our dead enemies is worthy those
Who can forgive them living.
Sieg. But I did not
Forgive this man. I loathed him to the last,
As he did me. I do not love him now,
But—
Prior. Best of all! for this is pure religion!
You fain would rescue him you hate from hell—
An evangelical compassion—with
Your own gold too!
Sieg. Father, 'tis not my gold.
Prior. Whose then? You said it was no legacy.
Sieg. No matter whose—of this be sure, that he
Who own'd it never more will need it, save
In that which it may purchase from your altars:
'Tis yours, or theirs.
Prior. Is there no blood upon it?
Sieg. No; but there's worse than blood—eternal shame!
Prior. Did he who own'd it die in his *bed?*
Sieg. Alas!
He did.

Prior. Son! you relapse into revenge,
If you regret your enemy's bloodless death.
    Sieg. His death was fathomlessly deep in blood.
    Prior. You said he died in his bed, not battle.
    Sieg.   He
Died, I scarce know—but—he was stabb'd i' the dark,
And now you have it—perish'd on his pillow
By a cut-throat!—Ay!—you may look upon me!
I am not the man. I'll meet your eye on that point,
As I can one day God's.
    Prior.   Nor did he die
By means, or men, or instrument of yours?
    Sieg. No! by the God who sees and strikes!
    Prior.   Nor know you
Who slew him?
    Sieg.   I could only guess at *one,*
And he to me a stranger, unconnected,
As unemploy'd. Except by one day's knowledge,
I never saw the man who was suspected.
    Prior. Then you are free from guilt.
    Sieg. (eagerly).   Oh! *am* I?—say!
    Prior. You have said so, and know best.
    Sieg.   Father, I have spoken
The truth, and nought but truth, if *not* the *whole:*
Yet say I am *not* guilty! for the blood
Of this man weighs on me, as if I shed it,
Though, by the Power who abhorreth human blood,
I did not!—nay, once spared it, when I might
And *could*—ay, perhaps, *should* (if our self-safety
Be e'er excusable in such defences
Against the attacks of over-potent foes):
But pray for him, for me, and all my house;
For, as I said, though I be innocent,
I know not why, a like remorse is on me,
As if he had fallen by me or mine. Pray for me,
Father! I have pray'd myself in vain.
    Prior.   I will.

Be comforted! You are innocent, and should
Be calm as innocence.
  Sieg.   But calmness is not
Always the attribute of innocence.
I feel it is not.
  Prior. But it will be so,
When the mind gathers up its truth within it.
Remember the great festival to-morrow,
In which you rank amidst our chiefest nobles,
As well as your brave son; and smooth your aspect;
Nor in the general orison of thanks
For bloodshed stopt, let blood you shed not rise
A cloud upon your thoughts. This were to be
Too sensitive. Take comfort, and forget
Such things, and leave remorse unto the guilty. [*Exeunt.*

ACT V.

SCENE I.

*A large and magnificent Gothic Hall in the Castle of Siegendorf,
decorated with Trophies, Banners, and Arms of that Family.*

Enter ARNHEIM *and* MEISTER, *attendants of* COUNT SIEGENDORF.

  Arn. Be quick! the count will soon return: the ladies
Already are at the portal. Have you sent
The messengers in search of him he seeks for?
  Meis. I have, in all directions, over Prague,
As far as the man's dress and figure could
By your description track him. The devil take
These revels and processions! All the pleasure
(If such there be) must fall to the spectators.
I'm sure none doth to us who make the show.
  Arn. Go to! my lady countess comes.
  Meis.   I'd rather
Ride a day's hunting on an outworn jade,
Than follow in the train of a great man
In these dull pageantries.

Arn. Begone! and rail
Within. [*Exeunt.*

Enter the COUNTESS JOSEPHINE SIEGENDORF *and* IDA STRALEN-
HEIM.

Jos. Well, Heaven be praised, the show is over!
Ida. How can you say so! never have I dreamt
Of aught so beautiful. The flowers, the boughs,
The banners, and the nobles, and the knights,
The gems, the robes, the plumes, the happy faces,
The coursers, and the incense, and the sun
Streaming through the stain'd windows, even the *tombs*,
Which look'd so calm, and the celestial hymns,
Which seem'd as if they rather came from heaven
Than mounted there. The bursting organ's peal
Rolling on high like an harmonious thunder;
The white robes and the lifted eyes; the world
At peace! and all at peace with one another!
Oh, my sweet mother! [*Embracing* JOSEPHINE.
Jos. My beloved child!
For such, I trust, thou shalt be shortly.
Ida. Oh!
I am so already. Feel how my heart beats!
Jos. It does, my love; and never may it throb
With aught more bitter.
Ida. Never shall it do so!
How should it? What should make us grieve? I hate
To hear of sorrow: how can we be sad,
Who love each other so entirely? You,
The count, and Ulric, and your daughter Ida.
Jos. Poor child!
Ida. Do you pity me?
Jos. No; I but envy,
And that in sorrow, not in the world's sense
Of the universal vice, if one vice be
More general than another.
Ida. I'll not hear
A word against a world which still contains

You and my Ulric. Did you ever see
Aught like him? How he tower'd amongst them all!
How all eyes follow'd him! The flowers fell faster—
Rain'd from each lattice at his feet, methought,
Than before all the rest; and where he trod
I dare be sworn that they grow still, nor e'er
Will wither.
  Jos. You will spoil him, little flatterer,
If he should hear you.
  Ida. But he never will.
I dare not say so much to him—I fear him.
  Jos. Why so? he loves you well.
  Ida. But I can never
Shape my thoughts *of* him into words *to* him.
Besides, he sometimes frightens me.
  Jos. How so?
  Ida. A cloud comes o'er his blue eyes suddenly,
Yet he says nothing.
  Jos. It is nothing: all men,
Especially in these dark troublous times,
Have much to think of.
  Ida. But I cannot think
Of aught save him.
  Jos. Yet there are other men,
In the world's eye, as goodly. There's, for instance,
The young Count Waldorf, who scarce once withdrew
His eyes from yours to-day.
  Ida. I did not see him,
But Ulric. Did you not see at the moment
When all knelt, and I wept? and yet methought,
Through my fast tears, though they were thick and warm,
I saw him smiling on me.
  Jos. I could not
See aught save heaven, to which my eyes were raised
Together with the people's.
  Ida. I thought too
Of heaven, although I look'd on Ulric.

ACT V.

Jos.   Come,
Let us retire; they will be here anon
Expectant of the banquet. We will lay
Aside these nodding plumes and dragging trains.
    Ida. And, above all, these stiff and heavy jewels,
Which make my head and heart ache, as both throb
Beneath their glitter o'er my brow and zone.
Dear mother, I am with you.

Enter COUNT SIEGENDORF, *in full dress, from the solemnity, and* LUDWIG.
    Sieg.   Is he not found?
    Lud. Strict search is making every where; and if
The man be in Prague, be sure he will be found.
    Sieg. Where's Ulric?
    Lud.   He rode round the other way
With some young nobles; but he left them soon;
And, if I err not, not a minute since
I heard his excellency, with his train,
Gallop o'er the west drawbridge.

Enter ULRIC, *splendidly dressed.*
    Sieg. (*to* LUDWIG).   See they cease not
Their quest of him I have described.   [*Exit* LUDWIG.
                        Oh, Ulric!
How have I long'd for thee!
    Ulr.   Your wish is granted—
Behold me!
    Sieg. I have seen the murderer.
    Ulr. Whom? Where?
    Sieg.   ·   The Hungarian, who slew Stralenheim.
    Ulr. You dream.
    Sieg.   I live! and as I live, I saw him—
Heard him! he dared to utter even my name.
    Ulr. What name?
    Sieg.   Werner! '*twas* mine.
    Ulr.   It must be so
No more: forget it.

Sieg.   Never! never! all
My destinies were woven in that name:
It will not be engraved upon my tomb,
But it may lead me there.
   Ulr.   To the point—the Hungarian?
   Sieg. Listen!—The church was throng'd; the hymn was
        raised;
"*Te Deum*" peal'd from nations, rather than
From choirs, in one great cry of "God be praised"
For one day's peace, after thrice ten dread years,
Each bloodier than the former: I arose,
With all the nobles, and as I look'd down
Along the lines of lifted faces,—from
Our banner'd and escutcheon'd gallery, I
Saw, like a flash of lightning (for I saw
A moment and no more), what struck me sightless
To all else—the Hungarian's face! I grew
Sick; and when I recover'd from the mist
Which curl'd about my senses, and again
Look'd down, I saw him not. The thanksgiving
Was over, and we march'd back in procession.
   Ulr. Continue.
   Sieg.   When we reach'd the Muldau's bridge,
The joyous crowd above, the numberless
Barks mann'd with revellers in their best garbs,
Which shot along the glancing tide below,
The decorated street, the long array,
The clashing music, and the thundering
Of far artillery, which seem'd to bid
A long and loud farewell to its great doings,
The standards o'er me, and the tramplings round,
The roar of rushing thousands,—all—all could not
Chase this man from my mind, although my senses
No longer held him palpable.
   Ulr.   You saw him
No more, then?
   Sieg.   I look'd, as a dying soldier

Looks at a draught of water, for this man:
But still I saw him not; but in his stead—
    Ulr. What in his stead?
    Sieg.   My eye for ever fell
Upon your dancing crest; the loftiest,
As on the loftiest and the loveliest head
It rose the highest of the stream of plumes,
Which overflow'd the glittering streets of Prague.
    Ulr. What's this to the Hungarian?
    Sieg.   Much; for I
Had almost then forgot him in my son;
When just as the artillery ceased, and paused
The music, and the crowd embraced in lieu
Of shouting, I heard in a deep, low voice,
Distinct and keener far upon my ear
Than the late cannon's volume, this word—"*Werner!*"
    Ulr. Uttered by—
    Sieg.   Him! I turn'd—and saw—and fell.
    Ulr. And wherefore? Were you seen?
    Sieg.   The officious care
Of those around me dragg'd me from the spot,
Seeing my faintness, ignorant of the cause;
You, too, were too remote in the procession
(The old nobles being divided from their children)
To aid me.
    Ulr.   But I'll aid you now.
    Sieg.   In what?
    Ulr. In searching for this man, or—When he's found
What shall we do with him?
    Sieg.   I know not that.
    Ulr. Then wherefore seek?
    Sieg.   Because I cannot rest
Till he is found. His fate, and Stralenheim's,
And ours, seem intertwisted! nor can be
Unravell'd, till—

Enter an ATTENDANT.

Atten. A stranger to wait on
Your excellency.
 Sieg. Who?
 Atten. He gave no name.
 Sieg. Admit him, ne'ertheless.
  [*The* ATTENDANT *introduces* GABOR, *and afterwards exit.*
         Ah!
 Gab. 'Tis, then, Werner!
 Sieg. (*haughtily*). The same you knew, sir, by that name;
  and you!
 Gab. (*looking round*). I recognise you both: father and son,
It seems. Count, I have heard that you, or yours,
Have lately been in search of me: I am here.
 Sieg. I have sought you, and have found you: you are
  charged
(Your own heart may inform you why) with such
A crime as—   [*He pauses.*
 Gab. Give it utterance, and then
I'll meet the consequences.
 Sieg. You shall do so—
Unless—
 Gab. First, who accuses me?
 Sieg. All things,
If not all men: the universal rumour—
My own presence on the spot—the place—the time—
And every speck of circumstance unite
To fix the blot on you.
 Gab. And on *me only?*
Pause ere you answer: is no other name,
Save mine, stain'd in this business?
 Sieg. Trifling villain!
Who play'st with thine own guilt? Of all that breathe
Thou best dost know the innocence of him
'Gainst whom thy breath would blow thy bloody slander.
But I will talk no further with a wretch,

Further than justice asks. Answer at once,
And without quibbling, to my charge.
    Gab.   'Tis false!
    Sieg. Who says so?
    Gab.   I.
    Sieg.   And how disprove it?
    Gab.   By
The presence of the murderer.
    Sieg.   Name him!
    Gab.   He
May have more names than one. Your lordship had so
Once on a time.
    Sieg.   If you mean me, I dare
Your utmost.
    Gab.   You may do so, and in safety;
I know the assassin.
    Sieg.   Where is he?
    Gab. (*pointing to* ULRIC).   Beside you!
        [ULRIC *rushes forward to attack* GABOR; SIEGENDORF
            interposes.
    Sieg. Liar and fiend! but you shall not be slain;
These walls are mine, and you are safe within them.
                                    [*He turns to* ULRIC.
Ulric, repel this calumny, as I
Will do. I avow it is a growth so monstrous,
I could not deem it earth-born: but be calm;
It will refute itself. But touch him not.
                         [ULRIC *endeavours to compose himself.*
    Gab. Look at *him*, count, and then *hear me.*
    Sieg. (*first to* GABOR, *and then looking at* ULRIC).
                                          I hear thee.
My God! you look—
    Ulr.   How?
    Sieg.   As on that dread night
When we met in the garden.
    Ulr. (*composes himself*).   It is nothing.
    Gab. Count, you are bound to hear me. I came hither

Not seeking you, but sought. When I knelt down
Amidst the people in the church, I dream'd not
To find the beggar'd Werner in the seat
Of senators and princes; but you have call'd me,
And we have met.
 Sieg.   Go on, sir.
 Gab.   Ere I do so,
Allow me to inquire who profited
By Stralenheim's death? Was't I—as poor as ever;
And poorer by suspicion on my name!
The baron lost in that last outrage neither
Jewels nor gold; his life alone was sought,—
A life which stood between the claims of others
To honours and estates scarce less than princely.
 Sieg. These hints, as vague as vain, attach no less
To me than to my son.
 Gab.   I can't help that.
But let the consequence alight on him
Who feels himself the guilty one amongst us.
I speak to you, Count Siegendorf, because
I know you innocent, and deem you just.
But ere I can proceed—*dare* you protect me?
Dare you command me?

    [SIEGENDORF *first looks at the Hungarian, and then
     at* ULRIC, *who has unbuckled his sabre, and is
     drawing lines with it on the floor — still in its sheath.*

 Ulr. (*looks at his father and says*)
       Let the man go on!
 Gab. I am unarm'd, count—bid your son lay down
His sabre.
 Ulr. (*offers it to him contemptuously*).
    Take it.
 Gab.   No, sir, 'tis enough
That we are both unarm'd—I would not choose
To wear a steel which may be stain'd with more
Blood than came there in battle.
 Ulr. (*casts the sabre from him in contempt*).

                It—or some
Such other weapon, in my hands—spared yours
Once when disarm'd and at my mercy.
    Gab.   True—
I have not forgotten it: you spared me for
Your own especial purpose—to sustain
An ignominy not my own.
    Ulr.   Proceed.
The tale is doubtless worthy the relater.
But is it of my father to hear further?   [*To* SIEGENDORF.
    Sieg. (*takes his son by the hand*).
My son, I know my own innocence, and doubt not
Of yours—but I have promised this man patience;
Let him continue.
    Gab.   I will not detain you
By speaking of myself much; I began
Life early—and am what the world has made me.
At Frankfort on the Oder, where I pass'd
A winter in obscurity, it was
My chance at several places of resort
(Which I frequented sometimes but not often)
To hear related a strange circumstance
In February last. A martial force,
Sent by the state, had, after strong resistance,
Secured a band of desperate men, supposed
Marauders from the hostile camp.—They proved,
However, not to be so—but banditti,
Whom either accident or enterprise
Had carried from their usual haunt—the forests
Which skirt Bohemia—even into Lusatia.
Many amongst them were reported of
High rank—and martial law slept for a time.
At last they were escorted o'er the frontiers,
And placed beneath the civil jurisdiction
Of the free town of Frankfort. Of *their* fate,
I know no more.
    Sieg.   And what is this to Ulric?

Gab. Amongst them there was said to be one man
Of wonderful endowments:—birth and fortune,
Youth, strength, and beauty, almost superhuman,
And courage as unrivall'd, were proclaim'd
His by the public rumour; and his sway,
Not only over his associates, but
His judges, was attributed to witchcraft.
Such was his influence:—I have no great faith
In any magic save that of the mine—
I therefore deem'd him wealthy.—But my soul
Was roused with various feelings to seek out
This prodigy, if only to behold him.
   Sieg. And did you so?
   Gab.   You'll hear. Chance favour'd me:
A popular affray in the public square
Drew crowds together—it was one of those
Occasions where men's souls look out of them,
And show them as they are—even in their faces:
The moment my eye met his, I exclaim'd,
"This is the man!" though he was then, as since,
With the nobles of the city. I felt sure
I had not err'd, and watch'd him long and nearly:
I noted down his form—his gesture—features,
Stature, and bearing—and amidst them all,
Midst every natural and acquired distinction,
I could discern, methought, the assassin's eye
And gladiator's heart.
   Ulr. (*smiling*).   The tale sounds well.
   Gab. And may sound better.—He appear'd to me
One of those beings to whom Fortune bends
As she doth to the daring—and on whom
The fates of others oft depend; besides,
An indescribable sensation drew me
Near to this man, as if my point of fortune
Was to be fix'd by him.—There I was wrong.
   Sieg. And may not be right now.
   Gab.   I follow'd him,

Solicited his notice—and obtain'd it—
Though not his friendship:—it was his intention
To leave the city privately—we left it
Together—and together we arrived
In the poor town where Werner was conceal'd,
And Stralenheim was succour'd—Now we are on
The verge—*dare* you hear further?
    Sieg.   I must do so—
Or I have heard too much.
    Gab.   I saw in you
A man above his station—and if not
So high, as now I find you, in my then
Conceptions, 'twas that I had rarely seen
Men such as you appear'd in height of mind
In the most high of worldly rank; you were
Poor, even to all save rags: I would have shared
My purse, though slender, with you—you refused it.
    Sieg. Doth my refusal make a debt to you,
That thus you urge it?
    Gab.   Still you owe me something,
Though not for that; and I owed you my safety,
At least my seeming safety, when the slaves
Of Stralenheim pursued me on the grounds
That *I* had robb'd him.
    Sieg.   *I* conceal'd you—I,
Whom and whose house you arraign, reviving viper!
    Gab. I accuse no man—save in my defence.
You, count, have made yourself accuser—judge:
Your hall's my court, your heart is my tribunal.
Be just, and *I* 'll be merciful!
    Sieg.   You merciful!
You! Base calumniator!
    Gab.   I. 'T will rest
With me at last to be so. You conceal'd me—
In secret passages known to yourself,
You said, and to none else. At dead of night,
Weary with watching in the dark, and dubious

Of tracing back my way, I saw a glimmer,
Through distant crannies, of a twinkling light:
I follow'd it, and reach'd a door—a secret
Portal—which open'd to the chamber, where,
With cautious hand and slow, having first undone
As much as made a crevice of the fastening,
I look'd through and beheld a purple bed,
And on it Stralenheim!—

   Sieg.   Asleep! And yet
You slew him!—Wretch!

   Gab.   He was already slain,
And bleeding like a sacrifice. My own
Blood became ice.

   Sieg.   But he was all alone!
You saw none else? You did not see the—
                       [*He pauses from agitation.*

   Gab.   No,
He, whom you dare not name, or even I
Scarce dare to recollect, was not then in
The chamber.

   Sieg. (*to* ULRIC). Then, my boy! thou art guiltless still—
Thou bad'st me say *I* was so once—Oh! now
Do thou as much!

   Gab.   Be patient! I can *not*
Recede now, though it shake the very walls
Which frown above us. You remember,—or
If not, your son does,—that the locks were changed
Beneath *his* chief inspection on the morn
Which led to this same night: how he had enter'd
He best knows—but within an antechamber,
The door of which was half ajar, I saw
A man who wash'd his bloody hands, and oft
With stern and anxious glance gazed back upon
The bleeding body—but it moved no more.

   Sieg. Oh! God of fathers!

   Gab.   I beheld his features
As I see yours—but yours they were not, though

Resembling them—behold them in Count Ulric's!
Distinct as I beheld them, though the expression
Is not now what it then was;—but it was so
When I first charged him with the crime—so lately.

   Sieg. This is so—

   Gab. (*interrupting him*). Nay—but hear me to the end!
Now you must do so.—I conceived myself
Betray'd by you and *him* (for now I saw
There was some tie between you) into this
Pretended den of refuge, to become
The victim of your guilt; and my first thought
Was vengeance: but though arm'd with a short poniard
(Having left my sword without) I was no match
For him at any time, as had been proved
That morning—either in address or force.
I turn'd, and fled—i' the dark: chance rather than
Skill made me gain the secret door of the hall,
And thence the chamber where you slept: if I
Had found you *waking*, Heaven alone can tell
What vengeance and suspicion might have prompted;
But ne'er slept guilt as Werner slept that night.

   Sieg. And yet I had horrid dreams! and such brief sleep,
The stars had not gone down when I awoke.
Why didst thou spare me? I dreamt of my father—
And now my dream is out!

   Gab.   'Tis not my fault,
If I have read it.—Well! I fled and hid me—
Chance led me here after so many moons—
And show'd me Werner in Count Siegendorf!
Werner, whom I had sought in huts in vain,
Inhabited the palace of a sovereign!
You sought me and have found me—now you know
My secret, and may weigh its worth.

   Sieg. (*after a pause*).   Indeed!

   Gab. Is it revenge or justice which inspires
Your meditation?

Sieg. Neither—I was weighing
The value of your secret.
Gab. You shall know it
At once:—When you were poor, and I, though poor,
Rich enough to relieve such poverty
As might have envied mine, I offer'd you
My purse—you would not share it:—I'll be franker
With you: you are wealthy, noble, trusted by
The imperial powers—you understand me?
Sieg. Yes.
Gab. Not quite. You think me venal, and scarce true:
'Tis no less true, however, that my fortunes
Have made me both at present. You shall aid me:
I would have aided you—and also have
Been somewhat damaged in my name to save
Yours and your son's. Weigh well what I have said,
Sieg. Dare you await the event of a few minutes'
Deliberation?
Gab. (*casts his eyes on* ULRIC, *who is leaning against a pillar.*)
If I should do so?
Sieg. I pledge my life for yours. Withdraw into
This tower. [*Opens a turret door.*
Gab. (*hesitatingly*). This is the second safe asylum
You have offer'd me.
Sieg. And was not the first so?
Gab. I know not that even now—but will approve
The second. I have still a further shield.—
I did not enter Prague alone; and should I
Be put to rest with Stralenheim, there are
Some tongues without will wag in my behalf.
Be brief in your decision!
Sieg. I will be so.—
My word is sacred and irrevocable
Within *these* walls, but it extends no further.
Gab. I'll take it for so much.
Sieg. (*points to* ULRIC'*s sabre still upon the ground*).
Take also that—

I saw you eye it eagerly, and him
Distrustfully.
 Gab. (*takes up the sabre*). I will; and so provide
To sell my life—not cheaply.
   [GABOR *goes into the turret, which* SIEGENDORF *closes.*
 Sieg. (*advances to* ULRIC). Now, Count Ulric!
For son I dare not call thee—What say'st thou?
 Ulr. His tale is true.
 Sieg.   True, monster!
 Ulr.   Most true, father!
And you did well to listen to it: what
We know, we can provide against. He must
Be silenced.
 Sieg. Ay, with half of my domains;
And with the other half, could he and thou
Unsay this villany.
 Ulr.   It is no time
For trifling or dissembling. I have said
His story's true; and he too must be silenced.
 Sieg. How so?
 Ulr.   As Stralenheim is. Are you so dull
As never to have hit on this before?
When we met in the garden, what except
Discovery in the act would make me know
His death? Or had the prince's household been
Then summon'd, would the cry for the police
Been left to such a stranger? Or should I
Have loiter'd on the way? Or could *you*, *Werner*,
The object of the baron's hate and fears,
Have fled, unless by many an hour before
Suspicion woke? I sought and fathom'd you,
Doubting if you were false or feeble: I
Perceived you were the latter; and yet so
Confiding have I found you, that I doubted
At times your weakness.
 Sieg.   Parricide! no less
Than common stabber! What deed of my life,

Or thought of mine, could make you deem me fit
For your accomplice?
    Ulr.   Father, do not raise
The devil you cannot lay between us. This
Is time for union and for action, not
For family disputes. While *you* were tortured,
Could *I* be calm? Think you that I have heard
This fellow's tale without some feeling?—You
Have taught me feeling for *you* and myself;
For whom or what else did you ever teach it?
    Sieg. Oh! my dead father's curse! 'tis working now.
    Ulr. Let it work on! the grave will keep it down!
Ashes are feeble foes: it is more easy
To baffle such, than countermine a mole,
Which winds its blind but living path beneath you.
Yet hear me still!—If *you* condemn me, yet
Remember *who* hath taught me once too often
To listen to him! *Who* proclaim'd to me
That *there were crimes* made venial by the occasion?
That passion was our nature? that the goods
Of Heaven waited on the goods of fortune?
Who show'd me his humanity secured
By his *nerves* only? *Who* deprived me of
All power to vindicate myself and race
In open day? By his disgrace which stamp'd
(It might be) bastardy on me, and on
Himself—a *felon*'s brand! The man who is
At once both warm and weak invites to deeds
He longs to do, but dare not. Is it strange
That I should *act* what you could *think?* We have done
With right and wrong; and now must only ponder
Upon effects, not causes. Stralenheim,
Whose life I saved from impulse, as *unknown*,
I would have saved a peasant's or a dog's, I slew
Known as our foe—but not from vengeance. He
Was a rock in our way which I cut through,
As doth the bolt, because it stood between us

And our true destination—but not idly.
As stranger I preserved him, and he *owed me
His life:* when due, I but resumed the debt.
He, you, and I stood o'er a gulf wherein
I have plunged our enemy. *You* kindled first
The torch—*you* show'd the path; now trace me that
Of safety—or let me!
    Sieg.   I have done with life!
    Ulr. Let us have done with that which cankers life—
Familiar feuds and vain recriminations
Of things which cannot be undone. We have
No more to learn or hide: I know no fear,
And have within these very walls men who
(Although you know them not) dare venture all things.
You stand high with the state; what passes here
Will not excite her too great curiosity:
Keep your own secret, keep a steady eye,
Stir not, and speak not;—leave the rest to me:
We must have no *third* babblers thrust between us.
                                          [*Exit* ULRIC.
    Sieg. (*solus*). Am I awake? are these my father's halls?
And yon—my son? *My* son! *mine!* who have ever
Abhorr'd both mystery and blood, and yet
Am plunged into the deepest hell of both!
I must be speedy, or more will be shed—
The Hungarian's!—Ulric—he hath partisans,
It seems: I might have guess'd as much. Oh fool!
Wolves prowl in company. He hath the key
(As I too) of the opposite door which leads
Into the turret. Now then! or once more
To be the father of fresh crimes, no less
Than of the criminal! Ho! Gabor! Gabor!
                [*Exit into the turret, closing the door after him.*

SCENE II.
The Interior of the Turret.
GABOR *and* SIEGENDORF.

Gab. Who calls?
Sieg. I—Siegendorf! Take these, and fly!
Lose not a moment!
[*Tears off a diamond star and other jewels, and thrusts them into* GABOR's *hand.*

Gab. What am I to do
With these?
Sieg. Whate'er you will: sell them, or hoard,
And prosper; but delay not, or you are lost!
Gab. You pledged your honour for my safety!
Sieg. And
Must thus redeem it. Fly! I am not master,
It seems, of my own castle—of my own
Retainers—nay, even of these very walls,
Or I would bid them fall and crush me! Fly!
Or you will be slain by—
Gab. Is it even so?
Farewell, then! Recollect, however, Count,
You sought this fatal interview!
Sieg. I did:
Let it not be more fatal still!—Begone!
Gab. By the same path I enter'd?
Sieg. Yes; that's safe still,
But loiter not in Prague;—you do not know
With whom you have to deal.
Gab. I know too well—
And knew it ere yourself, unhappy sire!
Farewell! [*Exit* GABOR
Sieg. (*solus and listening*). He hath clear'd the staircase
Ah! I hear
The door sound loud behind him! He is safe!
Safe!—Oh, my father's spirit!—I am faint—
[*He leans down upon a stone seat, near the wall of the tower, in a drooping posture.*

Enter ULRIC, *with others armed, and with weapons drawn.*
  Ulr. Despatch!—he's there!
  Lud.   The count, my lord!
  Ulr. (*recognising* SIEGENDORF). *You* here, sir!
  Sieg. Yes: if you want another victim, strike!
  Ulr. (*seeing him stript of his jewels*). Where is the ruffian
        who hath plunder'd you?
Vassals, despatch in search of him! You see
"T was as I said—the wretch hath stript my father
Of jewels which might form a prince's heir-loom!
Away! I'll follow you forthwith.
                        [*Exeunt all but* SIEGENDORF *and* ULRIC.
                        What's this?
Where is the villain?
  Sieg.   There are *two*, sir: which
Are you in quest of?
  Ulr.   Let us hear no more
Of this: he must be found. You have not let him
Escape?
  Sieg. He's gone.
  Ulr.   With your connivance?
  Sieg.   With
My fullest, freest aid.
  Ulr.   Then fare you well! [ULRIC *is going*.
  Sieg. Stop! I command—entreat—implore! Oh, Ulric!
Will you then leave me?
  Ulr.   What! remain to be
Denounced—dragg'd, it may be, in chains; and all
By your inherent weakness, half-humanity,
Selfish remorse, and temporising pity,
That sacrifices your whole race to save
A wretch to profit by our ruin! No, count,
Henceforth you have no son!
  Sieg.   I never had one;
And would you ne'er had borne the useless name!
Where will you go? I would not send you forth
Without protection.

Ulr.   Leave that unto me.
I am not alone; nor merely the vain heir
Of your domains; a thousand, ay, ten thousand
Swords, hearts, and hands, are mine.
    Sieg.   The foresters!
With whom the Hungarian found you first at Frankfort!
    Ulr. Yes — men — who are worthy of the name! Go te
Your senators that they look well to Prague;
Their feast of peace was early for the times;
There are more spirits abroad than have been laid
With Wallenstein!
                   Enter JOSEPHINE *and* IDA.
    Jos.   What is't we hear? My Siegendorf!
Thank Heav'n, I see you safe!
    Sieg.   Safe!
    Ida.   Yes, dear father!
    Sieg. No, no; I have no children: never more
Call me by that worst name of parent.
    Jos.   What
Means my good lord?
    Sieg.   That you have given birth
To a demon!
    Ida. (*taking* ULRIC's *hand*). Who shall dare say this of Ulric
    Sieg. Ida, beware! there's blood upon that hand.
    Ida. (*stooping to kiss it*). I'd kiss it off, though it were mine
    Sieg.   It is so
    Ulr. Away! it is your father's!   [*Exit* ULRIC
    Ida.   Oh, great God!
And I have loved this man!
    [IDA *falls senseless —* JOSEPHINE *stands speechless with horror*
    Sieg.   The wretch hath slain
Them both! — My Josephine! we are now alone!
Would we had ever been so! — All is over
For me! — Now open wide, my sire, thy grave;
Thy curse hath dug it deeper for thy son
In mine! — The race of Siegendorf is past!

APPENDIX.

A FRAGMENT.

June 17. 1816.

In the year 17—, having for some time determined on a journey through countries not hitherto much frequented by travellers, I set out, accompanied by a friend, whom I shall designate by the name of Augustus Darvell. He was a few years my elder, and a man of considerable fortune and ancient family; advantages which an extensive capacity prevented him alike from undervaluing or overrating. Some peculiar circumstances in his private history had rendered him to me an object of attention, of interest, and even of regard, which neither the reserve of his manners, nor occasional indications of an inquietude at times nearly approaching to alienation of mind, could extinguish.

I was yet young in life, which I had begun early; but my intimacy with him was of a recent date: we had been educated at the same schools and university; but his progress through these had preceded mine, and he had been deeply initiated into what is called the world, while I was yet in my noviciate. While thus engaged, I heard much both of his past and present life; and, although in these accounts there were many and irreconcileable contradictions, I could still gather from the whole that he was a being of no common order, and one who, whatever pains he might take to avoid remark, would still be remarkable. I had cultivated his acquaintance subsequently, and endeavoured to obtain his friendship, but this last appeared to be unattainable; whatever affections he might have possessed, seemed now, some to have been extinguished, and others to be concentred: that his feelings were acute, I had sufficient opportunities of observing; for, although he could control, he could not altogether disguise them; still he had a power of giving to one passion the appearance of another, in such a manner that it was difficult to define the nature of what was working within him; and the expressions of his features would vary so rapidly, though slightly, that it was useless to trace them to their sources. It was evident that he was a prey to some careless disquiet; but whether it arose from ambition, love, remorse, grief, from one or all of these, or merely from a morbid temperament akin to disease, I could not discover: there were circumstances alleged, which might have justified the application to each of these causes; but, as I have before said, these were so contradictory and contradicted, that none could be fixed upon with accuracy. Where there is mystery, it is generally supposed that there must also be evil: I know how this may be, but in him there certainly was the one, though I co not ascertain the extent of the other—and felt loth, as far as regarded h self, to believe in its existence. My advances were received with suffici coldness; but I was young, and not easily discouraged, and at length s ceeded in obtaining, to a certain degree, that common-place intercou and moderate confidence of common and every-day concerns, created n cemented by similarity of pursuit and frequency of meeting, which is call intimacy, or friendship, according to the ideas of him who uses those wo to express them.

Darvell had already travelled extensively; and to him I had applied information with regard to the conduct of my intended journey. It was secret wish that he might be prevailed on to accompany me; it was als probable hope, founded upon the shadowy restlessness which I observed him, and to which the animation which he appeared to feel on such su jects, and his apparent indifference to all by which he was more imm diately surrounded, gave fresh strength. This wish I first hinted, and th expressed: his answer, though I had partly expected it, gave me all t pleasure of surprise—he consented; and, after the requisite arrangemer we commenced our voyages. After journeying through various countries the south of Europe, our attention was turned towards the East, accordin to our original destination; and it was in my progress through those regio that the incident occurred upon which will turn what I may have to relat

The constitution of Darvell, which must from his appearance hav been in early life more than usually robust, had been for some time grad ally giving way, without the intervention of any apparent disease: he ha neither cough nor hectic, yet he became daily more enfeebled: his habi were temperate, and he neither declined nor complained of fatigue: yet h was evidently wasting away: he became more and more silent and sleep less, and at length so seriously altered, that my alarm grew proportionat to what I conceived to be his danger.

We had determined, on our arrival at Smyrna, on an excursion to th ruins of Ephesus and Sardis, from which I endeavoured to dissuade him i his present state of indisposition—but in vain: there appeared to be a oppression on his mind, and a solemnity in his manner, which ill corre sponded with his eagerness to proceed on what I regarded as a mere party o pleasure, little suited to a valetudinarian; but I opposed him no longer— and in a few days we set off together, accompanied only by a serrugee an a single janizary.

We had passed halfway towards the remains of Ephesus, leaving be hind us the more fertile environs of Smyrna, and were entering upon tha wild and tenantless track through the marshes and defiles which lead to th few huts yet lingering over the broken columns of Diana—the rooflees walls of expelled Christianity, and the still more recent but complete de solation of abandoned mosques—when the sudden and rapid illness of m companion obliged us to halt at a Turkish cemetery, the turbaned tomb stones of which were the sole indication that human life had ever been sojourner in this wilderness. The only caravansera we had seen was left some hours behind us, not a vestige of a town or even cottage was within sight or hope, and this "city of the dead" appeared to be the sole refuge for my unfortunate friend, who seemed on the verge of becoming the last of its inhabitants.

In this situation, I looked round for a place where he might most conveniently repose:—contrary to the usual aspect of Mahometan burial-grounds, the cypresses were in this few in number, and these thinly scattered over its extent: the tombstones were mostly fallen, and worn with age:—upon one of the most considerable of these, and beneath one of the most spreading trees, Darvell supported himself, in a half-reclining posture, with great difficulty. He asked for water. I had some doubts of our being able to find any, and prepared to go in search of it with hesitating despondency: but he desired me to remain; and turning to Suleiman, our janizary, who stood by us smoking with great tranquillity, he said, "Suleiman, verbana su," (i. e. bring some water,) and went on describing the spot where it was to be found with great minuteness, at a small well for camels, a few hundred yards to the right: the janizary obeyed. I said to Darvell, "How did you know this?"—He replied, "From our situation; you must perceive that this place was once inhabited, and could not have been so without springs: I have also been here before."

"You have been here before!—How came you never to mention this to me? and what could you be doing in a place where no one would remain a moment longer than they could help it?"

To this question I received no answer. In the mean time Suleiman returned with the water, leaving the serrugee and the horses at the fountain. The quenching of his thirst had the appearance of reviving him for a moment; and I conceived hopes of his being able to proceed, or at least to return, and I urged the attempt. He was silent—and appeared to be collecting his spirits for an effort to speak. He began.

"This is the end of my journey, and of my life;—I came here to die: but I have a request to make, a command—for such my last words must be.—You will observe it?"

"Most certainly; but have better hopes."

"I have no hopes, nor wishes, but this—conceal my death from every human being."

"I hope there will be no occasion; that you will recover, and—"

"Peace!—it must be so; promise this."

"I do."

"Swear it, by all that"—He here dictated an oath of great solemnity.

"There is no occasion for this—I will observe your request; and to doubt me is—"

"It cannot be helped,—you must swear."

I took the oath: it appeared to relieve him. He removed a seal ring from his finger, on which were some Arabic characters, and presented it to me. He proceeded—

"On the ninth day of the month, at noon precisely (what month you please, but this must be the day), you must fling this ring into the salt springs which run into the Bay of Eleusis: the day after, at the same hour, you must repair to the ruins of the temple of Ceres, and wait on hour."

"Why?"

"You will see."

"The ninth day of the month, you say?"

"The ninth."

As I observed that the present was the ninth day of the month, his countenance changed, and he paused. As he sat, evidently becoming more feeble, a stork, with a snake in her beak, perched upon a tombstone near us; and, without devouring her prey, appeared to be steadfastly regarding us. I know not what impelled me to drive it away, but the attempt was useless; she made a few circles in the air, and returned exactly to the same spot. Darvell pointed to it, and smiled: he spoke—I know not whether to himself or to me—but the words were only, "T is well!"

"What is well? what do you mean?"

"No matter: you must bury me here this evening, and exactly where that bird is now perched. You know the rest of my injunctions."

He then proceeded to give me several directions as to the manner in which his death might be best concealed. After these were finished, he exclaimed, "You perceive that bird?"

"Certainly."

"And the serpent writhing in her beak?"

"Doubtless: there is nothing uncommon in it; it is her natural prey. But it is odd that she does not devour it."

He smiled in a ghastly manner, and said, faintly, "It is not yet time!" As he spoke, the stork flew away. My eyes followed it for a moment—it could hardly be longer than ten might be counted. I felt Darvell's weight, as it were, increase upon my shoulder, and, turning to look upon his face, perceived that he was dead!

I was shocked with the sudden certainty which could not be mistaken —his countenance in a few minutes became nearly black. I should have attributed so rapid a change to poison, had I not been aware that he had no opportunity of receiving it unperceived. The day was declining, the body was rapidly altering, and nothing remained but to fulfil his request. With the aid of Suleiman's ataghan and my own sabre, we scooped a shallow grave upon the spot which Darvell had indicated: the earth easily gave way, having already received some Mahometan tenant. We dug as deeply as the time permitted us, and throwing the dry earth upon all that remained of the singular being so lately departed, we cut a few sods of greener turf from the less withered soil around us, and laid them upon his sepulchre.

Between astonishment and grief, I was tearless.

* * * * *

PARLIAMENTARY SPEECHES.

DEBATE ON THE FRAME-WORK BILL, IN THE HOUSE OF LORDS, FEBRUARY 27. 1812.

The order of the day for the second reading of this Bill being read,
Lord BYRON rose, and (for the first time) addressed their Lordships as follows:—

My Lords! the subject now submitted to your Lordships for the first time, though new to the House, is by no means new to the country. I believe it had occupied the serious thoughts of all descriptions of persons, long before its introduction to the notice of that legislature, whose interference alone could be of real service. As a person in some degree connected with the suffering county, though a stranger not only to this House in general, but to almost every individual whose attention I presume to solicit, I must claim some portion of your Lordships' indulgence, whilst I offer a few observations on a question in which I confess myself deeply interested.

To enter into any detail of the riots would be superfluous: the House is already aware that every outrage short of actual bloodshed has been perpetrated, and that the proprietors of the Frames obnoxious to the rioters, and all persons supposed to be connected with them, have been liable to insult and violence. During the short time I recently passed in Nottinghamshire, not twelve hours elapsed without some fresh act of violence; and on the day I left the county I was informed that forty Frames had been broken the preceding evening, as usual, without resistance and without detection.

Such was then the state of that county, and such I have reason to believe it to be at this moment. But whilst these outrages must be admitted to exist to an alarming extent, it cannot be denied that they have arisen from circumstances of the most unparalleled distress: the perseverance of these miserable men in their proceedings, tends to prove that nothing but absolute want could have driven a large, and once honest and industrious, body of the people, into the commission of excesses so hazardous to themselves, their families, and the community. At the time to which I allude, the town and county were burdened with large detachments of the military; the police was in motion, the magistrates assembled, yet all the movements, civil and military, had led to—nothing. Not a single instance had occurred of the apprehension of any real delinquent actually taken in the fact, against whom there existed legal evidence sufficient for conviction But the police, however useless, were by no means idle: several notoriou delinquents had been detected: men, liable to conviction, on the cleares evidence, of the capital crime of poverty; men, who had been nefariously guilty of lawfully begetting several children, whom, thanks to the times they were unable to maintain. Considerable injury has been done to the proprietors of the improved Frames. These machines were to them an ad vantage, inasmuch as they superseded the necessity of employing a number of workmen, who were left in consequence to starve. By the adoption o one species of Frame in particular, one man performed the work of many and the superfluous labourers were thrown out of employment. Yet it i to be observed, that the work thus executed was inferior in quality; not marketable at home, and merely hurried over with a view to exportation. It was called, in the cant of the trade, by the name of "Spider work." The rejected workmen, in the blindness of their ignorance, instead of rejoicing at these improvements in arts so beneficial to mankind, conceived themselves to be sacrificed to improvements in mechanism. In the foolishness of their hearts they imagined, that the maintenance and well doing of the industrious poor, were objects of greater consequence than the enrichment of a few individuals by any improvement, in the implements of trade, which threw the workmen out of employment, and rendered the labourer unworthy of his hire. And it must be confessed that although the adoption of the enlarged machinery in that state of our commerce which the country once boasted, might have been beneficial to the master without being detrimental to the servant; yet, in the present situation of our manufactures, rotting in warehouses, without a prospect of exportation, with the demand for work and workmen equally diminished, Frames of this description tend materially to aggravate the distress and discontent of the disappointed sufferers. But the real cause of these distresses and consequent disturbances lies deeper. When we are told that these men are leagued together not only for the destruction of their own comfort, but of their very means of subsistence, can we forget that it is the bitter policy, the destructive warfare of the last eighteen years, which has destroyed their comfort, your comfort, all men's comfort? That policy, which, originating with "great statesmen now no more," has survived the dead to become a curse on the living, unto the third and fourth generation! These men never destroyed their looms till they were become useless, worse than useless; till they were become actual impediments to their exertions in obtaining their daily bread. Can you, then, wonder that in times like these, when bankruptcy, convicted fraud, and imputed felony, are found in a station not far beneath that of your Lordships, the lowest, though once most useful portion of the people, should forget their duty in their distresses, and become only less guilty than one of their representatives? But while the exalted offender can find means to baffle the law, new capital punishments must be devised, new snares of death must be spread for the wretched mechanic, who is famished into guilt. These men were willing to dig, but the spade was in other hands: they were not ashamed to beg, but there was none to relieve them: their own means of subsistence were cut off, all other employments pre-occupied;

and their excesses, however to be deplored and condemned, can hardly be subject of surprise.

It has been stated that the persons in the temporary possession of frames connive at their destruction; if this be proved upon enquiry, it were necessary that such material accessories to the crime should be principals in the punishment. But I did hope, that any measure proposed by his Majesty's government, for your Lordships' decision, would have had conciliation for its basis; or, if that were hopeless, that some previous enquiry, some deliberation would have been deemed requisite; not that we should have been called at once without examination, and without cause, to pass sentences by wholesale, and sign death-warrants blindfold. But, admitting that these men had no cause of complaint; that the grievances of them and their employers were alike groundless; that they deserved the worst; what inefficiency, what imbecility has been evinced in the method chosen to reduce them! Why were the military called out to be made a mockery of, if they were to be called out at all? As far as the difference of seasons would permit, they have merely parodied the summer campaign of Major Sturgeon; and, indeed, the whole proceedings, civil and military, seemed on the model of those of the mayor and corporation of Garratt.—Such marchings and counter-marchings! from Nottingham to Bullwell, from Bullwell to Banford, from Banford to Mansfield! and when at length the detachments arrived at their destination, in all "the pride, pomp, and circumstance of glorious war," they came just in time to witness the mischief which had been done, and ascertain the escape of the perpetrators, to collect the *"spolia opima"* in the fragments of broken frames, and return to their quarters amidst the derision of old women, and the hootings of children. Now, though, in a free country, it were to be wished, that our military should never be too formidable, at least to ourselves, I cannot see the policy of placing them in situations where they can only be made ridiculous. As the sword is the worst argument that can be used, so should it be the last. In this instance it has been the first; but providentially as yet only in the scabbard. The present measure will, indeed, pluck it from the sheath; yet had proper meetings been held in the earlier stages of these riots, had the grievances of these men and their masters (for they also had their grievances) been fairly weighed and justly examined, I do think that means might have been devised to restore these workmen to their avocations, and tranquillity to the county. At present the county suffers from the double infliction of an idle military and a starving population. In what state of apathy have we been plunged so long, that now for the first time the house has been officially apprised of these disturbances! All this has been transacting within 130 miles of London, and yet we, "good easy men, have deemed full sure our greatness was a ripening," and have sat down to enjoy our foreign triumphs in the midst of domestic calamity. But all the cities you have taken, all the armies which have retreated before your leaders, are but paltry subjects of self-congratulation, if your land divides against itself, and your dragoons and your executioners must be let loose against your fellow-citizens.—You call these men a mob, desperate, dangerous, and ignorant; and seem to think that the only way to quiet the *"Bellua multorum capitum*" is to lop off a few of its superfluous heads. But even mob may be better reduced to reason by a mixture of conciliation and firmness, than by additional irritation and redoubled penalties. Are we aware of our obligations to a mob? It is the mob that labour in your fields an serve in your houses, — that man your navy, and recruit your army, — that have enabled you to defy all the world, and can also defy you when neglect and calamity have driven them to despair! You may call the people a mob but do not forget, that a mob too often speaks the sentiments of the people And here I must remark, with what alacrity you are accustomed to fly to the succour of your distressed allies, leaving the distressed of your own country to the care of Providence or — the parish. When the Portuguese suffered under the retreat of the French, every arm was stretched out every hand was opened, from the rich man's largess to the widow's mite all was bestowed, to enable them to rebuild their villages and replenish their granaries. And at this moment, when thousands of misguided but most unfortunate fellow-countrymen are struggling with the extremes of hardships and hunger, as your charity began abroad it should end at home. A much less sum, a tithe of the bounty bestowed on Portugal, even if those men (which I cannot admit without enquiry) could not have been restored to their employments, would have rendered unnecessary the tender mercies of the bayonet and the gibbet. But doubtless our friends have too many foreign claims to admit a prospect of domestic relief; though never did such objects demand it. I have traversed the seat of war in the Peninsula, I have been in some of the most oppressed provinces of Turkey, but never under the most despotic of infidel governments did I behold such squalid wretchedness as I have seen since my return in the very heart of a Christian country. And what are your remedies? After months of inaction, and months of action worse than inactivity, at length comes forth the grand specific, the never-failing nostrum of all state physicians, from the days of Draco to the present time. After feeling the pulse and shaking the head over the patient, prescribing the usual course of warm water and bleeding, the warm water of your mawkish police, and the lancets of your military, these convulsions must terminate in death, the sure consummation of the prescriptions of all political Sangrados. Setting aside the palpable injustice and the certain inefficiency of the bill, are there not capital punishments sufficient in your statutes? Is there not blood enough upon your penal code, that more must be poured forth to ascend to Heaven and testify against you? How will you carry the bill into effect? Can you commit a whole county to their own prisons? Will you erect a gibbet in every field, and hang up men like scarecrows? or will you proceed (as you must to bring this measure into effect) by decimation? place the county under martial law? depopulate and lay waste all around you? and restore Sherwood Forest as an acceptable gift to the crown, in its former condition of a royal chase and an asylum for outlaws? Are these the remedies for a starving and desperate populace? Will the famished wretch who has braved your bayonets be appalled by your gibbets? When death is a relief, and the only relief it appears that you will afford him, will he be dragooned into tranquillity? Will that which could not be effected by your grenadiers, be accomplished by your executioners? If you proceed by the forms of law, where is your evidence? Those who have refused to impeach their accomplices, when transportation only was the punishment, will hardly be tempted to witness against them when death is the penalty. With all due deference to the noble lords opposite, I think a little investigation, some previous enquiry would induce even them to change their purpose. That most favourite state measure, so marvellously efficacious in many and recent instances, temporizing, would not be without its advantages in this. When a proposal is made to emancipate or relieve, you hesitate, you deliberate for years, you temporize and tamper with the minds of men; but a death-bill must be passed off hand, without a thought of the consequences. Sure I am, from what I have heard, and from what I have seen, that to pass the bill under all the existing circumstances, without enquiry, without deliberation, would only be to add injustice to irritation, and barbarity to neglect. The framers of such a bill must be content to inherit the honours of that Athenian lawgiver whose edicts were said to be written not in ink but in blood. But suppose it past; suppose one of these men, as I have seen them,—meagre with famine, sullen with despair, careless of a life which your Lordships are perhaps about to value at something less than the price of a stocking-frame;—suppose this man surrounded by the children for whom he is unable to procure bread at the hazard of his existence, about to be torn for ever from a family which he lately supported in peaceful industry, and which it is not his fault that he can no longer so support;—suppose this man, and there are ten thousand such from whom you may select your victims, dragged into court, to be tried for this new offence, by this new law; still, there are two things wanting to convict and condemn him; and these are, in my opinion,—twelve butchers for a jury, and a Jefferies for a judge!

DEBATE ON THE EARL OF DONOUGHMORE'S MOTION FOR A COMMITTEE ON THE ROMAN CATHOLIC CLAIMS, APRIL 21. 1812.

Lord BYRON rose and said:—

MY LORDS,—The question before the House has been so frequently, fully, and ably discussed, and never perhaps more ably than on this night, that it would be difficult to adduce new arguments for or against it. But with each discussion, difficulties have been removed, objections have been canvassed and refuted, and some of the former opponents of Catholic emancipation have at length conceded to the expediency of relieving the petitioners. In conceding thus much, however, a new objection is started; it is not the time, say they, or it is an improper time, or there is time enough yet. In some degree I concur with those who say, it is not the time exactly; that time is passed; better had it been for the country, that the Catholics possessed at this moment their proportion of our privileges, that their nobles held their due weight in our councils, than that we should be assembled to discuss their claims. It had indeed been better—

"Non tempore tali
"Cogere concilium cum muros obsidet hostis."

The enemy is without, and distress within. It is too late to cavil on doctrinal points, when we must unite in defence of things more important than the mere ceremonies of religion. It is indeed singular, that we are called together to deliberate, not on the God we adore, for in that we are agreed; not about the king we obey, for to him we are loyal; but how far a difference in the ceremonials of worship, how far believing not too little, but too much (the worst that can be imputed to the Catholics), how far too much devotion to their God may incapacitate our fellow-subjects from effectually serving their king.

Much has been said, within and without doors, of church and state, and although those venerable words have been too often prostituted to the most despicable of party purposes, we cannot hear them too often; all, I presume, are the advocates of church and state,—the church of Christ, and the state of Great Britain; but not a state of exclusion and despotism, not an intolerant church, not a church militant, which renders itself liable to the very objection urged against the Romish communion, and in a greater degree, for the Catholic merely withholds its spiritual benediction (and even that is doubtful), but our church, or rather our churchmen, not only refuse to the Catholic their spiritual grace, but all temporal blessings whatsoever. It was an observation of the great Lord Peterborough, made within these walls, or within the walls where the Lords then assembled, that he was for a "parliamentary king and a parliamentary constitution, but not a parliamentary God and a parliamentary religion." The interval of a century has not weakened the force of the remark. It is indeed time that we should leave off these petty cavils on frivolous points, these Lilliputian sophistries, whether our "eggs are best broken at the broad or narrow end."

The opponents of the Catholics may be divided into two classes; those who assert that the Catholics have too much already, and those who allege that the lower orders, at least, have nothing more to require. We are told by the former, that the Catholics never will be contented: by the latter, that they are already too happy. The last paradox is sufficiently refuted by the present as by all past petitions; it might as well be said, that the negroes did not desire to be emancipated, but this is an unfortunate comparison, for you have already delivered them out of the house of bondage without any petition on their part, but many from their task-masters to a contrary effect; and for myself, when I consider this, I pity the Catholic peasantry for not having the good fortune to be born black. But the Catholics are contented, or at least ought to be, as we are told; I shall, therefore, proceed to touch on a few of those circumstances which so marvellously contribute to their exceeding contentment. They are not allowed the free exercise of their religion in the regular army; the Catholic soldier cannot absent himself from the service of the Protestant clergyman, and unless he is quartered in Ireland or in Spain, where can he find eligible opportunities of attending his own? The permission of Catholic chaplains to the Irish militia regiments was conceded as a special favour, and not till after years of remonstrance, although an act, passed in 1793, established it as a right. But are the Catholics properly protected in Ireland? Can the church purchase a rood of land whereon to erect a chapel? No! all the places of worship are built on leases of trust or sufferance from the laity, easily broken, and often betrayed. The moment any irregular wish, any casual caprice of the benevolent landlord meets with opposition, the doors are barred against the congregation. This has happened continually, but in no instance more glaringly, than at the town of Newton-Barry, in the county of Wexford. The Catholics enjoying no regular chapel, as a temporary expedient, hired two barns; which, being thrown into one, served for public worship. At this time, there was quartered opposite to the spot an officer whose mind appears to have been deeply imbued with those prejudices which the Protestant petitions now on the table prove to have been fortunately eradicated from the more rational portion of the people; and when the Catholics were assembled on the Sabbath as usual, in peace and good-will towards men, for the worship of their God and yours, they found the chapel door closed, and were told that if they did not immediately retire (and they were told this by a yeoman officer and a magistrate), the riot act should be read, and the assembly dispersed at the point of the bayonet! This was complained of to the middle man of government, the secretary at the castle in 1806, and the answer was (in lieu of redress), that he would cause a letter to be written to the colonel, to prevent, if possible, the recurrence of similar disturbances. Upon this fact, no very great stress need be laid; but it tends to prove that while the Catholic church has not power to purchase land for its chapels to stand upon, the laws for its protection are of no avail. In the mean time, the Catholics are at the mercy of every "pelting potty officer," who may choose to play his "fantastic tricks before high heaven," to insult his God, and injure his fellow-creatures.

Every school-boy, any foot-boy (such have hold commissions in our service), any foot-boy who can exchange his shoulder-knot for an epaulette, may perform all this and more against the Catholic by virtue of that very authority delegated to him by his sovereign, for the express purpose of defending his fellow subjects to the last drop of his blood, without discrimination or distinction between Catholic and Protestant.

Have the Irish Catholics the full benefit of trial by jury? They have not; they never can have until they are permitted to share the privilege of serving as sheriffs and under-sheriffs. Of this a striking example occurred at the last Enniskillen assizes. A yeoman was arraigned for the murder of a Catholic named Macvournagh: three respectable, uncontradicted witnesses deposed that they saw the prisoner load, take aim, fire at, and kill the said Macvournagh. This was properly commented on by the Judge: but to the astonishment of the bar, and indignation of the court, the Protestant jury acquitted the accused. So glaring was the partiality, that Mr. Justice Osborne felt it his duty to bind over the acquitted, but not absolved assassin, in large recognizances; thus for a time taking away his license to kill Catholics.

Are the very laws passed in their favour observed? They are rendered nugatory in trivial as in serious cases. By a late act, Catholic chaplains are permitted in gaols, but in Fermanagh county the grand jury lately persisted in presenting a suspended clergyman for the office, thereby evading the statute, notwithstanding the most pressing remonstrances of a most respectable magistrate, named Flotcher, to the contrary. Such is law, such is justice, for the happy, free, contented Catholic!

It has been asked, in another place, Why do not the rich Catholics endow foundations for the education of the priesthood? Why do you not permit them to do so? Why are all such bequests subject to the interference, the vexatious, arbitrary, peculating interference of the Orange commissioners for charitable donations?

As to Maynooth college, in no instance, except at the time of its foundation, when a noble Lord (Camden), at the head of the Irish administration, did appear to interest himself in its advancement; and during the government of a noble Duke (Bedford), who, like his ancestors, has ever been the friend of freedom and mankind, and who has not so far adopted the selfish policy of the day as to exclude the Catholics from the number of his follow-creatures; with these exceptions, in no instance has that institution been properly encouraged. There was indeed a time when the Catholic clergy were conciliated, while the Union was pending, that Union which could not be carried without them, while their assistance was requisite in procuring addresses from the Catholic counties; then they were cajoled and caressed, feared and flattered, and given to understand that "the Union would do every thing;" but the moment it was passed, they were driven back with contempt into their former obscurity.

In the conduct pursued towards Maynooth college, every thing is done to irritate and perplex — every thing is done to efface the slightest impression of gratitude from the Catholic mind; the very hay made upon the lawn, the fat and tallow of the beef and mutton allowed, must be paid for and accounted upon oath. It is true, this economy in miniature cannot sufficiently be commended, particularly at a time when only the insec defaulters of the Treasury, your Hunts and your Chinnerys, when only those "gilded bugs" can escape the microscopic eye of ministers. But when you come forward, session after session, as your paltry pittance is wrung from you with wrangling and reluctance, to boast of your liberality, well might the Catholic exclaim, in the words of Prior:—

> "To John I owe some obligation,
> But John unluckily thinks fit
> To publish it to all the nation,
> So John and I are more than quit."

Some persons have compared the Catholics to the beggar in Gil Blas who made them beggars? Who are enriched with the spoils of their ancestors? And cannot you relieve the beggar when your fathers have made him such? If you are disposed to relieve him at all, cannot you do it without flinging your farthings in his face? As a contrast, however, to this beggarly benevolence, let us look at the Protestant Charter Schools; to them you have lately granted 41,000*l.*: thus are they supported, and how are they recruited? Montesquieu observes on the English constitution, that the model may be found in Tacitus, where the historian describes the policy of the Germans, and adds, "This beautiful system was taken from the woods;" so in speaking of the charter schools, it may be observed, that this beautiful system was taken from the gipsies. These schools are recruited in the same manner as the Janissaries at the time of their enrolment under Amurath, and the gipsies of the present day with stolen children, with children decoyed and kidnapped from their Catholic connections by their rich and powerful Protestant neighbours; this is notorious, and one instance may suffice to show in what manner:— The sister of a Mr. Carthy (a Catholic gentleman of very considerable property) died, leaving two girls, who were immediately marked out as proselytes, and conveyed to the charter school of Coolgreny; their uncle, on being apprised of the fact, which took place during his absence, applied for the restitution of his nieces, offering to settle an independence on these his relations; his request was refused, and not till after five years' struggle, and the interference of very high authority, could this Catholic gentleman obtain back his nearest of kindred from a charity charter school. In this manner are proselytes obtained, and mingled with the offspring of such Protestants as may avail themselves of the institution. And how are they taught? A catechism is put into their hands, consisting of, I believe, forty-five pages, in which are three questions relative to the Protestant religion; one of these queries is, "Where was the Protestant religion before Luther?" Answer, "In the Gospel." The remaining forty-four pages and a half regard the damnable idolatry of Papists!

Allow me to ask our spiritual pastors and masters, is this training up a child in the way which he should go? Is this the religion of the Gospel before the time of Luther? that religion which preaches "Peace on earth, and glory to God?" Is it bringing up infants to be men or devils? Better would it be to send them any where than teach them such doctrines; better send them to those islands in the South Seas, where they might more humanely learn to become cannibals; it would be less disgusting that they were brought up to devour the dead, than persecute the living. Schools do you call them? call them rather dunghills, where the viper of intolerance deposits her young, that when their teeth are cut and their poison is mature, they may issue forth, filthy and venomous, to sting the Catholic. But are these the doctrines of the Church of England, or of churchmen? No, the most enlightened churchmen are of a different opinion. What says Paley? "I perceive no reason why men of different religious persuasions should not sit upon the same bench, deliberate in the same council, or fight in the same ranks, as well as men of various religious opinions, upon any controverted topic of natural history, philosophy, or ethics." It may be answered, that Paley was not strictly orthodox; I know nothing of his orthodoxy, but who will deny that he was an ornament to the church, to human nature, to Christianity?

I shall not dwell upon the grievance of tithes, so severely felt by the peasantry, but it may be proper to observe, that there is an addition to the burden, a per centage to the gatherer, whose interest it thus becomes to rate them as highly as possible, and we know that in many large livings in Ireland the only resident Protestants are the tithe proctor and his family.

Amongst many causes of irritation, too numerous for recapitulation, there is one in the militia not to be passed over,—I mean the existence of Orange lodges amongst the privates. Can the officers deny this? And if such lodges do exist, do they, can they, tend to promote harmony amongst the men, who are thus individually separated in society, although mingled in the ranks? And is this general system of persecution to be permitted; or is it to be believed that with such a system the Catholics can or ought to be contented? If they are, they belie human nature; they are then, indeed, unworthy to be any thing but the slaves you have made them. The facts stated are from most respectable authority, or I should not have dared in this place, or any place, to hazard this avowal. If exaggerated, there are plenty as willing, as I believe them to be unable, to disprove them. Should it be objected that I never was in Ireland, I beg leave to observe, that it is as easy to know something of Ireland without having been there, as it appears with some to have been born, bred, and cherished there, and yet remain ignorant of its best interests.

But there are who assert that the Catholics have already been too much indulged. See (cry they) what has been done: we have given them one entire college, we allow them food and raiment, the full enjoyment of the elements, and leave to fight for us as long as they have limbs and lives to offer, and yet they are never to be satisfied!—Generous and just declaimers! To this, and to this only, amount the whole of your arguments, when stript of their sophistry. Those personages remind me of a story of a certain drummer, who, being called upon in the course of duty to administer punishment to a friend tied to the halberts, was requested to flog high, he did—to flog low, he did—to flog in the middle, he did,—high, low, down the middle, and up again, but all in vain; the patient continued his complaints with the most provoking pertinacity, until the drummer, exhausted and angry, flung down his scourge, exclaiming, "The devil burn you, there's no pleasing you, flog where one will!" Thus it is, you have flogged the Catholic high, low, here, there, and every where, and then you wonder he is not pleased. It is true that time, experience, and that weariness which attends even the exercise of barbarity, have taught you to flog a little more gently; but still you continue to lay on the lash, and will so continue, till perhaps the rod may be wrested from your hands, and applied to the backs of yourselves and your posterity.

It was said by somebody in a former debate, (I forget by whom, and am not very anxious to remember,) if the Catholics are emancipated, why not the Jews? If this sentiment was dictated by compassion for the Jews, it might deserve attention, but as a sneer against the Catholic, what is it but the language of Shylock transferred from his daughter's marriage to Catholic emancipation—

> "Would any of the tribe of Barabbas
> Should have it rather than a Christian."

I presume a Catholic is a Christian, even in the opinion of him whose taste only can be called in question for his preference of the Jews.

It is a remark often quoted of Dr. Johnson, (whom I take to be almost as good authority as the gentle apostle of intolerance, Dr. Duigenan,) that he who could entertain serious apprehensions of danger to the church in these times, would have "cried fire in the deluge." This is more than a metaphor; for a remnant of these antediluvians appear actually to have come down to us, with fire in their mouths and water in their brains, to disturb and perplex mankind with their whimsical outcries. And as it is an infallible symptom of that distressing malady with which I conceive them to be afflicted (so any doctor will inform your Lordships), for the unhappy invalids to perceive a flame perpetually flashing before their eyes, particularly when their eyes are shut (as those of the persons to whom I allude have long been), it is impossible to convince these poor creatures, that the fire against which they are perpetually warning us and themselves is nothing but an *ignis fatuus* of their own drivelling imaginations. What rhubarb, senna, or "what purgative drug can scour that fancy thence?" — It is impossible, they are given over, theirs is the true

"Caput insanabile tribus Anticyris."

These are your true Protestants. Like Bayle, who protested against all sects whatsoever, so do they protest against Catholic petitions, Protestant petitions, all redress, all that reason, humanity, policy, justice, and common sense, can urge against the delusions of their absurd delirium. These are the persons who reverse the fable of the mountain that brought forth a mouse; they are the mice who conceive themselves in labour with mountains.

To return to the Catholics; suppose the Irish were actually contented under their disabilities; suppose them capable of such a bull as not to desire deliverance, ought we not to wish it for ourselves? Have we nothing to gain by their emancipation? What resources have been wasted? What talents have been lost by the selfish system of exclusion? You already know the value of Irish aid; at this moment the defence of England is intrusted to the Irish militia; at this moment, while the starving people are rising in the fierceness of despair, the Irish are faithful to their trust. But till equal energy is imparted throughout by the extension of freedom, you cannot enjoy the full benefit of the strength which you are glad to interpose between you and destruction. Ireland has done much, but will do more. At this moment the only triumph obtained through long years of continental disaster has been achieved by an Irish general: it is true he is not a Catholic; had he been so, we should have been deprived of his exertions: but I presume no one will assert that his religion would have impaired his talents or diminished his patriotism; though, in that case, he must have conquered in the ranks, for he never could have commanded an army.

But he is fighting the battles of the Catholics abroad; his noble brother has this night advocated their cause, with an eloquence which I shall not depreciate by the humble tribute of my panegyric; whilst a third of his kindred, as unlike as unequal, has been combating against his Catholic brethren in Dublin, with circular letters, edicts, proclamations, arrests, and dispersions;—all the vexatious implements of petty warfare that could be wielded by the mercenary guerillas of government, clad in the rust armour of their obsolete statutes. Your Lordships will, doubtless, divide new honours between the Saviour of Portugal, and the Dispenser of Delegates. It is singular, indeed, to observe the difference between our foreign and domestic policy; if Catholic Spain, faithful Portugal, or the no less Catholic and faithful king of the one Sicily, (of which, by the by, you have lately deprived him,) stand in need of succour, away goes a fleet and an army, an ambassador and a subsidy, sometimes to fight pretty hardly generally to negotiate very badly, and always to pay very dearly for our Popish allies. But let four millions of fellow-subjects pray for relief, who fight and pay and labour in your behalf, they must be treated as aliens and although their "father's house has many mansions," there is no resting-place for them. Allow me to ask, are you not fighting for the emancipation of Ferdinand VII., who certainly is a fool, and, consequently, in all probability a bigot? and have you more regard for a foreign sovereign than your own fellow-subjects, who are not fools, for they know your interest better than you know your own; who are not bigots, for they return you good for evil; but who are in worse durance than the prison of a usurper, inasmuch as the fetters of the mind are more galling than those of the body?

Upon the consequences of your not acceding to the claims of the petitioners, I shall not expatiate; you know them, you will feel them, and your children's children when you are passed away. Adieu to that Union so called, as "*Lucus a non lucendo*," a Union from never uniting, which in its first operation gave a death-blow to the independence of Ireland, and in its last may be the cause of her eternal separation from this country. If it must be called a Union, it is the union of the shark with his prey; the spoiler swallows up his victim, and thus they become one and indivisible. Thus has Great Britain swallowed up the parliament, the constitution, the independence of Ireland, and refuses to disgorge even a single privilege, although for the relief of her swollen and distempered body politic.

And now, my Lords, before I sit down, will his Majesty's ministers permit me to say a few words, not on their merits, for that would be superfluous, but on the degree of estimation in which they are held by the people of these realms? The esteem in which they are held has been boasted of in a triumphant tone on a late occasion within these walls, and a comparison instituted between their conduct and that of noble lords on this side of the House.

What portion of popularity may have fallen to the share of my noble friends (if such I may presume to call them), I shall not pretend to ascertain; but that of his Majesty's ministers it were vain to deny. It is, to be sure, a little like the wind, "no one knows whence it cometh or whither it goeth," but they feel it, they enjoy it, they boast of it. Indeed, modest and unostentatious as they are, to what part of the kingdom, even the most remote, can they flee to avoid the triumph which pursues them? If they plunge into the midland counties, there will they be greeted by the manufacturers, with spurned petitions in their hands, and those halters round their necks recently voted in their behalf, imploring blessings on the heads of those who so simply, yet ingeniously, contrived to remove them from their miseries in this to a better world. If they journey on to Scotland, from Glasgow to Johnny Groats, every where will they receive similar marks of approbation. If they take a trip from Portpatrick to Donaghadee, there will they rush at once into the embraces of four Catholic millions, to whom their vote of this night is about to endear them for ever. When they return to the metropolis, if they can pass under Temple Bar without unpleasant sensations at the sight of the greedy niches over that ominous gateway, they cannot escape the acclamations of the livery, and the more tremulous, but not less sincere, applause, the blessings, "not loud but deep," of bankrupt merchants and doubting stock-holders. If they look to the army, what wreaths, not of laurel, but of nightshade. are preparing for the heroes of Walcheren. It is true, there are few living deponents left to testify to their merits on that occasion; but a "cloud of witnesses" are gone above from that gallant army which they so generously and piously despatched, to recruit the "noble army of martyrs."

What if in the course of this triumphal career (in which they will gather as many pebbles as Caligula's army did on a similar triumph, the prototype of their own,) they do not perceive any of those memorials which a grateful people erect in honour of their benefactors; what although not even a signpost will condescend to depose the Saracen's head in favour of the likeness of the conquorors of Walcheren, they will not want a picture who can always have a caricature; or regret the omission of a statue who will so often see themselves exalted in effigy. But their popularity is not limited to the narrow bounds of an island; there are other countries where their measures, and above all, their conduct to the Catholics, must render them pre-eminently popular. If they are beloved here, in France they must be adored. There is no measure more repugnant to the designs and feelings of Bonaparte than Catholic emancipation; no line of conduct more propitious to his projects, than that which has been pursued, is pursuing, and, I fear, will be pursued, towards Ireland. What is England without Ireland, and what is Ireland without the Catholics? It is on the basis of your tyranny Napoleon hopes to build his own. So grateful must oppression of the Catholics be to his mind, that doubtless (as he has lately permitted some renewal of intercourse) the next cartel will convey to this country cargoes of sovrechina and blue ribands, (things in great request, and of equal value at this moment,) blue ribands of the Legion of Honour for Dr. Duigenan and his ministerial disciples. Such is that well-earned popularity, the result of those extraordinary expeditions, so expensive to ourselves, and so useless to our allies; of those singular enquiries, so exculpatory to the accused and so dissatisfactory to the people; of those paradoxical victories, so honourable, as we are told, to the British name, and so destructive to the best interests of the British nation: above all, such is the reward of a conduct pursued by ministers towards the Catholics.

I have to apologise to the House, who will, I trust, pardon one, not

often in the habit of intruding upon their indulgence, for so long attemp]
ing to engage their attention. My most decided opinion is, as my vote w
be, in favour of the motion.

DEBATE ON MAJOR CARTWRIGHT'S PETITION, JUNE 1. 1813.

Lord BYRON rose and said:

MY Lords,—The petition which I now hold for the purpose of presenting to the House, is one which I humbly conceive requires the particular attention of your Lordships, inasmuch as, though signed but by a single individual, it contains statements which (if not disproved) demand most serious investigation. The grievance of which the petitioner complains is neither selfish nor imaginary. It is not his own only, for it has been, and is still felt by numbers. No one without these walls, nor indeed within, but may to-morrow be made liable to the same insult and obstruction, in the discharge of an imperious duty for the restoration of the true constitution of these realms, by petitioning for reform in parliament. The petitioner, my Lords, is a man whose long life has been spent in one unceasing struggle for the liberty of the subject, against that undue influence which has increased, is increasing, and ought to be diminished; and whatever difference of opinion may exist as to his political tenets, few will be found to question the integrity of his intentions. Even now oppressed with years, and not exempt from the infirmities attendant on his age, but still unimpaired in talent, and unshaken in spirit—"*frangas non flectes*"—he has received many a wound in the combat against corruption; and the new grievance, the fresh insult of which he complains, may inflict another scar, but no dishonour. The petition is signed by John Cartwright, and it was in behalf of the people and parliament, in the lawful pursuit of that reform in the representation, which is the best service to be rendered both to parliament and people, that he encountered the wanton outrage which forms the subject-matter of his petition to your Lordships. It is couched in firm, yet respectful language—in the language of a man, not regardless of what is due to himself, but at the same time, I trust, equally mindful of the deference to be paid to this House. The petitioner states, amongst other matter of equal, if not greater importance, to all who are British in their feelings, as well as blood and birth, that on the 21st January, 1813, at Huddersfield, himself and six other persons, who, on hearing of his arrival, had waited on him merely as a testimony of respect, were seized by a military and civil force, and kept in close custody for several hours, subjected to gross and abusive insinuation from the commanding officer, relative to the character of the petitioner; that he (the petitioner) was finally carried before a magistrate, and not released till an examination of his papers proved that there was not only no just, but not even statutable charge against him; and that, notwithstanding the promise and order from the presiding magistrates of a copy of the warrant against your petitioner, it was afterwards withheld on divers pretexts, and has never until this hour been granted. The names and condition of the parties will be found in the petition. To the other topics touched upon in the petition, I shall not now advert, from a wish not to encroach upon the time of the House; but I do most sincerely call the attention of your Lordships to its general contents — it is in the cause of the parliament and people that the rights of this venerable freeman have been violated, and it is, in my opinion, the highest mark of respect that could be paid to the House, that to your justice, rather than by appeal to any inferior court, he now commits himself. Whatever may be the fate of his remonstrance, it is some satisfaction to me, though mixed with regret for the occasion, that I have this opportunity of publicly stating the obstruction to which the subject is liable, in the prosecution of the most lawful and imperious of his duties, the obtaining by petition reform in parliament. I have shortly stated his complaint; the petitioner has more fully expressed it. Your Lordships will, I hope, adopt some measure fully to protect and redress him, and not him alone, but the whole body of the people, insulted and aggrieved in his person, by the interposition of an abused civil, and unlawful military force between them and their right of petition to their own representatives.

His Lordship then presented the petition from Major Cartwright, which was read, complaining of the circumstances at Huddersfield, and of interruptions given to the right of petitioning in several places in the northern parts of the kingdom, and which his Lordship moved should be laid on the table.

Several lords having spoken on the question,

Lord Byron replied, that he had, from motives of duty, presented this petition to their Lordships' consideration. The noble Earl had contended, that it was not a petition, but a speech; and that, as it contained no prayer, it should not be received. What was the necessity of a prayer? If that word were to be used in its proper sense, their Lordships could not expect that any man should pray to others. He had only to say, that the petition, though in some parts expressed strongly perhaps, did not contain any improper mode of address, but was couched in respectful language towards their Lordships; he should therefore trust their Lordships would allow the petition to be received.

www.ingramcontent.com/pod-product-compliance
Lightning Source LLC
Chambersburg PA
CBHW032011300426
44117CB00008B/977